D0712907

ROME'S REVOLUTION

Ancient Warfare and Civilization

SERIES EDITORS:

RICHARD ALSTON   ROBIN WATERFIELD

In this series, leading historians offer compelling new narratives of the armed conflicts that shaped and reshaped the classical world, from the wars of Archaic Greece to the fall of the Roman Empire and the Arab conquests.

ROME'S REVOLUTION

Death of the Republic and
Birth of the Empire

Richard Alston

OXFORD
UNIVERSITY PRESS

OXFORD
UNIVERSITY PRESS

Oxford University Press is a department of the University of
Oxford. It furthers the University's objective of excellence in research,
scholarship, and education by publishing worldwide.

Oxford   New York
Auckland   Cape Town   Dar es Salaam   Hong Kong   Karachi
Kuala Lumpur   Madrid   Melbourne   Mexico City   Nairobi
New Delhi   Shanghai   Taipei   Toronto

With offices in
Argentina   Austria   Brazil   Chile   Czech Republic   France   Greece
Guatemala   Hungary   Italy   Japan   Poland   Portugal   Singapore
South Korea   Switzerland   Thailand   Turkey   Ukraine   Vietnam

Oxford is a registered trademark of Oxford University Press
in the UK and certain other countries.

Published in the United States of America by
Oxford University Press
198 Madison Avenue, New York, NY 10016

Library of Congress Cataloging-in-Publication Data
Alston, Richard, 1965–
Rome's revolution: death of the republic and birth of the empire / Richard Alston.
pages cm.—(Ancient warfare and civilization)
Includes bibliographical references.
ISBN 978-0-19-973976-9 (hardback)—ISBN 978-0-19-023160-6 (electronic text)—
ISBN 978-0-19-023161-3 (electronic text)   1. Rome—History—Republic, 265-30 B.C.
2. Rome—History—Augustus, 30 B.C.–14 A.D.   I. Title.
DG254.A47 2015
937'.05—dc23
2014049749

1 3 5 7 9 8 6 4 2
Printed in the United States of America
on acid-free paper

CONTENTS

Contents

PREFACE

O N MARCH 15TH, 44 B.C., a group of senators stabbed to death Julius Caesar. By this act, they hoped and believed, they had restored the Republic and freed Rome from the tyranny of a dictator. In fact, their actions brought an end to the Republic and ushered in a new political system, which we know as the Roman Empire. These were foundational events in Roman history. It is a matter of taste whether one emphasizes ends or beginnings, but in both ending and beginning, the events which are recounted in this book were violent, epochal, and revolutionary.

The violence of the revolution was intimate. Roman killed Roman. Family members turned against each other. The heads of enemies were displayed in the center of Rome. The dark heart of political power was there for all to see. It is this cataclysmic violence that has given historians and political thinkers pause over the centuries.

Rome was not just any state. It was a state that came to be associated with civilization, with grandeur, and with greatness. Rome has been a paradigmatic source of Western civilization. In politics, the republicanism of Rome has been long admired. At least until its last generation, Rome appeared to avoid the demagoguery and internal conflicts of classical Athens, and in so doing achieved a political stability that lasted at least four centuries and a community of purpose that brought a vast empire to this small Italian city-state. Great orators and political thinkers, such as Cicero and Cato, gave of their views as they stood before the people in the assemblies of state. This was the land of liberty and citizenship, those core values of Western political life. The historical imaginings of Rome's Republic fired the English civil war against their king and French revolutionary ardor throughout the seventeenth and eighteenth centuries, and inspired America to seize freedom from the remote, archaic, but powerful English monarchy.

But behind Rome's idealized Republic lurks the unpleasant fact of Rome's revolution, a revolution that suggested that corruption was latent in even the best of republics and moral and political decline went hand in hand with political and military success. Rome suggests that all the privileges of freedom, security, and wealth that were so hard-won over centuries of struggle could be dissipated in the blood of civil war.

This book looks once more at the trauma of the Roman revolution and attempts to understand that violent end. The problem is worth tackling not just because it was such a pivotal moment in world history, nor even because so much of our political thought since the sixteenth century has grappled with the problem of the failure of the Republic, but because, it seems to me, we have lost sight of the violence of the revolution.

In conventional historical narratives, the fall of the Republic and the birth of the empire have become bloodless, a constitutional adjustment or a worrying but brief exception in an extended golden age of rationalist, aristocratic rule. Not only does this distort events, but it civilizes them. The story I will tell here is of the fundamentals of politics: power, money, and violence.

In Western societies, we are fixated on political styles and the minor differences between our leaders. We have lost sight of the ability of power to destroy and, indeed, our reliance on political power to provide the basic necessities that get us from day to day and from generation to generation. Contemporary politics in the West is often described as dull and tedious, but if the state should fail, politics would suddenly become very interesting indeed.

The problem is one of perspective. If you are reading about the vicious violence that marks the Roman revolution in a comfortable seat in a library or lounge in Paris or Washington, London or New York, if you are warm and well fed and have no prospect of hunger or cold, then you can shudder with incomprehension and wonder at the darkness of the human soul that could tear such a system apart and bring forth anarchy onto the streets. You might shake your head at the dissipation of the freedoms of the Republic and the gradual and inexorable accumulation of power by the new imperial regime. You might thank your luck to be born in the current age, when such stories are things of the past. Or you might confine the story to the shelf of history books, remote from the realities of the modern world and with no meaning. But in many other parts of the world, if you are sitting reading this book, you may wonder what exactly the problem is: people, perfectly normal, rational people, can, under certain circumstances, take up arms and kill their neighbors. Governments, almost as a matter of course, use their resources corruptly to buy support and secure their political continuity.

In 44 B.C., the comfortable of the Roman world—the senators, the men who made the great decisions of state, led the armies, presided over the courts, and sacrificed to the gods—had no idea that their world was about to fall apart and a new regime would come to power. If any pessimists envisaged an end to the Republic, few, it seems, ever conceived of a new world order. But that new order emerged, and the old system was torn down. The senators did not understand the perilous and fragile nature of their position until a Roman legionary stood before them, armed and very dangerous.

The story that I tell is of a violent society. Rome was not a place of easy consensus and of shared values. In Rome, social order was maintained through the use of violent repression. Rome was, after all, a slave society, and the Romans were a people who had conquered Italy and large parts of the Mediterranean basin by the time this story begins. Violence is not, it seems to me, the normal way in which human relations are negotiated. I do not believe that left to our own devices, we will all start killing each other; the human heart is not the heart of darkness. But many societies are violent, and the potential for violence lies close to the surface. In many places, the political order is predatory, ensuring the acquiescence and service of its population through exploitation of their dependence and threats of violence.

This project started from a radical thought. I had been teaching the Roman revolution for years, but I did not like the books I got my students to read and I worried about the essays they wrote. Somehow, it was all too nice: the histories are full of "settlements," "consensus," "restorations," "peace," and, worst of all, "civilization." But the Roman accounts of their revolution are anything but nice. They were shocked and shocking. There was thus the kind of gap between modern perception and ancient sources that one worries about if one is a historian. I started to wonder how to think and write about that violence. I began to wonder why Rome was so violent. I could not just dismiss the violence as "one of those things," one cultural difference among many that separated us from them. And in worrying about the violence, I also started to worry about modern tales of violence, about the catastrophic and genocidal wars that we saw break out suddenly across the latter decades of the twentieth century. In the comfortable countries, that violence is also often seen as marking difference, a cultural and historical separation between us and them. Yet as soon as one digs a little and looks into what happened, "they," horrifying as it may seem, turn out to be quite like "us."

Much of our contemporary political terminology is classical: the classics gave us "democracy," "citizenship," and "freedom" (in at least some of its senses), and there is a temptation to read the classical states through the paradigmatic experience of the modern Western state, a state that has hidden its repressive powers and tendencies. Historians always imagine other societies from what they know of their own (making allowance for cultural difference). But what would happen to our histories if we thought of the Roman state not as a liberal consensual state, the basis of Western political thinking, but as a predatory state, its power resting in violence and in the poverty and dependence of its people? If we changed our perspective, we would have to start thinking about Roman politics and society again, starting not from the speeches and philosophical discourses of Cicero and his friends, nor from the values of citizenship and Roman political culture as they have been received and modified over generations of modern political thought, but from the perspective of the soldier in the camp, or the poor man in the street or the field. These were, after all, the vast mass of the individuals who fought and died in the civil wars. For what were they fighting? From their perspective, what were the values of Rome and the worth of Roman citizenship? Did they even participate in the values of the political elite, and did they have a stake in the state which demanded their services?

To understand these men, one had to begin at the beginning. One needed to think about what was important to them and how they interacted with political society and, crucially, how they survived from day to day and from generation to generation. The great truth of history, so often unspoken, is that for most of our ancestors the key issues were not those of political philosophy, the nature of freedom and the nation, but how to feed oneself and one's children. History is about food.

Once we start to think about the link between power and food, we can understand better the social divisions of Roman society and why so few people seem to have mourned the passing of the Roman Republic, a political system beloved of classical historians and political philosophers. Politics is not just, or even primarily, about great ideas and debates, the dramas of the great men and their conflicts and careers. Men and women may trade in ideas, but to live they need material: food and fuel and clothes and shelter.

From our comfortable seats, seduced by the glory and grandeur of Rome, this is a truth all too easy to forget. It is also a truth which is universal. Uncomfortably, one comes to suspect that lurking behind our politics of comfort might be another, harder world. If politics seems not to matter to many in the West, for billions of poorer people politics is profoundly important. Food, money, and violence are the realities of power, and this book reconnects to those realities.

The story of this book takes us from the murder of Caesar (chapter 2) to the accession of the second emperor, Tiberius. It shows us how and why the regime of Augustus was able to end five centuries of republic and replace it with a monarchy. The first chapter introduces some of the themes and theories of Roman politics. I use the chapter to explain some of the approaches that the book takes and why the Augustan period is paradoxical in its very nature. I have also made liberal use in this book of the word "revolution," a word which is provoking and dangerous. I use the chapter to explain why the Augustan period was revolutionary.

In the chapters that follow, I lead the reader through the great political events of the age, from the death of Caesar (and the background to

Preface

the assassination) to the emergence of a distinctive and new political order in Roman society. I show how the young Octavian and his allies broke the power of the old order and then how the new imperial system came into being. That new system was powerful and merciless. It allowed no opposition. Even after Octavian had changed his name to Augustus, the fundamentals of the regime remained unchanged. Augustus crushed his enemies. He bought supporters. The wealth of empire was exploited to maintain the new regime. In A.D. 14, Augustus died and was followed by a second emperor, Tiberius. By that time, the Republic was merely a ghostly memory, and it has remained such ever since.

There is a long road from idea to book. I persuaded the Arts and Humanities Research Council (UK) to give me some money, and that bought me time, for which I give them thanks. I also thank Stefan Vranka of OUP and Robin Waterfield for their endless patience, support, and detailed and deserved criticism. This is an infinitely better book as a result. I also thank the anonymous reviewer employed by OUP, whose detailed comments have saved me from many an infelicity and not a few errors. I thank those with whom I have talked about this project, mostly in passing: Dominic Rathbone, Henrik Mouritsen, Matthew Fox. Mostly, however, I thank my family, Sam, Josh, Vasilis, and Stefanos, for being endlessly wonderful.

I dedicate the book to Efi, in thanks for all the days and all the nights.

the assassination) to the emergence of a distinctive and new political order in Roman society. I show how the young Octavian and his allies broke the power of the old order and then how the new imperial system came into being. That new system was powerful and merciless. It allowed no opposition. Even after Octavian had changed his name to Augustus, the fundamentals of the regime remained unchanged. Augustus crushed his enemies. He bought supporters. The wealth of empire was exploited to maintain the new regime. In A.D. 14, Augustus died and was followed by a second emperor, Tiberius. By that time, the Republic was merely a ghostly memory, and it has remained such ever since.

There is a long road from idea to book. I persuaded the Arts and Humanities Research Council (UK) to give me some money, and that bought me time, for which I give them thanks. I also thank Stefan Vranka of OUP and Robin Waterfield for their endless patience, support, and detailed and deserved criticism. This is an infinitely better book as a result. I also thank the anonymous reviewer employed by OUP, whose detailed comments have saved me from many an infelicity and not a few errors. I thank those with whom I have talked about this project, mostly in passing: Dominic Rathbone, Henrik Mouritsen, Matthew Fox. Mostly, however, I thank my family, Sam, Josh, Vasilis, and Stefanos, for being endlessly wonderful.

I dedicate the book to Efi, in thanks for all the days and all the nights.

Preface

the assassination) to the emergence of a distinctive and new political order in Roman society. I show how the young Octavian and his allies broke the power of the old order and then how the new imperial system came into being. That new system was powerful and merciless. It allowed no opposition. Even after Octavian had changed his name to Augustus, the fundamentals of the regime remained unchanged. Augustus crushed his enemies. He bought supporters. The wealth of empire was exploited to maintain the new regime. In A.D. 14, Augustus died and was followed by a second emperor, Tiberius. By that time, the Republic was merely a ghostly memory, and it has remained such ever since.

There is a long road from idea to book. I persuaded the Arts and Humanities Research Council (UK) to give me some money, and that bought me time, for which I give them thanks. I also thank Stefan Vranka of OUP and Robin Waterfield for their endless patience, support, and detailed and deserved criticism. This is an infinitely better book as a result. I also thank the anonymous reviewer employed by OUP, whose detailed comments have saved me from many an infelicity and not a few errors. I thank those with whom I have talked about this project, mostly in passing: Dominic Rathbone, Henrik Mouritsen, Matthew Fox. Mostly, however, I thank my family, Sam, Josh, Vasilis, and Stefanos, for being endlessly wonderful.

I dedicate the book to Efi, in thanks for all the days and all the nights.

LIST OF ILLUSTRATIONS

LIST OF MAPS

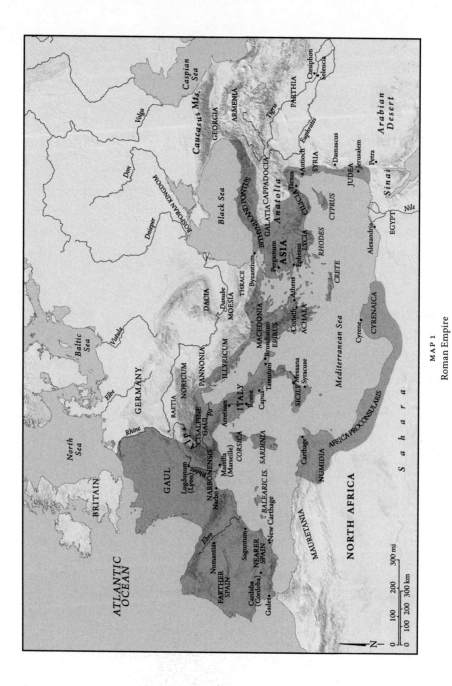

MAP 1
Roman Empire

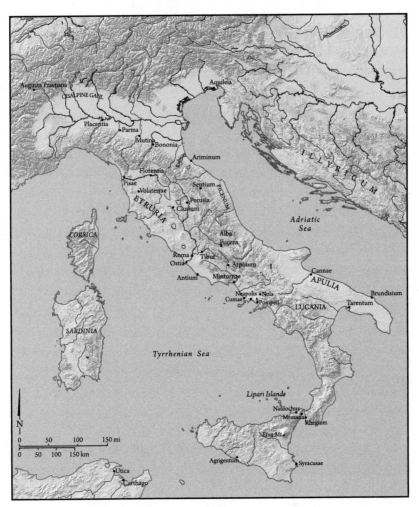

MAP 2
Roman Italy

∾

ROME'S REVOLUTION

1.

THE HISTORIAN'S PROBLEM: THE

AUGUSTAN PARADOX

I<small>N THE 2,000 YEARS SINCE</small> the death of the first Roman emperor, Augustus and Julius Caesar have been the subject of more learned debate than any other ancient political personalities. They capture our historical imaginations because they stand as central figures in a great historical transition, a shift in eras that was to shape subsequent world history. Julius Caesar has even given his name to a form of political governance, Caesarism, a reforming dictatorship favored by those who think that great individuals can transform societies and remake history in their own image. Caesar is thus the political precursor of Napoleon, after whom comes the sorry succession of delusional and murderous dictators of the twentieth century.

But Caesar has always been a somewhat unsatisfactory great man. It is true that he was a conqueror who brought Gaul into the Roman Empire. He was also victorious in civil wars and established a regime which might, eventually, have been transformed into a monarchy. His commentaries on his own wars portray a great and gifted leader. Yet there is very little evidence to suggest that he was a transformational presence in Roman politics and society. His period of dominance was cut short by his assassination, but historians struggle to find the radical and reforming agenda that might have stabilized the dangerous and violent politics of the late Republic. Transformation, when it came, was under the guidance of Caesar's heir, Octavian, later to be known as Augustus.

Even if Augustus is a better option for historical hero-worship, however, I see very little evidence that he had any firm grasp on the momentous nature of the political transformations that reshaped Rome under his rule. Augustus muddled through, like so many politicians, taking decisions contingent on the particular political circumstances. Of course, Augustus was a very able politician. He knew more about the day-to-day politics of his era than we ever will. He was also a supremely successful politician, and he established a stable imperial regime. As Augustus claimed on his deathbed, he played his part well. But in our admiration of his undoubted success and, indeed, of the cultural excellence that made Augustan Rome seem a golden age of literature, art, and architecture, it is easy to be blinded to the dark side of the regime.

The Roman revolution was a period of multiple paradoxes. The Republic had been astonishingly successful in the centuries following the expulsion of the kings in 509 B.C. In three centuries from ca. 350, Rome had conquered first Italy and then much of the Mediterranean region. And yet the Romans dropped the republican system, amid considerable political violence, at the end of the first century. In its stead, they adopted an imperial monarchy, a system which few contemporaries and few later theorists regarded as sensible or reasonable.

The key event that set the revolution in motion was the assassination of Julius Caesar in March 44, but when the assassins killed Caesar, a man honored by the Republic as one of its greatest leaders, they struck in the name of the Republic. They stabbed a senior magistrate in order to preserve the rights and privileges of Roman magistrates. They acted because they saw Caesar as a tyrant and because they knew that tyrants killed without due process and abused the rights of Roman citizens. Murder was used to prevent murders that had not as yet occurred. The assassins took the law into their own hands so as to defend the law. They killed a man notorious for his clemency, a man who had systematically forgiven his opponents after the recent civil war and who had consistently defended the rights of citizens to trial.

We can press the case. The "liberators of the Republic" were led by Marcus Junius Brutus. He was a friend of Caesar. His mother, Servilia, had been, it was widely believed, Caesar's lover and it may have been that the young Brutus got to know Caesar in his mother's rooms. In an era of personal politics, one would have expected Brutus to have tied his political career to the older man, but Brutus acted in conscious imitation of a mythical ancestor who had ended the rule of kings in Rome in 509 B.C. Rather than working through the paradigms and realities of contemporary political life, Brutus chose to re-enact a mythic event.

In itself, this stretches our imaginations. Who among our contemporary politicians would closely model their actions on acts acknowledged to be mythical? But the murder of Caesar was more than a nod to history, it was a reperformance of the events in the expectation that the same result would follow. Brutus appears to have believed that nothing fundamental had changed in the rules of Roman politics and society over the intervening 460 years and that his actions were likely to produce a historical repeat of the events around the foundation of the Republic (though we may note that the first Brutus expelled the tyrant rather than assassinate him). The assassins were educated men of considerable political experience who confidently expected that the outcome of their actions would be the restoration of the Republic.

For the assassins, the Republic had been suspended with the civil war between Caesar and his great rival, Pompey. The civil war of 49 had bubbled on until 45, though the outcome was decided by the battle of Pharsalus in August 48. Caesar had not, however, stepped back in 44 to a more normal role. It was in reaction to Caesar's continued predominance within Roman politics that the assassins acted. They desired to return Rome to the political status quo before the war. For this act of murder and political restoration, they would have fondly expected to receive the plaudits of a grateful Roman people. Perhaps they dreamed of statues in their honor in the Forum and of being remembered for generations to come as heroes of the Republic, as the first Brutus was remembered.

In this last regard were they right, but in all other respects they were wrong. The assassins misread the political outcome of their act. The conspirators had their supporters, for whom they were liberators, but for others they were enemies of the state, dangerous and violent murderers. They were hounded from the city and forced to fight a war, which they lost. That defeat led to a permanent monarchy in Rome, and so, to add to our list of paradoxes, Roman monarchy stemmed directly from the most famous attempt to restore a conservative republican political order.

The new monarchy was similarly paradoxical. In January of 27 B.C., the monarchy stabilized its political position through a series of acts that culminated in the first emperor declaring that he had restored the Republic. He maintained that position even in his final message to the Roman people, a list of achievements inscribed on large bronze pillars erected at the entrance to his mausoleum. That mausoleum was one of the grandest buildings of Rome and had been used as a family tomb long before A.D. 14, marking in the most obvious form the domination of Rome by a single family, a domination which seems to us and probably seemed to many contemporaries incompatible with republicanism.

The Roman revolution consistently wore the clothes of the Republic and of Roman traditionalism. The regime claimed to restore old ideas, old liberties, and old ways of behaving. The Augustan monarchy annexed the republican past to legitimize its existence. Augustan reforms of society aimed at restoration, not invention. Even when Augustus held a great festival to declare a new age, it was not, ultimately, supposed to be a new era but an old era returned. Yet nearly everyone seems to have thought that the Augustan world was radically new. Contemporaries noted the false conservatism of the regime and satirized it. Later historians discussed the nature of the revolution, proclaimed its completeness, and never doubted that it was a fundamental historical transformation.

The Augustan revolution is not easily categorized. There was no tsar to shoot or king to decapitate. There was no claimed sweeping away of social structures of oppression, either medieval or capitalistic. There was no "big idea" that animated radical political change. And yet I maintain that Rome experienced a revolution. There was a regime change. In spite of the fact that there was no new "big idea" which would challenge the dominance of the elite, the material realities of political power were such that the power of the political elite was broken and a new regime came into power. Many of those at the top of the political system in A.D. 14 were descendants of those who had been in power six decades earlier.

Nevertheless, the system that incorporated them in A.D. 14 was very different from that of 50 B.C. This transformation was far from a straight-forward process. The old system was extraordinarily resilient. It took civil wars, terrible state-sponsored violence, riots in the street, the cata-strophic political failure of the traditional elite, and the passing of a considerable amount of time to convince the elite that the nature of the Roman state had changed and that they lived in an empire with new rules and new modes of politics. It was that transformation in political culture that lay at the heart of the revolution.

A POLITICAL CULTURE

The senators were men of tradition, living in a traditional society. The hierarchical structures of Roman society were honored by history and tradition, and the weight of the past lay on the Roman elite. It was a heavy responsibility.

Over the last century of the Republic, there were numerous crises, but the Republic always bounced back. Between 133 and 31 B.C., Rome saw at least eleven major outbreaks of civil violence (discounting the occasional riot), several of which escalated into civil wars. The reason for the resil-ience of the Roman Republic lay not so much in the political and consti-tutional structures of the Roman state or in a reverence for political traditions as in the relationship between political structures and social structures. There was a fundamental integration of political and social life. This integration requires us to think about politics in the clas-sical period in a different way and to develop a particular terminology for the discussion of Greek and Roman politics.

Rome was a "political culture." Social hierarchies and political hierar-chies were integrated to the extent that they were inseparable. Whereas we envisage our societies as divided into a variety of loosely linked spheres of power and influence (e.g., media, business, civil society, the state, religious authority), such a division made no sense for the Romans.

We can understand this better by considering the social and politi-cal power of the senators. The senators were the wealthiest men in

Roman society. They were the cultural leaders, bringing literature, art, and architecture to Rome. They represented the Roman people to the gods. They sat in judgment on their fellow citizens in the courts. Crucially, they commanded the armies in war and wielded political authority. This authority was hallowed by tradition and success. To break senatorial power would (we might imagine) require a complete revolution in which the hierarchies of Roman society were also overthrown, the traditions of Rome lost, and every aspect of Roman society thrown into chaos. The embedding of the political in the social meant that to be Roman was to exist within the Republic, to enjoy its political privileges, to partake of its citizen culture, and to honor the hierarchies of Roman social life. A post-republican Rome was not Rome (or so it would seem). To imagine a Rome in which the political order had been subverted was to imagine a place without traditions and without social order; such a place would be anarchy. For Romans, such a development was not unthinkable, but it was cataclysmic and an end to Rome itself.[1]

Rome's political culture generated a consensus among the elite as to how Rome should be governed. The political hierarchies of Rome were integrated into its social and economic structures. Viewed from the outside, from the perspective of the partial record that we have from the late Roman Republic, one generated from within the educated political elite, this culture looks like a "total system" to which there was no alternative. There was plenty of competition in Roman society, but no obvious opposition.

But there were people outside the elite, people whose voices we rarely see reported. Rome was a city with a population in excess of 1,000,000. It sat at the heart of Italy, which had a population in excess of 5,000,000. Might the "masses" have had political views different from those of the elite? We might imagine differences of view, different interests, and different interpretations. The world of sub-elite thinking may not be recorded in our material, but we need not assume that the poorer members of Roman society just believed the same things in the same committed manner as the richer folk believed.[2]

THE NATURE OF ROME'S REVOLUTION

"Revolution" is a term laden with controversy. Its use and misuse throughout the political controversies of the twentieth century have given it complex layers of meanings. A revolution in the classical sense is a violent transition between forms of government. Classical political theory, transmitted through Aristotle, Polybius, Cicero, and Machiavelli, envisaged three basic forms of government: monarchy, aristocracy, and democracy. Each mode has its virtuous form, but each is subject to corruption, with monarchy degenerating to tyranny, aristocracy to oligarchy, and democracy to mob rule. The revolutionary moment comes when the citizens, recognizing the corruption within the government, violently overthrow the degenerate form and establish a moral form in its place.

From the nineteenth century onward, however, "revolution" has come to have a different meaning, in which not only is the form of government changed but a new "class" achieves political dominance. Such revolutions are sometimes seen as progressive, as elements in the march of progress towards the next, more developed, better historical stage. Much ink has been spilled in intellectual disputes over the definitions of revolution; much blood has been spilled in the furthering of revolutionary progress and the moral certainties of revolutionary and, indeed, counterrevolutionary activity.

The histories of revolutions are rarely so ordered. Revolutions are often against an existing order or seeming injustices embedded in that order; they are not necessarily "for" a particular new order. Ideologues and revolutionary leaders might be inspired by new ideas or by a preference for a new and different form of government, and ideological undercurrents might gradually strip away the legitimacy of the old regime, but mass popular uprisings are rarely responses to ideology. The mass ideological revolution, when it occurs, often comes after the fact.

Revolution begins when one system of values, an ideology dominant within a particular political culture, gives way.[3] Revolutions are normally incoherent, messy, violent affairs in which the existing order is rejected.

It is only later, sometimes much later, that a new order and a new social ideology take root, and very often that new order draws a great deal from the experience of the old. After 43 B.C., after the troops had marched on Rome and the triumvirs had consolidated their power, Roman society was turned upside down. Rome's traditions were denied. From 43 to 32 (the triumviral period), and especially in the early years of that period, every aspect of Roman society was thrown into chaos. As a result, a new political order emerged. Yet Rome continued.

Modern historians tend to be in denial about Rome's revolution. The last century of the Republic was marked by numerous violent civil dissensions: the killing of magistrates in riots and armed suppressions, violent assemblies, the murder of prominent politicians, and major civil wars. However one classifies these events, they do not speak of a healthy political system. And yet this age of disorder is notable for the absence of any serious attempt to address underlying causes or to reform Roman society.

There was no revolutionary agenda in Rome. The fundamental problems that modern historians can detect underlying the history of violence in the late Roman Republic (poverty of the lower classes, economic changes in Italian agriculture, the place of the minor aristocracy in the political system, increased divisions between rich and poor, the rewards of military service and access to the land) were hardly touched on in Roman political debate.[4] Fundamental reforms of Roman society were not discussed.

The Roman response to political trauma was conservative: the issue was that the social hierarchy was threatened. The threat stemmed from moral corruption, and the solution was not to re-establish social relations on a new and different sociological and economic basis or to provide a new political system, but to somehow return to an old set of moral and political values. Those ancient sources which discussed the problems of the late Republic were mostly pessimistic about a successful outcome to any attempt at conservative moral reform. Largely, this pessimism derived from the perception that imperial expansion had brought about fundamental changes in Roman social and moral relations on which politics had depended. As a result, there was no obvious means by which Rome could return to those antique social and moral relationships without giving up the wealth and power it had accumulated.[5]

If there was an absence of revolutionary ideology, a further paradox of the Augustan revolution is that by A.D. 14, we seem to be able to point to more continuities with the republican world order than dramatic divergences. In A.D. 14, the most powerful people in the state were landed aristocrats, many of whom were the sons and grandsons of senior figures in the republican aristocracy.[6] After the supposed "revolution," social structures were unreformed, the senate continued to meet throughout the triumviral period, laws continued to be passed, magistrates were elected (after a fashion), and the functions of Roman government continued. For some, the "revolution" has been reduced to a technical innovation, an improvement on a flawed political system.[7] Normally sober historians have been moved to lavish praise on the Augustan order; in this new regime, messy politics have been replaced by neat administration.[8] For Rome's modern interpreters, culture politics has replaced power politics; evolution has succeeded insurrection.[9] In the absence of evidence for systematic ideological debate, radical social reform, or the replacement of political institutions, the violence at the end of the Republic has become management failure. There was no social crisis, no radical agenda, and no revolutionary action.[10]

These interpretations run up against great problems. In 40 B.C., not only were there different people in power than four years earlier, but the political basis of their authority was different from that of the senators who had ruled Rome for the preceding centuries. The revolutionary government of the period crushed opposition, killing many of their opponents, and elevating their own supporters, most notably the troops. The contrast is marked if we consider that in 43 B.C. the senators had felt that they could not only insult senior soldiers sent to negotiate by Octavian, but that their power and political dignity required them to humiliate their inferiors. Three years later, those very same soldiers were masters of Italy. Rome still had its senators, but in 40 B.C. and throughout the subsequent centuries, anyone who believed that that the senators ruled Rome was deluded.

To understand exactly what happened, we have to break away from conventional modern ways of thinking and find a new paradigm for understanding Roman politics. Instead of thinking about politics in terms of classes, institutions, constitutions, and political structures, we should think of politics in terms of networks of power.

REVOLUTIONARY NETWORKS

It is perhaps only in the last decades that the contemporary political importance of networks has to come to be recognized by theorists. We are used to nineteenth-century conventions of class and national politics, but in the internet age and in a connected, globalised international financial system in which the nation-state seems so relatively impotent, political attention is once more being drawn to the network. And yet networks have always been an essential means of doing business in a society.

We can envisage Roman society as a series of networks. In the republican period, networks underpinned the hierarchy of the Roman political elite, but these networks were typically multiple small, flexible "friendship" groups in the Roman elite which did not control extensive resources.[11] There is one exception to the general rule, the Roman army. A Roman army came into being when a magistrate was given permission to raise an army to conduct a campaign. The magistrate, often a consul (the senior magistrate who chaired the senate) or of consular status, would then hold a levy, normally conducted by more junior magistrates, which would enlist the required number of troops to serve in the legions. Those legions would then serve, sometimes for extended periods, in the provinces. During that time, the legions could develop ties of dependence on their commanders, and their commanders developed ties of loyalty to the troops. At the end of a successful war, the soldiers would often be rewarded financially and would then be discharged from the army. Exceptionally, soldiers would be granted lands on their discharge.

But even though a general might expect a political bonus from a successful campaign when he brought back his soldiers healthy and wealthier and the granting of land to discharged troops through coloni-zation allowed institutionalization of the military network, military networks did not translate into political dominance. None of the great generals of the late Republic had "private armies" of troops and voters. The best a general seems to have hoped for is that his reputation would be enhanced by a successful campaign, leading to people seeking his advice and trusting him if it came to another election, or, if Roman politics hit a crisis sufficient to demand military intervention, his former troops and perhaps new recruits might offer their armed support.

By the end of the Republic, military networks were becoming more powerful. Julius Caesar's network consisted of the 50,000 troops that served with him, but would also have included the families and close associates of the soldiers; the businessmen who won the contracts to supply Caesar's army with food, clothing, and equipment; the traders who worked the camps; the officers whose careers Caesar supported; and the men who sold the captured slaves, and through whom Caesar's new wealth found its way back to the city. The great armies of the late Republic were an industry, and the conquests funded a great network by which the wealth of empire was cycled through Rome.[12] We may estimate that perhaps 20 percent of the population of Rome benefited directly from Caesar's military activities. Such a network had the potential to become patrimonial—that is, to establish an almost monopolistic control of resources (economic, social, and political) such as to marginalize or exclude opposing groups and to seize control of the state. Even if the Roman military networks had the potential to become dominant, however, prior to the triumviral period no network achieved long-term stability sufficient to turn short-term political control into a new form of governmental control. Without a regular flow of resources through the network, it simply dissolved. Without resources to distribute, there was no interest in maintaining such networks. Crucially, networks are non-ideological: they do not depend on a "big idea."

But this all changed with the death of Caesar. In simple terms, after Caesar's murder, the legions of Octavian, Antony, and Lepidus seized control of the Roman state. The extended period of violence and an extensive distribution of resources brought stability to this particular military network. The leaders of the network, Octavian and Antony, preserved their political and military power over a ten-year period. After the civil war between Octavian and Antony, Octavian further institutionalized his political network, and that network become more hierarchical. After 27 B.C., Augustus, the leader formerly known as Octavian, enhanced the power of his network by securing key state assets. These were, most notably, the provinces of the empire. Augustus made permanent the network's control of Rome. The political achievement of the triumvirs, and later of Augustus, was to transform that network from a revolutionary insurgency to a permanent feature of Roman political life. The patrimonial network was not just a military network; it extended eventually to encompass many different elements of Roman society, and that capacity to incorporate different groups was the basis of its success. What mattered was who had control over what resources, not the ideological, legal, or constitutional rules by which the dance of politics was conducted.

The great Roman historian Tacitus describes this patrimonial network:

> Augustus seduced the soldiers with gifts, the people with grain, and all with the sweetness of leisure, and little by little grew greater. He amassed in himself and without opposition the functions of the senate, the magistrates, and the laws. For the most fierce had fallen in battle or by proscription, while the rest of the nobles, who were more ready for slavery, were raised up by honours and wealth and so elevated by the new order they preferred present safety to past dangers . . . At home matters were quiet. The titles of the magistrates were the same. The younger men had been born after the Actian victory. Even many of the old were born in the civil wars. How many remained who had seen the Republic?[13]

Although the institutions remained the same and the names of magistrates were maintained, the Republic was over. To think otherwise is to fall into the trap of mistaking form for substance. Politics had become quiet because opposition had been crushed—to oppose was futile or suicidal. The senators were cowed by violence, paid off with honors and wealth. The Republic had become but a memory;

Augustan hegemony had become normal. The patrimonial state had replaced the Republic. Soldiers, plebs, and senators were subsumed by it, bought by its gifts. Real power lay with this Augustan patrimonial network.[14]

Rome itself was transformed during the triumvirate. On the Palatine Hill, a new marble temple of Apollo began to take shape. In the Forum itself, a great temple to Julius Caesar was being constructed, a memorial to a new human god. Nearby, a grand theater was being built, which was to be named after Octavian's nephew Marcellus. Further afield, Agrippa's pantheon was being built on the Campus Martius, adorned with a cult statue of Octavian. And by the river, the grand mausoleum of the still youthful Octavian was built on a scale to dwarf all earlier tombs. The old city disappeared beneath the monuments of the new regime.

A century after the civil wars, in his astonishingly violent retelling of the story of the conflict between Caesar and Pompey, the poet Lucan described the time thus:

> And so when the frame comes apart and the final hour sees the end of the ages of the world and we return once more to the primeval chaos, the constellations shall run together and the fiery stars fall into the sea and the earth refuses to stretch out the shores and throws off its waters and the Moon will turn against her brother and refuse to drive her chariot on its oblique course, demanding for herself the day, and the whole discordant mechanic of the universe will overthrow the laws of the torn-apart world.[15]

The old order was swept away together with all its rules. Roman politics was transformed. Although Lucan locates this change in the Caesarian war, it was the triumvirate that saw the revolution take shape. It was as if the old fiery stars had fallen from heaven and plunged into the sea, and in their place new constellations took the sky. Can one imagine a better description of revolution?

2.

DEATH OF A DICTATOR

EARLY ON THE MORNING of March 15, 44 B.C., the Ides of March, Rome's senators donned their official togas, white with a purple trim. They followed the normal morning rituals (making libations to the gods, perhaps consulting for omens), said farewell to their families, and gathered those who would attend on them (their entourages varied with the status of each senator). Only then did they commence their journeys across Rome from their grand and busy houses. Most of the senators probably walked through the bustle of the streets of the imperial capital, though some, the elderly or the unfit or those who just wished to display their wealth, would have been carried in litters by slaves.

The senators were all heading to the Theater of Pompey just to the northwest of the center of the city. As they got closer to the Theater, they met and greeted other senators, exchanged the normal pleasantries, and no doubt gossiped about the business of the day, the scandals and rumors that afflict and enliven small political communities. The great and good of Rome were gathering, a concentration of status and political power, of tradition, authority, and political experience. The senators, perhaps something over 600 men in a city of 1,000,000, reached the appointed place and the preparations began for a meeting of the senate.

Procedurally, there was nothing especially unusual about this meeting. The senate met on regular days but was sometimes called together if there was a particular issue or an emergency. If one assessed this meeting from the perspective of the last 450 years of Roman history, however—a history of nearly unbroken republican governance—this meeting was anything but normal. It was likely to be overseen by Julius Caesar, who would attend the senate as dictator, an exceptional position in the Roman constitution that could only be justified by an emergency that threatened the very existence of the Roman state.

This particular state of emergency had been extended. By March 44, it had lasted for almost five years. This was in marked contrast to the historical precedent of the dictatorship of the semilegendary farmer Cincinnatus, who had held office for a mere fifteen days. And even after such an extended period, there was no prospect of the state of emergency coming to an end or of Caesar laying down the powers that he had taken. Within this usual context, this meeting of the senate was particularly unusual: it was to be the last meeting that Julius Caesar would attend before his planned departure on March 19 for a new and ambitious campaign in the East.[1] The Ides of March presented the last, best opportunity to rid Rome of the dictator.

The Theater of Pompey, where the meeting was to be held, was a huge stone structure erected by Caesar's great enemy, Pompeius Magnus, Pompey the Great. The location of the senate's meeting was in itself a symbol of the traumatic politics of Rome over the previous decades. It was not unusual for the senate to meet in spaces other than the senate house; a meeting of the senate merely required its summoning to a particular place by the empowered magistrates, and the place itself was not crucial. Yet, the senate's regular meeting point, the Curia, was probably unavailable, being in a process of repeated elaboration and restoration since its destruction in popular rioting eight years earlier. The burning of the Curia had, arguably, set in train the events that were to lead to Caesar's dictatorship.

In 53–52 B.C., Rome had been riven by violence, and in January 52 the people's favorite, Publius Clodius, had been murdered. The crowd focused their fury on the senate house, blaming, with some justification, the senators for the murder.. The leader of the gang that had killed Clodius, a man named Milo, was the favorite of a leading figure in the senate, Marcus Tullius Cicero. Clodius and Cicero had clashed violently in the past, and Clodius had been responsible for the passing of a bill that had exiled Cicero for his actions in ordering the summary execution of Roman citizens who had been implicated in a conspiracy to seize power in 63 B.C. (the so-called Catilinarian conspiracy). Clodius had celebrated Cicero's exile by burning down Cicero's house and erecting an altar to Liberty in the ruins. But others had been drawn into the conflict, notably Cicero's brother and Milo. When the situation changed so that Cicero was able to return to Rome, Clodius and Cicero continued to clash, though the worst violence was between armed gangs led by Milo and Clodius. This violence culminated in the death of Clodius and the subsequent exile of Milo.[2]

Cicero played a central role in the events that were to follow. Many of his speeches, letters, and philosophical tracts have come down to us. He is by far the best-known Roman writer of the age, and as a result his words and views have dominated much of our understanding of the events at the end of the Republic. Yet he was a controversial figure. His facility with words made his career, but also got him into trouble. He had a typically Roman fondness for display and acclaim, and from time to time he appears to have been dazzled by his own brilliance. Politicians sometimes require us to forget words uttered in haste or *in extremis*, but that act of forgetting becomes more difficult the more memorable the words and occasion. Cicero sometimes found himself politically isolated, haunted by his own words.

More grievously, his acts—and especially his trampling over the basic rights and protections of Roman citizens—allowed him to be painted as an extremist. His behavior in the Catilinarian conspiracy, for instance, earned him the reputation of a man willing to kill his political enemies; Cicero was capable of persuading people to actions which, in retrospect, might seem extreme, violent, and regrettable. The extra-judicial executions of the conspirators of 63 were to haunt Cicero. Since protection from the violence of magistrates was the most valued of Roman citizenship rights, Cicero was identified as an enemy of the people, a potential tyrant who would crush the civil liberties of those who opposed him. Clodius's death merely confirmed Cicero's reputation as a violent opponent of popular leaders. Whatever Cicero's responsibility for the violence of 53–52, he was tarnished.

Riots were a familiar feature of Roman political life, but the Clodius-Cicero-Milo riots were unusual in their severity. The senate, the ruling council of Rome, lost control of the streets, the Forum, and their very own meeting hall. The burning of the senate house demonstrated the impotence of the senators and the scale of the threat they faced from at least some of the Roman plebeians. The senate responded to the rioting by summoning Pompey, the leading general of the day, and Pompey responded by summoning troops. The soldiers were veterans of Pompey's campaigns in the East, campaigns in which he had brought much of the territory of modern Turkey, Syria, Lebanon, Israel, and Palestine under Roman control. His veterans had been given land and established in communities in various regions of Italy within easy reach of Rome. These soldiers turned farmers were now summoned back to support their old general.

The crowds were no match for the troops, who quickly established control of the streets. Pompey became sole consul, an innovation given that the consulship was normally a joint post held by two equally powerful magistrates. Pompey, who had long been the most important figure in Roman political life, entered into an understanding with some of the more conservative senators. They accepted his hegemony, and together they worked to restore order in Rome.

Once Milo had been dispatched into exile and the streets of Rome calmed, the crucial problem that the new allies faced was Julius Caesar. Caesar was in Gaul. Even before his posting to Gaul, he had been a major figure on the Roman political scene. In 63 B.C., Caesar risked further controversy by speaking against the proposal that the Catilinarian conspirators should be summarily executed. In such dangerous times, his stance in support of the law and the rights of Roman citizens and against the majority of the senate was remarkable. Caesar's acts in 63 added to the controversy that surrounded him but cemented his support among those in Rome who feared the arrogance of the senators.

Caesar's rise was unstoppable. He was elected to the consulship of 59 and used that position to establish an alliance between himself; Pompey (possibly as early as 60), the leading general of Rome; and Crassus, reputedly the wealthiest man in the city. On their behalf, he pushed through a range of measures, including a colonization program which provided Pompey's veterans with land. Caesar's measures were achieved by employing a mixture of violence and charisma, often in violation of strict legal and constitutional procedures and against the opposition of his fellow consul. His reward was the governorship of Gaul and the enmity of many in the senate.

Caesar stayed in Gaul for ten years. He had left Rome as a figure of controversy, clearly junior to Pompey, but a rising figure in Roman politics. His consulship may have marginalized him: many neither liked him nor trusted him. But the Gallic command brought him wealth, prestige, and power. He intervened in Roman politics from Gaul, and his growing power base allowed him to secure the support of some of the senators in Rome. His real power, however, came from his military reputation, the vast wealth he managed to extract from the Gauls, and the loyalty of his troops. His victories over an enemy which had once threatened the very existence of Rome established Caesar as a general to rival any in Rome's glorious military history. By 49, no one could doubt that Caesar (depicted below as a victorious general) was a potential rival to Pompey in Roman politics.

FIG 1
A statue of Julius Caesar as dictator, sporting a laurel wreath
which symbolized his victories.

In the aftermath of the rioting of 52, Caesar's enemies included many of those with whom Pompey was now allied. Those enemies desired to destroy Caesar, but had been constrained when Pompey was allied to Caesar. Now, with an emerging rivalry between the two leading figures in the Roman state, they had an opportunity to strike at Caesar.

A serving magistrate could not be prosecuted in the courts, but Caesar's tenure of the governorship was coming to an end. The moment Caesar laid down his governorship in Gaul and returned to Rome, he was vulnerable, the charge being almost immaterial. Caesar feared that any trial would be conducted under armed guard, as Milo had been tried, the verdict determined by the political interests of Pompey.[3] Caesar was unwilling to throw himself on the mercy of Pompey and still less to rely on the charity of his enemies. He sought to move directly from the governorship to the consulship, which would provide immunity from prosecution, and from there he could expect another provincial command. Pompey and the leading figures of the senate were unwilling to oversee such a seamless transition. Negotiations opened and broke down. The majority of the senators urged the intransigent to compromise. The issues were personal rather than ideological and the immediate problem seemed little more than a legalistic technicality, which, with a little imagination and goodwill, could be circumvented: there had to be way to satisfy everyone. The people favored Caesar, and the people's representatives, the tribunes, were Caesar's men.

But compromise could not be reached. For what look to modern eyes like feeble reasons, Caesar's dignity (*dignitas*) and the protection of unclear constitutional precedents, the Roman world moved to the verge of civil war.[4]

In 49, perhaps reluctantly, Caesar led his legions to the small river that marked the boundary between his province of Gaul and Italy. As Caesar camped on the bank of the river, supposedly worrying about the momentous decision that lay before him and perhaps gripped by the moral quandaries that should beset a man about to plunge his land into civil war, he was supposedly given a sign. A god appeared, identified by his size and beauty. The local shepherds gathered round him and the soldiers came to see. At this point, he seized a trumpet from the soldiers and ran across the river and the soldiers followed. In so doing, they violated the frontier. The Romans believed in omens, chance signs from the gods that would lead them forward. "The die is cast," Caesar supposedly said. The game was in play and the gods would decide the outcome. Caesar crossed the Rubicon.[5]

Five years later, Caesar was master of Rome. He had led his legions into Spain and across the Adriatic in search of Pompeian forces. He had defeated Pompey at the battle of Pharsalus (in Greece) and pursued the fleeing general to Egypt, where he had been killed by the young King Ptolemy. Caesar had rewarded Pompey's murder by deposing Ptolemy in favor of his sister, Cleopatra. In the vicious local war that followed, Caesar was trapped in Alexandria and his position threatened by superior local forces. Eventually, however, Ptolemy was killed, and Caesar found some respite from the traumas of war in the arms of the young Queen Cleopatra. The last serious senatorial opposition was defeated at Utica in North Africa; after that battle, the leader of the anti-Caesarian group, Cato, a man of legendary moral resolution, killed himself and became a martyr to the republican cause.

Defeated in battle and politically crushed, the anti-Caesarian survivors were forgiven by Caesar. The senators' lack of power was such that Caesar could afford to be generous and to make a display of clemency. Caesar invited his enemies back to Rome.

Caesar was now unrivalled in Rome, perhaps unrivalled in Roman history. He had successfully conquered the Gauls, the historic enemies of Rome, and had in consequence brought the Roman people a vast province north of the Alps. He had even crossed the ocean to that semimythical island of Britain, though his raids had been short and inconclusive. His Alexandrian war had brought Egypt firmly under Roman control. His victory in the civil wars had removed any military or political competitor.

After the Alexandrian war, Egypt had not been made into a province, but the Egyptian queen, Cleopatra, was dependent on his power. Cleopatra was to prove herself staunch in her loyalty to Caesar and, indeed, to Caesar's memory. The sexual liaison between the two, whatever its romantic basis, suited them both. Caesar gained the prestige of a regal lover and an association with the romance and allure of Egypt; Cleopatra had access to Roman power and prestige in support of her own somewhat uncertain control over Egypt. Her regal predecessors had maintained a fragile independence in the face of Roman power, but Cleopatra now firmly tied the future of her dynasty to Rome. It was no passing affair; in 44, Cleopatra was resident in Rome, in a palatial villa across the Tiber from the historic centre of the city. Caesar had used her as a model for the statue of Venus that adorned the Temple of Venus Genetrix (Venus the Mother) that was the centerpiece of his new Forum in Rome. The use of Cleopatra's image had the probably intended consequence that Romans worshipped Venus/Cleopatra, lover of Caesar and mother of Caesar's only child.

And still more greatness beckoned. Caesar was planning a campaign to the East to exact revenge for a Roman defeat in 53. The prospective conquests would consign Pompey's achievements to the shade, Pompey having conquered much of what became the Roman East in a series of campaigns in the mid-60s. Caesar intended to emulate that other great hero of the Eastern Mediterranean world, Alexander the Great, founder of dynasties, destroyer of empires.

There were, undoubtedly, flickerings of opposition in Rome. A man who is victorious in civil war and establishes a personal domination on the scale of that enjoyed by Caesar was certain to make enemies. Even the very act of forgiving his enemies was a further display of his hegemony. Those who had been forgiven were indebted to Caesar, and were supposedly and openly grateful, but they were unlikely to rest easy. Those who depend on the charity of others do not always love the hand that saves them, their dependence reminding them of their political failures and their lesser status in the new world order.

Caesar's own position remained anomalous and perhaps unsatisfactorily resolved. Caesar was a supreme individual in a republican system. He had taken the legal position of dictator, which was technically and traditionally an emergency post to deal with specific political or military problems. That magistracy had been renewed and he had become *dictator perpetuus*, Permanent Dictator, a position for which there was no precedent in Roman tradition. Rome remained, technically, a republic, with magistrates supposedly chosen by the people and executive power wielded by those magistrates. But, in fact, Caesar chose the magistrates, designating them for office long in advance. He chose the governors for the provinces, who commanded the various armies that were located across Rome's empire. He had also rewarded some of his followers with seats in the senate, effectively packing the senate with his own support-ers. Caesar's power and position were incompatible with tradition, and tradition was a powerful force in Roman culture and political life.

It is likely that these innovations sparked dissatisfaction and rumblings of discontent and these may in turn explain an elaborate piece of politi-cal theater. Caesar's acolyte, Mark Antony, was performing at the Lupercalia, a riotous and traditional festival in which scantily dressed aristocratic men ran through the city in search of young women whose fertility would be enhanced by the ritual. At the culmination of the festi-val, Antony had offered Caesar a diadem, a mark of royalty.[6] The people had expressed their disapproval, and the offer was rejected. There were probably also murmurs as to Caesar's lack of respect for the senate: when he had been engaged in business, seated at the temple of Venus Genetrix, the senate approached in order to communicate a number of decrees in his honor. Caesar failed to rise to greet them and they took offence.[7] Rumors circulated that only a king could conquer in the East, but still he did not take the title.

The Romans knew all about kingship. Their own age of kings had come to an end in 509 B.C., when the Roman people had revolted to claim their liberty from Tarquinius Superbus, Tarquin the Arrogant. They knew about kings in the Greek and barbarian worlds. But a king was no part of their current political culture. Kings were associated with random, tyrannical power, which would override the hard-won rights of the Roman people. Kings were subject to no authority external to their own power.

The people's rejection of these regal overtures suggests their uneasi-ness with such a dangerous precedent and their desire to protect their citizenship privileges: they did not wish to become subjects. Nevertheless, these political theatrics did not mean that the Roman people were opposed to Caesar's dominance. Furthermore, as we shall see, ultimately the Roman people were not opposed to the idea of a single individual having quasi-monarchic authority.

There is a danger in seeing the political discontents in the light of the assassination and of perceiving a seething mass of indignation and rebellion just waiting for the opportunity to rise up against the dictator. Conservatives have fondly admired a Roman people hating the idea of kingship and clinging desperately to the ideals of their Republic. In fact, the situation is likely to have been far more complex. For every senator ready to die for the Republic, there were many others, senators and plebs, who cared more for their own security and wealth and who had little commitment to any particular form of government. There were many who had done well from Caesar, and we may suspect that there were many who saw no problem in Caesar's continuing dominance. Perhaps there were even some prepared to think in terms of a new Roman kingship; there were kings in the East, and their rule was widely accepted as legitimate.

By contrast with the myths that have grown up around the assassination, there is every reason to believe that in March 44, Caesar would have been in a confident mood. Politically, he was under no pressure to lay down his power or his titles; the pressure was if anything pushing in the opposite direction, towards a regularization of his position. The grumblings of the senators were just that, grumblings. There was no organized opposition, either through the electoral assemblies or through any other means. Caesar was a man who had ridden roughshod over the opinions and political sensitivities of his peers throughout the whole of his career. He was hardly likely, at the age of 55, suddenly to become worried as to his popularity among the leading men of Rome, and if he did start to value his reputation, he was unlikely to be able to do anything that would materially improve his status among the senators. His ambitious proposed campaign against the Parthians in the East was the act of a man confident in his power and position, not that of someone seeking foreign glory to support a domestic political position in disintegration.

It is, nevertheless, possible that there were rumors of conspiracy. The conspiracy that led to Caesar's death was enormous: no "lone gunman" here. More than sixty senators were involved.[8] Unlike the secret, small cabals of modern conspiracies, real or imagined, the assassins were far more of a political movement. We should not think of the conspirators as a conspiratorial cell but as a group of friends and associates. These men would have been engaged in the normal business of sociability among the Roman aristocracy: travelling to each others' houses, either those in Rome or the villas in the countryside; attending dinner parties, birthdays, significant family events, and literary receptions; going to the festivals together; in short, making and reinforcing the friendships crucial to getting on in Roman life. Such informal ways of doing business create an ideal environment for gossip, for hatching of plans, and for minor political concordats.

If debate took place in public, in the sessions of the senate and in public meetings in the Forum, politics took place in the semiprivate. Such a system was ideal for the formation of a large political conspiracy. One can imagine senators grumbling about Caesar until someone said "Something must be done" and actually meant it. But one can also imagine how those grumblings might be reported to Caesar, part of the normal tittle-tattle of Roman political life: who was meeting whom, who was at whose house, what one senator had said in an unguarded moment at his dining table during a long, wine-soaked meal.

The way of doing business in Roman political life, the personal connections, the formation of alliances, the face-to-face interactions, was paradoxically also ideal for covering up conspiracy, because everyone was conspiring all of the time. If Caesar heard about one particular discussion at one particular gathering of friends, how could he differentiate between normal social and political discussions and something that was dangerous? As emperors were to find out in the subsequent century, once one started to detect and act against conspiracy, conspirators and rumors of conspiracies multiplied. Imperial figures, much like our modern political leaders, needed to learn to ignore gossip.

At some point, someone in some group must have suggested that Caesar should be killed. Rome's politics were particularly violent, but political assassination was rare, and to conspire to murder an individual for political reasons seems to have been unusual. Before March 44, Romans had preferred to remove their enemies through riots and mass assaults, or even civil wars, rather than assassination. And Caesar was just not any individual. He was, by any standards, a hero of Rome. His victories in wars; his political standing; his religious position as Pontifex Maximus, possibly the most important priesthood in Rome; his connections and friendships (Caesar was a sociable man) across the Roman elite; and the standing in which he was held by the Roman plebs, all elevated him above the norms of Roman society.

Roman citizens were protected by the law, and Roman magistrates doubly so. An attack on a magistrate could be seen as an attack on Rome itself; the murder of a Roman citizen, without due process, was an abrogation of law and the constitution. It could also be seen as an act of betrayal, since many of those of the conspiracy had benefited directly or indirectly from Caesar's friendship and from Caesar's gift of clemency. There was no guarantee that the people would support the conspirators.

Indeed, it was likely that the people would turn against Caesar's murderers. The radical step that the conspirators were contemplating required that they form a large conspiracy of the powerful and prominent, for only if they could put together a potent coalition of friends and associates would they have a chance of controlling Rome when the city reacted to Caesar's death. Even so, their position was precarious, and the risks they faced were great.

On the other hand, there was a tradition in Rome, as there was in Greece, of heroic tyrannicide. The most famous instance in Rome's history of the violent removal of a tyrant went right back to the foundation of the Republic four and half centuries earlier. In a myth that was retold through the generations, the son of the tyrant Tarquin was received into the house of Collatinus, a Roman noble, by his wife, Lucretia. Collatinus was away and known to be so, but Roman aristocratic women were public figures with a certain responsibility. The house could not be closed to such a powerful guest.

Lucretia received the younger Tarquin with due decorum, and when he was accommodated, she retired to bed. In the darkness, Tarquin stole into Lucretia's bedroom and raped her at knifepoint. Once Tarquin left, Lucretia summoned her husband and father. They came with their friends, one of whom was Lucius Junius Brutus. Lucretia gave her account of the rape, pulled a dagger from her dress, and stabbed herself to death. Brutus took the knife from the wound, and swore vengeance. He raised an army and marched on the Tarquins. The tyrant was overthrown, and Lucius Junius Brutus became one of the first consuls on the foundation of the Republic in 509 B.C.[9]

In 44, another Junius Brutus stood ready to take on the mantle of his illustrious ancestor. Junius Brutus provided the ideological link between the foundation of the Republic in 509 and its supposed salvation in 44. But whereas the earlier Brutus was to be revered for acts which led to nearly five centuries of republican rule, the actions of Caesar's assassins were to usher in the final act of that Republic and prepare Rome for more than five centuries of rule by emperors.

The sources are full of stories of omens of Caesar's death. His wife dreamed of his bleeding body. Caesar consulted the omens before leaving his house for the Theater of Pompey, and they were dire.[10] A priest, Spurinna, warned Caesar of the Ides of March (March 15).[11] It is suggested that Caesar took fright and decided to cancel the meeting of the senate. Yet our Roman histories are full of omens reported before momentous events, and somehow never find or recall prodigies which turned out to have been insignificant. By their very nature, omens can only be understood after the event.

But Caesar did not cancel the senate meeting. There is nothing that might lead us to suspect that he was aware of any dangers. Caesar had entertained a leading conspirator in his house the night before. Another was with him in conversation as he made his way to the senate. A third man, supposedly aware of the conspiracy, chatted to Caesar as they entered the meeting.

Caesar took his place in the assembly. Before the meeting was called to order, the senators met and greeted each other. A powerful man would expect to be surrounded by those seeking favors or just greeting the man on whom, one day, they might have to rely. In this chaotic milieu of meeting and greeting, this flow of favors and friendship, business was conducted. A senator, Cimber, approached Caesar. His brother was in exile, and now he petitioned for his return. Caesar would not agree. The issue could not be decided there. Cimber was insistent. He grabbed

Caesar's toga, the ample cloth of which provided an easy hold. Caesar objected, "But this is violence!" Casca, who had been standing behind Caesar, stabbed at him. He missed, and Caesar rose. He threw off Cimber and grabbed at Casca's arm. Another knife went in. Caesar was struck in the face. Another knife. He fought on, but was surrounded. Then Brutus stepped up. Caesar had pulled his toga across his face; supposedly, on seeing Brutus, he said, "*kai su teknon*" ("and you, child?"), his last words, words in which he employed a familiar Greek rather than formal Latin.

Caesar fell to 23 knife wounds. He died at the base of a statue of Pompey, his blood spreading across the floor. To those who saw him, he must have seemed like a sacrificial victim, revenge exacted finally on behalf of his one-time friend and great enemy. But it is a different name that was exalted by the assassins. Leaving the senate, Junius Brutus raised his dagger and called out for Cicero.

Caesar's last words were to Brutus. Caesar had been the lover of Brutus's mother, but was not his father. The use of Greek, informal and friendly, a language that aristocratic Romans sometimes used in their homes, acknowledged a long and personal association. They were not just friends but people who had lived their lives together, and now one had killed the other. Caesar the dictator lay dead, killed by the child of his lover.

AFTERMATH

Time makes a difference to how we see things. People may think about the future when they act, but it is the past which shapes their actions. It is from their understanding of the past that they work out what they should do, what is right, and it is from the past that we learn to predict what will happen next. Historians, on the other hand, look at events from the future, their opinions shaped not so much from their knowledge of what happened before a particular event but what happened after. Caesar's death is always understood in retrospect, and from the perspective of the historian the assassination looks like a great mistake. For what happens next is civil war and then monarchy. In retrospect, Julius Caesar appears as the first quasi-monarch in a long line of monarchs, all of whom bore his name, Caesar, as a title. It is tempting to see the disorder that marked the last century of the Republic as demanding change, a monarchy of Caesars that would be "the answer" to Rome's woes.

But as the assassins left the theater that day, bloody from their victory, they could hardly have predicted what was to follow. For them, it is likely that Caesar's death was, or was least hoped to be, an end to a particularly difficult episode in Rome's history. With the death of Caesar, the normal practices of Roman political life, and of the Republic, could be resumed. In spite of the difficulties that the Republic faced in March 44, the assassins and their allies behaved not only as if a restoration of the normal workings of the Republic were possible, but as if it were inevitable. Whatever would happen next, whatever forces were unleashed in Roman political life, however the leading men of the Caesarian group behaved, whatever the attitudes of the ordinary people and of the troops, there was no alternative to senatorial government.

And although they proved to be spectacularly wrong, and oblivious to the catastrophe that was to befall them, their confidence was not without reason. If events had followed their expected course, republican normality would have been restored and they would have been heroes.

The rest of this book is about why that restoration did not happen. The war that followed the assassination of Caesar, breaking out at the northern Italian town of Mutina in late 44, became a revolutionary war in which the old order of Roman society was destroyed. Seventeen years after the death of Caesar, when his still young great-nephew stood before the senate and received the title of Augustus, few could have been unaware of the changes that had befallen Rome. Augustus stood at the head of a vast network of power and influence, a patrimonial network that encompassed the troops, the veterans of the legions settled in the towns across Italy, the plebs of Rome, and many others who had directly benefited from the resources that Augustus deployed to secure support. It was this network that dominated Roman society and politics and provided the new emperor with the power he needed in order to assert his individual and monarchic control. The senators, who had collectively dominated the Roman political scene, now held power only in so far as individuals were members of the patrimonial network. All eyes looked to the emperor.

And yet there is little or nothing from the literature on the eve of this revolution to suggest that contemporaries envisaged these sorts of political change. There was a sense of dismay at the events of the last century of the Republic and perhaps even worry that Rome was facing destruction, but no inkling that an alternative system of power was emerging. The last century of the Republic is notable for its violence, but it is also notable for the restorations of order that followed that violence. The Republic was resilient, and it recovered from trauma. It was this experience of restoration that will have encouraged the conspirators.

As the assassins fled the Theater of Pompey in March 44 and celebrated their success, they could not have believed that because of their actions the Republic that had lasted more than 450 years was in its last days.

3.

THE CRISIS OF THE REPUBLIC

J ULIUS CAESAR WAS BORN in 100 B.C. to a prominent political and aristocratic family. Like many aristocratic families of the period, the Julians had equipped themselves with a distinguished pedigree. They traced their origins back before the beginnings of Rome, traditionally dated to 753 B.C., to the mythical age of Homeric heroes. Someone had suggested that their name may have originated from Iulus and that Iulus was quite like Ilium, one of the names of Troy. Armed with such etymological inventiveness, it was an easy step to associate the Iulii with Aeneas, the legendary son of King Priam of Troy, who was taken by Venus as a lover. Hence, the ultimate ancestor of the Julian family became the goddess of love.

Caesar's family may have been distinguished by ancestry, but they had not enjoyed particular political prominence since the mid-republican centuries. Caesar's father had been elected as praetor (the second most senior position in the hierarchy of magistrates after the consulship) and was then made governor of Asia; he died in 85 B.C. Caesar's uncle, Sextus Julius Caesar, was consul in 91 and was killed in the early stages of the Social War, which broke out in 90 between Rome and her *socii* (allies) in Italy. Those allies had been conscripted into Rome's armies and may have contributed more than half of Rome's military forces, but the benefits of imperial conquest were not equally shared and the allies remained politically inferior.

The young Julius Caesar's early importance stemmed neither from his father nor his uncle but from the women of the family.[1] Caesar's aunt,

Julia, was married to the great general Marius. Marius was not from the highest echelons of Roman society, but the alliance must have seemed inspired while Marius enjoyed successive consulships and great military success. The association will have contributed to the political success of Caesar's uncle. But in 88, Roman political life was thrown into chaos. The consul Sulla clashed with a tribune, Sulpicius. The dispute escalated into street violence. Sulpicius sought the support of Marius and organized the transfer of a prestigious military command in the East from Sulla to Marius. In reaction, Sulla staged a coup that drove Marius and his supporters from Rome and inaugurated an extended period of civil war which came to an end in Italy in 81, but lasted in the provinces until 72 (somewhat intermittently). Sulla was victorious, and his victory left Julius Caesar on the wrong side in a civil war. From the first days of his adult life, Julius Caesar made his career in the knowledge that many powerful men would have preferred him dead.

Caesar, like all those who played a major part in the last days of the Republic, was born into an era of political violence. The century of violence opened in 133 B.C. with an attack on a tribune of the plebs, Tiberius Sempronius Gracchus. History might not repeat itself, but it does create expectations on the basis of which people act. Caesar's decision to cross the Rubicon in 49 was based on a particular understanding of Roman politics and an expectation of how his enemies in the senate were likely to behave. Caesar's enemies acted as their education had taught them to act. They expected certain outcomes to follow. But it was not just the major politicians who were shaped by the events of the previous century. Soldiers and plebs had to make their political decisions. The order of Roman society had been progressively undermined by repeated episodes of civil violence. Each episode of violence made the next episode more expected and less problematic. The violence created an expectation of violence.

The first act in this repetitive violence was the attack on the tribune Tiberius Gracchus. The tribunate had emerged centuries earlier as the people's representatives. After the overthrow of the monarchy, executive power was concentrated in the hands of the senior magistrates, the consuls and the praetors. These magistrates had the right to discipline Roman citizens and even to impose summary justice. Such powers were the subject of dispute, and political freedom for the Romans became identified with freedom from violent oppression. Ten tribunes upheld the laws and rights of the Roman people. These tribunes could convene the assembly of the Roman people and pass laws through that assembly. They could also interpose a veto on the actions of a magistrate. ("Veto" is simply the Latin for "I forbid.") The person of the tribune was declared sacrosanct for the period of their office, and in extreme circumstances a tribune could physically interpose himself between a magistrate and a citizen in order to protect that citizen. The attack on Tiberius Gracchus was a crisis for the political traditions of Rome and for the political contract between the senators and the rest of the Roman people. It was from the long shadow of these events and the subsequent civil wars that Caesar and his contemporaries drew their political education.

TRIBUNES AGAINST THE SENATE: THE FALL OF THE BROTHERS GRACCHI

The Gracchan crisis emerged in the context of a long series of wars in Spain in the middle of the second century B.C. In 136, the Romans were driving into the mountainous regions where they attacked the Numantians, a tribal group centered on the hill town of Numantia (modern Garray, between Valladolid and Zaragoza). The Numantians defeated the Roman army in battle and trapped the troops on a hillside. Unable to fight their way out and with no hope of relief, the Roman troops faced a defeat of historic proportions and an enormous loss of life. It was at this moment that Tiberius Sempronius Gracchus, who was serving as a junior officer, came to prominence. Tiberius's father—also, in the Roman tradition, Tiberius Sempronius Gracchus—had been a much respected general, renowned for his old-fashioned discipline and moral fiber. He had fought in Spain and earned himself a reputation for fair dealing. The younger Tiberius Gracchus made use of his father's reputation to open negotiations. The Numantians imposed a humiliating surrender on the Romans and the soldiers lost their arms and equipment, but Gracchus negotiated the lives of his troops. The soldiers were saved and peace was arranged.[2]

Yet, when the treaty was brought to Rome, the senators reacted critically. They rejected the treaty. They must, tacitly or explicitly, have suggested that the troops should have fought their way out of the trap, or have suffered a further defeat and its consequences. Tiberius, on whose reputation the treaty had been made, was thereby dishonored.

A new army was required. Troops were raised by a levy. All Roman adult males were liable to serve, except for those who were almost destitute (*proletarii*) and those who had already served for a considerable number of campaigns (probably sixteen). Technically, the levy was a form of conscription in which all Roman males were reminded of their duty as citizens, but it was simply assumed that men would serve willingly and would present themselves at the appointed time and places. The process of conscription was more efficient than requiring an act of volunteering, and ensured that troops could be found if those who were eager to serve proved insufficient. Rome had consistently raised large armies without much visible opposition, and, indeed, it is difficult to imagine that the state would have easily been able to raise troops against popular opinion. Many of the troops were probably drawn from agricultural workers (the smallholders and rural laborers), who were often very poor, and the benefits of military service, in terms of wages and the wealth that was to be looted from defeated enemies, encouraged military participation.[3]

The defeat of the army entailed a loss of life and of equipment, much of which would have been the soldiers' personal property. Roman soldiers served for financial gain, and to make service attractive the soldiers needed to have a reasonable expectation that they would survive and win. The soldiers returning from the Numantian campaign would have come back poorer than when they left. The soldiers were also unlikely to have taken kindly to the political humiliation of Tiberius Gracchus, the man who had saved their lives. When the senators tried to raise a new army for the Spanish war, there was discontent, which was only resolved when the old and trusted general Scipio Aemilianus was given charge of the campaign.[4]

But the political crisis was not over. The Spanish war pointed to fundamental problems in Roman society and politics. Tiberius Gracchus, elected tribune of the plebs for 133, came with a program of reforms. The centerpiece of that program was a *lex agraria*. This was a law for the distribution of public land (*ager publicus*) to Roman citizens.

Land distributions were a traditional feature of Roman political life. In legend, Romulus and Remus had founded Rome partly by the distribution of land to citizens. Landholding and citizenship were closely connected, and the obligation to serve in the army (the duty of the citizen) was related to an entitlement to hold land. For this reason, those who had no land were not allowed to serve in the army.[5] The establishment of the Republic in 509 is also associated with a distribution of land to the Roman people.[6] During the period of Italian conquest, normally, after a successful campaign, some of the land of the defeated was confiscated by the Roman state to be redistributed to its citizens.[7] From 393 to 177, more than 40 colonies were established, and although population numbers cannot be established with much certainty, it seems likely that more than 160,000 male settlers were sent out to the colonies.[8]

The exchange of military service for land may not have been direct (there was no automatic assumption that soldiers would form the colonizing group), but the numbers of distributed plots and the high proportion of Roman manpower that was enlisted for military service meant that there was an obvious connection between service and land distributions. There was thus a set of obligations and entitlements that animated Roman politics. The citizens were obliged to serve in the army, and in return they had some entitlement to land. That entitlement could only be met through sustained imperial expansion. But in the middle decades of the second century, the senate ceased to distribute land. After the sending out of 19 colonies between 194 and 177, there was a six-year break in colonial settlement, before the foundation of a single colony at Veleia. There may have been some settlements in Spain and in North Italy, perhaps providing for Roman veterans, but the scale of the settlements between 194 and 177 was not repeated.[9] The reduction in colonization closed off one of the means by which the Roman poor had benefited from military service and imperial expansion and undermined the network of obligation and entitlement at the heart of Roman political life. Tiberius Gracchus's *lex agraria* sought to honor the old obligations of the Roman state to its citizens and soldiers.[10]

The law was, however, controversial. Because there had been no conquests in Italy for more than a generation, the public land available in Italy was limited.[11] Further, that land was neither uncultivated nor unoccupied. Opposition to the Gracchan scheme probably came initially from local Italian communities enraged at the seizure of land perhaps more than a century after the initial conquest, as well as from the rich and powerful of Rome, some of whom had been able to acquire control over these public lands.[12]

The senators regarded the public land that they held as theirs by right, and they attempted to block the bill. One of the ten tribunes, Marcus Octavius, imposed a veto. Tiberius and his allies attempted to persuade him to withdraw his veto, but he refused. But Tiberius was not defeated. Arguing that the duty of the tribune was to protect the interests of the plebs and that Octavius was failing in that duty, he held a vote of the assembly to depose Octavius.

The assembly was divided into thirty-five tribes, which voted in sequence. Voting involved crossing wooden bridges to register one's vote and was a long, cumbersome, time-consuming process. It was not, however, necessary for all the thirty-five tribes to vote, just for enough tribes to vote for a decision to be made. Every tribe voted to depose Octavius and after the seventeenth tribe had crossed the bridges, Gracchus stopped the voting and tried once more to persuade Octavius to withdraw his veto. He refused. The next tribe voted, and Octavius was deposed. The land bill was carried.[13]

But the senators did not give up. The power of Roman magistrates was limited by the time they could serve in any one office, normally a single year. Faced with opposition from the senate sufficient to cripple his *lex agraria*, Tiberius decided to stand for election for a second successive year for the tribunate. This caused consternation, particularly as Tiberius was seeking to lay hold of the resources of the kingdom of Attalus, which had recently been bequeathed to the Roman state, and in so doing interfered with the senate's traditional control over foreign policy.

On the day of the electoral assembly, violence erupted. The election was at first delayed, and then on the following day the Gracchans took control of the temple area where the assembly was supposed to happen. The crowd was disorderly and there was a fear of violence from both sides, and, as is characteristic of such events, the accounts we have are confused about the details of what happened next. The anti-Gracchan group, led by Scipio Nasica, a cousin of Tiberius Gracchus and the Pontifex Maximus (the leading priest of Rome), gathered reinforcements and led them into the assembly. Some had perhaps come ready armed, others broke up the wooden benches that lay around the assembly, and others may have disarmed those guarding Tiberius Gracchus. Scipio's supporters set about the Gracchans. This time, the Gracchans were driven out of the assembly on to the Capitoline Hill. The steep slopes of the Capitoline were not sufficient to protect Gracchus and his supporters. The Gracchans were routed, and we are told that "more than 300" were killed (though not one by a sword). Gracchus himself was struck down and beaten to death.[14]

The killing of a tribune was a political and religious crime. It is possible that the murder was an accidental consequence of the rioting, even if the scale of the violence meant that such an outcome was at least possible, though one of our two main accounts suggests that it was planned.[15] The very function of the tribune was to defend the citizens from arbitrary violence and protect the security of the citizen. The killing of a citizen was a fundamental assault on one of the mainstays of the political order of Rome, which had limited social discontent between the wealthy and powerful and the lower orders over the previous three centuries. One might imagine that the senators would have been chastened, perhaps even shocked, by the death of Tiberius Gracchus, who was, after all, one of their own, a noble son of a noble family. But the mood appears to have been triumphal. There was no attempt at reconciliation. Some of the Gracchans were exiled by magisterial fiat and without due process of law or a trial. The most prominent of the Gracchans, Gaius Gracchus (the younger brother of the murdered tribune); Appius Claudius, from perhaps the most distinguished family in the city; and Fulvius Flaccus avoided exile, perhaps being too powerful and well connected to be touched, but there is no doubt that their influence was restricted. The senate had restored order and its control over the political process, but at the cost of murder, and in the long term this callous political attitude and lack of respect for fellow citizens had deleterious consequences.

The death of Tiberius Gracchus did not mean the end of his land law. Tiberius had appointed his father-in-law, the distinguished senator Appius Claudius, and his young brother, Gaius Sempronius Gracchus, to assist him on the commission for the division of land. But many obstacles were placed in its path, and the process of land redistribution ground to a halt.

The political issues that had inspired the program remained. In 124, Gaius Gracchus stood for the tribunate and was elected for 123. He used his position to continue his brother's work. Gaius relaunched the program of colonization. His first measures, however, were directed at changing the political landscape and demonstrating the power of his political mandate. If the opponents of his brother had shown no sympathy, political or otherwise, to the defeated, so Gracchus was now to exercise his power without respect for his enemies. He passed laws exiling those who had condemned any magistrates or who had killed Romans without trial. He also introduced a sustained and innovative policy of poverty alleviation. Soldiers were provided with free clothing. More radically, he passed a law for the provision of grain to the city of Rome.[16]

Gaius's grain scheme was the beginning of the Roman grain dole, a scheme that has been subject to the ire of conservative politicians and historians almost ever since. The scheme involved the sale of grain at fixed rates.[17] In a preindustrial city, the provision of food to the population was a major enterprise, and Rome was a great city. The population of the city was particularly vulnerable to speculations in grain, and extreme price variations were probably quite regular.[18] Gaius's measures insured against such problems by guaranteeing a certain level of supply at a fixed price. The major beneficiaries of grain speculation were the senators and large landowners.

Gaius also proposed a return to colonization.[19] The colonization program promised to put people back on the land and provided them with a means of subsistence, and we can be reasonably confident that this was the major plank of Gaius's policies. In 123, two major colonies were designated for southern Italy: Neptunia, near Taranto, and Minervia, modern Squillace. A third colony, to be called Junonia, was to be sent to Carthage.[20] We have virtually no information on the Italian colonies, but Junonia appears to have been planned as a major settlement of 6,000.[21] We may be looking at settlements being planned for 20,000 men, perhaps as much as 5 percent of the male population.

Gaius was able to stand for the tribunate a second time and secured the post for 122. But he met with problems from a different quarter. The senate seems to have given its support to another tribune, Livius Drusus, who put forward an even more radical set of proposals. He suggested not three but twelve colonies of 3,000 settlers each.[22] The proposal was to resettle over 9 percent of the Roman male population; if we add in the Gracchan colonies (though Drusus's proposal might have included those colonies), this would suggest a resettlement program that would benefit almost 15 percent of the male population.

Gaius's political difficulties were not limited to competition with Drusus. The colony at Junonia appears to have caused problems. This particular colony was a new development, since it was located in Africa. The colonists would have been distant from Rome and their families. Furthermore, the colony was associated with Carthage, and the three long wars against Carthage were still recent in the memory of Romans. Rumors circulated that any community on Carthaginian land would be inimical to Rome. Stories were told that wolves (the symbolic animal of Rome) ripped up the boundary markers of the new city, symbolizing divine disapproval of the resettlement of the site.[23] Whatever the accuracy of the accusations of lupine vandalism, there was a gathering opposition to Junonia.

One of the consuls for 122 was Lucius Opimius, a personal enemy of Gaius Gracchus. After his election, he let it be known that he intended to abrogate the law founding the colony. Gaius was in Africa, administering the foundation of his new colony and presumably hunting wolves. On receiving the news of Opimius's intentions, Gracchus returned to Rome to dispute with the consul.

There are two stories as to what happened next. In one, as Gracchus gathered his thoughts before the assembly that was to discuss the law, a man named Antyllus approached him. He seems to have reached out to Gracchus, but Gracchus moved away. A member of Gracchus's guard, seeing the interchange, intervened. A knife was drawn, and Antyllus was killed.[24] In the other story, there was a melee on the Capitoline Hill as supporters of the various factions gathered. Antyllus, who was connected to Opimius, approached the supporters of Fulvius (a long-term ally of the Gracchi) and insulted them. In the confusion that followed, Antyllus was stabbed to death with the sharp pens with which the Romans inscribed their wax tablets.[25]

Antyllus's death was a disaster. However accidental and unplanned, it gave substance to accusations that Gracchus aimed at tyranny. Antyllus's corpse was displayed in the Forum. Opimius urged the senators to resist and instructed the equestrians (the second most eminent social order in Rome) to assemble the following morning, bringing with them at least two armed followers each. Gracchus and Flaccus withdrew from the Capitoline Hill and returned to their homes, probably to gather supporters and take counsel. A crowd gathered in the Forum, holding the centre of the city in a vigil.

The next morning, Opimius collected his supporters on the Capitoline and Gracchus and Flaccus went to the Aventine Hill. The Aventine is now an aristocratic refuge from the bustle of Rome, filled with ancient churches and monasteries and large houses, some of which are occupied by ambassadors. In antiquity, it was probably an artisanal quarter and a likely centre of support for Gracchus. As importantly, the hill is steep and could be defended, especially against anyone trying to approach from the Capitoline.

Opimius summoned Flaccus and Gracchus to the senate to answer for the murder of Antyllus. They refused to come and sent an embassy. The embassy (the son of Flaccus) was received, but Opimius was in no mood for compromise and demanded again that Flaccus and Gracchus come down to the Forum themselves. The Gracchans can hardly have been confident that they would gain a sympathetic hearing or that they would escape with their lives. Flaccus sent his son back to the senators to continue the negotiations, but Opimius had the advantage. He arrested Flaccus's son and led his supporters out to battle.

The fighting was one-sided. Opimius had taken the precaution of securing the services of some Cretan archers. The Gracchans were probably caught unawares. They may have been prepared for a riot and been equipped with clubs and staves, but had not provided themselves with any armor. The volleys of the archers were decisive. The Gracchans fled. Flaccus was captured in a bath house and killed, while Gracchus attempted to escape across the Tiber. He was trapped. Although there is some confusion as to whether he committed suicide, was slain on his own order by a slave, or died while fighting off Opimius's men, Gracchus was killed in the violence.

Opimius had promised that the man who brought him Gracchus's head would be rewarded with the weight of the head in gold. When it was brought and placed on the scales, it was surprisingly heavy. The brain had been removed and the cavity of the skull had been filled with lead.[26] Opimius paid.

The deaths of the Gracchi were a victory for the conservative forces of the Roman senate, but the victory came at a cost. The senators showed themselves willing to use force to suppress those whom they regarded as opponents and to legitimize violence against citizens as being in defense of the Republic. They also identified that Republic with their political hegemony. They were not, however, the only interest group. The plebs, the soldiers and the poor of the countryside could also be seen as members of the Roman political community and citizens with no small claim on the state. The Gracchi had attempted to honor that claim by providing for the poorer citizens. They thereby enhanced their own political support to the extent that they were seen as a threat to the conventional political order of Rome. The entitlements of the Roman citizens were honored by the passing of the agrarian legislation, but they were also crushed by the killing of the tribunes. Further, the killings themselves threw into question the basic rights of Roman citizens to be protected from civil violence.

Nevertheless, the inability of the Gracchi to build a political group capable of resisting their enemies and the dissolution of the Gracchan faction on the deaths of its leaders show that there was no substantial and organized popular grouping capable of resisting senatorial claims to authority. The Gracchi may have demonstrated the potential of the office of the tribune as a means of organizing a political agenda, but their failure also attested to the limitations of the position. In many respects, the senatorial conservatives emerged from the Gracchan crisis more powerful: their enemy had been defeated and their power displayed.

For Caesar and his generation, the lessons were clear. Senators would be merciless in crushing those who crossed or threatened them. For the plebs, the lessons were still clearer. The conservative senators had little interest in their plight or their rights. They could not easily enforce their traditional claim for land and livelihood. They could not even defend their right to the security of the person. It was a lesson that was repeated over the next century.

THE RISE OF THE GENERALS

The suppression of the Gracchans reasserted the political dominance of the conservatives within Rome, but it did not resolve the problems afflicting Roman society. Violence continued to be a political tool, and political consensus was fragile; in 100 B.C., for instance, at the request of the senators the general Marius armed citizens against a tribune, Saturninus.

Nevertheless, in spite of episodes which led to polarization of politics, stable political groupings (parties) did not emerge. Similarly, the social issues underlying the difficulties of Roman political life did not lead to the formation of coherent political groups. Roman politics remained personal and hierarchic rather than ideological. Perhaps because politics remained so personal, the Roman political elite was prone to fragmentation.

Some ancient analysis appears to have acknowledged the fundamental nature of the problems. The historian Sallust, writing about 41 B.C., traced the origins of the increased turbulence of Roman politics to the last decade of the second century. That period saw the emergence of the generals Marius and Sulla, who were then to fight a civil war. Both men came to prominence in a long and difficult war against Jugurtha, king of the African land of Numidia, in what is now eastern Algeria. Looking back at that war, Sallust wrote:

> I will write of the war which the people of Rome fought with Jugurtha, king of the Numidians: first, because it was great, fierce, and with varying fortunes; but also then for the first time there was resistance to the arrogance of the *nobilitas*—a contest which confused everything, human and divine, and reached such senselessness that political divisions resulted in war and the devastation of Italy.[27]

Sallust laments the political events of the last century of the Republic, which forced him to end his own political career and turn to the writing of history.

> Truly, magistracies and commands, indeed all public offices, seem to me to be least desirable in these turbulent times, since office is granted not for virtue, and those who have gained position through wrongs are neither safe nor more honored. For to rule one's fatherland or elders by violence, even if you have power to correct wrongs, is nevertheless ill-natured when all change entails slaughter, exile, and the other horrors of war. Moreover, to struggle in vain and wear oneself out to achieve nothing but hatred is the height of madness, unless by chance one has a destructive and wicked passion to make a gift of one's honor and liberty for the power of a few.[28]

The shift from a state which was ruled by magistrates, elected and honored and allowed to achieve great things, to a state in which the "few" had all the real power marks the end of the Republic, a revolution in which vice is rewarded and virtue has no recognition, in which taking public office brings no power or honor, and liberty is prostituted in the service of violent rulers.

Sallust attributes the violence to the "arrogance" of the *nobilitas* and the challenges to that arrogance. Arrogance (in Latin, "*superbia*") in Roman political conceptions is a powerful idea. The arrogant displayed their superiority over their fellow citizens, and in so doing they undermined the status of those citizens as free men and as equal participants within the political process. Arrogance was the characteristic feature of tyrants. Arrogance was more than an irritating personal trait; it was a serious political failing.

Nobilitas was a loose and nontechnical descriptor which referred to the high aristocracy of Rome. In the period from the mid-third century B.C. onwards, certain families had come to dominate the senior magisterial positions. Their political authority was such that they were able both to accumulate significant wealth and to support their sons in achieving political power. Although other families were able to rise into the senate and to secure the less important political posts, breaking through to the consulship was difficult. These families certainly did not exert a monopoly on political power, but did wield considerable and disproportionate influence which enabled them to exhibit the characteristics of a hereditary elite, notably arrogance. The expectation of power was such that the *nobilitas* identified their rule with the preservation and continuation of the Republic, and it was against these attitudes that Marius, Caesar, and later Octavian were forced to fight.

The war with Jugurtha, which Sallust chose as the starting point of this story, arose from a dynastic struggle. The Romans were drawn into the dispute, but its political significance in Rome stemmed from the supposed incompetence of the generals entrusted with the campaign and the corruption of the Roman political class, which meant that for a considerable period Jugurtha could get away with whatever he wanted, including the murder of Italian businessmen who were caught up in a siege.[29] Eventually, the Roman electorate rejected the mismanagement of the old order and turned to a "new man," Gaius Marius, to lead the war.

Marius came from Arpinum, a town south of Rome which was also to be the birthplace of Cicero. Although the family was probably rich and powerful in the locality, Arpinum was a Volscian town whose population had only become Roman citizens in 188.[30] No man from Arpinum had ever held high office in Rome. Marius had volunteered for military service as soon as he came of age and then served with distinction with Scipio Aemilianus at Numantia. His alliance with Scipio was matched by an association with the Metelli which gave the young man powerful allies and encouraged him to embark on a political career. As tribune, Marius clashed with the senatorial leadership, but also opposed measures to introduce a free supply of grain.[31] His candidature for the next office in the career ladder, the aedileship, was unsuccessful, but unperturbed he stood for the second most senior office in Rome, the praetorship. Roman elections ran in such a way that the multiple office holders were elected in order of popularity, and Marius managed to squeeze in as the last praetor to be elected.[32]

This election would have been seen as a significant success; few "new men" (those without a distinguished heritage of senatorial service) rose to such positions. Nevertheless, the fact that he had been elected last in the poll would have been taken as good evidence that he could progress no further in his electoral career. Marius went on to serve as governor in Spain and then returned to Rome before joining the army going to Numidia.

After a year in Africa, Marius returned to Rome to stand for the consulship. His campaign was unexpectedly successful. Marius was a military man. He led his troops with valor, and he was popular. The soldiers came to believe, probably encouraged by Marius himself, that only Marius could bring them victory, and they communicated their feelings to the Roman electorate.[33] The tribunes presented a bill to the people which appointed Marius as general for the Numidian campaign.

Marius proved as good as his word. With his allies under increasing pressure, Jugurtha was betrayed to a junior officer in Marius's army, Cornelius Sulla. The king was captured and the war was over.

Marius's victory vindicated his supporters, and they enjoyed their moment. Marius brought his troops back to Rome and they marched through the city in a ceremonial triumph. Marius received the adulation of the crowd. Jugurtha and two of his sons were paraded in the procession, as were the gold and silver that Marius had looted from Numidia. The captured king and princes were taken to the prison in the centre of Rome and executed.[34]

Yet, as the Romans celebrated their victory in Africa, a far greater danger faced them in the North. Two Germanic tribes, the Cimbri and the Teutones, appeared in Gaul. The Romans gathered significant forces under the consul Gnaeus Manlius and the former consul Quintus Servilius Caepio. These forces were divided into two armies and met the Germans at Arausio, near Orange, in October 105. The Romans were overwhelmed. The army was destroyed, and 120,000 men perished (including legionaries, allied soldiers, and various camp followers).[35]

Once more, Rome turned to Marius, and he was re-elected to the consulship. This re-election was repeated in subsequent years, though there appear to have been significant reservations about such an extended hold over the consulship. In 102, Marius inflicted a defeat on the German tribes in a battle at Aix-en-Provence; he followed it up in 101 at Vercellae, near Milan, with another major victory. In the celebratory aftermath, Marius was elected consul for the sixth time.

Yet, with no emergency to hand, Marius then reverted to being an ordinary member of the senate, if one with a particularly glorious and controversial career. His power was built around dissatisfaction with the *nobilitas* and a reaction against their corruption and incompetence. In this limited sense, he was oppositional, but he made no attempt to institutionalize his power or to separate himself from the traditions of senatorial government. In an outbreak of tribunician discontent in 100, Marius sided with the conservative senators, maintaining the authority of the senate.

Marius's one major political reform was military. In the aftermath of Arausio and in Rome's desperation for troops, he abolished the census requirement for military service. Now all Roman freeborn men were allowed to serve, no matter how poor. Historians have sometimes seen this as a significant change in the relationship between the Roman state and the Roman army, creating a proletarian army with no property and little engagement with the traditional political values of Rome, an army of mercenaries ready to serve anyone who would pay them enough. This is simply not true.

Marius's abolition of the census requirement was likely a popular measure. It allowed the very poorest men in Roman society to serve in the legions and provided employment to those who were probably almost destitute. But the entry point for the legions had been reduced at least twice during the second century, from an early figure of 5,000 sesterces worth of property to 1,600 sesterces to 375 sesterces. The requirement for military service changed from a small amount of property, perhaps enough to support a single man, to a very small plot, to a notional amount, to, with Marius, nothing. Furthermore, simply because the census level had been reduced, it did not mean that only the very poor served in the army: it seems unlikely that the social composition of the army and its political attitudes were radically changed.[36] Although the army intervened in politics in 100, this did not mark a radical break with traditions. Indeed, Marius's use of the army against Saturninus was, if anything, conservative, restoring the existing political order.

Marius had shown the capacity of a general to rise above the majority of the senators. His career had also shown that a charismatic and able general was likely to win popular trust and support and that the traditional *nobilitas* did not enjoy that trust and support. Corruption, incompetence, and arrogance were hardly the characteristics most desirable in a political class. In a crisis, the Roman people could turn away from the *nobilitas* and look for a new leader. However, the *nobilitas* retained its power. Marius was an exception and was tolerated as such. Ultimately, he was useful because he united Rome and got the city through its crisis, and as a result he was well rewarded. His job done, he stepped down from his official position and sat among his equals in the senate house.

As Marius retired from the consulship on January 1, 99, there was little to suggest the disasters about to befall the Roman state.

THE FIRST CIVIL WARS: MARIUS AGAINST SULLA

In 90, after a period of political turmoil, the Italian allies revolted, and so began the Social War. Predictably, the Romans turned once more to Marius, but Marius was now aged, and his caution left the glory of victory to others. The most notable part in the war was carried by Cornelius

Sulla, the man who, acting under Marius's authority, had engineered the capture of Jugurtha. On the back of his victories in the Social War, Sulla was elected as consul for 88 along with another successful general of the Social War, Quintus Pompeius. Part of the settlement of the war was the granting of Roman citizenship to to the most Italian communities, which gave the the allies the vote and, perhaps more importantly, the political protections that came with the citizenship.

Sulla's election led to his appointment as general for a major expedition to the East. In the previous year, Mithridates of Pontus, one of the great kings of the Eastern Mediterranean, had moved against Rome, perhaps hoping to benefit from the disruption caused by the Social War. Rome's campaign against Mithridates was likely to be prestigious. Campaigning in Greece and Asia had the potential to enrich the general and his army. One presumes that Sulla had little trouble raising troops for this war.

But before Sulla could set off for the campaign, he and his fellow consul were faced with a troublesome tribune, Sulpicius. The clash with Sulpicius was over the voting rights of those Italians enfranchised at the end of the Social War. The traditional aristocracy sought to minimize the Italians' potential power, and one can imagine that Sulla himself, who had pursued the war with notable brutality, would have been keen to avoid the Italians having influence in Roman politics. For almost exactly contrary reasons, Sulpicius supported the Italians. The debate came to blows and the consuls suspended business on religious grounds. Sulpicius and his supporters took to the streets in large numbers. At some point, Marius was brought into Sulpicius's group. There was violence in the streets, several people died, and Sulla was pursued through the city by a mob.[37] Sulpicius had proposed a law that would deprive Sulla of his command and appoint Marius in his place, and Marius accepted the honor.

Sulla, however, took refuge in Marius's house, though Sulla was later to claim that he merely sought out Marius for advice. Marius helped Sulla escape, and Sulla headed out of the city to join the legions in Campania. Sulla was nevertheless furious. He addressed the soldiers, 35,000 men (probably seven legions). He complained of the violence of Sulpicius and the insults of Marius. His troops encouraged him; his officers defected.

Sulla marched on Rome. The march was supposedly to restore order and defend the rights of the consuls. The main aim, however, was to secure the command against Mithridates.[38]

The coup was unprecedented, and the Marians were not prepared. Marius and Sulpicius gathered what forces they could and they fought through the streets of Rome, but it was an unequal contest. Sulla's legionaries were victorious.[39] Marius escaped. He hid where he could, supposedly once beneath a bed of leaves, and eventually took a boat to Africa. The six-time consul lived to fight another day.[40]

Sulla passed the laws required to reacquire the command against Mithridates, but the situation in Italy remained unstable. Quintus Pompeius, his fellow consul, had supported the march on Rome, but he was murdered by soldiers. Sulla left Rome and Italy, and set out against Mithridates.[41]

Sulla left two consuls in Rome, Lucius Cinna and Octavius, but there was no political resolution. Those exiled by Sulla had friends in Rome and many were shocked by the events of the previous year. With Sulla safely out of the way, Cinna sided with Marius and his supporters and clashed with his fellow consul. Marius returned to Italy, but with fewer than a thousand troops (no sign of a "private army" of loyal veterans). He called in all the favors he was owed. He sought support from the Italians for whom Sulpicius had originally been struggling. The Samnites in southeastern Italy had not been fully pacified after the Social War. Marius now joined forces with them. He captured Ostia and cut off grain supplies to the city, and the seventy-year-old general marched against Rome.[42]

Octavius resisted, but the population was not with him. Rome was a huge city and not easily defended from a determined enemy. Marius also had control of the food supply, and the city could not stand a siege. The gates were opened and Marius and Cinna were invited in. The consul Octavius, seemingly convinced that no harm would come to such a senior magistrate, approached the Janiculum Hill to the west of the city, where Marius and Cinna had set up their camp. The consul sat upon his curule chair (the consular chair of office) with his attendants and regalia to receive his enemies. They sent cavalry and Octavius was decapitated. His head was taken to the centre of the city and displayed on the speaker's platform.[43]

Marius and Cinna set about extracting their revenge. Gangs of soldiers sought out their enemies on the promise of reward. The Roman aristocracy was purged.[44] Cinna and Marius were elected consuls for the following year, Cinna for the second time and Marius for the seventh time, but Marius did not live long into the year of his final consulship. In 86, the aged general died.

By 84, Sulla was ready to return. His conquests in the East had been brutal and Mithridates had been pushed back into his kingdom, though he remained a power. Sulla's soldiers were enriched, not least by the sacking of Athens, and were supportive of their general. The Marian leadership were ready to fight Sulla in Greece, but their soldiers were unconvinced and mutinous. Cinna attempted to exert some discipline, and was killed in a military riot. When Sulla landed in Italy later in the same year, he faced organized opposition, but many of the senators sided with him, including the young Gnaeus Pompeius, who was to later become the leading general of his generation. Sulla himself led an army of about 40,000 troops.[45] The Marian consuls may have put as many as 100,000 men into the field.

It was a war few people wanted, but attempts at peace negotiations proved fruitless. There was little hope of reconciliation, and the record of violence and assassinations meant that few could have hoped for clemency in case of defeat. The soldiers were often reluctant to fight. One failed attempt at negotiation resulted in a whole army defecting to Sulla.[46] The war was not confined to a single decisive battle, but took place through multiple armies scattered across central Italy. The first large battle was in Campania. Sulla was victorious, forcing the consul to retreat, supposedly with the loss of 6,000 men.[47] But the battle came late in the season, and the main campaigning was reserved for the following two years.[48]

The final battle came at the Colline Gate of Rome. The armies met in the late afternoon. The Sullan left was routed and fled to the city, where many were killed in the crush to get into the gates. But Sulla was victorious on the right. Rather than break off the battle at nightfall, the combatants fought on, and in the middle of the night the Marian camp was stormed. The generals were captured or killed, and the remnants of the Marian army surrendered. Sulla showed no mercy: 8,000 prisoners were executed to add to the 50,000 who had lost their lives that night.[49]

Sulla published a list in Rome of prominent Romans who were marked out for death. This procedure, called proscription, was a new form of extrajudicial murder. Rewards were promised for heads. At least 40 senators and 1,600 of the lesser aristocracy, the equestrians, were named. Sulla extracted land and money from the Italian communities that had been loyal to the Marian cause (and, after all, Sulla was legally an enemy of the state when he returned to Italy) and established settlements for his soldiers on the land that he had acquired. Some of the Marians fled Italy to maintain resistance. The most successful of these was Sertorius, who was to establish an independent power base in Spain. But there was no question that the Sullans had won.

Our sources give casualty figures for the war that amount to 89,000, but it is difficult to believe that the war did not cost the lives of 150,000 or more Italian soldiers, and we can hardly estimate how many noncombatants were killed in the sieges and the devastation of lands that were a feature of the war.[50]

This was the world into which Caesar emerged as a political figure. Aristocratic, well-connected, but very young, Caesar found himself on the wrong side of the political divide. Connected to the Marians through his aunt, Caesar had been married off to Cornelia, the daughter of Cinna. With the Sullan victory, Caesar was required to repudiate his spouse and his family. He refused. The reaction of the Sullans was predictable, and a reward was placed in Caesar's head. Even before Caesar had held a single political office, those in control of Rome wished to see him dead.

4.

CAESAR AND POMPEY

SULLA CELEBRATED HIS VICTORY in Rome in the last days of 82 B.C. Contemporaries must have hoped that it would also herald the end of nine years of internecine war in Italy. Nevertheless, it would have taken little imagination or social sense to believe that the violence of the previous fifty years had arisen from fundamental problems in Roman society: the repeated outbreaks of violence can hardly be understood as merely an unfortunate concatenation of events. It was not enough for Sulla to kill his enemies; Sulla's settlement needed to reform Roman politics.

Sulla's solution was to restore the old order. In his diagnosis, the senatorial consensus had been weakened by democratic elements which had allowed tribunes to exercise power independently of their peers in the senate, the popular assemblies to pass laws against the advice of the senators, and great men (such as Marius and Sulla) to emerge who were difficult for the senators to control.

Consequently, Sulla's reforms limited the powers of the tribunes, especially in relation to the passing of legislation. Career structures of senators were to be more closely regulated. Governors were to be answerable to the senate. Implicitly, the blame for the conflict of the previous decades was placed on the populace and those who had sought their political support. The senate was seen as the repository of public responsibility, military experience, wisdom, and political authority. Sulla's plan was to offer Rome strong aristocratic government. Rome had democratic potential, but that potential was limited by the operation of politics in Roman society and was to become more limited by the Sullan reforms.[1]

The limited scope of the Sullan settlement reflected the fundamentals of Roman social and political thought. Whereas modern political thought tends to identify political turbulence with social problems and disruption with the emergence of a new and insurgent social group, the Roman view was that turbulence was a moral failure—that is, a failing of social discipline and social hierarchies.

Modern historians have tried to identify insurgent social and political groups who might be responsible for the destabilizing of Roman politics, but with no success.[2] Even the soldiers failed to establish any political unity. Many soldiers were drawn from relatively poor rural backgrounds; their service gave them an elementary political structure and certainly a collective identity and discipline. They also had immediate shared interests. But soldiers never operated as a unified political group. Soldiers fought on all sides in the civil wars, with determination and with considerable bravery. And there is no suggestion that soldiers were politically naive, pulled in whatever direction their leaders wished to take them. The soldiers were perfectly capable of expressing views contrary to those of their leaders, formulating and representing their views in the most forceful of ways, and, if matters did not go as they wished, mutinying until they achieved their goals.

That the Romans did not form coherent political and economic interest groups was not a failure of Roman political and social imagination but a reflection of the political culture of Rome. Rome simply did not do business in that way. Rome lacked many of the sorts of formal and informal political and social institutions that are taken for granted in the modern West and go to form what we tend to call "civil society." Instead of using institutions, the Romans used informal networks as a means of getting things done.[3]

These networks provided a social location in which one's friends established one's social status. The powerful had powerful friends, and the less powerful sought such friends. The networks allowed an infinite gradation of hierarchies, as each connection could be weighed and judged.[4] But the networks also distributed real benefits through the social system. A powerful man could enhance his power through the distribution of resources to his friends, both those of similar status and those of lesser status. It was important for those of the highest status to cultivate their peers. If a particular individual could not get a favor done, he could always seek to influence another man (or woman) of high status who might be able to deliver. The younger men needed older men to give them posts and offices, introductions and support, and the obligations created meant that the successful were later obliged to help the sons and grandsons of their friends and their friends' friends in their turn.

Friendships were cultivated across the elite, but were not limited to the elite. No one, rich or powerful, could possibly survive without a social network. The poor needed information about where there was work, access to the resources of the wealthy, and support from their peers. The rich needed contacts, favors, and information (without established mass media, information was always at a premium). Personalized processes of advancement worked through all echelons of Roman society. Even among the lesser elite, the equestrians, some of whom at least engaged in public contracts, the support of magistrates could be crucial, and the businessmen and merchants in the provinces benefited from the favors of prominent Romans, as those prominent Romans no doubt benefited from their local knowledge, connections, and, probably, money.

A man seeking office in the army, for instance, could secure that office only through a recognition of his qualities and experience. Such recognition could only be achieved through the attestation of his friends. In many poor societies today, what counts is who you know, on whom you can rely, what sources of support you can muster, and who might give you that crucial access. Rome worked in a similar way. Networks cut across classes, but also meant that people, though extremely conscious of status, did not think in terms of classes. Generals needed their soldiers and soldiers needed their generals. Peasant farmers needed their landlords to provide access to land, and landlords needed labor. Citizens needed magistrates and politicians needed votes.

Nevertheless, the networks bound members of the elite more closely to each other than to those people lower down the social hierarchy.[5] Among the elite, friendships extended into familial ties. Marriage was one way in which the social location of individuals within a network was reinforced. Daughters would be married off to cement a familial tie, often (though not always) to men of their fathers' generation. Marriage was a familial business and primarily an issue of lineage, not romance. Men would be similarly expected to marry women of an appropriate status and would look to their friends and associates to provide them a suitable marriage partner.

Roman networks tended both to reinforce the social hierarchy and to pressure individuals toward a social and political consensus and homogeneity. Since family was also a means by which social connections operated, status would follow the family line through the generations. The hierarchy would thus perpetuate itself within families, and some family histories inevitably generated a sense of entitlement among the rich and powerful. Political, economic, and social power were integrated, part of the same system. There were limited opportunities for men to rise from outside the boundaries of the elite. The "new men" (*homines novi*), such as Marius and later Cicero, were not outsiders, just from aristocratic families which, for one reason or another, had not had a member who had previously attained high office. The "new men" might not have had the background and lineage of the more established aristocracy, but their arrival (in very small numbers) in the senior magistracies caused no anxiety among the political elite.

It was this very homogeneity of the Roman political class that rendered the violence of the wars so brutal. Those judged to have stepped outside the restraints of the political order were perceived as a threat to that order and to the particular and individual standings of those who were opposed. To threaten the existing order was to threaten the status of those who represented that order; in a far more intense way than we can imagine, personal identities, social status, and the values of the state were all caught up within the existing order and its networks. As a result, politics was ferociously personal and major rifts within the political order were regarded with considerable anxiety—they threatened both individuals and the state.

In a politics that became easily polarized, the use of violence came at an enormous political cost. The Sullans, like the Marians before them, killed without compunction. But once the killing has started, repressive regimes face the problem of what limits to place upon the violence. What criteria sent the death squads to a particular door? In the Roman political class, everyone was connected to everyone else. There were no party boundaries that would allow an easy listing of who was "in" and who was "out." Civil war forced the drawing of lines, but loyalties would always be split. The deaths had cut a swathe across the Roman aristocracy; friends and family of those who sat in the Sullan senate had been killed or were in exile. There was always pressure for some sort of reconciliation, but equally there were those who feared the return of their enemies and were defensive of the power that they now held. All had suffered. All had lost friends. All had lost family. In the legendary aftermath of the Homeric wars, Helen offered the magical waters of Lethe to Menelaus and Telemachus so that they might forget their sorrows. No such waters were available for the Romans. The savage memories could not be erased.

After a civil war, it is in the interests of the victors to persuade the defeated to be pragmatic and to acquiesce. But it is difficult to be pragmatic when so many had been killed and so much had been lost. Healing the wounds was problematic when the victors rejoiced in their success and proclaimed that in bringing death to the streets and the fora and fields of Italy they had saved a society under threat. The legacy of the civil wars was that wounds were to be reopened as the losses and the victories were remembered. The defeated endured, but perhaps only because they had little choice.

CAESAR AND MARIUS

The young Julius Caesar was caught up in the legacy of the civil wars. Caesar himself, born in 100 B.C., was too young to have any direct involvement. Probably in 84, Caesar married Cornelia, daughter of Lucius Cinna, the man who had taken over the leadership of the Marian group on the death of the old general. Caesar's bride tied the young man yet more firmly to the Marian camp. It was clearly a political marriage. Aristocratic Roman men did not usually marry so young. Someone, maybe not even Caesar but those around him, decided that this was an important match. But for the last time in his career, Caesar had chosen the losing side. His youth may have saved him; he could not be held responsible, even in a time of civil war, for the marriage. Sulla tried to persuade Caesar to divorce Cornelia. It would have been the pragmatic and expected act. But Caesar remained married. In refusing to divorce, Caesar made a choice for which he was inescapably responsible.[6]

Caesar's uxoriousness might, if we were romantically inclined, be attributed to his love for the mother of his first child. Yet fidelity was not characteristic of Caesar. He later famously divorced a wife because of a passing association with a religious scandal, and Caesar himself was associated with a string of lovers. As the marriage was a political marriage, so Caesar's refusal to divorce was a political decision. We can read such open defiance of a violent and victorious regime as ambition. Deserting the Marians would have ensured a relatively easy progression through the early stages of his career, but Caesar would also have alienated those of his associates who were firmly excluded from the Sullan elite. Further, even if he had deserted the Marian cause, many of the Sullans would have continued to regard him with suspicion, and he would have been in danger of not belonging among his new friends. Caesar chose to stay loyal to those currently completely marginal to the political process.

Sulla's predictable response was to number Caesar among the proscribed, marking him down for death. Caesar's recalcitrance secured him a certain notoriety, and by this single act he won for himself a place in Roman political consciousness. It was a huge gamble. Yet, although he was forced into exile, Caesar had support in the inner circles of the Sullan group. Sulla was petitioned to pardon Caesar, but the dictator was reluctant; it took Sulla's closest associates to persuade him. Irritated, Sulla, who no doubt could make the same political calculations that Caesar had made, supposedly exclaimed "In Caesar there are many Mariuses."[7]

Sulla's decision to spare Caesar was pragmatic, since not all those with some connection to Marius or Cinna could be removed. But allowing the young man his political life was also a risk; it offered those who were sympathetic to the Marians' plight the prospect that as Caesar matured he might challenge the Sullan settlement. Indeed, in 68, Caesar was to pronounce a funeral oration for his aunt Julia, who had been the widow of Marius.[8] Two years after that, when Caesar was holding the office of aedile, he arranged for busts of Marius to be displayed.[9] Sulla had not quite been able to stamp out the memory of his formidable enemy. But by that time, Sulla himself was long dead.

AFTER SULLA

Sulla himself stepped down from office after his consulship in 80 B.C. and died of natural causes in 78. His death led to a brief resumption of civil disorder in which the consul of 78, Marcus Aemilius Lepidus, clashed with the other consul, Quintus Catulus.[10] The conflict escalated into violence and both consuls raised armies, but Catulus, who was defending Sulla's political legacy, was supported by the young Gnaeus Pompeius, whom we know as Pompey the Great, who, coincidentally, had an army to hand. Lepidus was easily defeated, and Pompey then marched on to face the more serious and robust resistance in Spain.[11]

While Pompey was in Spain, Italy was itself convulsed by the slave revolt of Spartacus, from 73 to 71. We know very little about Spartacus and his rebel slaves, though Spartacus remains an enduring symbol of valiant resistance to the brutalities of slavery. Licinius Crassus eventually brought an end to the revolt, and the remnants of the slave army were defeated by Pompey as he marched back into Italy from the victorious conclusion of the war in Spain.

The defeat of Spartacus and the return of Pompey allowed a new political settlement in Rome. In 70, Pompey and Crassus were consuls. Both men had impeccable Sullan credentials and were basking in the glory of their military triumphs.[12] The senators were confident in their power and their success. The Marian emergency was over, and they decided to remove the obviously authoritarian limitations on the tribunes and to give the people's representatives their voice. The Marian exiles were also allowed to return. Ten years after Sulla's retirement, the restoration of tribunician rights and the return of the exiles represented a return to the constitutional position of the pre-Sullan period, but politically the senatorial elite were more powerful, more numerous, and more confident.

For the next twenty years, the senatorial elite was to rule Rome. The senators did so using traditional means. Although there were discordant elements, opposition was mostly accommodated. Caesar's honoring of Marius, for instance, may have caused hackles to rise, but Caesar presented no challenge to the conservative hegemony of the senators, at least at this stage of his career. The legacies of Marius and, to a lesser extent, Sulla became primarily historical issues, marginal to the politics of the last generation of the Republic. And yet, that last generation bore the scars of the civil wars. They could scarcely forget the violence that had afflicted Roman society, and at least some of the political elite were convinced of their duty to crush those they perceived as enemies of the Republic.

The experience of the civil wars demonstrated the resilience of the Roman political elite. The networks of friendship through which power was articulated within Roman society survived the civil war, partly because there was no alternative way of managing political power in Roman society and partly because such political systems were flexible and adaptable enough to survive. The resilience of those networks meant that the Roman political elite retained its grip on power. The elite remained homogeneous, hostile to outsiders and committed to a high degree of cultural uniformity. The language of political debates was conservative and moral. Politicians were supposed to behave in certain ways, honor certain customs, and acknowledge the authority of their fellow senators. Roman cultural politics looked backwards to the traditions of the ancestors for their moral codes, and those codes tended to be powerfully conformist, hostile to innovation, and subservient to the values of the senatorial peer group. Competition within the group was contained and limited by a shared set of cultural values. Although our sources from this period tend to magnify moral and cultural differences within the group (as all small and culturally uniform groups tend to do), it is the homogeneity of the Roman political elite that stands out. Any perceived threat to the dominance of the political elite was met with violence. After all, the employment of violence had repeatedly been successful in asserting senatorial power over the previous decades.

THE ERA OF POMPEY

Gnaeus Pompeius Magnus, known to us as Pompey the Great, was the most powerful figure in the post-Sullan era. Pompey rose to prominence with Sulla's second march on Rome. An enemy of Cinna and his regime, he fought with distinction during the civil wars. In the aftermath of the Sullan victory, Pompey was sent to Africa to deal with Marian resistance. On his return, he joined with Catulus to defeat Lepidus, and immediately afterwards marched his troops into Spain to fight the Marian Sertorius and his Spanish allies. He returned to Italy in 71, just in time to defeat the remnants of Spartacus's army who were attempting to escape Italy after their revolt had been crushed by Crassus. By 70, he was beyond doubt Rome's leading general, and his election as consul in that year recognized and continued his distinguished career.

After his consulship, Pompey remained in Rome and did not seek a new military appointment. But in 67, Rome faced a crisis. The Mediterranean was suffering from a wave of pirate attacks, which seemed to emanate from Cilicia, on the southern coast of Anatolia. These pirates raided small coastal settlements and islands, seizing what they could. Pirates were an elusive foe and no respecters of borders, and they were difficult for land-based provincial governors to fight. Even Roman magistrates could be attacked, and we have a story that suggests that the young Julius Caesar was himself kidnapped by pirates, on whom he exacted terrible revenge.[13] The Romans decided that the pirate threat warranted an extended special command, with plenipotentiary powers which would stretch across the Mediterranean. These powers were voted in a special law, the Lex Gabinia, and the command was awarded to Pompey, who was given three years to rid the sea of pirates and vast resources with which to accomplish the task. There was considerable senatorial opposition to the law, which appeared to be making the greatest man among them considerably and dangerously greater.

Three months later, he declared victory. The Cilician pirates were dispersed.[14] At least some of the pirates were relocated to colonies established by Pompey in Syria on land he annexed for the purpose from the Syrian king Antiochus, an act of imperial hauteur that reflected Roman military hegemony.

Pompey moved straight from this victorious command to a yet larger military task. Rome had been engaged in an extended period of conflict with Mithridates of Pontus, against whom Sulla had previously campaigned. Mithridates had gradually been pushed back by armies led by the Roman general Lucullus. But Lucullus's relationship with his troops broke down. Mithridates went on to the offensive and defeated a Roman army.

Unable to resolve this long-running war, the Roman people turned to Pompey, and he was appointed to the command by the Lex Manilia of 66.[15] The war in the East was to last until 63 and saw Pompey vastly extend the scope of Roman operations. He eventually defeated Mithridates, captured Pontus, annexed Syria, and marched into Judaea, sacking Jerusalem. Pompey's victories marked the final dissolution of the Hellenistic kingdoms (established by the successors to Alexander). Of those kingdoms, only Egypt now remained, and the ruling Ptolemaic dynasty took great pains to ensure that they had Roman support.

The politics of this period were far from easy. Pompey had many rivals and many enemies. Leading senators, such as Catulus, spoke against his extended commands. The further elevation of Pompey was seen as a threat to the relative equality of the senators, creating an over-mighty senator who, like Marius, might threaten the political consensus. In 62, after Pompey had returned from his great victories, the senate pored over his settlement of the East, questioning his decisions. Pompey had established provinces, notably the Roman province of Syria, but he had also made kings, and these kings owed their loyalties at least as much to Pompey himself as to Rome. As with Caesar just over a decade later, there was a problem as to whether the great general was compatible with Republican traditionalism and whether his power and wealth threatened aristocratic rule.

Pompey responded to the hostility of the leading senators by tying his fortunes to Julius Caesar, whom he supported in the consular elections of 60. He renewed his association with Crassus, and the three of them formed a formidable alliance. With Caesar as consul, Pompey's settlement of the East was ratified and land was provided for his veterans. Caesar received the governorship of Gaul.

Caesar forced through these measures against considerable opposition, seemingly justifying in part Sulla's warnings about the young man. Caesar had hardly been a major player in Roman politics before 60. but he had been consistent in his support for Roman liberties in the face of senatorial authoritarianism Nevertheless, he had held no major commands and there had been no suggestion that he would or could mobilize plebeian support against the political establishment. In 60, Caesar seized the opportunities presented by Pompey's estrangement from at least some of the senators to secure a powerful ally and to deliver what Pompey needed. If his consulship confirmed the suspicions of his opponents, Caesar's reward, Gaul, gave him the chance to transform his political position.

Pompey remained the grandee of Roman political life. His influence was exerted most obviously in the suppression of an episode of street violence, an action which culminated in Pompey's election to an unprecedented sole consulship for 52. The "backstory" goes back a decade to the Catilinarian conspiracy of 63. In that year, Cicero was consul. He had been elected ahead of a prominent Roman aristocrat, Lucius Sergius Catilina. Catilina ran again in 63 for the consulship of the following year, but Cicero opposed his candidature and he was once more defeated. After the consular elections, Cicero discovered a conspiracy. Catilina was supposedly aiming to overthrow the senate, murder Cicero, and insert himself and his friends into positions of power.[16] Catilina fled Rome to an army that had been raised in Etruria. As Catilina's supporters attempted a nighttime flight from the city, Cicero's men intercepted them and discovered incriminating letters that gave proof of an attempt to involve a Gallic tribe, the Allobroges, in their revolt. Equipped with unimpeachable evidence of treason, Cicero called together the senate and announced the uncovering of the conspiracy.[17]

It was left to a further meeting of the senate to decide what was to be done with those who had been arrested.[18] Some, especially Cato, favored immediate execution in what was perceived as a national emergency. Caesar warned against such actions, arguing that they could remain under guard until the conflict was resolved and then dealt with by due process, but he lost the argument.[19,] Cicero was lavishly praised for his actions and clearly expected that when Pompey returned in the following year, the great general would acknowledge his achievements. After all, Cicero had loyally supported Pompey's interests.[20] Pompey was, however, under pressure from the very same men who were proclaiming Cicero's achievements and was not disposed to add his voice to the chorus of approval. Cicero appears to have been taken aback and, somewhat marginalized, he began to find himself under political pressure. The speeches that he delivered on the conspiracy were quickly published, but that was not enough to secure his reputation, and he spent considerable time trying to find a tame poet to commemorate his achievements.[21] When this failed, he took on the task himself, composing a long and sadly not quite completely lost poem on his consulship.[22]

Sensing his vulnerability, Cicero's enemies closed in. One of those enemies, Clodius, came from possibly the most distinguished family in Rome.[23] Clodius and Cicero had become enemies after Clodius had become involved in a religious scandal. He was supposedly found in an all-female religious event in which Bona Dea, the Good Goddess, was worshipped.[24] Clodius was tried for sacrilege, a charge which carried the death penalty, and Cicero gave evidence that disproved Clodius's alibi despite the fact that the two had previously been friends.Clodius escaped supposedly by lavishing money on the jurors.

Clodius now instituted a law exiling all those who had killed Roman citizens without trial (an echo of the Gracchan legislation), which appears to have specifically identified Cicero. He also gathered together gangs that allowed him to control the assemblies and public spaces of the city, much to the opprobrium of his aristocratic peers. But the response of the conservative senators was muted, and neither Pompey nor Caesar moved in Cicero's support. Cicero had little choice but to slip away to exile.

Clodius celebrated Cicero's departure by storming Cicero's house and dedicating an altar to Liberty on its grounds. The dedication of the altar was symbolic.[25] Clodius was restoring the liberties of the Roman people, and perhaps the most closely guarded civic right was freedom from the arbitrary violence of magistrates. Although our sources on the Catilinarian conspiracy are universally hostile, it seems clear that he had some measure of popular support, and the uprising in Etruria may also have reflected popular discontent. Even those who had not sided with Catilina might have seen the summary execution of Roman citizens, supposedly legalized through the declaration of a state of emergency, as a tyrannical act.

Cicero returned from exile in late 57, chastened and dependent on the support of Pompey. His return was again probably more related to putting Clodius back in his place than restoring a senatorial hero, since there had been in the meantime a breach between Pompey and Clodius. Cicero found a champion and Clodius a rival in a senator by the name of Annius Milo. Milo's gangs intervened to prevent Clodius from stopping Cicero's recall.[26]

There was a resurgence of violence in 53, when both Clodius and Milo were running for election. The violence culminated in the murder of Clodius. According to Cicero's defense of Milo (a speech published but never delivered), Milo just happened to be on the road along which Clodius and his supporters would travel to Rome. This unfortunate coincidence resulted in a brawl. Milo's supporters, acting in self-defense according to Cicero, killed Clodius.[27] When news reached Rome, the bereaved followers of Clodius rioted and focused their wrath on the senate house, probably suspecting (and with good reason) that many in the senate were sympathetic to Milo's murderous violence. The senate house was burned down. The senate responded by appointing Pompey sole consul for 52, and his troops cleared the streets. Milo was brought to trial and went into exile, perhaps sacrificed in an attempt to bring peace to the streets of Rome. Pompey emerged, once more, as the guarantor of Roman political order.

The events of 53–52 brought about a rapprochement between the more conservative senators and Pompey. Pompey was confirmed as the general and political leader on whom the Republic depended for its safety, and the senators acknowledged his predominance. Nevertheless, Pompey remained firmly within the long tradition of great Republican generals, a tradition that included men such as Scipio Africanus and Scipio Aemilianus. Pompey had consistently supported the Sullan settlement against those who might have undone the work of the dictator and maintained the authority of the senate. He may have been the greatest of the senators, but he remained a senator.

Within two years, however, the talk was once more of civil war. In late 50, Julius Caesar, after nearly ten years of successful campaigning in Gaul, marched south. He camped his victorious legions on the Rubicon, the river that marked the border between his province and Italy. On January 10, 49, he crossed into Italy, and Rome embarked on a renewed civil war.

CAESAR'S ACCIDENTAL WAR

In the "great man" tradition of writing history, Julius Caesar is one of the greatest of the great. Caesar is the man, for some of the more star-struck biographers and historians of the nineteenth century, who saw through the crises of the Late Republic, observed the tottering edifices of Roman power, and seized the moment.[28] If one were to read the German philosopher Hegel, one would find Caesar among the World Historical Individuals, those through whom the Spirit of the Age moved and who as a consequence advanced the course of History.[29] Yet, in the twentieth century's historical experience, the comforting dream of the great leader became the terrifying nightmare of genocide. These tyrants cast themselves in the image of Caesar, but our image of Caesar has also been cast in the image of these tyrants.[30]

Caesar was a gifted man. He was a fine writer, a skilled politician, a sublime orator, and a brilliant general. Like many of his contemporaries, he was impressively educated and hugely ambitious. Those ambitions were unusual in scope.[31] Few men have seriously attempted to rival Alexander the Great, though, fortunately, few have been in a position to try. There may also have been an unusual streak of ruthlessness to him.

Certainly, like so many great men, he left a massive trail of death and destruction in his wake. The events of 49 B.C. led to a great war that destabilized the political status quo and was a fundamental cause of the end of the Republic. These were, it turned out, events of great historical importance. But if Caesar crossed the Rubicon and launched the civil war in the service of some great idea or a great reforming agenda, there is little hint of what that idea might have been in all his writings or in everything that was written about him.

Caesar did carry out reforms, mostly from 46 onwards when he was able to devote significant time to nonmilitary matters. There was a technical reform of the calendar. There were reforms of the senate and the drafting in of large numbers of new senators. Perhaps more ambitious was the building of new forum in the centre of the city, at the heart of which was a temple to Venus. He looked after his constituencies: he adjusted and raised military pay, the levels of which had probably been set three centuries before. He extended Roman citizenship into previously Gallic lands in northern Italy. He took measures to secure the grain supply and reform the grain dole, reducing the number of citizens who were eligible from 320,000 to 150,000. This measure, which one might expected to have been unpopular, was probably offset by a program of colonization by which Caesar looked after his own veterans, but also sent some of the Roman poor from Italy.[32] Nevertheless, Caesar's policies appear to have been quite conservative; his aim, once he had eventually settled the civil wars and defeated most of the Pompeian resistance, was entirely traditional. It was to gather enough soldiers and resources to launch a major campaign against the Parthian empire, the major power to the east of Syria.

The civil war was to rage across the Mediterranean from Caesar's crossing of the Rubicon in January 49 to the death of Cato after the battle of Utica in April 46 or perhaps to the battle of Munda in Spain in March 45. Yet, other than a dispute as to who was to be the leading man, one has to wonder why the civil war needed to be fought. The reason offered by Caesar seems at first absurd. As the quarrel between Caesar and Pompey deepened in 50, Caesar's interests were represented by tribunes of the plebs. When it became clear that there would be no compromise, the tribunes fled to Caesar. Caesar's primary reason for invading was to defend the privileges of the tribunes, but those privileges would not have been threatened if the tribunes had not been acting in Caesar's interests.

In a debate in the senate that preceded Caesar's crossing of the Rubicon, all but 22 of the senators supported a motion urging Pompey and his supporters to reconcile themselves with Caesar. The vast majority of the senators, it might be argued, did not see that the problem should be allowed to escalate into civil war. The issue at stake in 50, as the war moved inexorably closer, was reduced to Caesar's *dignitas*. The obvious translation for *dignitas* is "dignity," but that does not capture the full force of the Latin conception; "standing" might be better. In a society which worked through networks, standing was a crucial social and political commodity. Without standing, a man was nothing, and his ability to help his friends (and harm his enemies) was negligible; Caesar plunged the Roman world into war for more than his pride.[33]

When Caesar had embarked on his conquest of Gaul a decade earlier, he had been the junior partner in the political alliance between himself, Pompey, and Crassus. In the intervening period, Crassus had been killed at Carrhae in Northern Mesopotamia in 53 on campaign against the Parthians, Pompey's political stock had risen yet further, and Caesar had become rich and had secured himself a reputation as a great conqueror. For the Romans, the Gauls were almost mythical enemies, different in dress, language, and culture.[34] Caesar intended to return from Gaul rich and great, in the grand tradition of Roman conquering heroes.

But the question that arose in 50 B.C. was how Caesar should return. He had many enemies in the senate, and those enemies were confident in their alliance with Pompey. If Caesar were to return without holding office, he would be liable to prosecution, but if he were to return as consul he would be immune from the attacks of his enemies. Caesar had achieved this precise privilege in 52 when, in the aftermath of the violence surrounding Milo and Clodius, the ten tribunes had passed a law allowing Caesar to stand for the consulship in absentia. Granting Caesar's wishes raised other problems, however: it effectively provided immunity from the law, but the law was the guarantor of the Republic. The senate had a right to question the actions of magistrates, and all had a right to bring cases against those who had broken the law during their period of office. On the other hand, the rights of the senators were balanced by the law that granted Caesar special privileges. To make an exception for Caesar was to put Caesar outside the reach of Republican institutions, but to refuse to make an exception was to act against the law on which all Republican institutions ultimately depended (or claimed to depend).

Yet, behind all these legal niceties was politics: what concerned Caesar and his supporters was that his enemies were determined to destroy Caesar—to insult him, and to break his political and personal influence. What concerned those in the senate was that a man of Caesar's standing could not be subordinated to the collective will of the senators, the very guiding principle of the post-Sullan system. Reluctantly, an exception had been made for Pompey, who had been the defender of the senate for three decades, but Caesar had more powerful enemies. Moreover, the senators had Pompey, and Pompey himself would allow no rival to his preeminence.

Caesar had a perfectly reasonable requirement that he would be protected from his personal enemies. As conqueror of Gaul, he had an expectation that his achievements would be honored and that he would be given the respect he was due. For his enemies, Caesar was a dangerous man whose history gave evidence that the power that he had secured in Gaul—the wealth, the prestige, the favors accumulated and the friend-ships made, and the loyalty of significant numbers of about to be veteran troops—would be used to destabilize a Republic which they (and Pompey) controlled. If Caesar refused to acknowledge their authority and the authority of the senate in general, then he was refusing to acknowledge the claims of the *res publica*, and this was evidence of his tyrannical and revolutionary intentions. Conversely, for Caesar to lay down his office was to risk political annihilation in a personalized and potentially violent conflict. The senatorial group had provided plenty of evidence of their preparedness to use any and all means to dispose of challengers.

The *dignitas* of Caesar was not just an issue for Caesar. His period of power in Gaul had allowed him to establish a patrimonial network. It involved the soldiers, their officers, the men who supplied the army, the men who had drawn benefits from Caesar's support, and those who had represented Caesar in the senate. Caesar was expected to continue to deliver political benefits for those who had supported him, and that could not be done if Caesar was to be humiliated or politically hamstrung. As no man was really an individual in Rome, the *dignitas* of any individual was never just about them, it was always also about those who were with them in the network. The rise and decline of individuals would bring benefits to those with whom they were most closely associated as well as to those who were dependent on the great man. Caesar's decision to stand against the senators who abused the rights of the tribunes pointed to a more general issue. For if Caesar were to be taken down, others would undoubtedly be caught up in his fall. Caesar's enemies seemed prepared to trample on the rights and protections of the tribunes, and Caesar and his friends would have been conscious of the history of senatorial violence directed against any who sought to oppose the hegemony of the traditional powers in the senate. Fundamentally, the issue was not one of law but of political good faith.

Rome was at an impasse. If some of the senators had wanted war, they were not ready for it. As the conflict drew closer, they rushed to gather troops, but when Caesar crossed the Rubicon, he faced a disorganized opposition. The senators' lack of preparedness may have been overconfidence, perhaps stemming from a view that Caesar would have to reach a settlement. Caesar's famous *celeritas* (swiftness) undid his enemies, but even as he moved through Italy, he negotiated. The crisis rushed up on the senators. They had underestimated Caesar.

Caesar's war was accidental. Caesar invaded to resolve a particular tactical problem: how he and his supporters could find their place in the Republic. Caesar and his supporters never threatened the Republic. They represented themselves, reasonably, as having been threatened and excluded by a faction within the senate. The war was personalized. Once the Pompeians had fled Italy, Caesar left those senators who remained in Rome in peace; he had no quarrel with them. Once the war was won, he made efforts to make peace. Unlike Marius and Sulla, he forgave his enemies. He did not store up for himself the resentments of the bereaved. He brought the defeated back into the senate; his enemies sat before him, as they should, since they were members of the senate and their presence was necessary for the proper workings of the Republic, which Caesar had fought to restore. Caesar's enemies suffered from his pre-eminence, as his friends benefited, but again that was how life should be.

Five years later, in March 44, the longevity of Caesar's rule raised further doubts as to the compatibility of Caesar and the Republic. His extended period of dominance meant that the operation of politics was being distorted. He was planning a great campaign to the East, and if he were to be victorious and return yet more powerful, then the Republic faced a man so great that the Republic's traditional elite would be subordinated (if they had not already been so). The problem was Caesar, and the solution was simple. The death of Caesar would inevitably entail a resumption of political normality, or so it seemed. The reasons the senators worried about Caesar's return in 49 were exactly the same reasons that led to his assassination in 44.

As the assassins left the theater and raised the bloody daggers, they called out Cicero's name. They were not just calling upon the distinguished senator to take the helm of the Roman state; they were asserting an interpretation of their actions. Killing Caesar was in the tradition of Cicero's disposal of the Catilinarians, a bloody act necessary to save the Republic in an extreme situation. Cicero linked his actions to the emergencies that had befallen the senators in the past, a tradition of violence that stretched back to the Gracchi. Nearly a century after Tiberius Gracchus had been beaten to death, Cassius and Brutus associated themselves with a senatorial tradition that justified their murder of a magistrate of the Republic. For the assassins, the murder of Caesar was just the latest stage in the honorable tradition of violent defense of Roman order.

5.

MUTINA: THE LAST BATTLE

OF THE REPUBLIC

IN SPRING 43 B.C., a year after the murder of Julius Caesar, five Roman armies gathered on the plain near the North Italian city of Mutina (modern Modena). Decimus Brutus was trapped inside the city. Besieging him was Mark Antony with at least four legions of well-trained troops and a large number of recent recruits. The joint army of the consul Aulus Hirtius and the young Octavian, great-nephew and posthumously adopted son of Caesar, was harassing Antony, awaiting any opportunity to relieve Brutus's army. Further to the south and east, the army of the other consul, Vibius Pansa, was cautiously approaching with the aim of reinforcing Hirtius and Octavian. Once Hirtius, Pansa, and Octavian were conjoined, they planned to bring Antony to a decisive battle. That battle came in April 43, and Antony was defeated.

The victory over Antony was celebrated lavishly by the senators in Rome. At last, it seemed, they had secured their power and authority, having been humbled by Julius Caesar. Mutina seemed to represent the culmination of the political process begun with the murder of Caesar. The defeat of Antony achieved the strategic aims of the assassination, finally crushing the Caesarian challenge. Once again, the conservative and traditional order had triumphed, as it had repeatedly since the victories of Sulla.

But the senators were proved wrong. The battle of Mutina did not represent the spectacular restoration of the fortunes of the old Roman

Republic. Victory on the plains of Northern Italy did not complete the task of ridding Rome of Caesar's legacy.

In the next days and weeks, defeat was plucked from the jaws of victory. In retrospect, Mutina was to prove the last battle of a beleaguered Republic.

CAESAR'S LEGACY

As *dictator perpetuus* (dictator for life), Julius Caesar had dominated Rome. He had supervised the "election" of the senior magistrates and governors of the Republic, appointing men several years in advance. The beneficiaries of Caesar's patronage included Hirtius and Pansa, who were to be consuls in 43, and Decimus Brutus, who was appointed by Caesar to the strategically important governorship of Cisalpine Gaul. The consuls of 43 were to lead armies against Antony, the man who portrayed himself as Caesar's heir, in support of Decimus Brutus, one of the assassins. The dictator's arrangement of the provinces had rewarded many who were to act against him directly or were to turn against those who saw themselves as Caesar's heirs. Some of these men, such as Hirtius, had been close to the dictator. Caesar's death threw all these established political relationships into the air. Everyone now had to decide on their loyalties and reposition themselves in the aftermath of the assassination.

Immediately after the assassination, Rome had been in turmoil. Mark Antony was in nominal control of the city. He had been the dictator's deputy and in 44 held the consulship. By a mixture of political pressure and veiled threats, Antony persuaded the assassins to withdraw. That withdrawal was a mixed blessing for Antony; he must have calculated that Decimus Brutus would head immediately to his province and take control of the legions stationed there. Antony thus allowed an enemy to become armed. But getting Decimus Brutus and the other assassins out of Rome bought him time.

Antony was short of political resources. He was faced with a significant and militant conspiracy whose violent intent had been demonstrated. He had no organization, no army, and probably little money. He had little choice but to play for time, to maintain some kind of order in Rome, and to make an uneasy peace with the senatorial assassins, many of whom were deeply suspicious of a consul who had been so closely associated with the dictator.

The absence of the assassins took the passion out of the immediate situation. The plebs had shown their loyalty to Caesar and their hostility to the assassins. Putting distance between the assassins and the angry crowd prevented an escalation of the situation. There were delays, maneuvers, and negotiations. In late March, April, and indeed through much of May, it was even unclear that there would be "sides" to choose between, and there was a strong possibility of a post-Caesarian consensus. Some sort of settlement in which the murder of the dictator was forgiven and Antony's political future was secured could not be ruled out. There were no firm political alliances, and even those who had owed the old dictator a personal debt of obligation or had been among his close friends had no commitment to Antony. Few of the elite manifested much desire to exact revenge for the dictator or to bring his assassins to court. The shifting sands of politics meant that it was unclear on what grounds they would choose one side or another. Antony could not assume that those who had been Caesar's men would be keen on accepting his leadership, and it is likely that many rejoiced in their release from their obligations to Caesar and looked forward to playing a more traditional senatorial role in a senate no longer controlled by the dictator.

The two leading figures in the plot, Marcus Junius Brutus and Gaius Cassius, stayed in the environs of Rome. Decimus Brutus arrived in Cisalpine Gaul in late April. This province was in Northern Italy in territory that had been occupied by the Gauls in the fourth century B.C.; it was from there that Caesar had launched his conquest of Gaul, and a decade later he had gathered his forces there for the invasion of Italy. Its legions were the closest to Rome, and in the uncertain atmosphere that followed the assassination of Caesar, Gallia Cisalpina was a major asset.

As the assassins awaited developments, Antony sought money from every available source, including the late dictator's estate and the treasuries of Rome. Military resources were more difficult to obtain. He could and did look to Caesar's veterans, settled in colonies in various Italian towns. More notably, he took advantage of a suspiciously convenient and false rumor of invasion by the Getae, a Thracian tribe, to secure an emergency command for himself in the province of Macedonia.[1] The great advantage of Macedonia was that it was the location of the legions that Caesar had been gathering for his expedition to the East.

Having secured the Macedonian legions and being assured of the falsity of the rumors of invasion, Antony discovered that it was unnecessary to make the journey to the province himself. Instead, he ordered the legions to return to Italy. By October, they were in the southern Italian port of Brundisium (now Brindisi).

By that time, the political situation in Rome had become clearer. The uneasy peace in Rome had not held. Two months after the assassination, on May 24, 44, rumors were circulating that Antony intended to upset Caesar's apportioning of provinces. Antony's intention was to gain control of those provinces in which significant military forces were located and to remove his enemies from any positions of authority. Foremost among those to be deposed was, of course, Decimus Brutus. In the first days of June, Antony moved against his enemies.[2] Antony was able to pass a plebiscite through the popular assembly that deprived Decimus Brutus of his province. Cassius and Marcus Brutus were put in charge of the grain supply and ordered to leave Italy. His fellow consul, Publius Cornelius Dolabella, who could potentially have made life very difficult for Antony, was secured by the award of the large and prestigious province of Syria for five years. Macedonia was formally transferred to Gaius Antonius, Antony's brother; Antony himself supplanted Decimus Brutus in Cisalpine Gaul. Legally, Antony and Dolabella had secured military forces certainly sufficient to guard against his main rivals.

The senators, who traditionally decided such matters, were infuriated, but the consuls were able to block any opposition in the senate. The senators themselves were unable to rouse popular support against Antony, and Antony—either because he was genuinely popular or through manipulation—was able to use the popular assembly to achieve his political goals. The consulship and the assembly effectively gave Antony control over the constitutional machinery of the Roman state, and there was little his enemies could do about it legally. The senators could only make their opposition felt through absence, and many stayed away from the senate.

Antony's actions must have reflected a political perception that his enemies meant him harm and that to some extent the work of the assassination was as yet incomplete. His provincial command had the potential to mirror that of Caesar after 59, establishing Antony in security away from Rome while political temperatures cooled and simultaneously preventing malicious prosecutions. Yet, equally, command in Gaul would give Antony a power base that might allow him eventually to strike at Rome, as Caesar had done. If his enemies saw Antony as a second Caesar, Antony could also perceive that his situation was perilous and that one tyrannicide might lead to a second. The uneasy peace of the aftermath of the assassination had unraveled.

On the Ides of March, Marcus Brutus had raised his bloody dagger to the sky and called for Cicero. Brutus's acclamation may have been something of a surprise to Cicero. In the extensive correspondence and the many speeches that survive, there is no evidence that Cicero was aware of the plot, and, given that he was hardly shy of advertising his importance, his silence may be taken as good evidence of ignorance. Cicero had been in and out of Rome since the assassination, uncertain as to whether to leave Italy, but meanwhile trying to help the assassins when he could, and build a coalition of support. He and Antony had maintained cordial relations in public, but that cordiality masked deep personal and political distrust.

On September 1, Antony called the senate into meeting and insisted that all senators appear. Cicero (depicted below in his senatorial toga) found himself detained by other business and appeared in the senate only on the following day, when Antony was absent. Cicero made use of the opportunity to deliver what came to be known as the first Philippic, the first of fourteen speeches published between September 44 and the end of April 43 in which Cicero attacked Antony. They are so called in recognition of their rhetorical model, the Philippics delivered by the

FIG 2
Marcus Tullius Cicero, the greatest orator of the Republic.

Greek orator Demosthenes to rally support against Philip of Macedon three centuries earlier. As Demosthenes had spoken for the freedom of Greece, now Cicero claimed to speak for the freedom of Rome.

Although Cicero claimed in his September speech to be a friend of Antony, due to past favors accumulated between the two of them, this public attack, far more gentle than what was to follow, was a declaration of enmity.[3] It was also an attempt to rally the senate and offer the senators leadership and the prospect of a post-Caesarian settlement in which the senators collectively, rather than Antony, would control political life. Cicero's plan was to complete the aims of the assassination by restoring senatorial hegemony. The failure of the assassins to achieve that aim had been proven by Antony's rearrangement of the provinces against senatorial opposition. The most significant block preventing a restoration of the old order was Antony himself, and Cicero was now seeking to break Antony's political power. He may have already decided that the matter would not be resolved without further violence.

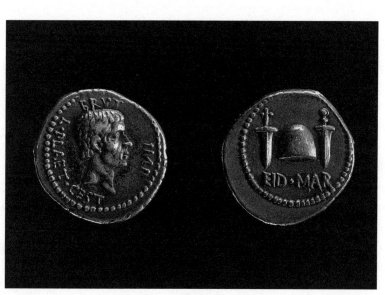

FIG 3

Coin of Junius Brutus. The coin depicts daggers and the cap of freedom which was given to slaves when they were released. The image claims that the assassination on the Ides of March brought Rome her freedom.

After some delay, Antony replied in kind. The normal language of politics in Rome was set in the vocabulary of friendship, reflecting an ideological mirage of unity and mutual respect in the senatorial group. In political terms, the speeches marked a formal break between Antony and Cicero.

After delivering his speech, Cicero returned to his villa, avoiding immediate conflict on the streets with Antony's supporters. Cicero had served notice that when Antony stepped down from the consulship, as he was bound to do at the end of the year, his acts against the assassins would not be forgiven, his rearrangement of the provinces would be taken as a threat to the Republic, Antonian hegemony would not be accepted, and Cicero and his supporters would be arrayed against him in Rome in defense of freedom.

As a result of the June plebiscite, Decimus Brutus had been ordered to quit his province. Brutus was understandably reluctant to give up his army, but was faced with a law that made his tenure of the province illegal and an instruction of the consul which he was bound to obey. He could resist only at the cost of civil war. His friends in Rome urged him not to give up his province, but he let it be known that he would abide by the law and turned his armies towards Italy. Given that his was a seemingly legal army on a "normal" march, each of the councils of the cities of Cisalpine Gaul ordered that their gates be opened and provided facilities and food for the army. But when Decimus Brutus reached Mutina, he stopped. Lying on an extensive fertile plain, Mutina had rivers to its west, south, and east that made it easy to defend. It was one of the larger and more prosperous cities of the region. Brutus had grain brought in, slaughtered cattle, and salted meat. And having secured a well-fortified and provisioned town, he settled down to wait.

As Decimus Brutus fortified Mutina, Marcus Brutus and Cassius began gathering their forces in the East. Cassius was taking control in Syria, where he was to be faced by Dolabella, whereas Marcus Brutus had his eyes set on Macedonia. In Rome, Antony continued to gather funds, but there he met with a further obstacle in the emergence of a new Caesar.

Julius Caesar had made his young great-nephew, Octavius, his heir and adopted him by will. Octavius immediately began to style himself Caesar, and he is so known in contemporary sources. In modern accounts, however, he is more often known as Octavian.[4] On his arrival in Rome, he posed not just as Caesar's personal heir (and demanded his father's money, which Antony had spent for his own cause), but also as his political heir. He used what money he had to pay the legacies of Caesar's will and he demanded that action be taken on the murder of his uncle-father. This put him into direct competition with Antony. At some point during 44, there were measures to deify Caesar, possibly led by Antony, but they enabled Octavian to pose as *divi filius*, son of the deified one, and to appeal to those who remained loyal to the memory of the late dictator. Octavian sought support from the plebs of Rome and from Caesar's veterans, and showed hostility toward Antony, who warmly reciprocated.[5] And yet, as early as June 44, Octavian had let it be known to Cicero that he was disposed to look favorably on Brutus and Cassius, offering a prospect of reconciliation between the assassins and the Caesarians.[6]

By October, hostility between Antony and Octavian had reached such a pitch that Octavian was gathering supporters among his father's old troops. Octavian's devotion to his uncle's veterans was expressed in offers of money, perhaps 2,000 sesterces per soldier (when annual pay was 900 sesterces), and the offer of cash as well as his stance as Caesar's heir and a friend to those who had been a friend to his uncle encouraged at least some of the veterans to his side.

Antony, though, was emboldened by the arrival of the Macedonian legions, which gave him a significant military advantage for the first time since the assassination. If the conflict were to become violent, these legions gave Antony the ability to overwhelm Decimus Brutus and take control of the Italian peninsula. But when Antony visited his five legions at Brundisium, he found them in restive mood, unsure of Antony's leadership. Antony offered them 400 sesterces, an offer which was not received well.[7] Antony responded violently to their reluctance. The traditional Roman punishment for mutiny was decimation, the execution of a randomly selected tenth of the mutineers. Antony ordered the arrest of the ringleaders of the mutiny. Lots were drawn, though fewer than the customary tenth were executed.[8] Order restored, Antony gathered a personal guard and instructed the remaining legions to march north along the east coast of Italy towards Ariminum (Rimini), while he himself returned to Rome. Armed for the first time since Caesar's death, Antony was in a strong position. It seemed that he could ignore the threat posed by the irritating, but very young and completely inexperienced, Octavian.

Such confidence was probably strengthened by events in Rome. In Antony's absence, Octavian had brought the veterans he had been able to raise from his father's colonies to Rome. But after an incendiary speech against Antony, he was unable to persuade them to take action.[9] The troops had gathered for revenge on Caesar's killers, not to quarrel with Antony. Their primary interest was to secure the land that Caesar had granted them, and Antony was the leader most likely to be able to confirm their claims. Antony was anyhow in a dominant position, and it was difficult to see how the soldiers' influence would be strengthened by his removal. Octavian's army melted away, and Octavian's hopes of posing as Caesar's political successor would seem to have vanished along with the veterans.

And yet this was the start of Antony's problems. The emergence of Octavian did provide the soldiers with an alternative leader for the Caesarian cause, and the legions decimated by Antony were out for revenge. On the road north, two of his legions, the Martian and the Fourth mutinied. They broke off from the rest of the army and marched towards Rome, stopping in the middle of the Apennines at Alba Fucens, about 100 km east of Rome. They took the political route that Antony had decided was closed to them when he decimated the legions. Antony left Rome with what forces he could muster and attempted to address his mutinous troops. They responded with missiles. Antony retired to Tibur, about 30 km north-east of Rome.

The defection was a substantial blow to Antony and a political lesson: the troops had a political will, and in the circumstances of the post-Caesarian crisis, they had the opportunity to make their political interests felt. But Antony's position was far from critical. He was met at Tibur by veterans from Caesar's armies, who must have been recruited previously by Antony's agents. Many of the senators also came out to meet him and present their respects, assuring him of their loyalty and friendship. But Octavian headed to Alba to meet what was now his army.

Antony marched from Tibur to join his other legions at Ariminum. He now had at least three legions, the Second, the Thirty-fifth, and the Alaudae ("larks"), about 15,000 troops in all; probably more than 6,000 irregularly raised veterans; and numerous new recruits. In December 44, Antony moved on towards Mutina to begin his circumvallation of the city.

Decimus Brutus's securing of Mutina was a military and political decision. His troops (probably 16,000–20,000 men) were not vastly outnumbered, but they lacked the experience of Antony's hardened veterans. Brutus would almost certainly have been defeated in battle. Yet, even allowing for Roman expertise in sieges, breaking into a fortified city was extremely hazardous and costly. The very skills that enabled the Roman armies to storm cities also enabled them to fortify cities, and Decimus Brutus had had considerable time to prepare his defenses. Locked into the city, Brutus was temporarily secure, but his eventual safety depended on help from elsewhere. His political calculation must have been that Antony's enemies in the senate would mobilize in sufficient numbers that relief would come. To win the war, he needed the conflict to mushroom from a local dispute over provincial control into a major civil war. He needed the politics to turn in his favor.

THE POLITICAL TIDE TURNS: THE CICERONIAN MOBILIZATION OF ROME

The senate was chaired by the consuls, and Antony had secured the complicity of his fellow consul, Dolabella. Consequently, until December 44 the senate was relatively muted. Cicero's dissension appears to have been the exception. The popular assemblies were, in general, supportive of Antony and loyal to Caesar's memory. Antony thus controlled the political mechanisms of Rome. But he had not been able to build a consensus. From June, his more determined enemies tended to stay away from the senate, their absence demonstrating their opposition, and it was for this reason that Antony attempted to require attendance. But after Dolabella and Antony himself finally left the city in late 44, Cicero and his allies gathered and seized the political initiative. On December 20, Cicero delivered his third Philippic. The senate decided that it would be a good idea to revoke Antony's arrangement of the provinces and asked Antony to leave Decimus Brutus unmolested and instructed Antony to head to his province (Macedonia). In constitutional terms, however, all the senate could do was to advise the consuls (neither of whom were likely to listen to their advice), and although they might express disapproval of a plebiscite, a decree of the people trumped a decree of the senate.

On January 1, 43, the Senate convened to witness the oaths of office of the new consuls, Aulus Hirtius and Vibius Pansa. Both of these men had been designated consuls by Julius Caesar and had been firm friends of the dictator. Hirtius was, it is often thought, the ghostwriter of Caesar's account of the Alexandrian wars. Neither man, however, was particularly fond of Antony. They were to preside over a senatorial debate about the brewing war to the north, and this debate provided Cicero and his allies with their opportunity.

Antony was unable to control the senate from Mutina or indeed, to defend himself from the accusations of his assembled enemies. Nevertheless, he had plenty of friends able and willing to speak on his behalf. Detailed accounts of the debate have come down to us, and these suggest that the discussion was long and fractious, with insults flying.[10] The supporters of Antony, led by Quintus Calenus and Lucius Piso, clashed with Cicero and his supporters. Antony's defenders reminded the senators that Antony was backed by the plebiscite. Cicero depicted Antony as a threat to the state. In an echo of the Catilinarian conspiracy, Cicero was proposing to have Antony declared an enemy without Antony having the opportunity to answer the charges laid against him.

The law was on Antony's side. Cicero's proposals were unconstitutional, and already in the fourth Philippic, delivered in late December, Cicero was drawing comparisons between Antony and Spartacus in order to justify emergency measures that would suspend the laws and the rights of citizens.[11] Cicero's attack drew attention to Antony's killing of the mutineers at Brundisium, dressing up the execution of Roman citizen-soldiers as the act of a tyrant, though this confused boundaries between legitimate military discipline and illegitimate violence. If Cicero could persuade the senators and people that Antony's actions at Brundisium were an act of quasi-war against the Roman people, it would add force to Cicero's demand that Antony be declared an enemy of the state.

Cicero also made explicit reference to decrees empowering the consuls to take actions required for the defense of the Republic, the so-called Final Decree of the Senate (*senatus consultum ultimum*).[12] In so doing, he recalled the measures he had taken in 63 against Catilina and similar measures taken against popular leaders over the previous eighty years. Cicero's claim was that this was an emergency of historic proportions, but also that the senators had repeated experience of dealing with just such a threat.

Such messages were unlikely to win Cicero much support before a popular audience, but even among the senators many of those who were not particularly fond of Antony or within his "group" were not persuaded. The Ciceronians had proposed a decree that would effectively declare war on Antony, but procedures were brought to a close by a veto issued by a tribune before a vote could be taken. All the tribune could do, however, was to buy time. The session closed with the senate to meet the next day and in the expectation that a condemnatory decree would then be passed.

It is notable that in this moment of near civil war, Antony's family and many of his supporters felt sufficiently safe to remain within the city. A frenzied night of lobbying followed in which Antony's family put on mourning and attempted to rally support, and their politicking had an effect. The following day did not go as the Ciceronians might have expected. Perhaps the enormity of the decisions being taken impressed the senators. Many of the senators will have been friends of Antony. The senate was, after all, a narrow elite of men many of whom had spent years working together or against each other, and, indeed, sharing each other's lives.[13] In the published version of the fifth Philippic, we have Cicero imagining pro-Antonian senators making excuses: "he is my friend" or "he is my relative" or "he lent me money." Although the last was a joke, pointing to Antony's notorious spending and consequent need for cash, Cicero nicely illustrates the mechanics of political and social relations among the elite in Rome. Antony himself had been prominent in the senate both in his own right and as Julius Caesar's close ally, enabling him to establish ties of friendship and loyalty with many of his fellow senators. This, together with his legendary sociability, which his enemies portrayed as an excessive fondness for alcohol, ensured that he was at the centre of an extensive social network.

Attempts to reconstruct these networks eventually fail, because the networks expand, potentially endlessly, and what is a centre and what a periphery is merely a matter of focus. Even if one could divide off particular elements of that network, say the friends of Antony or the friends of Cicero, there were still overlaps. Even among feuding enemies (such as Cicero and Clodius or Antony himself), there was often a prehistory of cordiality. Dolabella, Antony's ally and fellow consul, had been Cicero's son-in-law. As the connections were activated, individuals had a choice as to whether they felt a need to rally to their friend, sit on their hands, or turn against them, perhaps from loyalty to another part of their social network. A declaration of enmity within Roman social-political life, such as that between Cicero and Antony, was disruptive precisely because it divided the social network and attempted to impose the idea that one could be a friend of Antony or of Cicero, but not of both.

Some may have been convinced of the rectitude of Antony's cause and suspicious of Cicero's vehemence, and perhaps more fearful of Cicero's allies, who included the young, fiery, and almost unknown Octavian. Anyone reading the second Philippic, a pamphlet that published a speech never delivered, would encounter Cicero's highly charged defense of his own career, and vicious accusations against Antony: Cicero accused him of homosexuality, of drunkenness, of corruption, and of visiting veterans while "locked in the arms and the embrace" of an actress.[14] Readers might wonder whether these highly personal attacks were justified or a sufficient reason for civil war. Such readers might also recall Cicero's similar vehemence and the extrajudicial murders of twenty years earlier, also justified by the danger to the state, and to which Antony drew attention in his attack on Cicero. Antony's suggestion that Cicero was in a similar way responsible for the murder of Caesar and was the political advisor to the assassins continued the association between Cicero and extrajudicial violence, an association of which Cicero himself appears, if anything, rather proud.

To declare Antony an enemy was to suspend his citizenship and by extension the citizenship of his supporters. Suspending the most important protections of the citizen in order to defend citizens against a threat that Antony might suspend citizens' protection from arbitrary and tyrannical violence was, at best, a paradox. Selling that policy to a reluctant population required a rhetoric of extremity not justified by the events in the aftermath of Caesar's death; Antony had not, after all, proved himself a homicidal monster in his uneasy control of Rome. The debate was in large part about power: was Antony compatible with republican rule? The Roman political elite were in danger of replaying the civil war between Caesar and Pompey, and it is understandable that there was a reluctance to take an irrevocable decision. Some may have regarded the Ciceronians, with their violent rhetoric, as the most significant threat to a peaceful republican order.

In such decisions, ideology and political opportunism might play a part, but in moments of crisis such as this, senators, who were after all winners of the political and social game, the richest and most powerful men in Rome, were probably more acutely aware of what they had to lose than what might, if all went well, be won. Civil war presented individuals with difficult choices that, ultimately, could result in friends and relations facing each on the field of battle. At this stage in the political fragmentation of the Roman elite, it would have been unpredictable on which side of that battlefield particular individuals would find themselves. Even if there were individuals who were neutral about Antony and well disposed to Cicero, perhaps even persuaded by what Cicero was saying, they would also have friends and relatives committed to Antony's cause. It was one thing to agree with Cicero's general argument and another to go to war against those whom you had termed friends.

Most senators were probably stuck in the middle, indecisive, with no strong commitment to either side. Civil war was a disaster with which the Romans had long been familiar. It was a certainty that friends and family would be killed and properties seized, and the eventual outcome was unpredictable. As a result of such doubts and fears, Antony's supporters made progress on the second day of the debate.[15] Cicero failed to win approval for his hard-line policy, but the senate agreed that an ultimatum be sent to Antony, and it is possible that at this point measures were passed to legalize Octavian's military command; he was in camp at Alba with two legions and a body of other troops. The ultimatum was to be drafted by Cicero, and Cicero demanded that Antony withdraw from Gaul and submit to the authority of the senate.[16]

Antony responded. He wrote back to the senate to say that he would, of course, follow their advice in all matters, but that he was obliged by law to act against Decimus Brutus.[17] In late January 43, Cicero delivered his seventh Philippic, in which he describes the consuls raising troops and draws attention to the arms factories in the city itself. Cicero called on the senate not to compromise with Antony. His argument was that Rome was already in a state of war, and peace was impossible. He was concerned that the levy was being hampered by a lack of resolve from the senators. Reading between the lines, Cicero was concerned over the wavering of senators still to be convinced of the necessity of a war which, Cicero claimed, was already upon them. One may imagine that some were still in search of peace, but peace would require agreeing on terms for Antony's security.

On February 3, Antony's reply was received, and it contained a plan for peace. Lucius Caesar, a relative of Antony's, spoke on his behalf. Antony's solution was that he withdraw from Gallia Cisalpina and be given Gallia Comata (central and northern Gaul) instead. He was to be granted six legions for five years. He also demanded that his acts as consul, which included the setting up of colonies for Caesar's veteran troops, be confirmed by the senate.

Cicero's view was that this was not war prevented but war delayed. In this, Cicero was recalling Julius Caesar's ten-year tenure of Gaul, which enabled him to build up such resources that not even Pompey was able to defeat him. Cicero pressed the senate to remain firm. The senate refused the compromise, and it seems to be only at this point that it decided on war. Antony's soldiers were offered a temporary amnesty, provided that they desert. Cicero's orations through the remainder of February show a confidence in the senate's resolve that his previous speeches had lacked.

These seem to have been real negotiations, not just a formalistic process by which both sides could justify military action. Antony's offer to exchange Cisalpine Gaul for Gallia Comata was realistic, since his position outside Mutina was far from certain. Although he had considerable support in Italy among Caesar's veterans, he may have calculated that even a temporary peace would provide him with the opportunity to further augment his army and his reputation. It would also provide Rome with five years of uneasy peace through which to negotiate a settlement in which all parties would be secure.

Nevertheless, the fundamentals of the situation remained difficult. The assassins and the Ciceronians were distrustful of and ill disposed toward Antony. Antony was being pushed into a position analogous to that of Caesar in 49, and it is difficult to believe that, given the history of violence in Roman politics, the result would not have been the same. Cicero, for all his bellicosity, may have been right. Antony's proposal was merely to delay the inevitable reckoning. It is perfectly possible that Antony had made the same calculation.

Furthermore, delay suited Antony. Antony had infiltrated Mutina. There is a story of Decimus Brutus detecting Antony's spies by the simple measure of ordering a crowd to divide to different sides of a square with soldiers going one way and civilians the other; Antony's spies could not work out whether they were soldiers or civilians and were discovered.[18] Nevertheless, the arrest of some of the least quick-witted spies in world history is unlikely to have stemmed the flow of information from the city. As winter turned to spring, food supplies started to run dangerously low. If Antony could take Mutina quickly, the senators would be faced with a fait accompli, and if they declared war anyway, Antony could concentrate his troops on the more serious threat posed by Octavian and the consuls.

TO WAR: THE ARMIES GATHER

On declaring Antony a public enemy, the senators passed a series of measures that put their position beyond doubt. This was a political victory for the Ciceronians, and Cicero now acted to build an unlikely coalition against Antony. With war upon them, the senators declared a state of emergency and instructed the consuls to raise troops. The senators themselves gave up wearing togas and dressed in their military cloaks. They elevated Octavian to magisterial status and granted a statue in his honor.[19] They also transferred commands in the East to Marcus Junius Brutus and Cassius, supporting their previously illegal actions in gathering arms and throwing their authority behind the assassins in the coming war. The assassins were not the only group to find their position legitimized. The senators recognized the remnants of the old Pompeians who had gathered under the leadership of Sextus Pompeius, Pompey the

Great's son. This loose coalition was, nominally at least, under senatorial control. The senators also sent orders to the various governors in the West—notably Marcus Lepidus, with four legions in Spain, and Asinius Pollio and Munatius Plancus, who had three and four legions respectively—to march against Antony.

The loyalties of these last three men were uncertain, particularly since they had all been close associates of Caesar. None of them had made a move in the months since the assassination of Caesar, nor had their troops expressed a political view; Caesar's loyal supporters had disappeared like winter snow on a warm spring day. The instructions from the senators were effectively both warnings and a drawing of battle lines. The governors in the West needed to decide which side to support. Although prior loyalties would play a part in such decisions, in practical terms the generals and their soldiers would be swayed by more immediate concerns. They needed to calculate whose victory would be to their advantage, and, crucially, who was likely to emerge with power. Of course, if the consuls and Octavian could deal with Antony before the Gallic and Spanish legions came into play, then there would be no difficult decisions for these governors to take. Timing was crucial.

The strategy of Cicero and his group was clear and consistent. They sought to break Antony as quickly as possible. By February 43, military matters in the East appeared to be going the way of the assassins, and this probably induced more confidence among the Ciceronians. Brutus controlled Macedonia and had captured Antony's brother Gaius, while Dolabella's foray into Asia and Syria went disastrously. He was besieged by the assassins' armies and, with no hope of relief, committed suicide. Effectively, the East (excepting Cleopatra's Egypt) belonged to the assassins. In the West, Lepidus and Plancus appear to have stated their loyalty to the senate, though there was uncertainty as to what would happen should they be tested. Pollio was a known friend of Antony, but he was effectively powerless to intervene, since he would need to march through Lepidus's province. In January 43, Cicero had proposed honors for Lepidus for his inaction, a policy which recognized both that Lepidus's legions could crucially tip the balance in Italy and that Lepidus was prevaricating.[20]

Cicero appears to have been confident that he could use the senate's authority to isolate Antony from any potential allies and that ultimately the risks of civil war against the senate and their allies, Brutus and Cassius, were too great for any coalition of former Caesarians to form. Further, they seem to have believed that they had incorporated the young Octavian into their party. In December 44, after Octavian had managed to secure the support of two veteran legions, Cicero was lavish in his praise of the young man. Octavian appeared to offer a means of reconciliation between those Caesarians reluctant to support Antony and the Ciceronians. Not only were Octavian's legions invaluable, but the political symbolism of Caesar's heir marching alongside the senate's legions gave Cicero and his allies hope of a lasting victory. By contrast, Antony seemed isolated.

The legalizing of these various senatorial forces may have had limited real effects, but it created a perception of constitutional normality and conservatism in which the armies of the Republic marched at the behest of the senate and under the authority of senatorial magistrates. Even if considerable preparations had been undertaken before February, it was only with the declaration of war that the consuls sprang into action. Aulus Hirtius joined Octavian's swelling army and took control of two of his legions. Alongside the grant of magisterial status to Octavian, the consul's command transformed those legions into an army of the Republic. Vibius Pansa, the other consul, went to the countryside to recruit troops. Both armies were under the direct command of the consuls, as instructed by the senate and in accord with long-established traditional practices. The armies of the Republic gathered to make war on the Republic's behalf.

Hirtius and Octavian marched slowly north, not intending to do much before they could be joined by Vibius Pansa's new recruits. However, news of the parlous state of Decimus Brutus's forces reached them, and they hurried their approach. Hirtius and Octavian seized Bononia (modern Bologna), about 42 km southeast of Mutina, without a battle, but found that the rivers of the plain were in flood and restricted their movements. Antony responded by sending his cavalry against them, and an inconclusive series of skirmishes followed that were enough to deter

Octavian and Hirtius from a direct attack on Antony and to bolster the determination of the defenders of Mutina. Four of the armies were now gathered, and a fifth was awaited.[21]

In Rome, Cicero and his supporters exercised their authority and sought to raise resources to conduct their campaign. New taxes were imposed. For more than 120 years, Roman citizens had not been subject to direct taxation; the revenues necessary for the state were mainly extracted from the provinces. But in the preceding years of turmoil, the treasuries had been denuded, and it seems likely that before his assassination Julius Caesar had transferred a considerable amount of money out of Italy to Greece in order fund his planned campaign against the Parthians. Furthermore, Antony had gathered as a much as he could to fund his own war effort. Now short of money to fund the war, the senate levied a 4 percent tax on the wealth of senators and what Dio describes as a "four-obol tax" on each roof tile of all the houses owned by senators in the city of Rome.[22]

This last figure was not arbitrary, but was the daily wage of a Roman legionary. The levy provided one soldier for one day for each roof tile on the urban property of the senators in Rome, and in this tax we get some measure of the inequalities of ancient Rome. These monetary taxes were levied only on the senators, perhaps in keeping with a tradition that in times of trouble the wealthy would pool their resources in order to defend the state, perhaps because money could be levied from the senators with minimal political strife, or perhaps because the "donations" could be seen as an enforced badge of loyalty on the resurgent senate. Pro-Antonian senators who might have acquiesced in the war, sitting it out in Rome, were now faced with prospect of paying for it, and there is some suggestion that those suspected of siding with Antony were subject to extraordinary levies.[23]

The situation was fluid and uncertain. In December, many senators had pledged loyalty to Antony at Tibur, but now they were funding a war against him. Those tending towards Antony must have been especially nervous, given the parallel dangers of fleeing to his army or of remaining in a Rome controlled by a hostile party. Nevertheless, those Antonians who had stayed in Rome, working on Antony's behalf, were protected by a show of legality on the part of the Ciceronians, and perhaps by a reluctance to suffer the generalized bloodletting that had marked the civil wars of Sulla and Marius less than fifty years earlier.[24]

The Ciceronians were far from having Rome locked down at this point, and one of these supporters of Antony, Publius Ventidius, who had served under Caesar, left for Campania and started to recruit among Caesar's veterans. He enjoyed considerable success and quickly raised two legions. Suddenly, he had the largest effective military force in the region of Rome (Octavian and the consuls being in the North). A feint on Rome caused panic. His intended target was probably Cicero, but Cicero fled, and Ventidius crossed the Apennines and marched north to join up with Antony. The outcome of the war would not be settled in Rome.

Ventidius was prevented from joining up with Antony by the senatorial armies and retreated to the district of Picenum on the eastern flank of Italy. Picenum was Ventidius's native district, and there he was able to raise yet another legion and prepare for the next stage of the conflict. His was the sixth army in North Italy.

MUTINA: THE REPUBLIC'S VICTORY

By April, Pansa had levied a sizeable force, perhaps 16,000–20,000 men, and he marched to join up with the armies outside Mutina. On April 13, worried that Antony might intercept the new recruits, Octavian and Hirtius sent some of their best troops, the Martian legion and Octavian's personal guard, probably about 10,000 troops in all, under the command of Decimus Carfulenus to escort the new troops into their camps near Mutina. But the next day, as the armies advanced, Antony's troops were waiting for them. Two legions, perhaps 10,000 troops, lay hidden in marshes alongside the causeway across which Pansa's troops and their escorts had to pass. Carfulenus's men spotted the ambush, but as they assessed the situation, Antony's personal guard appeared, partially hemming them in. Carfulenus's troops divided in two and advanced into the swamp to meet their ambushers. Appian gives a description of the ensuing battle.

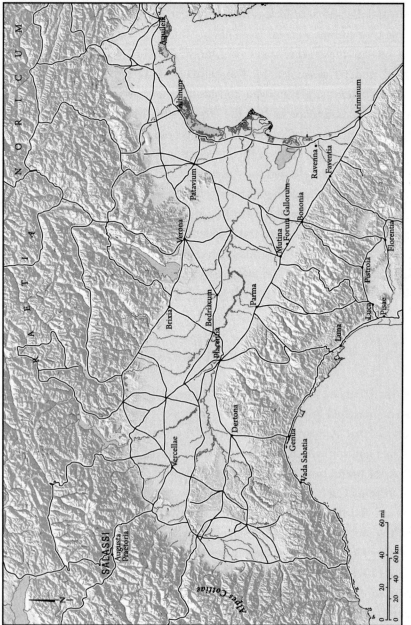

MAP 3: Northern Italy

Fired by anger and by ambition they fell on each other in the belief that this battle was more about their own concerns than those of their commanders. Because of their experience, they raised no battle-cry, which would have terrified neither side, nor did any of them utter a sound as they fought, whether they were winning or losing. Since the marshes and ditches provided no opportunities for charging or flanking and they were unable to push each other back, they were locked together with their swords as if wrestling. Every blow found its target, but instead of cries, there were only wounds, and men dying, and groans. If a man fell, he was immediately carried away and another took his place. They had no need for encouragement or cheering on, because each man's experience made him his own commanding officer. When they were tired, they separated for a few moments to recover, and then grappled with each other again. When the new recruits arrived they were amazed to see this going on with such discipline and silence.[25]

Veteran units met each other in disciplined and bloody conflict. In such a physically exhausting environment as the ancient battlefield, intimidating your opponents, making them fearful and getting them to take that step backward that would begin to break up the formations, was crucial. Ferocity of appearance, the battle cry, the sounds of the soldiers charging were central to the psychology of battle; an intimidated enemy would step back whatever their numbers, and an army going backwards was but a moment away from an army in flight. But in this battle, the soldiers showed respect for each others' discipline. They knew that their opponents would not be intimidated; they recognized a shared experience of war. The first battle of Mutina especially was a soldiers' battle, a battle without tactics, just man against man in a brutal and bloody struggle.

The new recruits joined the battle, but even so it was inconclusive until Pansa was wounded. His troops extracted him and some of them carried him back to Bononia. But deprived of their leader, the inexperienced troops started to give way, slowly at first but then faster, until it became a disorderly retreat. The veterans were similarly forced to retreat, but in good order, covering as best they could the fleeing recruits. Those who had not been directly involved in the battle had been engaged in building a camp in case of retreat, and it was to this bastion that the defeated troops returned. Antony's veterans caught the new recruits in the open and inflicted heavy casualties, though Carfulenus's veterans retained their integrity and were relatively unscathed. Antony's troops, satisfied with their victory, appear not to have tried to break them.[26]

Antony's army marched back towards Mutina. But en route they met Hirtius with a fresh legion. Exhausted from the physical demands of the earlier battle and now cut off from their camp, Antony's troops were forced to fight once more. This time Hirtius's legion scattered the Antonians, driving them into the marshes. As night fell, Antony's cavalry arrived to scour the marshes in search of survivors and bring them to the small town of Forum Gallorum. The town was sufficiently protected that the Antonians could shelter for the night without having to further fortify it. The next day, the survivors made their way to the camps at Mutina. According to another source, a letter from a certain Galba written to Cicero on April 20, Hirtius captured two legionary eagles and 60 standards of centuries. Galba suggests the almost complete disintegration of Antony's army, but from later events, his report seems a gross exaggeration.[27]

It is difficult to piece together the topography of this battle in a landscape that has probably changed a great deal since antiquity. Pansa's troops had assembled at Bononia and were intending to march along the Via Aemilia, which runs about 42 km in a straight line across the plain to Mutina. The plain is traversed by numerous small rivers draining from the Apennines in the south and west toward the Adriatic in a roughly northeasterly direction, as shown in Map 3. Various wetlands lay a few kilometers outside the historic centre of Bononia, near the River Reno, but these are too close to the town to be the site of the battle, which has to have taken place at a sufficient distance from the city that even though Pansa himself could be evacuated to Bononia, the legions needed an intermediate camp to which to retreat. This makes the more likely spot for the battle the wetlands near modern Ponte Samoggia (probably ancient Ad Medias), about halfway between Bologna and Modena. Antony's forces were caught on the way back to camp, much closer to Modena. We are told that they retreated to Forum Gallorum, and although this village cannot be firmly located on the map, locals seem of the view that it lies under the modern Castelfranco Emilia, 14 km from Modena.

With his force depleted, the tactical and strategic situation changed. Antony avoided battle. Hirtius and Octavian now faced a predicament. With the situation within Mutina becoming desperate, they could not risk a direct assault on Antony's fortifications, and Antony could afford to starve out Decimus Brutus. On April 21, in an effort to break the siege or draw Antony out, Hirtius and Octavian marched round the city to attack a perceived weak point in the circumvallation. Fearing that the siege would be lifted, Antony counterattacked. The battle went badly for Antony's forces, in part because they were divided into various camps around the city. By the time they had concentrated, the first two legions had already been defeated. Hirtius managed to storm one of the camps, but was killed in the fighting, possibly as Antony's troops rallied and were reinforced. As Hirtius's troops were being driven from the camp, Octavian launched another attack and managed to secure Hirtius's body, but was again forced to retreat.

Although Octavian pronounced the encounter another major victory, Antony still held Mutina under siege and his camps were intact. Further, one of the three generals opposing him was dead and another injured. Antony still had options. But instead of pressing the siege and daring Octavian to assault his fortifications, he decided to withdraw.

The recapture of his camp and the repelling of the attempt to lift the siege had not resolved Antony's difficulties. Although our sources tell us that he only decided to quit Mutina after the second battle, the decision may already have been made. He could have simply waited until Decimus Brutus surrendered, but even if he captured Mutina, his troops would not necessarily have been able to defeat Octavian's and Pansa's combined forces, and he himself could have ended up trapped in a city that had already endured a long siege. Mutina's military importance was anyhow declining. Ventidius and his legions lay south of Bononia. Munatius Plancus and Lepidus were approaching from the north. Pollio was also heading towards Italy, but at some distance. Although they were of uncertain intentions, they would be unlikely to side with a decisively defeated Antonian army. If he were to break off and meet them, he would force them to make a decision; it is improbable in the extreme that Antony had not been in touch with his former comrades in the Gallic and Spanish legions. As Hirtius and Octavian had been reluctant to force the issue before Pansa's arrival, now Antony had the potential to bolster his chances through gathering reinforcements. Once united with them, he would be possessed of a formidable force with which to press his case. He chose mobility, and broke off the siege. Mutina was relieved.

The first and second battles of Mutina had been won by the conservatively constructed senatorial forces; the armies were led by the consuls and under the authority of the senate. It was to be the last time Rome's armies fought under such a constitutional and legal framework. As Antony's troops departed hastily to the north, it seems unlikely that anyone had an inkling that the last battle of the Roman Republic had been fought.

6.

A VICTORY LOST: THE

DEFEAT OF THE SENATE

A NTONY'S NECESSARILY RAPID MARCH away from Mutina did not lead to an immediate pursuit. The aftermath of the battles was chaotic. Although the senatorial side were loud in their proclamations of victory, the battles had been hard-fought. There were undoubtedly many injured, and in the disorder after the battle it would be difficult to gather fit troops ready for a rapid pursuit. More crucially, even with the siege lifted Decimus Brutus was in dire need of supplies and would not have the animals necessary to transport his men and equipment. But even if the military and logistical issues could be quickly solved, the armies faced questions of leadership.

In fact, as Antony headed away from Mutina, Octavian turned in the opposite direction and marched to Bononia. There he met the ailing Pansa and both men wrote separately to the senate to inform them of their victories. In a letter of May 9, Decimus Brutus puts down at least some of the delay in pursuing Antony to a desire to discuss matters with Pansa. Octavian, Pansa, and Decimus Brutus needed to decide what would happen with Hirtius's legions. Pansa was the senior magistrate in the field, and his authority was crucial. Octavian was the junior figure, yet it was likely that he would have views, and these would need to be addressed. They needed to decide how to pursue the next stage of the war.[1] But before Decimus Brutus reached Bononia, Pansa died.

A whole new set of problems then arose. It seems inconceivable that the senate had given instructions as to what should happen in the extremely unlikely circumstance of the deaths of both consuls (Roman generals were only rarely killed in battle). Now the division of labor and command of the various legions needed to be resolved. Not only were Hirtius's legions to be assigned, but also Pansa's. We may assume that Octavian held onto the troops he himself had raised, but there were two sizeable armies without commanders to be divided between Decimus Brutus and Octavian.

Relations between the two men do not appear to have been good. Decimus Brutus was, after all, one of the assassins. In one account, the two men did not meet, but instead had an angry exchange of letters and delegations which culminated in Decimus Brutus standing on the edge of one of the rivers reading as loudly as he could a letter from the senate that gave Brutus authority in Gaul, and then forbidding Octavian from pursuing Antony or crossing the river into Mutina.[2] This would seem to be an exaggeration, perhaps for dramatic purposes. In April and May and for some time later, there was no open breach between them. In fact, they almost certainly did meet. Decimus Brutus's own account comes from the same letter of May 9. Not much detail is given of the meeting, though a slightly earlier letter of May 5 points to friction between the generals, Decimus Brutus complaining that Octavian did not follow his orders.[3] Octavian did, however, allow some of Pansa's troops to join Decimus Brutus, hardly the actions of a man bent on conflict, and the letters from Decimus Brutus to Cicero do not suggest that Octavian was hostile. However the issue was decided, it fell to Decimus Brutus and his troops to pursue Antony.

Even if the issues of command were problematic, probably the key factor that delayed the pursuit was the state of Brutus's army. All the Republican armies had taken a battering during the Mutina conflict, and although the forces of Hirtius, Pansa, and Octavian may have been in better condition, the consuls' forces were the least experienced, and Octavian's legions, presumably being mainly composed of Caesarian veterans, may have been unhappy at the prospect of serving under Caesar's assassin.

Brutus needed to transform his army from one organized and equipped to resist a siege to one which could march in pursuit of a rapidly retreating foe. He needed food and transport animals, and perhaps additional or new equipment for the troops. Those troops who had undergone the privations of the siege may not have been immediately capable of forced marches. This was a big army, and the logistics of moving such a force were far from straightforward. When Decimus Brutus eventually gathered his various legions and set off after Antony, Antony had several days' start, and Brutus himself acknowledged that his march was not rapid.[4]

News of the first victory reached Rome by April 20.[5] Cicero and his supporters were jubilant. Cicero read the consul Pansa's announcement to the people (in seeming acknowledgement of Cicero's pre-eminence in Rome itself), while Octavian's letter was read only to the senate.[6] Fifty days of public thanksgiving were announced.

Cicero was carried up to the Capitol, the traditional location of triumphal celebrations, to offer sacrifice and thanksgiving. The state of emergency was suspended, and the senators took off their military cloaks and donned their togas in recognition of the restoration of normal government. It was not just that the Republic had been saved, but the senators could congratulate themselves on the manner of the victory: it had been engineered by the senate, led by the consuls, fought for by armies raised in republican fashion. It was thus a victory for the conservatives, using the established institutions and won in traditional style.

In their new confidence, the senate passed resolutions which reasserted their constitutional authority. Crucial to senatorial power was the ability of the senators to influence the actions of magistrates and prevent the emergence of a "mighty" individual who could maintain power beyond that senatorial sphere of influence. The senators therefore decreed a return to annual officeholding, which meant that magistrates would be subject to the law on their withdrawal from a particular post. They also reasserted the normal age limits on the career structure, which had meant that men would progress gradually through the offices in Rome until at age 42 they could be appointed consul. The most obvious contemporary exception to the rule was the 19-year-old Octavian, who in 43 B.C.

enjoyed praetorian status and had been permitted to stand for office ten years earlier than the norm. But even this privilege would mean a wait of another twelve years before Octavian could take the most senior magistracy.[7]

The immediate issue facing the senate was, however, what to do about the armies outside Mutina. News of Pansa's death in Bononia and Hirtius's in Mutina reached Rome less than a week after news of the first victory.[8] The two consular armies had both lost their generals, and the senate needed to make arrangements for their command and the pursuit of what Cicero regarded as the mere remnants of Antony's army. Of the two possible commanders, Octavian was of praetorian status, whereas Decimus Brutus was of consular rank. Brutus held the provincial command, and authority over his own troops; it seems likely that Octavian's command had been legally subordinated to that of the consuls.

Later historians are astonished by the senate's decision to transfer command of the legions to Decimus Brutus, seeing it as a deliberate snub of Octavian which inevitably led to Octavian's defection. One source gives Pansa a clearly fictional secret deathbed speech in which he tells Octavian that the senate intended eventually to eliminate him.[9] Yet there does not appear to have been very much doubt at the time as to the appropriate course of action, and appointing Decimus Brutus was in keeping with the senate's commitment to constitutionalism and magisterial control. Nor does it seem that Octavian made any attempt to resist the new order; the new legions were transferred to Decimus Brutus (and may even have been transferred before the senate ruled on the matter), though those which had been raised by Octavian or had defected to him remained with the young general.[10] Furthermore, Octavian appears not to have taken offence for several months and until after several further provocations.

The gratitude of the senate and the honors granted by it were focused on the leading commanders under whose authority the war had been fought: Decimus Brutus, Hirtius, and Pansa. In Roman military practice, the commanding officers conducted the religious offices before battle in order to determine the will of the gods, and subsequently battle was joined under their auspices and on their responsibility. Junior officers, no matter how important, could not expect major honors. Given that Hirtius and Pansa were dead and thus in no position to participate in the honors, it was solely on Decimus Brutus that the rewards for victory concentrated. Again, later historians find in this a deliberate insult towards Octavian, and perhaps there was a reluctance to further elevate Caesar's heir among the leading senators of Rome, but the failure of the senators to specifically honor Octavian while being extravagant in their celebration of the victory itself and fulsome in their praise of Decimus Brutus seems conventional, if misguided.

The strategic situation of the senatorial forces was, in fact, deteriorating. Antony and his supporters were not wasting time. The normal assumption is that Roman troops were able to cover up to 30 km a day (18–19 miles), but marching any number of troops that fast over an extended period was a major logistical and athletic feat. He first headed northwest and reached Parma. En route, he appears to have liberated the slaves from the work gangs operating in the region and recruited them into his army. His army ravaged the land to secure supplies, animals, labor, and anything else of which they had need. On arrival at Parma, he looted the city, probably to reward his troops, restore morale, and equip his forces with supplies necessary for the coming struggle.[11] Antony's troops then probably continued north through Placentia (modern Piacenza) to Dertona (Tortona) and then down to Genua (Genoa) and along the coast to Vada Sabatia (Vado Ligure). He is reported as having been there in a letter of May 5.[12] He had covered 300 km (185 miles) in a maximum of 14 days (see Map 3: North Italy).

Vada was the rendezvous with Ventidius and his three legions. They had been last heard of in Picenum. The most direct route from Picenum to Vada would have been difficult and long, covering almost 600 km (370 miles). Such a journey would probably have taken nearly 30 days, meaning that to be at Vada on May 5 Ventidius would have had to depart by April 5, long before even the first battle of Mutina on April 14. It seems more likely that he had moved north during April so as to be closer to events at Mutina, perhaps to Ariminum or even closer to Bononia. If Ventidius was south of Bononia, his position after the first battle of Mutina would have had been perilous. There were two armies between him and Antony, and as the Republicans held Bononia, it was difficult to see how he could join with Antony unless both he and Antony could press on to Bononia together. It is thus possible that they decided after the first battle that the only way in which Ventidius could contribute was by marching around the Republican armies.

Even from south of Bononia, Ventidius faced a formidable march to reach Vada. He might have cut directly across the Apennines, taking a road from Florentia (Firenze) to Pisae (Pisa). Then he could have turned northward along the coast, a journey of somewhere between 425 and 480 km (265–300 miles). That journey might in normal circumstances have taken 20 to 24 days. Marching at breakneck speed, they might just have covered the distance in 16 days. If Antony had taken the decision to leave Mutina on April 21 or 22, after the second battle, a message would need to have been sent to Ventidius, and Ventidius would then have needed to order the march. He could hardly have set out before April 23. To be in Vada Sabatia earlier than May 5, his troops would have needed to leave by April 20, before the second battle of Mutina. This would mean that Antony had already decided to lift the siege before the second battle, and his retreat was far from a panicked response to a failed storming of his fortifications.

After the first battle of Mutina, Antony must have decided that it was unlikely that he could win a decisive victory on the plains of Mutina. Topography and numbers were against him. By regrouping, the equation could be changed. The second battle of Mutina was a sideshow, and even if Antony was defeated, the death of Hirtius worked in his favor in delaying the Republicans. With two armies in the field and the possibility of more support from his friends in Gaul and Spain, he was in a strong position. Senatorial celebrations were considerably premature.

In Rome, Cicero believed that the war was over. His letter to Marcus Junius Brutus of April 27, announcing the deaths of Hirtius and Pansa, is dismissive of Antony, seemingly believing that Antony's forces would be easily destroyed by Decimus Brutus.[13] In the competitive culture of Roman politics, it was not in a general's interest to be modest as to his own achievements, a trait with which Cicero should have been abundantly familiar. Decimus Brutus, however, was rather less confident than Cicero. In a letter of April 29, he expressed his worries about Lepidus and Pollio, fearing the loyalty of the former and his fear that the latter would take any opportunity to join Antony, though he appears relatively unconcerned about Antony's own legions.[14]

Decimus Brutus could, potentially, have raced Antony to try to catch him before he met Ventidius. Yet, in the letter of April 29, eight days after the battle, he was only a day's march north of Mutina, probably gathering the supplies and animals necessary for the march. One might imagine that Cicero read the address line of the letter with some distress. The pursuit sped up notably after that and by May 5 had reached Dertona, about 75 km (45 miles) north of the coast at Genua but about 110 km (70 miles) from Antony. Brutus's legions were five days behind and had failed to prevent the Antonians' union with Ventidius's legions.[15] It seems possible that Cicero expressed his displeasure. A letter from Decimus Brutus from May 9 is cast as a defense in the face of an accusation that he had mishandled the situation in allowing Antony to escape his clutches.[16] He complains that he was forced to pursue Antony without baggage animals and without cavalry. Antony's greater maneuverability posed considerable problems, and Decimus Brutus was fearful that he would be ambushed by Antony's cavalry. After all, Antony had already attempted an ambush in the first battle of Mutina. He could not entirely predict which way Antony would turn; Decimus Brutus details a sudden attack by Antony's troops on the town of Pollentia. He was able to save the town, and Brutus represents this as yet another worthy victory, though, as we shall see, this attack was probably nothing more than a feint.[17]

It is already evident from the letter of May 5 that Decimus Brutus was losing confidence.[18] Antony's army was far from negligible, and the tasks Decimus Brutus faced were rather more taxing than the "mopping up" of residual resistance which Cicero envisaged. The strategic situation is summarized in a letter from early June from Pollio to Cicero (news perhaps not traveling very quickly to Spain). Pollio claims that Antony had four legions (one of which was ill equipped) and 5,000 cavalry. With the addition of Ventidius's three legions, at least two of which consisted of veterans, he was leading a considerable army. Brutus's forces may have amounted on paper to as many as ten legions, but the quality of those legions was questionable. Pollio voices his doubts, suggesting that Brutus may have been down to as few as four effective legions, only one of which had had much experience, and we know from elsewhere that they were suffering an outbreak of disease in the aftermath of the siege.[19] If Pollio was right, though as a closet supporter of Antony he had reason to underestimate Brutus's capabilities, any battle between Antony and Decimus Brutus might well have been one-sided and have resulted in a decisive Antonian victory.

Decimus Brutus was hoping for support from Munatius Plancus, who although a former Caesarian, showed remarkable loyalty to the senatorial cause. He was approaching from the north with four legions. Yet even with Plancus, the situation was far from straightforward. In an undated letter to Cicero (which must come from the end of April), Plancus reports a mutiny: the Tenth legion, one of the more experienced of his army, had wanted to join Antony, but Plancus had managed to bring them back under control.[20] Plancus's loyalty was evidently not shared by his troops. If Antony were to cross the Alps, Plancus was far from confident that that his four legions would be able to mount any significant resistance. He might have been able to hold onto his troops as they marched south, but the soldiers' calculations might have changed once they were on the battlefield. Plancus faced the distinctly uncomfortable scenario that if he met Antony in battle, the Tenth legion would defect and bring others with them.

If Antony could encourage the mutiny of Plancus's troops or secure union with Lepidus and Pollio, he would be reinforced by up to eleven additional and experienced legions, making a total of eighteen. Whatever Cicero may have been thinking in Rome, Antony was not just a power in the land but had the potential to overwhelm the senatorial forces.

ANTONY RESURGENT

We have considerably less information about what was happening in the Antonian camp; they were not communicating their plans to Cicero. In a letter to Cicero justifying his actions after Mutina, Decimus Brutus explained that he could not guess what Antony intended following his union with Ventidius. Antony might continue into Gaul towards Lepidus, but he feared that the Antonians would turn south towards Etruria, aiming to recruit more troops, and then march on Rome.[21] At first sight, this might seem an unlikely tactic, and one might imagine that the possibility was intended as a justification for Brutus's hesitation. Yet, it was a feasible strategy. Brutus reports news of a meeting in which the Ventidian legions had refused to leave Italy. He does not explain why. As is typical of conventional accounts, both modern and ancient, the soldiers' logic is simply ignored as not worth considering or dismissed as perverse. But in this case, one has to believe that these legionaries, at least two-thirds of whom were seasoned veterans and many of whom had not been involved in the battles of the previous month, were spoiling for a fight. They might have felt, and with considerable reason, that Decimus Brutus was in no position to defend Italy against them.

Antony appears to have had all the options. A strike to the south would have brought him control over Rome and its manpower, as well as access to the resources of southern Italy. It would have left Decimus Brutus isolated in northern Italy. But there were several unknowns, the most significant of which was the slowly approaching Lepidus. No one, and perhaps not even Lepidus, appears to have been certain of his intentions, and if Lepidus sat out the conflict, then the military balance between Antony and the Republicans was more even. Further, Antony was aware of the hostility of Plancus; after the war, he wanted revenge for Plancus's enmity in these crucial months. The other great unknown was Octavian. If Octavian had continued to work against Antony, a march south might separate Antony from his potential allies to the north and the balance would have tipped once more.

Antony turned his forces north, towards Decimus Brutus, striking towards Pollentia. The town of Pollentia was of strategic importance, since it controlled the valley that led up to Dertona and hence to Parma, but Brutus got to Pollentia first. Once he was inside the town, Antony would have difficulty forcing a battle. The feint was an aggressive move. It demonstrated Antony's confidence in his newly augmented force and was a warning to Brutus. One may also imagine that the strike was in part for the benefit of his own troops, to show them that they were not running scared but engaged in a strategic retreat.

Antony had the advantage, but a battle at this stage was an unnecessary risk. Instead, he left Italy and headed towards Lepidus and his troops in Gaul, presumably confident that Lepidus and his legions would come over to his side.

Lepidus himself had been very quiet. He was in contact with several of the main participants, notably Plancus, whose own legions were relatively close by. Perhaps sometime towards the middle of May, news reached Rome via Plancus of a meeting of Lepidus's troops in which the troops proclaimed that the war was over now that both consuls were dead and that no more Roman citizens should be killed. Such a declaration of peace could be read as suggesting that the legions were unwilling to fight Antony.[22] But Lepidus was still not decided. He had sent troops ahead of his main column to hold the Alpine passes against Antony. This should have rendered Antony's progress difficult, but two of Lepidus's leading officers, Culleo and Silanus, defected and opened the passes, raising further doubts as to the loyalty of Lepidus's legions.[23]

By May 15, Antony, who had met up with his brother Lucius, arrived at Forum Iulii, about 200 km (125 miles) from his rendezvous with the Ventidians. According to Plancus, Lepidus was at Forum Voconii, about 24 Roman miles away (just under 40 km).[24] At this point, there was a pause. Lepidus and Plancus were in communication. Cicero was urging Decimus Brutus to take decisive action against Antony; Brutus was writing back to say he did not have troops of sufficient numbers or experience.[25] He must have feared that if Antony turned on him, he would lose a battle, and if he lost, the chances of retaining the loyalty of the various commanders of the West were negligible.

Lepidus wrote to Cicero to announce Antony's arrival in his province, and claimed to be receiving deserters from Antony. Given Antony's record of infiltration, Lepidus might perhaps have been advised to worry about those who were joining him rather than celebrate their arrival. More significantly, he was also losing men.[26] The loss of Culleo and Silanus demonstrated the fluid loyalties of his troops and their officers.

Lepidus was still, however, moving very slowly towards Antony and had reached the Argens River, to the west of Forum Iulii, by May 22.[27] The snail's pace of his march demonstrates a considerable reluctance to make a decision and declare his hand. Still, he wrote a letter from the banks of the river assuring Cicero of his loyalty.[28] Two large and evenly matched armies lay close to each other, seemingly ready for battle.

Eight days later, on May 30, Lepidus wrote to the senate and people of Rome:

> I call gods and men to witness, fathers of the senate, in what mind and spirit I have regard to the Republic, and that I have judged nothing to be important other than common safety and liberty. I would have proved this to you shortly, but fate has torn away from me the opportunity of following my policy. For my whole army has mutinied and following its desire to maintain the common peace and the lives of citizens, has forced me, to tell the truth, to preserve the safety and security of so great a number of Roman citizens.[29]

Lepidus had lost his army. The soldiers had taken the decision out of his hands and gone over to Antony. Lepidus's letter concludes by begging the senators to have regard to the lives of citizens. The implication is clear: the senate had lost; Antony had won. The senators could choose between defeat in civil war or recognizing Antony's dominance.

Lepidus's letter to the senate explains and justifies his position. His claim was to have been loyal to the senatorial cause throughout, but defeated by circumstance. Still, he was unwilling to commit to one side or the other. In the situation of May 30, when he was perforce to be identified with Antony's cause, such ambivalence was redundant.

Like many others, Lepidus had sought to avoid involvement in civil war. The Ciceronians had always been dubious of his loyalty, and he would thus have been uncertain of his position in a Cicero-led Rome. He was no enthusiast for Antony, but the decision had been made by others.

As Lepidus had made his ever-so-slow approach towards Forum Iulii, Antony had marched out to meet him. He had camped near the Lepidan forces and encouraged fraternization among the troops. In Lepidus's army was a Tenth legion, which had been commanded by Antony and was loyal to him, and it was this legion which seems to have spoken for Antony with Lepidus's other forces.[30] The officers became aware that the legions were of changeable loyalty and informed Lepidus. But Lepidus did nothing to shore up support among his troops. He divided his army into three, set them to guard duties, and went to bed.

The final watch of the night opened the gates of the camp and summoned Antony. Antony arrived, and Lepidus was roused. In front of Antony and the assembled army, Lepidus struggled to get dressed. Antony then indulged in a little political theatre and asked Lepidus to make peace.[31]

Even if Antony had not been confident of winning over Lepidus himself, he trusted in his ability to secure Lepidus's troops. It seems likely that officers in Lepidus's army were transmitting information and that a network of former comrades from Caesar's army was at work. The choice the soldiers had was between fighting Antony's formidable army and joining it. Given that Lepidus's soldiers had no reason to hate Antony, and some had reason to support him, the decision was probably not, in the end, too difficult. Furthermore, we cannot know what attitude these soldiers were taking to events in Italy. It seems unlikely that they would have had much sympathy with Cicero and his ilk. To turn against Antony would have been to support Decimus Brutus and the assassins, and they may have calculated that Antony was likely to be generous in his gratitude. Antony could rely on the political self-interest of the soldiers.

Antony could have deposed Lepidus and perhaps had him killed, but the theatrical request for peace made the point that he wanted to preserve the lives of citizens. Such a performance recalled the declaration of the Lepidan legionaries after the death of the consuls at Mutina for the preservation of the lives of Roman citizens. Antony's peaceful stance may also be seen as an appeal to other former Caesarians to join forces and avoid conflict. The soldierless general struggling to dress himself in the midst of the camp retained his importance, and his life, because he could be made a symbol of Antony's policy of reconciliation and of a desire to bring peace to Rome and her armies. In that policy, there was a claim to represent the forces of legitimacy and order and an assertion that Antony was fighting for more than his own gain.

News of the unification of the armies of Lepidus and Antony must have reached Rome in early June, about a week later. Cicero wrote to Cassius telling him that all the hopes of the Republic lay with him.[32] Indeed, the situation of the Ciceronians was now desperate. The senate sought support from the legions located in Africa, summoning them back to provide a defense for Rome.[33] Of the other armies in the field, Pollio had not officially joined the Antonians by June 6, when he informed Cicero that Antony was asking for one his three legions and offering bounties to the others, but it seems that Pollio hardly delayed a defection that all believed inevitable.[34] Plancus, however, remained steadfast. He withdrew to meet Decimus Brutus, with whom he joined forces on June 10 at Cularo (Grenoble).[35] Plancus and Decimus Brutus were still at or near Cularo a month later. Near the end of July, Plancus wrote to Cicero in affectionate terms:

> I hope, however, that you approve of our policy, though I know how eager our side is for a decisive victory. For if anything were to befall this army, what substantial reserve would the Republic have by which to resist a sudden charge or raid by the parricides? I think that the forces at our disposal are known to you. There are three veteran legions in my camp, one of recruits (perhaps the finest of all). In [Decimus] Brutus's camp there is one veteran legion, another in the second year of service and eight newly recruited. So altogether our army is fine in number but in resolve it is weak. For we have enough experience of how much we can rely on the recruits in the battle line. If we could add to the trunk of our armies either

the African army, which is veteran, or that of Caesar, we could dispute the Republic in battle without any qualms. Of those, Caesar's is the closest as we can see. I have, therefore, never stopped from encouraging him by letter, and he has confirmed each time that he is coming without delay, while in the meanwhile he has turned away from that thought and has another plan.[36]

Although Plancus and Brutus had thirteen legions, probably in excess of 55,000 troops, they had considerable doubts as to the quality of those troops. Antony may, in fact, have had a similar force, depending on how much damage had been inflicted on his forces at Mutina and how many troops Pollio had sent, but nearly all Antony's troops were experienced. The distant African legions might have made a significant difference, but if the order had been sent out in mid-June, getting them to Rome before August was unlikely, and it would take yet longer before they could be committed to any conflict in northern Italy. Octavian was, therefore, crucial to the balance of power. But Octavian and his troops are almost a blank. Little in Cicero's letters gives any suggestion as to what Octavian was thinking. It is almost as if Octavian had been forgotten.

OCTAVIAN'S COUP: THE MARCH ON ROME

In our narrative, we left Octavian in Bononia in the aftermath of the second battle of Mutina. When Brutus's forces set off after Antony, Octavian remained in Bononia. There was perhaps at that moment an opportunity to pursue the Ventidian legions, but Octavian did not march out, or if he did, it was a token act. Decimus Brutus suggested that Octavian was unable and unwilling to move his troops: "But one cannot order Caesar, nor Caesar his army: both of which are very bad."[37] The soldiers themselves were uneasy, considering their options in the aftermath of battle.

The silence on Octavian is broken by a letter from Decimus Brutus to Cicero from mid-May. Brutus complained about the way matters were being handled in Rome. A commission of ten had been established to look into Antony's acts as consul, including his establishing of colonies for veterans. This was causing disquiet among the troops, in part because Cicero himself was seen as the arbiter of all decisions and in part because the land settlements were the major resource for the soldiers in their retirement. Decimus Brutus begged Cicero to accede to the veterans' demands. He may have been talking only about the veterans in his own forces, but whatever anxieties applied to Brutus's veterans would also have applied to those with Octavian.

Decimus Brutus also inquires about a bon mot from Cicero in connection with Octavian: "laudandum adulescentem, ornandum, tollendum." The epigrammatic quality of this cannot easily be captured in English, and it contained within it an ambiguity. It could mean that "the young man must be praised, rewarded, and disposed of"; a charitable translation might suggest "raised up" rather than "disposed of," but the implication was surely that Octavian could be marginalized. Cicero was relaxed enough about Octavian that he could make this witticism.[38]

Cicero's unbridled rhetorical facility could as easily lose him friends as secure him allies. Brutus clearly reads the event as Cicero foolishly showing his wit. That the phrase had reached him in his pursuit of Antony should not surprise us, and, indeed, it shows that there is little new in the business of politics: the much-used and much-derided political sound bite—the phrase which owes it power to its repeatability, to the fact that it will stick in the mind when the complexities of argument have long gone—was as powerful and prominent a political weapon in the Roman Republic as it is in the American Republic, and as prone to return to haunt the unwary politician. In Cicero's reply to Decimus Brutus, he does not seem unduly worried by the publicity his phrase has attracted, which may just be acceptance that what is said cannot be unsaid.[39]

Cicero's phrase is in line with his consistent policy towards the young Caesar. He had supported and perhaps even initiated the elevation and praise of the young man, and Octavian, in spite of the more radical elements of his agenda, appears to have consulted Cicero and made an attempt to secure his support (which was reassuring for the older man).

But Cicero appears to have believed that this new Caesar should be and could be confined within the traditions of the Roman constitution. He may have felt that the "young man" did not have the political weight or the experience to be a power in his own right, or that the options open to Octavian were distinctly limited: he could not join Antony after the events of Mutina and their hostility throughout 44 B.C., and so he was bound to the senate and its cause. Brutus, who had more experience of Octavian and his army, was not so sure. He might perhaps have felt that a man, however cornered, with more than 15,000 veteran troops behind him should not be treated lightly.

Octavian had done nothing by the end of July 43 that gave any indication of what was to come. He may have been recruiting. Appian tells us that Octavian had eight legions plus additional forces, suggesting 50,000–60,000 troops.[40] The first signs of activity from Octavian came with the sending of an embassy to Rome. This embassy came from the soldiers, who asked the senate for money. The senate partially acceded to the request, sending half the money promised, but the money was not delivered to Octavian's army but to that of Decimus Brutus.[41] There may have been a delay after this, but a further embassy, also led by centurions, was sent to the senate. Before entering the senate, they laid aside their swords, and then made their demands. They requested that Octavian be made consul in place of either Hirtius or Pansa. The senators objected. They cited Octavian's youth, but the centurions, who clearly knew their Roman history, drew parallels with Scipio Africanus during the Hannibalic war; Scipio Aemilianus, who had been entrusted with commands in Spain; and Marcus Valerius Maximus Corvus (or Corvinus), who had held a consulship in 348 at the age of 23. The debate became heated, and one or more of the senators either rebuked or struck one of the centurions for their insolence. According to Dio, at least one of the centurions left and returned with his sword. Indicating that sword, he cried out "If you do not give the consulship to Caesar, this will give it." Cicero supposedly replied "If you make demands in this way, he will get it" (meaning the sword).[42] Even at this point, Cicero and the senators had no inkling of what was to happen.

It is easy to attribute these events to the Machiavellian Octavian, playing a complex political game, making the soldiers do his work. But the soldiers had their own agenda. Octavian's legions appear to have been restless since Mutina. Decimus Brutus regarded them as being beyond Octavian's control. The veterans had asserted their power and defeated Antony, but what was their longer-term political interest? The senators had not provided the promised rewards. Brutus seemed to be the real winner of Mutina, his army relieved and reinforced, but he was Caesar's assassin. In Rome, Cicero and his allies were reconsidering Antony's settlements of Caesar's troops, and in this, Octavian's legions had a direct financial interest. If it is clear to us that Octavian's legions had the power to turn the war against the senators, then it is likely that it was clear to the soldiers themselves. They knew their political power and they were about to use it. Octavian was hardly a passive beneficiary of what was about to happen, but his interests were fundamentally tied to and dependent on those of his soldiers.

Equally notably, Cicero and his allies in the senate appear to have had a very different understanding of the political and strategic situation. They expected the soldiers to do what the senators ordered them to do. They were offended by the centurions debating with them and making demands. This was an insult to Rome's social and political order. It seems to have been inconceivable that those subordinate within the traditional hierarchy could threaten the senators, and certainly that the soldiers could act of their own accord within a political sphere; the senators seem not to have considered the possibility that the soldiers might step outside that hierarchy and invent a new kind of order. The decision to reopen the question of Caesar's land settlements was an assertion of senatorial authority, but also of the traditional power of the landed elite of Italy and of the values of the social hierarchy of Rome. From our perspective (and perhaps from that of Decimus Brutus), the policy seems courageous to the point of naiveté, but for the senators, this hierarchy was precisely what they were fighting for. Reinforcing the hierarchy cemented their political control on Italy and the coherence of the Italian elite against Antony and his followers.

If one wants to understand the scale of the revolution and the immensity of the political misconceptions of the Roman senatorial class, secure as they were in their own ideological bubble, convinced that their mastery of Rome was endorsed by the gods, one needs only to remember the senators quibbling over the land and money that had been given to the soldiers and rebuking the centurions in whose hands their fates ultimately lay.

The earliest feasible date for the second debate between the senators and Octavian's soldiers is the end of July (formerly the month of Quintilis, which had been renamed in honour of Julius Caesar), but it is more probable that it took place in the first days of the following month, Sextilis, which, in turn, was, many years later, renamed after Augustus. When the centurions reached their camp and gave their account of the debate, Octavian split his army into columns and marched on Rome.

The senate, perhaps understandably, showed signs of panic. They sent promises of money not just to the two legions that Octavian had led at Mutina, but to all his other forces. They promised him the consulship—anything rather than have him take the city by storm. But while the embassy was negotiating, resolve stiffened. The two legions they had summoned from Africa arrived. They already had a legion left to them by Pansa, and they started to recruit anyone they could persuade or intimidate to join up. With this force they believed they could hold off Octavian until Decimus Brutus and Plancus could be summoned. Cicero, who had disappeared with news of Octavian's march, reappeared to lead the resistance.

The defense of Rome was a farce. Octavian's legions quickly reached the suburbs. Rome, a vast and sprawling city, was no Mutina behind whose relatively short walls an army could hide. The defenders were split into small groups and sent to strongpoints throughout the city. But as Octavian paused on Rome's outskirts, the senators and the leading men of Rome made their calculations. The military reality was obvious. A steady stream of senators and other individuals made their way to Octavian's camp to welcome the new master of Rome. The next day, Octavian entered the city accompanied only by a bodyguard, a sign that he expected no serious resistance. The senate's resolve had crumbled. The two veteran legions defected: they had previously served with Julius Caesar. Their commander killed himself, and the others who had been placed in charge of the strongpoints deserted.

Eventually, Cicero himself emerged and went to greet his old friend. He seemingly made a long speech on how he had always supported Octavian's cause. It is not one of those that Cicero was to publish. We can only imagine the convoluted history that Cicero was forced to tell. Octavian listened to his old mentor and drily noted that Cicero was the last of his friends to meet him.[43] This was political theatre, and it dramatized a revolution. Whatever explanations Cicero offered as he stood to welcome Octavian to Rome, however he rewrote recent events to put himself in the most favorable light and to represent himself as a loyal and trustworthy friend of Octavian, his undoubted rhetorical brilliance hardly mattered. Cicero was politically bankrupt, and it was obvious to everyone. He could do nothing to oppose the soldiers who controlled the city. His political vision of a Rome governed by the senators in accord with a social and political hierarchy dominated by the traditional values of the traditional aristocracy of the city was exposed as flawed and failed by the very fact that he had to explain himself to Octavian. Octavian did not have to listen to the great consular. He did not have to grant Cicero an audience. The respect that Cicero had been able to demand as of right from the younger men, from his juniors within the hierarchy of Roman society, was granted as a gesture which everyone knew that Octavian had no need to make. The senators who watched their former leader being indulged by the "young man" about whom Cicero had so recently quipped, could have been in no doubt as to which man had power. That power did not stem from office or tradition or from the conventional hierarchies of Roman social life, but from the soldiers who stood at Octavian's side.

Octavian made arrangements for his election as the youngest-ever consul and acted with generosity to his enemies. His policy must have recalled that of his adoptive father, Julius, who had proclaimed his clemency in an attempt to bring peace after his civil war. But acts which recalled the dictator merely emphasized what the senators already knew, that a new Caesar held Rome, and the rights, powers, and lives of the senators subsisted merely because the new Caesar willed it so. One wonders whether as they greeted the young consul the senators recalled the aftermath of Mutina and carrying Cicero to the Capitoline to give their gratitude to the gods and commence the days of thanksgiving for which they had voted. Mutina, the last battle of the Republic, had been won, but as Octavian sat before the senate as consul four months later, the war was lost.

7.

THE REVOLUTION BEGINS

OCTAVIAN'S CAPTURE OF ROME brought an end to the first stage of the civil war. The alliance that Cicero had forged between Octavian and the senate was in tatters. Octavian's march on Rome marginalized the senators as political players. But the impotence of the Ciceronian senate was almost the only certainty in an extremely fluid situation. Antony and Lepidus remained in Gaul, opposed by the armies of Decimus Brutus and Plancus. Spain and much of Gaul were under Antonian control, while Octavian was dominant in Italy.

Sicily was under the sway of Sextus Pompeius, the son of Pompey the Great.[1] Sextus had survived his father's defeat by Julius Caesar and fled to Spain. There he had raised an army and fought a bandit war. He had also gathered a fleet and engaged in piracy. Lepidus and Pollio had been sent by Caesar to repress the Pompeians, and they had succeeded in driving him out of Spain, but his fleet had enabled Sextus to transfer to Sicily, and, if anything, Sicily was a better base for operations than Spain. He was sufficiently close to Italy that he could launch raids on the Italian coast and make use of whatever political opportunities came his way.

Sicily also had a number of great estates which relied heavily on slave labor, and Sextus is alleged by his enemies to have recruited from these slaves. Although the accusation is clearly propagandistic, and equally clearly Sextus recruited from the disaffected free in Italy and elsewhere, it is unlikely that he could afford to ignore the ready supply of manpower offered by the Sicilian slaves. The legitimation of Sextus Pompeius by the Ciceronians in the aftermath of Mutina offered Sextus the briefest of possibilities of a return to respectability, and there can be little doubt that every effort would have been made to negotiate a transition from outlaw to statesman if Cicero and his allies had managed to hold on to Rome. But Octavian did not welcome a potential reconciliation with the son of Julius Caesar's great enemy. Sextus returned to his role as pirate king.

In the East, Marcus Brutus and Cassius had established themselves as the dominant powers. They had first taken control in Macedonia and Syria, and from there had expanded their authority through Asia Minor. Somewhat surprisingly, they were often resisted, and at least some of the Greek city states were secured through violence. Brutus and Cassius enjoyed naval hegemony, and their military control over the Eastern Mediterranean was threatened only by Cleopatra of Egypt. Cleopatra remained loyal to her late lover, Julius Caesar, and sought to support Antony and Octavian whenever possible, but although she had signifi-cant naval forces, she was geographically isolated, remote from the main Caesarian forces, and Brutus and Cassius were threatening her Eastern borders.

There were thus at least six major military groupings across the Roman Empire: Octavian; Antony and Lepidus; Marcus Brutus and Cassius; Decimus Brutus and Plancus; Sextus Pompeius; and finally Cleopatra. No single group could achieve dominance, and it was this knowledge that brought Antony, Lepidus, and Octavian together. They needed to unite to defeat Brutus and Cassius. But the unity they achieved rested on suffi-ciently firm foundations that these men were to remain in alliance for the next eleven years. The alliance that emerged was not just to dispose of the assassins and their supporters, but was also to secure the settlement after the war. The major beneficiaries of that settlement were the soldiers, and it was in the soldiers' interests that the alliance was maintained.

The political role of the soldiers over the next decade was a revolution-ary change. As was to become clear very quickly to the Roman political elite, the moment Octavian's troops reached the outskirts of Rome, aristo-cratic control came to an end. In the conditions of civil war, when all is turned upside down, this reversal of the political and social hierarchy could be seen as an accidental consequence of the political turbulence, a revolutionary moment after which the traditional balance of power and social hierarchy would be quickly restored. This may have been what the Roman elite expected, and perhaps with some reason, given their historical experience of the previous century. But the Caesarians did not give up their power, and consequently the Roman political landscape was transformed.

CAESAR'S LEGACY AND THE FORMATION OF THE REVOLUTION

Octavian's capture of Rome was almost bloodless, and the full implications of the event took some time to work through. His cordial reception of the senators established an interlude of uncertain peace. The soldiers brought him control of the city, but it was not immediately clear how his coup would affect political relations with those in arms outside Italy. Octavian can have had few illusions that a senate which had shown considerable reluctance to honor and reward him when he was their hero would acquiesce in his seizure of power. He must also have realized that whatever their formulaic expressions of friendship, many senators wished him dead and, if the opportunity had arisen, would have acted to make that wish come true. After all, it had been Caesar's "friends" who had stabbed him to death, and if that act of political assassination had been hard, a departure even in the violent norms of Roman politics, a second act of assassination would be much easier.

However, Octavian did not at this stage move against his senatorial enemies, nor did the most prominent of those enemies flee Rome. The senators did not expect a purge. The reasons for this misplaced sense of security are obscure. After Julius Caesar had marched on Rome, many of those who had no sympathy with him were able to remain in Italy, living in quiescent security. It seems possible that the senators were still convinced that Octavian would seek reconciliation. Even given the duplicity with which they had behaved, the offence that they had caused, and the violence which they had shown to Caesar and the Caesarians, individual senators appear to have been confident of their personal safety. Even Cicero himself awaited events in Italy.

Octavian's first task was to reward his troops. He seized the money that had been collected by the senate to fund the resistance to Antony and distributed it to his soldiers. He then secured a consulship. Octavian was elected with Quintus Pedius as his colleague, a man who had been at Octavian's side almost since his arrival in Italy in 44. The election was not in itself violent, but it was carried out under military supervision and Octavian's soldiers guaranteed that the electors made the right decision. Such an electoral process, following in its essentials constitutional procedures, established a characteristic discrepancy of the period that was to follow: legal process was maintained in a transformed political reality.

One of Octavian's first acts as consul was to call a special assembly, the *comitia curiata*. This was an archaic assembly which existed only in a reduced and ceremonial form in the thirty lictors who accompanied the consuls. These lictors carried the rods and axes, the fasces, which represented consuls' powers to discipline and, indeed, kill Roman citizens, a symbol of violence more familiar to us through its adoption in the 1920s by the Italian fascists. One of the few remaining functions of the *comitia curiata* was to ratify adoptions among the patricians (an old aristocratic status group). This assembly now passed a law, a *lex curiata*, to legalize Julius Caesar's adoption of Octavian. Contemporaries had been calling Octavian "Caesar" since the will of Julius Caesar had become known, and the meeting of the *comitia curiata* was possibly redundant, but the passing of the law gave Octavian the opportunity to proclaim his continued fidelity to Caesar's memory.[2] Octavian owed much of his authority to a name, as Antony put it: the name of Caesar.

Octavian's initial complaint against Antony was that Antony had sought reconciliation with the assassins rather than revenge for Caesar's murder.[3] This was, of course, calculated to appeal to those who were loyal to Caesar's memory, but as a tactic, it had limited effect. The legionary veterans certainly did not flock to his side demanding the heads of the assassins. Octavian's subsequent alliance with the senate and their open support of the assassins against Antony seem, at the very least, in tension. But it can hardly have been perceived as such at the time. Although the assassins clearly distrusted Octavian (rightly, as it turned out), there is nothing that suggests that they viewed him as being in a political bind, caught by his dependence on his political inheritance from Caesar. We must assume that Octavian and the Ciceronians foresaw ways in which the assassins and Octavian could be reconciled.

This possibility leads us to question the very nature of Caesar's legacy. Clearly, Caesar was not a revolutionary and his actions were not designed to bring about a new order. The assassins may have been acting to "restore" liberty, but Caesar's own actions appear to have been aimed at reconciliation and at establishing a mode of operation by which he could continue to exert political authority within the traditions of the Republic (including maintaining *libertas*). In this light, the assassination was controversial; it could be seen as an extreme reaction to Caesar's dominance, unjustified by the political actions of Caesar himself and based on an extreme understanding of Roman politics.

Caesar's assassination was not, then, a counterrevolution, for the very reason that there had been no revolution to counter, and Octavian's position in the aftermath of Caesar's death was equally not revolutionary, since he had no revolutionary legacy to adopt. Caesar's heir might be expected to work alongside the traditional powers in Roman society, for there was no obvious alternative, and if a personal reconciliation could be achieved with the assassins, there was nothing fundamental about which Octavian and the assassins disagreed. The ideological conflict between the two parties was limited to the assassination itself, and it probably seemed possible that Marcus Brutus, Cassius, and Octavian could have some way of agreeing to differ on that action without engaging in violent conflict; after all, both Decimus Brutus and Cicero had managed to find ways of working with Octavian, if uneasily in the first instance.

The problem of late 44 and early 43 was Antony, not the young Caesar. Octavian's position was anomalous, but from the perspective of the senators in 43 it was neither threatening nor particularly disturbing until he turned his troops around and marched on Rome.

The senators' position and actions in 43 seem perfectly sensible and logical if we assume their political prejudices, in which the senators themselves were the key to political power and in which it was only the senators who mattered. The problem is that their prejudices and their political ideology did not match the realities of political power. Those realities were money and muscle. Muscle came in the form of the soldiers. The senators may have had far more money than any other group in Roman society, but Antony and Octavian were able to use the military to strip the senators of all the cash that they could.

The troops were the missing element in the senators' calculations; despised and ignored, probably drawn from the least powerful, least wealthy, and least influential echelons of Roman society, they were simply not seen as a power worthy of consideration. Even as their political position collapsed, the senators still appear to have been thinking in traditional terms, unaware of the shifts of power in Roman society that were happening before their eyes, still confident of their ability to manage and control the soldiery and unaware that the legacy of Caesar's assassination was not so much the somewhat surprising and unprecedented elevation of Octavian as the breach between themselves and Caesar's legionaries and the emergence of those legionaries into Roman political life. If revolutions are built around insurgent groups, the Roman revolution's insurgents were Caesar's veterans.

RETURN TO MUTINA: THE FOUNDATION OF THE TRIUMVIRAL ALLIANCE

Any residual ambiguity about Octavian's position was dispelled in the first actions of the new consuls. Not only was there the adoption, a ceremonial acknowledgment of Octavian's political and personal debt to Caesar and a reassertion of his claim to be Caesar's true heir, but the consul Pedius introduced a law which banished Caesar's assassins.[4] This law revoked amnesties granted in the aftermath of the assassination and extended the remit of the crime of Caesar's murder to include not only those many senators who had taken an active role in the killing, but also those who had been aware of or involved in the conspiracy. This inevitably allowed charges to be brought against a much wider circle and the purging of those enemies of Octavian who might conveniently be suspected of having had prior knowledge of the assassination.

Charges were brought against the assassins; they were tried en masse, on a single day and in absentia. Octavian presided over the court. The jury, which would have been composed of more than 50 members of the higher echelons of Roman society, unsurprisingly voted to convict. Only one juror, a senator, Silicius Corona, stood out against the young Caesar's wishes and voted to acquit, a brave act of resistance to the regime and an assertion of senatorial independence.[5] Silicius survived for the moment. By these measures, Octavian established the legal framework which would underpin the coming war against Marcus Brutus and Cassius, and it is notable that in spite of the circumstance of an approaching civil war, Octavian felt the necessity to equip himself with such legal backing.

Octavian was still in conflict with Antony, who was still an enemy of the Roman state. Furthermore, Decimus Brutus and Plancus were in command of powerful armies on the borders of Italy. The uncertainties of the time are reflected in a somewhat delayed reaction to events in Rome. Decimus Brutus had not immediately begun a retreat from Cularo once news of Octavian's coup became known. It seems possible that he was waiting to see what the young man intended to do. But once Octavian had committed to a policy of war against Marcus Brutus and Cassius, a war neither he nor Antony could hope to win alone, reconciliation between the Caesarians became inevitable. Octavian and Pedius paved the way for this reconciliation by persuading the senate to revoke its decrees against Lepidus and Antony.

Octavian thus signaled his willingness to negotiate.[6] When news of the decrees reached Decimus Brutus and Plancus, they must have realized that their position at Cularo was untenable. By this time, Lepidus and Antony had been joined by Pollio, and they now marched on Plancus and Decimus Brutus. Faced with a much larger army approaching from the south and with no prospect of victory or reinforcement, Plancus sought reconciliation. Antony had been annoyed that in spite of their prior ties Plancus had been so firmly in the Ciceronian camp. Yet, as one of Caesar's former officers, Plancus had many friends with influence over Antony, and making peace with Plancus was less problematic than the personal and political contortions that Antony and Octavian would have to go through. Pollio mediated, and Antony and Plancus were reconciled.

Plancus's troops, who were anyhow hardly the most reliable of the senate's legions, joined with the army of Antony.

Decimus Brutus, however, did not have such connections and as one of the assassins of Caesar had no prospect of pardon. With Plancus gone, Decimus Brutus's only option was to join with Marcus Brutus in the East. The most obvious route was to cross the Alps, march through northern Italy, and to exit the peninsula near Aquileia before crossing the Balkans. But Octavian had started to send troops north, and Antony was in a position to pursue closely. It seemed unlikely that Decimus Brutus would get to Aquileia before Octavian or without being caught by Antony. Decimus Brutus devised an alternative plan to march north of the Alps. But this was a desperate venture. He would need to cross the Rhine and travel through areas which were beyond Roman control.

His soldiers were understandably unconvinced. They defected. The new recruits who had served with Pansa went first, heading off to join Octavian. Those who had served longer turned the other way and went to join Antony. Decimus Brutus was left with only a bodyguard of Gallic cavalry. He discharged most of these, and adopted a disguise.

Now in a small party, Decimus Brutus shifted his route again. He aimed to cross into Italy incognito and then find his way to Marcus Brutus. But the Alpine region was not peaceful, being controlled by numerous small tribes that were perhaps diplomatically subservient to Rome, but largely independent powers. Decimus Brutus's party attracted the attention of one of the bandit groups of the region, and he and his companions were captured. The bandits quickly realized that they had secured an unusual and dangerous prize and passed him on to their tribal chief, Camilus, a friend of Decimus Brutus. Camilus was placed in a quandary, but the choices he had to make were not too difficult. In spite of their prior friendship (probably a convenient political friendship anyhow), Camilus could hardly resist Antony's legions and he could not risk making powerful enemies. The chief informed Antony, and Antony ordered that Decimus Brutus be killed. The last resistance in northern Italy was brought to an end.[7]

Octavian and his army returned to Bononia and there awaited Antony and Lepidus.[8] Antony and Lepidus meanwhile marched into

Italy and camped at Mutina. The two sides had returned to the scenes
of the previous year's battles, and lined up on the same plain. In spite
of all that had happened between them, Antony and Octavian needed
each other.

The three men must have realized long before this meeting that it was
necessary to pool resources to meet their military enemies in the East
and in Sicily and to combat their political enemies in Rome. They had to
look beyond their differences and personal animosities and beyond the
vicious fighting of the previous months. Such a reunification of Caesar's
men may have been Antony's aim ever since his decision to raise the siege
of Mutina. Although there was every reason to believe that the period to
follow would be marred by a cordial hatred between the three men,
resolving those issues would have to wait. Furthermore, it seems unlikely
that the troops, some of whom had already declared their unwillingness
to fight each other, would accept anything other than a wholehearted
alliance against their common enemies. The veterans wanted the
Caesarian settlement guaranteed, the promised rewards paid, and a
security for their newfound power and influence. They demanded that
the Caesarians be reunited.

Lepidus, Antony and Octavian met near Mutina on an island in the
Lavinus River. The most important issues to resolve were probably the
mechanics of power: how to establish their alliances, their zones of
activity, the basis of their authority, and what they would do next.
After two days of discussions, they announced the inevitable accommodation. It was resolved that Octavian would resign the consulship
and that the three of them would hold new offices, innovations in the
conservative Roman constitution, with absolute power.[9] Then they
turned to Rome.

THE RULE OF THE TRIUMVIRS

The three Caesarians divided the world between them. Octavian was
given control over Africa, Sardinia, and Sicily; Lepidus took Spain and
Gallia Narbonensis (Southern France); Antony held the rest of Gaul (on

both sides of the Alps). They agreed that Lepidus would be elected consul for the following year. Lepidus was to have three legions with which to control Italy. He gave the rest of his legions to Antony and Octavian so that they had twenty legions each to pursue the war against Brutus and Cassius. The provinces were to be governed by legates (picked representatives of the triumvirs). This gave each triumvir the opportunity to reward his close and loyal friends, and also a source of wealth and power with which to support his political and military adventures.[10]

The basis of the agreement was announced to the soldiers at a general meeting. The soldiers approved and asked that this new alliance be recognized in the marriage of the young Octavian to Clodia, who was the daughter of Antony's wife, Fulvia, and Cicero's old enemy Clodius, further illustrating the small world that was the Roman aristocracy.

Part of the agreement that was not announced to the soldiers was to dispose of the political enemies of the triumvirs. As the new allies approached Rome, four prominent men were killed either at dinner or on the streets. There was no decree, no announcement, and certainly no legal process. Rome was a city in which rumor was the main means for the dissemination of information. News travelled quickly through the tight-knit social networks of the Roman upper classes. It became clear during the night that armed men were searching Rome, looking for certain individuals, but other than those in the gang, no one knew who was being targeted or how many. Even later, there was uncertainty as whether there were to be 12 or 17 victims. In the dark of an unlit city, the commotion caused panic. The consul tried to assert a measure of control, touring the city with heralds urging calm, and at dawn, against the intentions of the triumvirs, he posted the names of the intended victims, announcing that the blame for the civil war was to be limited to these men. Soon afterwards, Pedius died. Somewhat implausibly, it is claimed that the stress of the night led to his death. He was the third consul to die in service that year.[11]

The three Caesarians entered the city soon after. Each man brought his praetorian guard and a single legion. The tribune Marcus Titius was then encouraged to put a bill before the people. The convention was that a period of three market days would pass between the publication of the bill and voting on the proposal, which might mean a delay of the best part of a month, but in this case, the vote took place on the day the bill was published. On November 27, 43, the Lex Titia came into being and with it the new magistracy of the *triumviri rei publicae constituendae* (which we might translate as the "three magistrates for the establishment of the Republic").[12]

The provisions of the Lex Titia are obscure.[13] The law was time-limited, and the magistracy was to lapse after five years. It would seem to have granted the triumviri plenipotentiary powers, at least those of the consul, and probably also powers over the provinces, for that period. One might reconstruct the bill on the basis of what we find the triumvirs doing over the next years, and imagine provisions relating to the designation of magistracies and the abrogation of the civil rights of the Roman people. But it is perhaps more likely that the law was very short, on the model of the decrees which empowered a dictator or of the emergency decrees of the senate that instructed the consuls to do all in their power to ensure the preservation of the Republic. Perhaps there was also an empowering clause similar to that which we find in the later laws which elevated individuals to the imperial position (*leges de imperio*). Those laws had a clause which legalized all actions deemed necessary by the emperor. Probably the best evidence for the law lies in the title of the magistrates, *triumviri rei publicae constituendae*.

Although the Romans gave us the modern term "republic," with its connotations of a government of citizens rather than a monarchy or a tyranny, the Latin original, *res publica*, means simply "public matters," as opposed to the *res privata*, the "private matters" of household and family. The vagueness of the Roman notion of republic reflects the absence of constitutional formality in Roman political culture. Rome was ruled through a mix of customs and practices, some of which were enshrined in law, some of which depended on the behavior of the Roman political class and the general citizenry to work. Such flexibility was both a strength and a weakness within a political system. It was a strength because it allowed the system to accommodate different circumstances and to evolve as needs required. It was a weakness because it also allowed unscrupulous politicians to manipulate the system. Furthermore, the lack of formal rules and the absence of any body to decide what the informal rules might be, such as an independent judiciary or a supreme court, left considerable opportunities for interpretative disputes, as politicians could argue as to whether the "spirit" of the constitution overrode established practices.

The openness of *"res publica"* to interpretation did not, however, render the term meaningless. The *res publica* was associated with other political concepts which were of great value, most notably *libertas* (freedom) and *pietas* (respect for the gods and ancestors), both of which are difficult to define but had considerable moral force. Precisely because there was no written constitution and the Romans relied on this cluster of practices, behaviors, and laws, a vague terminology was necessary. *Res publica* thus could come to mean "the way we do public affairs" and although there might be arguments at times, there was a general knowledge of past customs and a generally agreed set of practices that could be described as the Roman republican constitution, or, perhaps better, "Roman republican political culture." The importance of the *res publica* is displayed by the vehemence with which the term was deployed in political arguments and the prevalence of the term in political life, and by the fact that people were prepared to fight and die for the Republic.

The Lex Titia created the new triumviral magistracies for the "establishment of the political system." The function associated with the title is paralleled by the title associated with Sulla's dictatorship in 82, which was probably *dictator legibus faciendis et rei publicae constituendae* (dictator for the making of laws and the establishment of the political system) or *dictator rei publicae constituendae*.[14] It is likely that Sulla's title was innovative, since dictators had previously been appointed either for the purpose of holding elections or to deal with a particular crisis, normally military.

The title of the triumvirs implied that the political system had ceased. The triumvirs represented themselves as stepping in to resolve an absence, an absence of a political system.[15] That absence, however, was not institutional. All the institutions that we associate with the Republic continued to function. Further, the triumvirate was called into being by law, and although the Lex Titia was passed in an unorthodox manner, the foundational act of the triumvirate acknowledged both the sovereignty of the people and the institutional means by which that sovereignty was enacted. Similarly, the triumvirs operated in a close institutional relationship with the senate during their period of office and sought senatorial ratification of at least some of their acts.[16]

Still, the failure of the traditions of political life must have been profound. Something of the triumviral diagnosis can be seen in a decree preserved in Appian.

Marcus Lepidus, Marcus Antonius, and Octavius Caesar, chosen by the people to set right and regulate the republic, state: if wicked traitors had not begged for clemency and once they had received such benefits become enemies of their benefactors and conspired against them, Gaius Caesar would not have been killed by those many whom he had taken prisoner in war and saved by his clemency and allowed his friendship and upon whom he had bestowed offices, honors, and gifts; nor would we have been compelled to act against those who have insulted us and declared us public enemies. But now, as things are, realizing from the conspiracies against us and what was suffered by Gaius Caesar that such evil cannot be overcome by kindness, we prefer to anticipate our enemies rather than suffer at their hands. Let no one regard such acts as unjust or cruel or disproportionate, knowing what both Caesar and ourselves have suffered. Although Caesar was dictator and Pontifex Maximus, although he had conquered and added to our empire nations most feared by the Romans, although he was the first man to venture on the unsailed seas beyond the pillars of Hercules and discover a country previously unknown to the Romans, in the middle of the senate, which is designated as sacred, and under the eyes of the gods, he received twenty-three evil wounds and was murdered by men whom he had taken prisoner in war and spared, some of whom he had even made heirs to his wealth. The others, instead of punishing those guilty of this crime, sent them out as magistrates and commanders, in which offices they seized the public money, and are raising an army against us and seeking the support of barbarians who have been enemies to our empire and Roman cities which they cannot secure are burnt, ravaged, or razed, while other have been forced by fear to fight the nation and us . . . One task yet remains, that is to campaign across the sea against Caesar's assassins. As we prepare to undertake this war for you, we do not consider it safe, either for us or for you, to leave our other enemies behind to take advantage of our absence and watch for opportunities in the events of war; nor further that we should delay such a task on their account, but rather that we should dispose of them at once, since it is they who began the war against us when they decreed us and our armies enemies.[17]

The case that the triumvirs supposedly placed before the people of Rome was simple. The murder of Caesar, a man who had done so much for Rome and who held such a high position, demonstrated the bankruptcy of the Roman political system. The subsequent actions of individuals which were aimed at the destruction of the triumvirs themselves merely confirmed that bankruptcy. Caesar's assassins were men who had been forgiven by Caesar for their opposition during the civil war, reintegrated into the political system, and honored, even recognized in his will. Their betrayal of that personal relationship demonstrated that peace was impossible with them. Their offence stood against the political and social customs of friendship and personal obligation. They could not be trusted. They acted outside the norms of Roman political culture. Their urging on of war had brought the Roman citizenry huge losses, and more were to come. These leading men had turned away from the traditions of Rome, and their rejection of those values demonstrated their contempt for Roman political culture as well as the corruption that had overtaken it.

Late in life, Octavian, long established in power, drew up the account of his career to be published on his tomb and across the empire. He summarized these events of 44–42:

At the age of nineteen, by my private initiative and on my private resources, I raised an army through which I won liberty for the Republic, which had been oppressed by the domination of a faction. For which the

senate, with honorific resolutions, elected me into its order, in the consulship of Gaius Pansa and Aulus Hirtius, at the same time giving me a
consular place in voting; it also gave me *imperium* [legal power]. It
ordered me as propraetor, along with the consuls, "to see that the Republic
suffered no harm." In the same year, moreover, when both consuls had
fallen in war, the people made me consul and triumvir for establishing
the Republic. Those who had killed my father I drove into exile, revenging
their deed by legitimate legal action, and afterwards when they waged
war on the Republic I twice defeated them in battle.[18]

Allowing for the passage of half a century to have dimmed political
memories of these violent events and an elderly politician's polishing of
his reputation for posthumous consumption, Octavian's account notably
employs a traditional political vocabulary. His acts against Antony are
described as restoring freedom (*libertas*). He fought on behalf of the *res
publica*. His virtue was recognized by official constitutional bodies, the
senate and people. He opposed the tyranny of a clique in order to restore
normal political life. His actions against the assassins were legal, following proper procedures, and the war which was to follow was also in
defense of the Republic. The conservatism of the presentation is largely in
keeping with Appian's report of the triumviral decree. The elderly
emperor presents his younger self as engaged in heroic efforts to establish
and defend a Republic threatened with extinction. But that threat is
nowhere described as having been constitutional or institutional; it is
attributed to the political actions of individuals.

Taught by our modern constitutionalists, we tend to think of constitutions in terms of checks and balances, the ways in which the powers of
the executive are limited and responsibility and accountability are generated within the system. In modern systems, the legislature supervises the
executive and the judiciary, and investigative authorities ensure that
proper procedures, appropriate openness, and general fair play are
employed by the legislators and executive. The Roman system was
substantially different. Power always had the potential to be untram-
meled; the senior magistrates were the judiciary, the executive, and the
military commanders. The power of the magistrates extended to capital

punishment. From the fifth century B.C., Roman citizens had secured various means of protecting themselves from a magistrate, including a right of appeal to the people (probably through the tribunes, who would then intercede, perhaps even physically standing between the magistrate and the citizen). From 17 B.C., it was the emperor who protected Roman citizens from their magistrates.[19] But the real limitations on magisterial violence were the customary practices by which politics was conducted, which required that magistrates behave with decorum, seek advice from consultative bodies such as the senate itself, and treat Roman citizens of all status levels with respect.

The triumviral argument was about political morality, and it bore similarities to the messages that had been coming from the Caesarians for some time. Lepidus's soldiers had announced that the war was over once the consuls were dead, and asserted that the lives of Roman citizens should be preserved by ending the fighting. Antony had asked the resourceless Lepidus to make peace. Lepidus himself had advised the senate to accept the military and political reality of the victory of Antony and so preserve Roman lives. In late 43, the triumvirs made an offer of peace to the people so that the *res publica* could be formed once more and the Roman "way of doing business," so obviously lost in the violence of March 44 and later, could be restored. But that restoration would take time. In the interim, before the peace and security of the Roman people could be secured, power, pure and simple, would rule, and those who had proved themselves inimical to peace must be removed. This was not an argument about constitutionalism or legality but about political culture, and in default of that political culture, a failure made obvious by the murder of Caesar and the actions taken against Antony and Octavian, all that remained was the politics of violence.

8.

DEATH IN ROME

THE TRIUMVIRAL DECREE IS a long, angry preamble to slaughter. It concludes by outlining what will happen next:

We shall not strike angrily at the crowd, nor take vengeance against all who have opposed us or conspired against us, or those who are merely rich, wealthy, or honored; nor as many as a previous dictator killed, a man who held the supreme power before us, when he, too, was regulating the city in civil war, and whom you named Felix for his success, though necessarily three have more enemies than one. But we shall seek revenge only on the worst and most deserving. This we shall do for you no less than for us: for it follows that while we are in conflict all will necessarily suffer terribly, and we must also appease the army, which has been insulted, provoked, and made an enemy by our common foe. Although we could summarily arrest whomsoever we had decided on, we choose to proscribe rather than seize them unaware; and this, also, we do for you, so that the enraged soldiers are prevented from surpassing their limits and exceeding their orders and acting against those not responsible, but that they are limited to a certain number of known names, and spare others by order.

Good fortune! Let no one support or hide or help escape or receive money to aid any whose names are listed beneath. If anyone is found saving, or helping, or conspiring with those listed, we will add them to the proscribed without listening to excuses or pleas. Let killers of the proscribed bring us their heads and receive the rewards: to a free man 25,000 Attic drachmas for each; to a slave freedom and 10,000 Attic drachmas and his master's citizenship. Those who place information shall receive the same rewards. So that they may remain unknown, none of the recipients will be inscribed in our registers.[1]

This decree was posted on the very night that the Lex Titia was passed. One hundred and thirty names were posted as an appendix to the decree, and another 150 were to follow soon after. The list was published by being painted up on two white boards in the Forum. On one of those boards the names of senators were written up, while the other board was reserved for nonsenators. The separation reflects the seeming desire of the triumvirs to give their massacre an air of formality and order. The irony of the preservation of status designations in the face of the equality of death was not lost on contemporaries.[2]

Sulla had employed a similar procedure at the end of the civil war of 81 B.C. Names were posted, and rewards were given for proof of the deaths of those individuals. The proof demanded was the head, and the heads of the slain were displayed in the Forum. But whereas Sulla seems to have recorded the names of the informers and killers as recipients of public reward, the triumvirs guaranteed anonymity in order to provide the killers with protection from the enraged friends and family of the killed. They probably hoped that anonymity would free the killers from any social restraints.

Our sources have many stories of the horror that befell Rome. Appian has the most detailed and extensive collection, but one finds a similar compilation in Dio and in *Memorable Deeds and Sayings* by Valerius Maximus. This last is a very unusual collection of anecdotes, usually devoid of historical context and organized according to certain moral or political categories (loyalty of slaves, patriotism, etc.), normally subdivided by Roman and non-Roman examples. Valerius probably collected these anecdotes so that Romans could learn from the deeds of their predecessors, historical examples being a source of moral guidance. Valerius returns again and again to the triumviral proscriptions, and Appian tells us that the events of the proscriptions were recorded in numerous books and that he repeated only a small number of the instances available to him.[3] The events of the proscriptions were remembered for generations.

Although the triumviral decree envisaged the forthcoming slaughter as an orderly process that would affect a limited number of the Roman elite, only the fiercest of the triumvirs' enemies, the most diehard of the opponents of Caesar and his successors, the reality was different. The terror that gripped Rome was general. The narratives suggest anarchy even as the triumvirs justified the process by claiming that it would prevent the soldiers from instituting anarchy.[4] The breakdown of social order was almost as shocking as the killings themselves. In Roman society's hierarchical arrangement, power resided with the master of his house. That power was exercised over the *familia*, despotically in the case of slaves, and with more moderation with regard to children and wives. But the proscriptions meant a radical shift of power. Because of their potential to inform, slaves and wives now had power over masters. Furthermore, neighbors, creditors, "friends." those bound by social ties, those seeking redress for real or imagined wrongs, the envious, the covetous, and those predisposed towards violence could now prove themselves killers.

One is forcibly reminded of modern accounts of intercommunal violence in which people who had lived alongside each other all their lives suddenly take up arms and enact a murderous hatred. Social tensions, social competition, and the general disaffection that so often mark everyday interactions could in certain political situations be resolved by murder. Societies work because of a certain amount of trust, but in civil conflicts such as these, there could be no trust. In circumstances of social breakdown and pervasive violence, people find that joining with the violent is a means of self-preservation.

The proscription list was not fixed, and individuals could petition for people to be removed or added. It meant that even if one was safe initially, one might not be safe the next day. One never knew if someone, somewhere, was whispering into the ear of one of the triumvirs, trying to persuade them to add another name to the list in pursuance of a feud; an estate; a sudden, extreme, and final dissolution of a marriage; or an early inheritance. In such circumstances, social relations collapsed in a welter of suspicion and fear. If someone was proscribed, they were immediately deprived of rights; their property technically came to belong to the state, but in the anarchy that raged across the city, no one had the duty, responsibility, or interest to preserve a property (certainly not the proscribed), and so an estate was unprotected and subject to looting by neighbors or associates or those passing who sensed an opportunity. Slaves may have taken the opportunity to disappear, either temporarily or permanently, secure in the knowledge that there was only the faintest possibility that anybody would remember them, find their records, or come looking for them to exact the penalties due on fugitives.

The corruption of normal social relations is emphasized by the inclusion of those closest to the triumvirs on the list: Antony proscribed his uncle, Lepidus his brother, Octavian his former guardian. Other figures with high connections were also proscribed, such as Asinius Pollio's father-in-law and Munatius Plancus's brother. In the face of such ruthlessness, few will have had much hope of appealing to the sympathies of the triumvirs.[5]

Appian, reflecting the hierarchical thinking that was second nature to Romans (and Greeks) of the imperial period, organizes his stories by social and political status, and then by the closeness of familial relations (and hence the extent of corruption). He leads with stories of magistrates killed, then moves to fathers betrayed by sons, brothers killed together, masters given up by slaves, and wives who took the opportunity to dispose of inconvenient husbands. Balancing such tales of horror are examples of familial unity—of magistrates or former generals saved by loyal individuals, wives hiding husbands and helping them to escape, fathers and sons and brothers attempting to flee together, and slaves accompanying their masters and sometimes sacrificing themselves for them.

The tribune Salvius threw a dinner party as the triumvirs approached the city.[6] A centurion and his detachment broke into Salvius's house, and ordered the diners to remain in place. He pulled Salvius down on to the table by his hair and beheaded him. The guests were forced to remain at table, next to the headless corpse of their host.

A praetor, Annalis, was campaigning for votes when the news came through that he was proscribed. His attendants fled, and Annalis rushed off to the house of a freedman who lived in the suburbs. His son, though, guessing or informed that he would flee to this friend, led the soldiers to him. His son was rewarded with his father's property, but was later killed by the same soldiers in a drunken brawl. A former praetor, Thouranius, was arrested by soldiers and begged them to delay so that his son could intercede with Antony on his behalf. The soldiers told him that his son had already interceded with Antony so as to include his father on the list in the expectation of an early inheritance.[7]

Quintus Cicero, brother of the orator, and his son were captured together. The executioners killed them at the same moment. Another father and son were decapitated with a single blow, leaving their headless corpses still embracing. Balbus and his son managed to escape Rome. Balbus sent his son ahead, but his son drowned at sea and Balbus returned to Rome to meet his death. The son of Arruntius refused to flee without his father, but as the killers closed in, he was persuaded to head off to sea, where he also drowned. His mother, having performed the funeral rites for her executed husband, killed herself.

Two brothers hid themselves in an oven. When their slaves found them, they killed one brother, while the other escaped. On realizing that his brother was dead, the surviving brother threw himself off a bridge, only to be rescued by some fishermen. The fishermen tried to help, but they were seen by soldiers, who cut off the remaining brother's head. One man intervened to protect his brother, offering himself in his place. The centurion informed him that both men were proscribed and beheaded the brothers.

Another man was hidden by his wife. Her slave came to know and betrayed them and then headed to the Forum for her reward. The woman starved herself to death. A certain Septimius, unaware of his wife's adultery, fled to his wife's house. She accepted him and locked the doors, but not before sending for the killers. On the very day of her husband's death, she married her lover.

Statius, an elderly senator, finding himself on the list of the proscribed, gave away all his property to his neighbors and then set his house on fire while remaining inside. Naso was informed on by a freedman who was also his lover; he broke away from his captors just long enough to kill his betrayer. Labienus, who had led one of Sulla's death squads, sat outside the front door of his house to await the next generation of murderers. Aemilius, unaware that he was himself proscribed, attempted to distract a centurion who was pursuing a victim; the centurion killed both men. Silicius, the senator who had bravely voted to acquit Brutus, attempted to flee the city, but finding the gates guarded, attached himself to a group of pallbearers. The soldiers noticed the unusual number of bearers and Silicius was given away. Rufus owned a block of houses next to property belonging to Fulvia, Antony's wife. Fulvia had previously wanted to buy the property, but Rufus had refused to sell. When Antony rose to power, he had given her the property, but he still found himself on the list. Antony sent Rufus's head to Fulvia, who had it displayed on the block rather than in the Forum.[8]

Alongside these stories, Appian has a number of successful escapes and notable stories of familial loyalty. Antony's uncle was protected by his sister, Antony's mother, who openly dared Antony to add matricide to his list of crimes. Reginus left Rome disguised as a charcoal burner, his wife traveling in a litter behind him. A soldier decided to search the litter. Reginus interceded. The soldier recognized Reginus, but sent him and his wife on his way—he had once served under him. Geta's son held funeral rites for his father and then kept him in hiding. Caponius's wife gave herself to Antony to secure her husband's pardon. Oppius was carried from the city by his son in a manner which recollected the mythical stories of Aeneas fleeing the burning city of Troy; somehow the soldiers failed to notice him.[9]

The most detailed story comes from an inscription, the so-called Laudatio Turiae, a very long and fragmentary account (more than 120 lines of Latin) of a woman's exceptional loyalty to her husband.[10] When her husband was listed, she, her sister and brother-in-law hid him and petitioned Octavian for his restoration. They managed to achieve this, but their real enemy was Lepidus. When the loyal wife presented Octavian's edict of restoration, she was beaten, but she returned again and forced Lepidus to accept the edict.

The most notable victim of the proscription was Cicero. He attempted to flee Italy, but was driven back by the weather. He then vacillated. As the search closed in, he entered a litter and fled towards the sea. A certain Laenas, whom Cicero had once defended, discovered where he was and led the party of killers towards him. Cicero's slaves resisted; on finding himself outnumbered, Laenas called for reinforcements, though he knew that none existed. Cicero's attendants fled, and Cicero was pulled from the litter. Accounts of how the 63-year-old met his death vary slightly and were probably improved in the various retellings. After three blows, Cicero's head was removed. His right hand was cut off, the hand that had composed the Philippics. These body parts were sent to Rome and were displayed on the rostrum in the Forum from where Cicero had delivered some of his most scathing attacks on Antony.[11]

We can reconstruct something of the mechanics of the massacre from these stories. The lists were posted in the Forum, and possibly then copied and distributed across the city. News filtered through relatively slowly. Some individuals were struck down before they knew that they had been proscribed, which must have added considerably to the fear of the population. Once the gangs began to scour the city, it would have been a brave individual who ventured down to the Forum to check whether he was listed. Some soldiers guarded gates and bridges; others went in search of their victims. The killers appear to have had few difficulties in recognizing their targets. Such familiarity can only have stemmed from the culture of display in Roman political life: prominent men were seen as they were accompanied to the Forum and to the temples, to the courts and in the performance of their business. These were individuals who had lived at least partly in public, and it was their celebrity which allowed them to be hunted down.

It is unclear how many were proscribed and how many escaped. It would seem likely that the 280 listed individuals (to whom we should probably add the 12 or 17 unlisted individuals who were attacked as the triumvirs approached Rome) were prominent members of the political class, certainly men of sufficient import to win the enmity of the triumvirs. Not all were senators. One must imagine that there were also other casualties of the purge: those judged to have aided the proscribed in their attempted escapes, those added later, and those whose deaths were the "collateral damage" of the proscriptions. Dio claims that names were regularly wiped from the boards, and new names added.[12] Appian gives 300 senators and 2,000 equestrians as the eventual number of victims, but this is little more than a guess, and it was hardly in the interests of the triumvirs to keep good accounts. There are no numbers for those below this status level.[13] One should also imagine that many fled to join Brutus or Sextus Pompeius. Whatever the true number of killed and exiled, the proscriptions cut a swath across the Roman political class.[14]

There was no attempt to hide the brutality of these events. The proscribed were not "disappeared," nor were they transported to specialized places of death as has been the practice of modern totalitarian states. The grisly proof of the slaughter was displayed in the most important public space of all Rome, the Forum. An ever-expanding exhibition of heads gave a visual context to the performance of politics in triumviral Rome, representing the power of the triumvirs and the reality of military control of the city. Cicero's head and hand were displayed from the rostrum, a gory, silent, but eloquent spectacle.

Romans were not squeamish about death; they lived in a militaristic, slave-owning society in which death as spectacle was a public entertainment. Nevertheless, displaying the heads of your political enemies was an extreme representation of the violence of the regime. The stories that circulated dramatized the arbitrary workings of violent power—the pardons received, the deaths secured by petitioning the triumvirs, the seemingly trivial offences revenged and old scores settled through execution, the prostitution of a wife to save her husband. There was a terroristic element to this violence, scaring any who might think of opposing the regime. The purge left no doubt as to what would happen to opponents of the regime. After the worst of the violence was over, those orators who clambered onto the rostrum to address the Roman people would have found themselves standing next to the head of Cicero. It may be assumed that they would take note. Even once the grisly remains had been removed, the memories of the atrocities would be strongly associated with the public spaces of Rome and bear heavily on the minds of the people. It is difficult to imagine that many senators would enter the Forum without being haunted by the specters of the proscriptions.

The display of violence operated at another level. The Forum was the monumental center of Roman politics and of the Roman state. It was loaded with symbols that represented the political culture of the city. One needs to compare it with the other symbols of nations and their politics with which we are familiar. Whenever filmmakers want to show us the end of the modern political system, they show us the White House in ruins, Parliament ablaze, the Eiffel Tower fallen. Such ruination comes to represent the revolutionary overthrow of the state. The display of heads in the Forum is such a ruination, turning the spaces of Roman political culture (of respect for the citizen, of honor for the senators and the leading men of the city) into a display of destruction. The symbolism would be almost as potent as displaying impaled heads and hands on the White House lawn.

There was a revolutionary element to this violence. Civil rights and normal political customs were suspended. The emergency was not a temporary state, a moment of anarchy which, even if not forgotten, could be rapidly consigned to the past. Instead, it was an extended emergency. When Lepidus spoke to the senate and gave them hope that this emergency state would lapse and something more approaching normality would resume, Octavian is said to have explicitly differed. Octavian asserted that although the worst might be over, he must be free to resume the proscriptions in the future: the state of terror was suspended, not ended.[15] Power at its most wild sat at the heart of the triumviral regime, and Octavian was not prepared to let the senators forget it.

FINANCING THE REVOLUTION: MONEY AND POWER

Alongside the accounts of extreme violence, our sources do not lose sight of that other lever of power, money. The triumvirs made generous offers to their soldiers to secure their loyalty, but this generosity was not just a bribe, it was a major transfer of resources. Since money could be translated into power, the impoverishment of the traditional aristocracy and the enriching of a new social class established a more stable power base for the triumvirs while weakening the opponents of the new regime.

The property of the proscribed was forfeit to the state, but the triumvirs, as Dio explains, guaranteed a fraction to the sons of the proscribed
(a tenth) and a smaller fraction to their daughters (a twentieth). The
dowries of wives were also to be repaid.[16] In the Roman Republic, wealth
was the surest defense of status. Most wealth was invested in land, and a
respectable Roman would expect to pass down to his children the estates
that he himself had inherited and property at least sufficient to maintain
his children at his status level. This bequest was enhanced by the dowry
that his wife brought to the marriage, and, of course, any other property
that she owned separate from the dowry. The inherited nature of wealth
and status meant that the landed wealthy were recipients of estates which
had, at least in theory, been built up over generations and were expected
to be preserved over the generations. Each generation was a short-term
tenant of the property, responsible for preserving the family estates and
transmitting them to the next generation.

In addition to the murder of the leading member of the family,
proscription entailed a devastating financial loss. There is, of course,
every reason to doubt that the widows and heirs of the proscribed were
able to secure their shares. In the first instance, it is highly unlikely that
the triumvirs would have been minded to be generous to those whose
close relatives they had killed. In other circumstances, a financial disaster might be offset by networks of family and friends who might step in
to soften the blow. But the proscriptions were generalized and aimed
precisely at those networks of power and influence. Even if there were
some relations or friends sufficiently unscathed and sufficiently brave to
lend a hand, the surviving members of even a prominent family were
condemned to relative poverty for generations.

The crisis was translated into a general economic problem, a collapse
in the land market. That collapse affected the ability of the landed to
raise money to meet the exactions of the triumvirs as well as the ability
of the triumvirs to convert their newly acquired and vast property
portfolio into the cash that they required to meet the demands of the
soldiers.

The price falls were probably in part due to a disappearance of buyers
from the market. Anyone buying an estate would advertise his individual

wealth just as the cash-strapped triumviral regime searched for resources.[17] Some may also have felt a moral repugnance at the prospect of benefiting financially from the wholesale social disaster around them. Large estates could only be bought by the richest within Roman society, of whom there were now substantially fewer. In the dramatic uncertainties of the violence and confiscations, large amounts of ready cash would be very difficult to secure, and any potential lenders would be loath to let people know that they had cash available. With a shortage of cash, an absence of buyers, and a glut of supply, one would expect a market collapse.[18]

The triumvirs may have been somewhat surprised by the market failure. In the Sullan proscriptions, 350,000,000 sesterces were raised.[19] The triumvirs supposedly missed their revenue target by 200,000,000 sesterces, but we do not know what that target was. Although many in the last generation of the Republic were able to enrich themselves from the profits of empire, the really wealthy were probably the exception and the norms of senatorial wealth were likely to have been much lower, perhaps in the region of 2,000,000–5,000,000 sesterces, which gives some idea of the scale of the triumviral requirements and the financial issues that they continued to face after the proscriptions.[20] An attempt to tax the wealth of women also failed; instead, a 2 percent tax was introduced on the wealth of all those who had a census of more than 400,000 sesterces charged at double rate for the first year.[21]

A further tax was introduced in 42 B.C., levied on the richer within Rome and set at a tenth of their property. If one starts to add up the percentages, one may be looking at the richer in Roman society paying up to 15 percent of the notional value of their estates, perhaps as much as two years' income. Given the difficulties of raising cash in the depressed market conditions, the amount of land transferred from the richer element in Roman society was significant.[22]

Much of the money raised was to go to the soldiers. Roman public finances had previously been faced with a norm of supporting fewer than 100,000 troops in the field, at perhaps an annual cost of slightly more than 90,000,000 sesterces. This was almost certainly the major drain on the treasury in the Republican period.[23] But in 43, the revenues had to meet the wages of 193,000 legionaries in the triumviral armies alone (173,700,000 sesterces per year), to which we need to add legions in Spain and Gaul. The normal wage requirements of the military would have more than doubled the expenses of the state. Furthermore, Octavian had promised his troops 20,000 sesterces each.[24] We must assume that similar amounts were to be distributed to Antony's and Lepidus's armies. There were at least 43 legions in these three armies. This would suggest a distribution of something in the region of 3,870,000,000 sesterces, 43 times the normal military pay budget.[25] This financial challenge needed to be met without the resources of the East, which were being used to fund Brutus's and Cassius's armies, or of Sicily (under Sextus Pompeius) and perhaps also Africa. Understandably, then, the triumvirs were desperately short of ready cash. The accusation leveled consistently in our sources that the rich were targeted merely to raise money seems likely to have been true, adding a further layer of class conflict to the political crisis.[26]

At an individual level, the rewards paid to the soldiery were large. The annual salary of a legionary was 900 sesterces, from which he was expected to meet his basic expenses. The reward of 20,000 sesterces was considerably more than a soldier might expect to earn over a long military career. Furthermore, the money was free from deductions, whereas the notional pay of a Roman legionary was used to fund the food, equipment, and other goods that the army's logistical systems provided. If we assume that the average soldier was drawn from the less wealthy echelons of Roman society, such rewards had the potential to transform his social status. And the rewards to be paid out to the gangs of killers who sought out the proscribed were significantly larger, and probably also directed at soldiers. The chosen figure, 100,000 sesterces, was the level of census requirement for the *prima classis* of Roman society and thus, in theory at least, each successful kill elevated the killer into the upper echelons of Roman society (though one assumes that each reward was normally divided among the gang members). For 2,300 victims, the bill for the proscriptions alone was 230,000,000 sesterces.

The triumvirs were thus engaged in a huge transfer of resources from the wealthy in Roman society to the soldiers. If we estimate the total bill in 43 and 42 as having been an amount in excess of 4,000,000,000 sesterces, then we are looking at over 4,000 senatorial fortunes.[27] If we assume that the money was distributed across the soldiers of the triumviral armies plus some others, the beneficiaries probably amounted to 200,000 men. If we count in the women and children likely associated with these males, perhaps 700,000 Romans out of a total free population of just over 4,000,000 were beneficiaries of the triumviral violence.[28] For all the stories of horror, the triumviral violence had its share of winners. It is difficult not to draw the conclusion that the triumvirs were buying mass political support.

We might perhaps imagine that the period of the proscriptions was the most extensive redistribution of wealth in Roman history. Even if the existing elite were disparaging about the nouveaux riches, horrified by the way they had made their money, and reluctant to admit such people into their social circles, eventually status would follow money.

Civil war is an exercise in building group loyalties. The trauma of civil war and massacre works not just to desocialize the victims but to socialize the killers into a particular ethical and political stance. Men who had killed together were bound together. Comrades in killing would offer loyalty to a regime that had encouraged their actions and rewarded murder. The wealth with which they were rewarded further bound these men, making them dependent on the regime that had elevated them and guaranteed their position. The triumvirs built a class of relatively wealthy, powerful individuals who could be relied upon to support the regime and who were tainted by the spilling of blood. The regime established a storehouse of political loyalty among the Italian beneficiaries of its violence. We should not imagine that those enriched by the revolution simply disappeared into prosperous obscurity.

The triumvirate was a period of revolution.[29] The revolution was felt throughout Roman society. The slaying of the wealthy and the consequent redistribution of resources provoked unprecedented social turmoil in a society which was hierarchical and traditional. Even though Rome had a history of violence, the brutality of the triumviral proscriptions was such that historians writing more than a century later would recall these events with horror. And yet, even as the legions marched off to meet the armies of Brutus and Cassius, the problems of Italy were far from over.

9.

THE TRIUMVIRS' VICTORY

THE PROSCRIPTIONS BROUGHT THE triumvirs complete control of Rome. After the violence, there could be no negotiated settlement. Too many people had been killed. Too many would bear the psychological scars of the traumatic events in Rome. The triumvirs had secured their power by making promises to the soldiers, and to make good those promises, the lands of the rich and powerful were forfeit. Their political options were limited, and Octavian, Antony, and Lepidus could not turn back.

The turmoil in Rome reinforced the position of their enemies. The triumvirs had managed to dislodge the senatorial governor, Quintus Cornificius, from Africa, but Sextus Pompeius was reinforced by those fleeing Italy.[1] The threat that had initially mobilized the assassins to take up arms against Antony, which was that Antony would institute tyrannous government, had been realized with a severity and violence which probably exceeded even the worst nightmares of the senatorial elite. The waverers could either join with the new regime or to Brutus and Cassius. For those who had already resolved to join with the assassins or who were tacit supporters of their cause, events in Italy confirmed their views: the regime of the triumvirs was revolutionary and threatened the security of all. For the triumvirs, the Republic needed remaking after the murder of Caesar and the battles of Mutina; for their opponents, the Republic had been overthrown by triumviral violence.

The proscriptions were announced as a necessary prelude to the campaign against Brutus and Cassius. They were intended to secure

Rome and Italy for the triumvirs. With opposition in Italy crushed, Antony and Octavian turned their attention to the East.

THE DEFEAT OF THE ASSASSINS: PHILIPPI

Antony and Octavian faced severe difficulties. Although they had a significant number of troops, they needed to transport those troops across the Adriatic and supply them once they were in what is now northern Greece. Under normal circumstances, that would not have been a problem for a Roman army, but these were not normal times.

Sextus Pompeius controlled the sea lanes around Italy. In the East, Brutus and Cassius enjoyed naval superiority. The triumvirs had hopes of Cleopatra, whose Egyptian fleet was strong enough that she could potentially challenge Brutus and Cassius. But naval warfare in the Mediterranean was a deeply uncertain business. One of those uncertainties was meteorological. All one could do to predict the weather was look at the sky. If one was in a single craft and the weather started to turn, one could run for shore, but it was more difficult for a fleet to secure a viable harbor. Cleopatra's fleet put to sea, sailed against Brutus and Cassius, hit a storm, and was wrecked. She was forced to sail for home, and because re-equipping a fleet took considerable time, she was unable to make any further contribution to the war.[2]

The triumvirs' naval inferiority was complete. Even crossing the Adriatic was a matter of luck, exploiting an unexpected absence of Sextus Pompeius's fleet, and once the army was in Greece it was on its own, unable to rely on logistical support from Italy and unable to secure reinforcement.

Meanwhile, Brutus and Cassius had been engaged in Syria and Asia Minor. The very fact that they were fighting so far to the east suggests that they were not particularly concerned to repel any invasion and perhaps did not even expect Antony and Octavian to manage the Adriatic crossing. Their strategy appears to have been to secure control of the resources of the eastern empire and use that resource base to build their military power. In response to the invasion, Brutus and Cassius began a long march from Asia Minor to meet the triumviral armies.

Brutus and Cassius crossed into Europe and then marched round the coast through Thrace towards Macedonia. The road to Macedonia ran between mountains and marshes, and in some places the mountains reach down to the sea. Octavian and Antony wanted to delay Brutus and Cassius as long as they could and had sent out an advanced guard of eight legions under two trusted senior commanders, Lucius Decidius and Gaius Norbanus, to hold the passes, but Brutus and Cassius crossed the mountains aided by local guides who led the army by unexpected routes, and a naval detachment threatened to outflank the triumvirs' advanced guard. Norbanus and Decidius fell back, and Cassius and

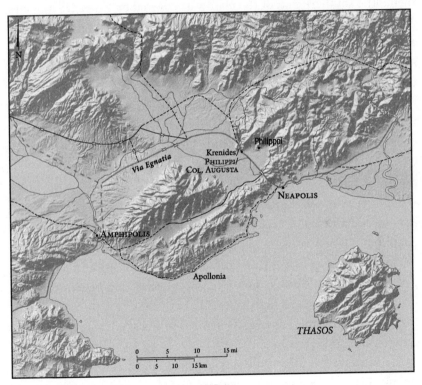

MAP 4
Philippi and Environs

Brutus descended on the small town of Philippi, on the edge of a wide and fertile plain, the main town of which is now Drama.

Modern Philippi lies a couple of miles from the ancient site, which is on the edge of the village of Krinides. The town, named after the father of Alexander the Great, was founded by the Macedonians both to watch the mountain passes and to exploit nearby gold mines. The exact location of the town was probably recommended by the abundant springs which give Krinides its name. The older parts of the town may well have been on the hill above the plain and there was perhaps a scatter of small settlements across the mountain approaches, very much as there is today. Brutus and Cassius camped on two hills just over two miles from the center of Philippi itself, a mile apart.[3] It would seem that the camps were positioned to the west of Philippi so as to have the mountains behind them. The southern end of the plain was covered by extensive marshes. The road across these marshes ran down past the mountains to the sea and allowed easy supply of the troops. Brutus and Cassius's control of the sea meant that supplies could be brought in from across the East and then transported to their camps.

Norbanus and Decidius, almost outflanked by the surprise arrival of Brutus and Cassius, had retreated to the town of Amphipolis, about 60 kilometers from Philippi. The town controlled the main routes to the west and was a valuable base where they could collect supplies. There they awaited Antony and Octavian.

On arrival in Amphipolis, with a sick Octavian trailing in his wake, Antony embarked on a typically daring approach. Leaving one legion in Amphipolis to secure his supply lines against naval harassment, he struck out toward Philippi. He pitched camp very close to Brutus and Cassius, perhaps only a mile away, on low, damp ground, and began to fortify. Brutus and Cassius held higher ground, but Antony's activity and assertiveness were intimidating. Octavian made his way more slowly, and camped alongside Antony.

The forces were almost evenly matched. Both sides had nineteen legions, Brutus's legions being perhaps under strength. But Brutus and Cassius had 20,000 cavalry, while Antony and Octavian had only 13,000. Two hundred thousand men faced one other across the plain.

In the circumstances of ancient warfare, any small advantage could prove crucial. An army that thought itself at a tactical disadvantage would, if possible, avoid battle, remaining behind fortifications. Thus, ancient battles were sometimes fought by negotiation, at places and times where both sides were in agreement. On an open plain, the two sides deploy their full forces and meet their opponents on equal terms, and both could hope for a decisive victory. The plain before Philippi was an ideal place for the battle that would bring the war to an end. Both sides barricaded themselves behind fortifications, securing a place of retreat in case the battle should go against them, and engaged in skirmishes, but battle was not joined. Each day, Antony and Octavian led their armies out to offer battle. They may, thereby, have boosted the morale of their troops, suggesting that their opponents were scared, but they could not force Brutus and Cassius from their camps.

Delay was to the advantage of Brutus and Cassius. Their position on the higher ground seemed unassailable. Furthermore, their control over the sea and of the eastern provinces meant that they were well supplied. Antony and Octavian, having crossed the Adriatic with difficulty, could not easily bring supplies from Italy, the supply route being threatened by Sextus Pompeius's and the assassins' fleets. Southern Greece could not easily be exploited, in part for topographical reasons which meant that supplies were most easily transported by ship. Octavian and Antony were therefore reliant on the relatively rich grain fields of Thessaly and Macedonia. Feeding and equipping 100,000 men, their horses, and the supply train itself was no easy matter. It was the equivalent of feeding three large ancient cities, but cities which had no established supply infrastructure. Although Macedonia and Thessaly could be scoured for supplies, there was a limit to how long they could feed the triumviral armies. At least some of the supplies were provided by private merchants, and they could charge "famine prices," much to the distress of the soldiers. Brutus and Cassius could simply wait until the food ran out, forcing Antony and Octavian to either attack their fortified positions or lead a vulnerable army in a hungry and perhaps mutinous retreat.[4]

Antony was, however, not a general predisposed to waiting upon events. He sneaked a detachment into the marshes to cut a path through to the hills south of Philippi. Unseen by Cassius until too late, Antony used the route to establish outposts from which his troops could close the supply lines to Philippi. Cassius responded with a similar feat of military engineering. He drove a fortified causeway into the marshes with the aim of cutting Antony off from his outposts. The troops engaged where the causeways met, and Cassius managed to cut Antony's road, thereby isolating his outposts to the south. But Antony took advantage of Cassius's commitment of forces to the marshes by charging from his lines to attack the causeway on solid ground near the camp. If he could cut the causeway there, he would separate Cassius and the troops in the marsh from the troops in the camp, repeating the tactics employed by Cassius, but on a larger scale. The charge was oblique, leading his forces—which were, presumably, facing east—to the south and east. With Antony's legions turning away, Brutus's forces saw their chance. Some charged the exposed flank of Antony's army; others engaged Octavian's army. Battle was now joined across the plain.

Octavian's army, perhaps caught by surprise by the sudden turn of events, was rapidly pushed back and Octavian's camp was seized. Brutus's soldiers fell to looting, securing the precious supplies, equipment, and personal possessions of the soldiers, without which it would have been very difficult for them to continue the war. To the south, Antony's troops stormed the fortified causeway. He now had an obvious choice. He could attack Cassius in the marshes, pushing him back down the causeway, or he could turn his attention to the victorious army of Brutus and try to recoup the ground lost by Octavian. But Antony took a third option. Holding off Brutus's forces on one flank and keeping Cassius and the portion of his army that was trapped on the causeway penned in the marsh, Antony himself led a daring attack on Cassius's camp. Fighting their way across the fortifications and filling up the ditches with their dead, the Antonians, with Antony at their head, forced their way into the camp. Cassius's army had been defeated. Antony had won a victory to parallel that of Brutus.

Cassius, unable to return to his camp, turned east and headed to the hill of Philippi. There he tried to make sense of the battle. In the noise and dust, with so many troops similarly equipped, it was difficult to gain reliable information. He sent an officer to find Brutus. There are two stories as to what happened next. In one, news reached Cassius of Brutus's victory. But Cassius, in shame at having lost, asked his slave to cut his throat. In the second story, the messenger was seen approaching a body of cavalry. Cassius thought they were enemies who had captured his officer. He returned to his tent and was helped in his suicide by his slave.[5]

Although the tradition would appear to represent the battle as a draw, one army on each side being defeated, it seems likely that this first battle changed the tactical situation, even if not decisively. There followed a period of maneuvers in which Octavian and Antony attempted to put Brutus under siege, shifting their fortifications in an attempt to cut him off from the sea. Short of supplies themselves, and with autumn approaching, even if they could establish a circumvallation, there was a question as to which side would starve first.

On October 23, Brutus led his army out to fight. It is not clear why he decided to risk a decisive engagement. Appian speculates that his enthusiastic army, flushed with their victory over Octavian, were eager for a fight and believed that with a strongly fortified position, even if the battle went against them they would be able to retreat securely. Appian even suggests that Brutus feared that his troops might mutiny if he did not allow them to join battle.[6]

The armies were evenly matched. They lined up opposite each other and then charged. No subtle tactics were deployed. This was a Roman battle fought straight, man against man, legion against legion. When the front line tired, they retreated and were replaced by the second line, and then by the third until the first returned and the circulation recommenced. The discipline required to complete such maneuvers while under attack was extreme. But, eventually, as if they were lifting a very heavy machine, the triumviral forces started to push their opponents backwards. Brutus's front line stepped back to the second line, and the lines became compressed. Slowly, the tipping point was reached. The lines started to become confused, and ordered circulation became impossible. The formation began to break up, giving their opponents the opportunity to strike. As more men fell, more were exposed, so the pressure grew and the lines lost ground and their shape. And then they turned and fled. But the triumvirs' legions kept up the pursuit, even to the very gates of the camp. Those guarding the gates fired missiles at the attacking troops, but still they came, attacking the soldiers struggling to get through the narrow gates, crushed and unable to oppose the forces behind them. Eventually, the army broke up, some heading for the sea, some for the hills, and some getting back into the camp.

The battle was over. Antony and Octavian hunted down the fleeing troops and attacked the outposts by which Brutus and Cassius had fortified their portion of the plain. They posted guards on the camp and began a circumvallation. Brutus himself could not reach his own camp and retreated into the mountains with what troops he could gather. He probably intended to head to the sea or cross the mountains, but Antony was in pursuit. By nightfall, Brutus was surrounded.[7] Antony waited, supposedly lurking behind a rampart of the dead.

When day broke, Brutus reviewed the situation. He had the remnants of four legions. The main camp was under siege, but had not been taken. His only option was to attempt a breakout. He could charge through Antony's forces and then through Octavian's legions and rejoin his troops in the main camp, but the soldiers had no stomach for a plan with such a limited chance of success and high probability of death. A negotiated surrender would at least preserve their lives. Brutus supposedly proclaimed "And so then I am no longer of use to my country, if these men are so disposed," and called for a friend, Strato of Epirus. He asked Strato to stab him. Strato refused. Brutus summoned a slave. But Strato was shamed that a slave would do this final service; he stabbed his friend, who never flinched.[8]

Appian's account, which is the basis of our detailed understanding of the battle, displays a very good understanding of the topography and logistics that underpinned events. Nevertheless, there are reasons to doubt its absolute veracity. It has novelistic elements and even, at certain points, tends towards romance. Some ancient historians were prone to adding drama to their accounts, producing versions of "what must have happened." The very fact that Appian has two versions of Cassius's suicide suggests that he was dealing with accounts that had been developed in ancient literary imaginations. Brutus and Cassius were later adopted as martyrs of the Republican cause, men whose deaths were to inspire resistance to the more tyrannical emperors over the next century and a half. The drama of these moments was bound to excite literary ambitions, and it is almost impossible to separate fact from fiction, reality from mythology. Indeed, part of the point of these accounts was that the events of Philippi were mythologized, remembered as the dramatic moments when Republican resistance was brought to an end. The great literary endeavor was, and to an extent still is, to overlay the battle with symbolism and to make it a last, great, tragic moment in the fall of the Republic. Brutus and Cassius, then, had to die as martyrs to a cause at once moral and political.

In the absence of a magic formula that would allow us to distinguish fact from fiction, all we can do is note the predominant tendencies of the version of the battle that has come down to us. Brutus and Cassius emerge from the story as heroic figures, boldly and bravely facing their defeats and meeting their deaths (if somewhat prematurely in Cassius's case). Each man faces his martyrdom without emotion, making an exemplary death that would later be imitated and matched by those facing murderous emperors. They are given memorable and patriotic final words. Even the detail of the narrative is strongly in their favor: they are rational, good generals, who, mostly, make the right decisions. By contrast, Antony is consistently depicted as rash to the point of madness, brutal and bloody. He marches too close to the camps of Brutus and Cassius; he storms Cassius's lines in a reckless manner; he diverts to the camp rather than deal with Brutus's forces. And everywhere he is associated with death and a disregard for the lives of his troops and the bodies of the slain; that is until he is faced with the body of Brutus. Then, overcome by the nobility of his opponent, he wraps him in the purple robe of the general and performs the proper funeral rites, sending the ashes to Brutus's wife.

Antony's victory seems against all logic. Yet Antony was the most experienced general of all those on the field. It was Antony who broke the deadlock. It was Antony who defeated Cassius. Antony's troops managed to storm the fortifications, turning the battle. The account minimizes the scale of Antony's victory in the first battle, balancing it with Octavian's defeat, which, of course, leaves a problem with Cassius's suicide. Antony's maneuvers and fortifications over the three weeks between the two battles are given little importance, but it was such maneuvers that had initially provoked Cassius to battle, and it seems unlikely that Antony ceased his efforts to break Brutus's supply lines.

Furthermore, the decision to fight the second battle is attributed to the rash impetuosity of Brutus's troops, persuading their all-wise general. However, educated elite writers were fond of opposing the rationality of the elite with the lack of reason of those of lesser status. The neatness with which the relationship between the wise Brutus and the foolish masses falls into this trope should cause suspicion. It seems more likely that rather than being filled with a completely irrational confidence, especially after the losses of the first battle, Brutus and his troops feared being trapped, surrounded by Octavian and Antony's fortifications. Cut off from the sea and the possibility of retreat through the mountains, Brutus and his army could attempt to starve out their besiegers, or pay the cost in lives of breaking out of their prison. They fought because three weeks after the first battle, the alternative seemed worse.

As the account denigrates the soldiers in Brutus' army, blaming them for the defeat, so it emphasizes their inconsistency in failing to fight on the following day. No blame can fall on Brutus: it is the soldiers who were at fault, soldiers who had fought so long and so hard, who had lost so many comrades, and who now refused almost certain death. In the end, the soldiers were not prepared to be martyrs for a republican cause not their own, unwilling to accompany their general to his posthumous glory and act as suicidal support players in the tragedy of Brutus. They negotiated a transfer into the armies of the triumvirs. In keeping with the rich traditions of elite historiography, the noble general is abandoned by the morally suspect soldiers. We have a powerful instance of losers' history.

For Appian, this was a battle to end all (civil) wars.[9] Although there were pockets of resistance, most notably Sextus Pompeius in Sicily, it is difficult to demur from his judgment that the war was indeed over. Caesar was avenged. Antony and Octavian (with Lepidus as the support act) were masters of the Roman world. Furthermore, it is also difficult to avoid his view that Philippi marked the end of an epoch. Philippi confirmed a shift in power in Roman society that went beyond the obvious change at the top. It was a victory that confirmed the hegemony of a new regime in which power was initially exercised by and for the soldiers and was later employed to the benefit of a wider imperial network.

Defeat plunged the conservative senators into a helpless nostalgia in which the suicides of Brutus and Cassius were replayed time and again. After Philippi, Rome was no longer a place suitable for real republican heroes. Such heroism could only survive in the literary imaginations and romanticized histories of an elite that portrayed their predecessors nobly dying in fruitless opposition to a brutal new world in which the realities of political power were forever against them.

10.

THE SOLDIERS' PEACE

IN THE AFTERMATH OF their victory, the triumvirs divided the world once more between them. Lepidus was confined to Africa, while Spain went to Octavian and Gaul to Antony. Antony turned to the East to receive the allegiance and excuses of the cities and kings who had given their loyalty to Brutus and Cassius, and to subdue any opposition that remained. His most notable meeting was with Cleopatra in Cilicia. The two had met several times before, when she was sixteen and he was in Alexandria with the army of Gabinius, and when she was in Rome as Caesar's consort. Plutarch in his *Life of Antony* describes their meeting in grand colors, her bark progressing up the river Cydnus (now the Berdan):

> She came sailing up the river Cydnus, on a golden-prowed barge with sails of purple outspread and rowers pulling on silver oars to the sound of a reed pipe blended with wind pipes and lyres. She herself reclined beneath a gold-embroidered canopy, adorned like a painting of Aphrodite, flanked by slave-boys, each made to resemble Eros, who cooled her with their fans. Likewise her most beautiful female slaves, dressed as Nereids and Graces, were stationed at the rudders and the ropes. The wonderful smell of numerous burning spices filled the banks of the river. Some people formed an escort for her on either side all the way from the river, while others came down from the city to see the spectacle. The crowd filling the city square trickled away, until at last Antony himself was left alone, seated on a dais. The notion spread through the city that Aphrodite had come in revelry to Dionysus, for the good of Asia. . .

According to my sources, in itself her beauty was not absolutely without parallel, not the kind to astonish those who saw her; but her presence exerted an inevitable fascination, and her physical attractions, combined with the persuasive charm of her conversation and the aura she somehow projected around herself in company, did have a certain ability to stimulate others. The sound of her voice was also charming and she had a facility with languages that enabled her to turn her tongue, like a many-stringed instrument, to any language she wanted, with the result that it was extremely rare for her to need a translator in her meetings with foreigners; in most cases she could answer their questions herself, whether they were Ethiopians, Trogodytae, Hebrews, Arabs, Syrians, Medes, or Parthians.[1]

Antony was not disposed to resist the charms of the Egyptian queen, and after the natural passage of time, Cleopatra gave birth to twins, Alexander Helios and Cleopatra Selene, brother and sister to Caesarion, her son by Julius Caesar. Thus begins another romantic trope of this period, the story of the hard-bitten, fast-living general seduced by the mysteries of the oriental queen.

Octavian had a rather less entertaining time than his triumviral colleague. Ill before and during the battles at Philippi, illness further delayed his journey home. He only arrived back in Italy in 41 B.C., when Publius Servilius and Lucius Antonius, brother of Antony, were consuls. His main task was to pay the bills that the triumvirs had built up in the last two years of warfare—he needed to make good the promises to the soldiers.

A traditional demand of the soldiers was land. Rome had long had a system of colonization in which settlers were established in communities, often on newly conquered land. These communities had been the "bulwarks of empire" (*propugnacula imperii*) which defended and secured the centre of Italy from rebels and external enemies.[2] But whereas in earlier centuries colonies could be established on land confiscated as a result of conquest, once Italy was a Roman dominion such lands were no longer available. Colonies in Italy would have to be established on land newly confiscated. The towns to suffer the imposition of colonies had been listed as early as the negotiations to form the triumvirate; 18 towns were identified.[3]

The triumvirs were in no position to offer recompense to those whose property they now seized. The displacement was such that petitioners and refugees flocked to Rome. The towns affected appealed for the burdens to be shared more widely, but Octavian had no room for maneuver. Furthermore, the land grants did not prevent the soldiers, organized and armed and with a monopoly on political power, from encroaching on neighboring lands and further extending their estates.[4]

It was at this point, and perhaps unexpectedly, that serious opposition emerged. That opposition centered on Lucius Antonius, Antony's brother, and Fulvia, Antony's wife. The key to understanding these events lies in uncovering the motivations of these two.

The tradition that has come down to us is favorable to Octavian and hostile towards Lucius Antonius and, especially, Fulvia. Throughout his account, Dio denigrates Lucius Antonius and portrays Fulvia as the power behind the very weak consul.[5] Appian has a rather different picture in which Antony and Fulvia were actually enemies, differing over policy towards colonization, until a certain Manius (who appears regularly in the tale as a woefully incompetent advisor to Antonius and Fulvia) suggested that if there was to be a conflict with Octavian, Mark Antony would come rushing back from the East to his betrayed wife. In a gross trivialization of events, the story leads us to believe that Fulvia went to war from sexual jealousy.[6]

In a further sexual twist, as the relationship between Octavian and Lucius Antonius and Fulvia worsened, Octavian divorced Clodia, Fulvia's daughter, whom he had married after the agreement at Mutina. Octavian took an oath that she was still a virgin. The point of the oath is far from clear; later writers were bemused by it as well.[7]

LUCIUS ANTONIUS, THE SOLDIERS, AND
THE POLITICS OF REVOLUTIONARY ROME

If Fulvia's political actions are demeaned in the tradition, we have a rather more balanced account of Lucius Antonius and his motivations. Although Lucius had loyally supported his brother and his brother's children, even supposedly adding Pietas (loyalty) to his name, it is claimed that he held republican views and disapproved of the triumvirate.[8] Thus, we have a paradox: Lucius the republican claims to revolt against the triumvirate in honor and support of his brother, the triumvir.

One of the few consistent elements in the story is an association between Lucius and those dispossessed in the colonization program.[9] As consul, Lucius received their petitions and complaints and was perhaps the only one of the leading men of Rome brave enough to give the Italian dispossessed a hearing.[10] This put him on a collision course with the soldiers, and it is possible that Fulvia also was not pleased at Lucius's stance.[11] But it seems that Lucius did not oppose the colonization program itself; rather, he disapproved of the uncontrolled, violent seizure of land by the soldiers.[12] Lucius Antonius's advisor Manius supposedly claimed that Octavian was exceeding his remit, taking land throughout Italy rather than from the 18 towns which had been identified, and settling 34 legions rather than the 28 agreed upon.[13] The settlement program was out of control, and the accusation was that Octavian was allowing the soldiers free rein. Lucius wished to bring the process back under effective magisterial supervision and also to ensure that Antony's part in the colonization program was recognized.

As a result of the gathering dispute with Octavian, Fulvia and Antony's children were paraded in front of the soldiers, presumably in camp in Rome, and the soldiers were asked to intercede so that Antony would not be deprived of the glory of helping them achieve their settlements. The glory belonged not just to Antony himself, but to his household. There was a dynastic aspect to the process. Furthermore, Octavian acceded to the requests, thereby acknowledging the power of the case being made, and appointed Antony's supporters to the commission in charge of assigning land.[14]

But still there was no peace between the two men. When Octavian left to supervise the foundation of colonies, Lucius and Antony's children followed. They were to attend the religious ceremonials that marked the establishing of any new community. But as Lucius was progressing southwards, he was spooked by a detachment of Octavian's cavalry and took refuge in the small town of Teanum. It was there that the officers of the army attempted to affect a reconciliation between Lucius and Octavian.[15] Lucius went to Praeneste, claiming to fear Octavian. Another reconciliation was attempted, but both sides started to gather themselves for war.

Lucius's opposition to Octavian did not solely result from his loyalty to his brother. If the first issue that drove a wedge between Octavian and Lucius Antonius was the involvement of Mark Antony in the foundation of the colonies, the secondary issue appears to have been the colonies themselves. Appian gives Lucius dramatic speeches in which he asserts that he had never opposed the settlement scheme and had been slandered by Octavian to the troops. Indeed, he stresses that his demand was rather to be involved in the colonization program.[16] He claims to have been motivated not by a desire to oppose the land settlement, but to restore republican government.[17]

Lucius cannot have opposed the predominance of Antony and Octavian, but it seems that he understood that predominance as being located within the traditional political culture of Rome. That political culture required order. It required that the consul take charge of matters within Italy and that the law be upheld. In particular, it required that the soldiers be kept in some form of control.

Octavian's position was different. Octavian had no intention of subjecting himself to the rough and tumble of republican politics and the possibility of prosecution in the courts. Octavian's future depended on the soldiers continuing to hold power, and it was in his interest for the state of emergency inaugurated by the triumvirate to be continued. Furthermore, bringing the soldiers to order would have been extremely difficult. At some point in the year, Octavian attempted a reconciliation with the senatorial elite, exempting their property from further requisitions. The soldiers mutinied, killed their centurions, and turned on Octavian, who had little choice but to acquiesce in their demands. They secured exemptions from the confiscations of property for their own relatives and for the fathers and sons of those who had been killed in the battles of the civil war, and may well have reversed Octavian's peace offering to the senators.

We have other reported instances of the rebelliousness of the soldiers. A soldier was unable to find a seat in the theatre and decided to take a seat among the equestrians. Octavian was presiding, and had the soldier removed (reinforcing the old order of society). A story circulated that the soldier had been imprisoned or killed. The soldiers rioted and could only be calmed when the ejected soldier was produced. In another incident, soldiers gathered on the Campus Martius to receive notification of the apportioning of land. Octavian was late, and the troops became rowdy. A centurion, Nonius, intervened, but failed to restore discipline. The soldiers started to throw missiles, and Nonius ran. He threw himself into the Tiber but the soldiers were not to be put off. They fished him out and killed him. When Octavian eventually appeared, he was faced with Nonius's corpse.[18]

The program needed to settle at least 28 legions, somewhere in the neighborhood of 140,000 men. The procedures involved the soldiers gathering in Rome before being allocated to a colony. The feeding of a city of a million was a complex logistical problem anyhow, but the population was now swelled by the soldiers. Refugees from the land settlement program further increased the population. With the seas still under the control of Sextus Pompeius, supplies could not be brought in from Sicily or North Africa, and agriculture in Italy would have been disrupted by the wars and probably far more by the land settlement program itself: who would plant crops and cultivate land which was about to be confiscated for the soldiers? Unsurprisingly, there was famine in Rome.[19] In competition for food, the plebs of Rome clashed with the soldiers. The soldiers took control of the streets, but the rioters held the rooftops and pelted the troops with broken tiles.[20] A fire broke out. Fires were particularly dangerous in the cramped conditions of an ancient city without adequate water supplies. This was one of the more serious fires in Roman history, and a rent remission was put in place to help those who had suffered.

There is a strong sense that the city was no longer governable and, in an elite nightmare, the soldiers, irrational, changeable, impolitic, and heavily armed, were in charge.[21] But the soldiers' demonstrations against Octavian reflect a consistent political position. If Octavian was to be reconciled with the wealthy, then the political power of the soldiery was under threat. It was that power that guaranteed both the distribution of land and rewards and, crucially, the soldiers' security of tenure. If Octavian exempted the elite, the impositions would fall more heavily on the smaller farmers, the very group from which the soldiers were recruited. It would have been of limited benefit to the soldiers if their rewards were at the expense of their own families. The soldiers stood together to defend their mutual interests, recognizing that their coherence as a group was essential to maintaining their power.

If Lucius Antonius sought a restoration of the old order and reconciliation with the traditional elite (or what remained of it), Octavian maintained his revolutionary posture. Suetonius describes his behavior after Philippi:[22]

> He was not moderate after his victory, but once he had sent Brutus's head to Rome, to be cast at the feet of Caesar's statue, he exercised his anger at the most distinguished of his captives, not even resisting insulting them. So, to one who begged humbly for burial, it is said that he replied that this was now an issue for the birds. When two others, father and son, begged for their lives, he is said to have bidden them cast lots or play *mora* to decide who would be spared, and to have looked on as both died, the father killed because he offered to die, and the son who thereupon killed himself. Because of this the rest, including Marcus Favonius, the imitator of Cato, when they were led out in chains saluted Antonius respectfully as *imperator*, but abused Augustus in the strongest terms.[23]

Such brutality was a continuation of the politics of the proscriptions without forgiveness or mercy. Displaying honor to one's defeated enemies recognized a social relationship and a common set of values. The hailing of Antony as *imperator* acknowledged his success as a Roman general; it was a shared ritual of victory and defeat.[24] Moderation was a traditional characteristic of the good ruler which recognized the necessity of accommodation to make the political system work. Octavian's behavior demonstrated that the war had not been ended by the defeat of the assassins. There was to be no reconciliation and no closing over the wounds. The atrocities were a refusal of reconciliation.

When Octavian returned to Rome in 41, a crucial question was how politics could resume. Throughout the civil strife of the last 90 years, periods of violence and even civil war had been followed by a resumption of politics. This meant that the wealthy, landed citizens would recommence their management of the state. But in response to the suggestion in 41 that he might allow the senators security of property, Octavian is recorded as saying "from where then are we to give the veterans their prizes"? Octavian had no interest in denying the soldiers and probably no ability to oppose them.

PERUSIA

The lack of clarity in the political situation is reflected in Lucius Antonius's ability to raise troops. The issue for the troops may have been different from that facing Lucius. One presumes that those who sided with Lucius fought from loyalty to Antony, because they thought they might get a better deal from Antony as a result and because they presumed that they would win. Nevertheless, the soldiers had no enthusiasm for the conflict.

As Italy moved towards war, eight armies converged on northern and central Italy. Three of these were in the Alpine region under Asinius Pollio, Ventidius, and Calenus, all loyal to Antony. Lucius Antonius, who had probably the largest force in the field, marched on Rome. Octavian, who had been in Rome, retreated from the city and headed northeast with an army of probably four legions.[25] There were two other armies loyal to Octavian. One was formed by two legions under the command of Salvidienus Rufus (supposedly loyal to Octavian), which was in the north of Italy, having been on its way to Spain when war broke out. There is mention of a seventh force in central Italy which was harassing Octavian. Further south, Marcus Agrippa, Octavian's close friend, was gathering fresh troops.

Although Lucius may have had the greater number of troops in total, Octavian and Salvidienus Rufus lay between him and the Antonians in the north. Lucius marched north from Rome, perhaps hoping to find a route around Octavian and his allies. Salvidienus and Octavian took control of the via Aemilia, the main road north through Mutina and Bononia. Agrippa marched into Etruria and seized Sutrium (Sutri), 50 km north of Rome, and positioned himself to block any march up the northwest of the peninsula. Lucius abandoned his march north and turned to the Etruscan city of Perusia (Perugia). There he encamped to await reinforcements.

Perusia may have looked like an ideal city in which to wait out developments. Its hilltop location made it impregnable. With winter coming, Lucius may have felt that any besieging troops would suffer more than his armies, warmly secure in the city. But Octavian and his generals set about walling Lucius into Perusia. The circumvallation stretched for seven miles. Eventually, there were 1,500 towers along the siege works. The ditches, lined with stakes, were 30 feet deep. A second line was built to protect the siege works from any external attacker. Artillery fired into the city, probably not with sufficient force to do much damage, but the little lead pellets that have been found were inscribed with messages for the besieged, notably obscenities directed at Fulvia (though she was elsewhere). Octavian's plan was clear. He intended to starve Lucius out.

Lucius must have expected his allies to relieve Perusia, but they never appeared. Ventidius and Pollio were to the north. Calenus may also have come to join them. Munatius Plancus also raised a ninth army and approached from the south, reaching Spoletium. But none of these forces moved decisively against Octavian, and the longer they waited, the tighter and the less penetrable the siege works became. Lucius attempted a breakout on New Year's Eve, but was driven back from the ramparts.[26] Later, Ventidius and Pollio got to within 20 miles of Perusia and lit fires to let Lucius know that they were coming, but they were unable or unwilling to force their way through the lines.[27] Lucius tried a night attack, but was once more beaten back. A third attack followed, this time by day, but once more Octavian's men drove them back.[28] Food became short: they had already stopped feeding slaves. There was no hope of relief. Desertions became significant, and Octavian received the deserters into his lines, showing the defenders that they had little to fear. Lucius had little choice. He surrendered.

Octavian received the surrender in his camp. The army came first. The soldiers lined up in their legions before Octavian and were ordered to lay down their arms. Whatever Octavian's intentions, his own troops broke ranks and embraced their former colleagues. The triumviral legions were united.[29]

It was a different matter with the leaders. Lucius was followed by the senators and the equestrians who had joined him, and then the council of Perusia. The senators and equestrians were received and placed under arrest, discreetly. The council was received in the camp, detained, and put to death. Perusia itself was looted by the troops and burned. The troops clamored for revenge, and Octavian had a number of his senatorial and equestrian captives killed.[30] Three hundred equestrians and many senators are said to have been executed on an altar to Julius Caesar.[31] Suetonius has the captured begging to be pardoned, and Octavian replying to each request with the formulaic two words *"moriendum esse"* ("you must die"). The property of the captured was confiscated and distributed to the soldiers.[32] Octavian was still exacting revenge for the death of Caesar and blaming the rich and powerful. Several hundred more of the Roman aristocracy lost their lives. Lucius himself was spared, though we know nothing of his later life.

The war was still not settled. The Antonian armies that had failed to relieve Perusia were still in the field. And there was still Antony. The armies in northern Italy left. No one was willing to fight until Antony arrived, but Antony was on his way.

ENEMIES UNITED: THE PEACE OF BRUNDISIUM

Antony was in Alexandria when the war broke out. He needed to gather his troops and transport them across the eastern Mediterranean to Italy. This was not easy in winter. He hopped round the coast: to Tyre, Cyprus, Rhodes, Asia Minor (where he learned of the defeat at Perusia), and then Athens, where he was reunited with Fulvia. It is not recorded whether they found time to discuss how Antony had been spending his leisure hours in Alexandria.[33] Fulvia and Antony's mother, Julia, had been escorted to Greece by representatives of Sextus Pompeius. Pompeius made overtures to Antony and held out the prospect of an alliance. Another admiral, Domitius, who had controlled the Ionian coast in the aftermath of Philippi, defected to Antony.[34] Pompeius had been under pressure in 41 and 40 from Octavian and Agrippa, though they had made little progress. Yet, in the longer term, Pompeius's future could only be secured by reconciliation with the triumvirs. Antony's response to the embassy from Pompeius was to offer alliance in case of war and reconciliation in case of peace.[35] If we can trust this report, it would suggest that Antony was as yet not convinced that war was inevitable, in spite of all that had happened in Italy.

Antony's developing relationship with Pompeius provided an avenue by which former supporters of the assassins could negotiate their way back into the Roman mainstream. Lucius Domitius Ahenobarbus, who was one of the more prominent of the Pompeian military commanders, joined Antony on Cephalonia and accompanied his landing in Italy, near Brundisium. Brundisium was garrisoned by Octavian's troops, and it is possible that Ahenobarbus's presence in Antony's army encouraged resistance (Ahenobarbus had led raids in the region). Antony besieged the town. Octavian and Agrippa marched south, and although Agrippa levied troops on the march, he also suffered desertions as the soldiers made clear their reluctance to fight.[36] Octavian outnumbered Antony but could not into break into his defenses, and sea power gave Antony the ability to strike behind Octavian's lines. There was stalemate.

In this standoff, a mutual friend, Lucius Cocceius, began negotiations. Antony's mother, Julia, who was a relative of Octavian, also played a part. Officers and soldiers sent messages to Antony.[37] Since these approaches were not rebuffed, the soldiers formed a court and summoned both men. The soldiers had no interest in fighting. Ultimately, although there were hurt feelings, neither Antony nor Octavian were fully committed to conflict; they could work together. The soldiers' requirements were for a united regime that would guarantee them the promised rewards. If the soldiers would not fight, there had to be peace.

The settlement of Brundisium redivided the Roman world. Lepidus, increasingly irrelevant, kept Africa. The rest of the West—Gaul, Spain,

Sardinia, Dalmatia—all went to Octavian. The East went to Antony.[38] The alliance was cemented by another marriage. Fulvia had been taken ill and died in Greece, leaving Antony free (forgetting for a moment, as Antony appears to have done, Cleopatra) for Octavian's sister, Octavia, who was herself a recent widow. Octavian and Antony marched to Rome to celebrate the dynastic marriage. The settlement was not bloodless. Lucius Antonius's advisor, Manius, was made responsible for the war. More surprisingly, Salvidienus Rufus was summoned back from Gaul and killed. He was accused of perfidious dealings.

The war ended in a reformation of the alliance. This was the result demanded by the soldiers. Some form of reconciliation did follow from the peace: there was an amnesty for some of the proscribed. Some of those who had taken refuge with Pompeius took advantage of the rapprochement with Antony to find their way back to Rome. But the triumvirate was to continue, and Rome was to be ruled by Antony (largely in his absence) and Octavian. The arrangements suited the new brothers-in-law, as it suited the soldiers whose land arrangements were now guaranteed by a period of stable autocratic government.

The Perusine war was an attempt to close down the triumvirate and return to the traditions of Roman political culture; it was a war of a consul against a triumvir and a war for normality against emergency. Antony, the older man and the dominant political figure, had less to lose from such a restoration than the young, still inexperienced, and much-feared Octavian. But for those who had benefited from the revolution, most notably the soldiers, the triumvirs themselves, and their close allies, a return to the old ways had few attractions.

EPILOGUE: SONGS OF LOVE AND LAND

If we can read the traumas of the proscriptions in the histories and collections of famous deeds and sayings, the stress of the Perusine war and the associated land settlement can be seen in the poetry. Virgil was to write the epic of the Augustan age, the *Aeneid*, but his earlier works were short, dense poems in the pastoral tradition. The *Eclogues* invent an unreal Arcadian world in which the herders of goats compete in songs and love in a mythical countryside. But this is an idealized world that is under threat, disturbed by war, invaded by the impious soldier. In the first Eclogue, Tityrus and Meliboeus debate their contrasting fates. Meliboeus has had to leave his land.

> Some impious soldier will have my well-farmed lands.
> A barbarian has my cornfield. Civil strife
> has brought us misery.[39]

Tityrus is saved, however, by the real other world that is Rome. There, he meets Octavian, whom he describes as a god, and by whom his lands are returned.[40]

Eclogue 4 changes the format and the tone. Instead of singing goatherds, we have a poem in the first person which essays "a little grander subject." The poem is about many things, but the basic plot is that in 40 B.C. a new golden age is to dawn. This age is inaugurated by a child. The child will see a turning back of history in which a second Achilles will sail for Troy, a second Argo will set out in search of a second golden fleece. The earth will not need labor to produce food. Ships will no longer need to dare the seas. The ox will lie down with the lion. Finally, the sheep will turn purple and our poet will sing a great poem. The poem is messianic in its hope for this child who will bring about the new golden age, and the messianic element has encouraged wild interpretations. But the point is the fantasy: the hope of the future is not real, but is manifested in a miracle in which time will have its end and in which the history of the world will be repeated. Once that has been achieved and purple sheep are grazing on the hillside, then Virgil will write his great poem. Until that moment, he remains in retreat from the world in his rural, invented Arcadia, resisting a reality too horrible for poetry.

Propertius was a very different poet. His first collection, known as the *Monobiblos*, opens with a declaration of intent.

> Cynthia's eyes first captured me (wretch that I am), previously unhurt by
> desire. Then Love stamped down my constant stare of arrogance and

pressed down upon my head with his feet, until that disgraceful one taught me to hate chaste girls and to live without a plan.[41]

Twenty poems of love follow. He lives for this girl. He is a slave to love. He burns with desire. No masculine aloofness for Propertius. No random sexual encounters. This is love, powerful and controlling. Nothing else is of importance. The real world, the world of politics, is as meaningless and fleeting to the lover Propertius as it was to the goatherds of Arcadia. But that wit and brilliance and the love depart as the book closes. The last two poems are clearly meant to be read together.

> You who rush to escape my fate, a soldier wounded in the Etruscan ditches, why do you flash your eyes at my groan? I was at your side in service. So save yourself so that your parents can rejoice and a sister know what has happened just from your tears, that Gallus broke through the center of Caesar's swords, but could not avoid the clutches of an unknown assailant and whatever bones she finds dispersed up here on the Etruscan mountain, let her know these are mine.
>
> Tullus, you often ask on account of our friendship, of what stock and from where my home gods come. Do you know the Perusine tomb of our land, the death-rites of Italy in a hard time, when Roman citizens were driven by their dissension—so mourn for me, Tuscan dust, since you have allowed my kinsmen's bodies to be thrown out and you have no earth covering their wretched bones—Umbria, rich and fertile, where she most closely touches the plain, gave birth to me.[42]

The book of love ends with death: the lament of his dead friend Gallus, his bones scattered on the Tuscan hills. Unburied, his ghost would roam. Unsettled, the dead would have no peace. Without performing the rituals, his lover would have no end to her loss. Propertius's recollection of the destruction of his town and his kin and of all Italy becomes a reluctant admission of his Perusine origins; the stories of love mask a deeper regret. In the rich dust of Tuscany, there lies a richer dust. Blood and bones, sorrow and loss mark the Italian earth.

The war of Perusia was over, but it was not forgotten.

11.

THE TRIUMVIRAL WARS

WITH THE SETTLEMENT AT Brundisium and the celebration of the marriage between Antony and Octavia, the triumvirs were free to complete the business of the soldiers' settlement and use their power to extend their reputations and their dominance. For Antony, the East beckoned. He took his new wife Octavia to Athens for the winter and began to prepare for a major expedition against the Parthians. Antony had set himself the tasks of revenging the defeat of Crassus, killed in 53, and of fulfilling the promised campaign of Julius Caesar. For Octavian, there were pressing local concerns. The settlement of the troops needed to be completed, but the settlement had also left an anomaly: Sextus Pompeius, the son of Pompey the Great. Although peace had been made, it was an uneasy peace, and with Sextus Pompeius still armed and still in Sicily, it could hardly have been expected to last.

KILLING THE PIRATE KING

Sextus Pompeius had been engaged in military operations almost since the defeat of his father by Caesar. His main base was in Sicily, from where he was able to establish naval dominance and control the important sea lanes across the western Mediterranean. The naval support he had provided Antony and the hospitality he had shown to Antony's family created a debt, and Antony brokered a peace between the triumvirs and Pompeius, somewhat at the expense of Lepidus.[1] That peace allowed the return of the exiled aristocracy, cowed by their defeat and, though not forgiven, at least restored.

Peace was never likely to last. Relations between Octavian and Pompeius were strained, and nothing held them together. Octavian's control over Italy and its resources meant that in the longer term, in any competition between the two Octavian would be successful, and it is likely that Pompeius and his supporters could make that calculation. Similarly, Octavian must have been aware of the potential benefits of controlling Sicily's grain fields and also wary of the dangers of Pompeius's fleet. A season of stability would allow Octavian to invest in his naval power; conversely, delay weakened Pompeius. Fleets were expensive to build, man, and maintain. In the medium term, Pompeius's resources would be stretched and his ability to maintain his supporters diminished.

The *casus belli* was an accusation of piracy, but it brought war because one of Pompeius's more important admirals, Menodoros, defected to Octavian. Octavian now had a fleet with which to contend with Pompeius. War broke out in 38, and the first major battle was fought off Cumae in south Italy. Octavian's fleet was defeated. Although the defeat may not in itself have been particularly damaging, the relatively inexperienced commander got caught in a storm and many of the ships were wrecked. Octavian was thus unable to compete with Pompeius at sea, and Pompeius's maneuverability allowed him to raid along the Italian coast, making the following year uncomfortable for the triumvir.[2]

By 36, Octavian was re-equipped and rearmed. Antony had visited Italy and brought with him 120 ships for the campaign in return for a promise of 20,000 legionaries that he would employ against the Parthians in the East. Lepidus was given instructions to co-ordinate an attack from North Africa in a campaign starting on July 1. Once more Octavian's forces were caught by the weather; Lepidus also suffered naval reverses.[3] But the situation was moving inexorably against Pompeius. Lepidus managed to land twelve legions and laid siege to the city of Lilybaeum (modern Marsala), on the Western edge of Sicily. Pompeius now had to face a substantial army on Sicilian soil, and Octavian was not finished.

Agrippa, Octavian's close friend who had been at his side from the start of his great political adventure and who had led Octavian's campaign with distinction during the Perusine war, had established a base on the Aeolian Islands, west of mainland Italy. He now sailed almost due south against Pompeius, and the two met at Mylae, on the northeast coast of Sicily. For the first time, Octavian's forces got the better of a naval battle, and although the victory was far from decisive, Agrippa landed his troops and thus brought a second army into play. Octavian took advantage of Pompeius being engaged to the north of the island to cross from the Italian coast to Sicily and began to disembark his troops near Tauromenium (modern Taormina), on the east coast.

Octavian's crossing, however, ran into difficulties. Pompeius's naval and land forces retreated from Mylae, rounded the coast at Messana and headed south, and caught Octavian's army disembarking. They knew that Octavian was attempting a crossing, and once it had become clear that they could not stop Agrippa, they broke off the engagement in an attempt to surprise Octavian. With his troops in disarray and outnumbered on land and sea, Octavian's situation was difficult. His army was probably only saved by nightfall and the fatigue of Pompeius's troops. Octavian took advantage of the night to fortify his camp, and by morning the two sides were at a standoff.[4]

Octavian's position was, however, untenable. He loaded up his marines, embarked on a light boat, and led a breakout. Pompeius defeated the fleet, but Octavian himself escaped and fetched up on the Italian coast. If Pompeius had found him, the war would have had an unexpected outcome, but Octavian was rescued by locals who had been watching the battle from the hills and taken to rejoin his forces and organize reinforcements.

Meanwhile, Octavian's legions near Tauromenium were under pressure. The camp had not been selected with care, and it had to house about 19,000 men. Supplies were limited. More seriously, they lacked water. The general left in charge, Cornificius, offered battle, but the Pompeians were aware of the strength of their position and waited, and he was thus forced to march out in search of water and reinforcement.[5] Harried by the Pompeians, Cornificius led his troops inland, crossing the lava plains of

Etna, a harsh, dry, unshaded landscape into which the locals only ventured at night. At the best of times, this was a difficult crossing for an army. The Pompeians tried to hold the route against them, blocking passes while continuously menacing the march. The Pompeian cavalry were adept at hit-and-run attacks, and missiles wounded many of the soldiers, further slowing the march. Each fortification delayed them further, and increased their thirst and the number of wounded. Progress was slow. Without shelter and without water in the middle of summer, trudging across the Sicilian lava, the situation of the army was desperate.

Eventually, the soldiers sighted a spring, but the Pompeians held it in numbers. If they could not break through the lines, and quickly, thirst and fatigue would tell and the army would face destruction. As they approached the spring, another army was sighted approaching from the opposite direction, but they were at a great distance and could not be identified. If these were Pompeian reinforcements, Cornificius and his men were lost. The Pompeians, though, were closer and probably informed by scouts. The new army was led by Agrippa and was in search of Cornificius. The Pompeians marched off, and the army was saved.[6]

Having failed to prevent Octavian's legions joining with those of Agrippa, Pompeius was now in serious difficulties. He was faced by superior land forces in Sicily, and his fleet, his best weapon, no longer enjoyed complete dominance. He could hold some of the towns, but he could not prevent the free movement of the triumviral armies. Lepidus was effectively taking control over the west of the island, while Agrippa and Octavian were a formidable presence in the east. Pompeius's best chance was to offer battle at sea. If he could win back control of the sea, he might be able to cut off the triumviral armies from Italy and put pressure on the triumviral supply lines. On September 3, 36, Pompeius led out his fleet. It is a measure of Octavian's and Agrippa's confidence that they accepted the challenge, and the two fleets sailed into combat at Naulochus (probably modern Spadafora), west of Mylae.

Roman naval battles had a standard shape. Unlike the old trireme battles in which the object was to ram your opponents with your sleek, fast ships in the hope that the impact would break up your opposing ship, Roman naval battles were slow, steady affairs, centering on grappling and boarding.[7] As a result, ships tended to be large and high, fortified with towers from which the soldiers would fire missiles and with heavy defensive plates to repel missiles. The ships were thus lumbering craft, packed with marines and equipment. These stately castles of the sea formed a wooden and metal wall, and it was crucial that the ships maintain a line so that opposing craft could not ram them from the side or double up on a single opponent. The skill of the sailors was in holding the line, keeping close enough that opponents could not sail among them and break the line, but not getting so close that the oars would become fouled. The battle consisted of grappling and firing missiles, the rowers driving the ram forward, backing to extract themselves from the clutches of their enemies or to prepare another charge, maneuvering to hold their line or to break that of the enemy. The marines would be simultaneously targeting their missiles and avoiding whatever their opponents threw at them, watching for grappling irons, steadying themselves for the crash of the colliding craft, picking on seemingly weaker ships and avoiding the stronger, waiting and watching for the opportunities to board and throw themselves among their enemies. Battles were slow, attritional, and exhausting.

At Naulochus, Agrippa deployed a new device. His engineers had devised a grab. As the boats grappled, the grab dropped down on the Pompeians' decks in the hope of plucking off one of the marines or perhaps breaking up the deck fortifications or the missile engines. The weapon was probably more effective as a terror tactic than in inflicting physical damage on the opposing craft. Because it had not been seen before, the marines were not ready, and did not have poles to hold it off. It may just have given the triumviral fleet an edge, and an edge was enough.

Pompeius and his army were watching from their camp. Slowly, the battle turned against them. As the day ended, the triumviral troops began to sing a victory hymn. They were answered from the shore by Octavian's legions. The Pompeians were in despair. Pompeius himself left the scene and returned to Messana, which was his base of operation.

There, it is said, he remained silent and issued no orders. His legions had no hope. They surrendered.[8]

Pompeius himself still had cards to play, but his was a losing hand. He fled to the East, mustering troops as he went, and appealed to Antony on the grounds of his prior services to Antony and his family. At the same time, he sent embassies to the Parthians to establish a retreat of last resort. Antony received his embassy and promised to listen compassionately, provided Pompeius came in peace. But Pompeius had nothing to offer, and Antony had no reason to treat with him. As Pompeius settled in Asia Minor, Antony's generals began to assemble. Fleets neared Pompeius. Armies collected. The embassy to the Parthians was intercepted. Pompeius attempted to fight, and with some success, but he was trapped. Eventually he burnt the remainder of his fleet and set off overland for Parthia. His cause was lost, and his officers knew it. They defected, and eventually Pompeius was captured. After a short delay, he was executed.[9]

Events in Sicily took a stranger turn. The last of the Pompeian forces in the field defected not to Octavian but to Lepidus. Lepidus took the opportunity to declare himself master of Sicily and demand a better settlement in the triumviral arrangements. A standoff followed, but as in 40, it was not in the interests of the soldiers to fight. The Pompeian legions were demoralized by defeat and feared another battle in a cause far from their own. Octavian approached the Lepidan camp and offered amnesty. A skirmish followed in which one of Octavian's companions was wounded and Octavian beat a hurried retreat. Some of the Lepidan forces had been listening, however, and their resolve was weakened. Octavian waited, and in dribs and drabs, the Lepidans came over. Lepidus, who had experience of this very situation when facing Antony, changed from his military dress and went to Octavian. As Lepidus stooped to abase himself and beg for his life, Octavian left his tribunal to welcome him to the camp. His life was granted in an uncharacteristic act of clemency that echoed Antony's similar earlier generosity. Octavian perhaps intended to demonstrate to the Caesarians that whatever happened, the network stuck together. Ultimately, it showed that he had no fear of Lepidus. Stripped of his military authority, Lepidus retained the position of

Pontifex Maximus, the most important of the priesthoods of Rome; his political insignificance was such that he was not worth killing.[10]

Still, the war was not quite over. Octavian was faced by a mutiny. The troops demanded rewards on the scale of those given after Philippi. Octavian was reluctant and tried to hold firm. The assembly became riotous, and one particular tribune, Ofellius, took the lead. Octavian was forced to retreat to his tent. The next day he returned to the assembly of the troops in more confident mood. He offered some concessions and promised to lead the legions in a new campaign against the Illyrians. But Ofellius was missing. Octavian's supporters had, presumably, snatched him during the night and killed him. As the soldiers became conscious that their spokesman was absent, Octavian mixed concessions with threats. Those discharged would never serve again; this avenue would be closed to them. Octavian was asserting himself. The soldiers could exclude themselves from their rewarding participation in the triumviral network or they could be subject to the discipline that came with serving that network. In victory, Octavian's hegemony over the network was restored. He may have needed the soldiers, but the soldiers also needed him.[11]

This was Octavian's victory and his hour. He was able to guarantee access to the grain fields of Sicily and Africa and thus secure the grain supply for Rome. Not only had he defeated a rival to yet further cement the dominance of the triumvirs, but he was now in a position to bask in the appreciation of the plebs and to offer them some measure of food security. The aristocracy may have taken a different view. Some at least were recently returned from Pompeius's group. Others were still probably loyal to the ideas of Brutus and Cassius, but the victory demonstrated once more their irrelevance.

Octavian was not shy about his victory. The popular assembly voted him the right to sit on the benches of the tribunes (probably permanently) and also gave him the rights of protection that went with the position of tribune (*sacrosanctitas*), which made it a crime to injure his person. There is no doubt that this was an entirely honorary title; would-be assassins were unlikely to be cowed by such a privilege. But both privileges associated Octavian with the position of tribune and established that association on a long-lasting basis.[12] Octavian was posing as the protector of the people of Rome, acknowledging his obligations to the people, and asserting their dependence on him.

As a lasting memorial of the victory and a reminder to his opponents of the fate of those who opposed him, Octavian constructed an extraordinary monument right in the center of the city. In archaic Rome, naval victories were memorialized by the use of the rostra ("beaks"), the rams, of the enemy ships. These heavy metal-plated rams were cut from the ships and attached to a new monument. Octavian had a column built in the center of the Forum, a monument (now lost) that could be seen from all sides and dominated the most important political space in the city. The column was topped by a golden statue of Octavian.

Precious metal statues were normally reserved for divinities. Octavian was experimenting with his public image. He was the protector of his people, a man of great power. He sat at the heart of a new order in Rome, basking in the support of the soldiers and the gratitude of the plebs. Now he could be compared with the gods.

The only challenge to his position lay across the seas, with Antony and Cleopatra in Alexandria. But as Octavian celebrated victory, the triumvirate appeared stronger and more powerful than before. It was, after all, Antony who had finished off Pompeius. Antony had provided Octavian with ships to fight the war. Antony, whatever his relations with Cleopatra, was still married to Octavia, Octavian's sister. Neither Antony nor Octavian would have missed much the presence of Lepidus. Octavian sent back the ships borrowed from Antony and replaced those that had been lost from his own resources.[13] Octavian also ensured that Antony received credit for the victories over Pompeius. Victory games were held in Rome in honor of Antony's killing of Pompeius. A statue of Antony in a chariot was established in the Forum of Rome near the speaker's platform, and statues were placed in the Temple of Concord. Coins were issued carrying the heads of both men (see fig. 4). Antony, his wife (Octavia), and his children were given the right to hold banquets in the temple.[14] Octavian acknowledged the crucial role of his colleague and that the two men stood united. Any senator who might doubt their unity could look on Antony's statue in the Forum and be reminded of their

FIGURE 4
DENARIUS OF OCTAVIAN AND ANTONY: Silver coin issued to show the unity of
Octavian and Antony in the 30s B.C.

mutual dependence and their formidable joint authority. Rather than preparing to fight each other, both men now had the chance to do what Romans did best: expand the empire.

ANTONY IN THE EAST

The Parthians had been an ongoing problem for the Romans since the battle of Carrhae in 53, a major Roman defeat. The expeditionary force defeated at Carrhae had been led by Marcus Crassus and was composed of seven legions and associated support troops. They were caught by the Parthians and outmaneuvered by their cavalry: the Parthians made use of heavy armored cavalry and lighter archer cavalry which the Roman heavy infantry had difficulty engaging. The loss of Crassus and his legions would normally have encouraged the Romans to throw more troops into the battle, but the worsening political situation in the West meant that attention was distracted. Caesar had been preparing to avenge the defeat of Carrhae in 44 before his assassination. Now that civil order had returned to Rome, Parthia was a natural place for Antony to pursue his military ambitions.

After Philippi, Antony had set himself to securing the East, all of which, with the exception of Egypt, had eventually sided with Brutus and Cassius. His political and sexual union with Cleopatra effectively decided a good deal of Roman policy. Cleopatra's dynastic rivals were removed, and Antony extracted cash from various Greek communities before establishing a political base for operations in the East in Alexandria.[15]

The Parthians, meanwhile, perhaps realizing that once Rome was politically unified they could expect a Roman invasion, took up arms. They were led by Pacorus, a son of the king, and Quintus Labienus, a Roman. Labienus had been Caesar's right-hand man in Gaul, but had joined the Pompeians during the civil war. He had subsequently been liaising with the Parthians on behalf of Brutus and Cassius. When news of their defeat and deaths reached him, he chose to remain with the Parthians. In an age before nationalism, switching sides in this way was unusual, but far from unthinkable.

Labienus persuaded the Parthians to take the offensive and make use of the fickle loyalties of the various Roman garrisons in the region, most of which had been established by Brutus or Cassius. He was able to make progress in Syria. Apamea fell; Antioch followed. Labienus crossed into ancient Cilicia (southeast Turkey). Pacorus marched into Judaea and took control of Jerusalem. In a short campaign, the Parthians had taken control of the Roman Levant.[16] Before Antony could respond, messages summoned him to Italy, and his troops moved away from the Parthians.

In 39 B.C., Antony returned to the Parthian problem. Leaving Italy, he sent his friend and ally from the Mutina campaign, Ventidius, ahead with a significant legionary army while he himself made slower progress through Greece. Characteristically, our sources attribute his slow approach to lethargy and immorality; equally characteristically, Antony was moving at a pace that would confound his enemies.

The first Labienus knew of Ventidius's approach was when the legions came into contact. Labienus was in Asia Minor with his Roman troops and without Parthian cavalry; they were no match for Ventidius's legions, and one suspects that Antony knew as much. Labienus had little choice but to retreat into Syria. But Ventidius abandoned his heavy troops and used his cavalry and light troops to trap Labienus. Both sides waited for reinforcements.

The Parthian cavalry and the Roman infantry arrived together. Ventidius was encamped on the higher ground. Labienus and the

Parthians offered battle, but Ventidius did not want to expose his forces to the Parthian cavalry.[17] The Parthians attempted to draw the Romans out, moving closer and closer to the fortifications. Eventually, they charged up the slope towards Ventidius' barricades. Ventidius's troops sallied out. The Parthian cavalry was surprised and turned. They rushed away from Ventidius's infantry, which was the proper maneuver when closely engaged, but in this instance they careered into the next wave of advancing cavalry. In the confusion, Ventidius's infantry caught them. The Parthians were routed. Ventidius cut off their retreat towards the Parthian forces in Syria, and the remains of Labienus's army went west. There was no salvation. Trapped, Labienus's legions broke up and attempted to escape by circumventing Ventidius in small groups. Many were caught. Labienus himself donned civilian clothing and disappeared into Cilicia, a ruse that worked for a while, but he was eventually located and killed.[18]

The Parthians were not organized for a defensive war. Without a standing army and with many of their cavalry killed by Ventidius, they were unable either to meet the Romans on the field or to garrison towns against them. Those kings of the East who had acquiesced in their capture of the Roman Levant were equally ready to make peace with the Romans, and once the Romans were in Syria, Pacorus had little option but to retreat.[19]

The most prominent victim of Antony's reconquest of Syria was Antigonus, who was king in Judaea. He had sided with the Parthians and then resisted the Roman invasion. The Romans besieged and captured Jerusalem. Antigonus was tied to a cross and flogged, and either then or soon after, he was killed. He was replaced by Herod, who was not of his dynasty and, indeed, was something of an outsider to the traditional priestly elites of Judaean society. Herod the Great, as he was to become known, was an ideal king for the Romans, a military hard man capable of considerable brutality in maintaining local order, but a figure who was always ultimately dependent on Rome for his position.[20]

In 38, the Parthians took the offensive. Ventidius once more lured the Parthian heavy cavalry close to his fortification, from which he pelted them with missiles. The cavalry became confused and Ventidius attacked. This time, they managed to kill Pacorus, and although the Parthian cavalry fought hard to secure his body, the Romans drove them off. Ventidius had secured a second major victory.[21]

The war now paused. Antony needed to reassert Roman political control in Syria, and he was also distracted by the war in Italy between Octavian and Sextus Pompeius. The Parthians were in no position to resume the offensive and also now suffered one of their periodic bouts of dynastic bloodletting. The old king Orodes died, probably in 37, and with Pacorus also dead, the kingdom passed to Phraates, another son of Orodes. Phraates, however, had many enemies, and he moved against them. He killed his half-brothers, born to Orodes from the daughter of Antiochus of Commagene. When Antiochus objected to the murder of his grandchildren, he was also killed. At least some of the Parthian nobles now defected, including one Monaeses.[22]

Antony now took the offensive. He split his army in two, leaving his baggage train and much of his force with Oppius Statianus, and headed to the city of Praaspa in modern northwest Iran, a major city of the Median kingdom. The tactic was a good one. The Parthians were divided, and Antony sought to benefit from the internal divisions and encourage the disintegration of the Parthian empire. But if the Romans were learning how to fight the Parthians and their allies, so the kings of the East were learning how to fight the Romans. The Median king Artavasdes was determined not to get pinned down by the Romans and trapped into a long siege in which there were would only be one result. He left Praaspa garrisoned, avoided Antony, and marched on Statianus. He caught him on the march and routed Statianus's army.

Without reinforcements and with his supply train lost, Antony refused to withdraw. Artavasdes harassed Antony's lines. Antony tried to supply his forces off the land around Praaspa, but the Medians looked for opportunities to hit the foragers, and gradually Antony's food supplies ran low. Antony had little choice but to make for safer territory. As he withdrew, the Medians took the offensive, attacking his troops. Antony led one group into Armenia, but another group was turned from the usual road and found itself lost. In one attack, finding themselves assailed by Median archers, the Romans formed the *testudo*, a wall made of overlapping shields that covered the legionaries from all sides. The Medians had never seen this before and, thinking that the Romans had fallen, dismounted and attacked. The legionaries reformed and defeated the Median army. Escape became possible.[23]

Antony wintered in Egypt and summoned support from Octavian and from Cleopatra. Octavian took the rather unusual decision of sending Octavia with the troops to join her husband. Antony did not choose to have both his wives in the East at the same time and asked Octavia to return to Rome while the troops sailed on. Although the hostile sources emphasize the defeat of Antony in 36, Artavasdes was not convinced that the war was going his way. Probably by the end of 35, the Medians were in the Roman camp.[24] In early 34, Antony invaded Armenia. He captured the Armenian king and drove off a Parthian counterattack.[25] Antony had won his war: he had driven the Parthians from Syria; killed Pacorus, heir to the Parthian throne; intimidated Media; and captured Armenia. The later tradition, hostile to Antony, regards the war as a failure and a further example of the incompetence of a general distracted by affairs of the heart. But Antony could point to a series of political and military successes that had securely placed vast territories under Roman influence and weakened the other powers of the region. Antony might not have gotten all he had wanted, but he declared victory and headed to Alexandria to celebrate.

The return to Alexandria was to mark the last stage of Antony's hegemony in the East. While Antony had been engaged in his various conquests, Octavian too had been busy. With Sextus Pompeius dead, Octavian at first looked to go to Africa to quieten what had been Lepidus's province. He arrived in Sicily, but soon changed his mind. There was trouble in Dalmatia, and this provided him with the opportunity of imperial expansion. He raised troops for the war and for some reason, perhaps because he had need of the troops himself, decided not to send to the East the full allocation of troops that Antony had requested.[26]

The campaign in Dalmatia began in 35. The Romans had been influential in the region for a long time and had naval domination in the

Northern Adriatic. But as they pushed inland, resistance stiffened. Octavian was wounded during a siege, but seems to have thought the war over by the end of the campaigning season.[27] He left Dalmatia for Gaul, supposedly planning an invasion of Britain.[28] The Dalmatians were not convinced by their defeat, and the war resumed. Octavian returned, was once more wounded, and once more the Romans declared victory. The region was to resist Roman imperial expansion for decades. Still, Octavian had a victory of sorts and was awarded a triumph by a grateful and cowed senate.[29]

By 33, Octavian and Antony were freed from immediate military problems. No doubt both could have found, had they wished, places to invade and reasons to expand the imperial reach of Rome, but for reasons which are unclear, relations between Octavian and Antony were worsening. After a decade of uneasy cooperation, they and their various friends were sniping at each other, finding reasons to quarrel. The issues at stake are not obvious and were probably not insuperable; Rome was not faced with the same conundrum as when Caesar was poised on the Rubicon, and certainly the issues cannot be reduced to the romance of Antony and Cleopatra, but Rome was once more moving inexorably towards a civil war that would reduce the diarchy of Antony and Octavian to the monarchy of Augustus.

12.

ANTONY AND CLEOPATRA: LOVE

AND ITS ENEMIES

THE ROMAN REVOLUTION CHANGED the nature of politics in Rome. After the averting of war at Brundisium, the triumvirate was resilient. However stable the institutions of Rome, however much the forms of government were maintained from their Republican precedents, power rested in the hands of the triumvirs, and Antony and Octavian were not likely to set aside that power. Yet the peace of Brundisium, which may be seen as a last act in the story of the overthrow of the Republic, is traditionally not that story's end, but the start of another, much more famous tale, that of Antony and Cleopatra. It is that tale, with all its glamour, that continues to distract audiences, just as Antony was supposedly distracted by his Egyptian lover.

Armed with the considerable benefit of hindsight, it is easy to think of the war of Actium, the final reckoning between Antony and Octavian, as inevitable. They were hardly the best of friends and had fought each other in the past. Actium can be seen as the resolution of business postponed from 40 B.C., or even from 44, and a further stage in a slide to monarchy. But it would hardly have been obvious in 40 that the triumvirate would fail, or that the eventual resolution of the social and economic pressures would be a monarchy in the Augustan form. Not only had the triumviral regime been maintained through the Perusine War, but it also survived the war between Sextus Pompeius and Octavian, the tribulations of Antony on the Eastern frontier, the campaigns of Octavian, and the

FIGURE 5
Cleopatra: A head of Cleopatra depicting her in the
tradition of Greek queens.

removal of Lepidus. The alliance was maintained through three civil wars and lasted from 43 to 32, a span which many modern political regimes might envy. Over that period, the relationship must have withstood everyday frictions as two powerful men and their allies attempted to manage the politics of the Roman state. Furthermore, neither side behaved as if war were coming. Jealousies abounded, no doubt, and the two main protagonists probably fenced with each other, but Octavian did promise and deliver some support for Antony's campaigns in Parthia and Antony provided a fleet in the war against Pompeius. There were problems, but the resilience of the regime makes its eventual fall more problematic.

Antony and Cleopatra is the story that has everything, but as a story, it risks not making sense. In large part, that is because of the layers of interpretation and the multiple retellings with which we are faced. We cannot read about Antony and Cleopatra without acknowledging somewhere in the back of our heads the many films, plays, artworks, novels, and other representations that lie between us and the ancient pair. Nor is it enough to strip away those interpretations to get to the "real" story, not because there is no real story but because the first retellings of the story already have about them an aura of myth, and it seems likely that even while the couple held court in Alexandria, mythic stories circulated about their behavior.[1] Our main sources on Antony and Cleopatra are Plutarch and Dio. Plutarch, whose *Life of Antony* was the ultimate basis of the Shakespearean play, was writing after more than a century of myth building, and Dio composed his version another century later. Plutarch's interest was not primarily in the history and politics of the episode but in drawing moral lessons, and the mythic elements of the story suited his purposes rather more than any realistic historical evaluation of the pair.

This concern with morality has been shared by many of those who have turned their attention to Antony and Cleopatra. The result has been that the story has come to focus on their intimate relationship. The issue has become character, not power, partly because how to be good is a question that everyone has always needed to consider, while how to run an empire is of more specialist interest. Antony and Cleopatra could be depicted as having been very bad, and the bad are much more entertaining than the good. The historian Dio, from 250 years later, exemplifies the quality of the ancient analysis in his succinct summary: "Antony was enslaved to his desire and by the witchcraft of Cleopatra."[2]

The story became one of love, and love was separated from the politics, placed into a realm of irrationality as opposed to the supposedly always rational male realm of political life. Antony and Cleopatra were tragic heroes long before Shakespeare. Yet if Cleopatra, with her oriental sexuality, has been the dark, seductive heart of the tale for modern audiences, for the ancients it is Antony's fatal, tragic flaw that makes the drama. As Antony and Cleopatra became symbols of the madness of love, so Octavian and his allies, in their imperial grandeur, became the enemies of love. In such a universe of black and white, Roman history is made into a morality tale of sex versus empire, passion versus reason, which resonates across the ages in its emotional familiarity and simplicity.

For a slave to love, Antony was remarkably absent from his mistress. He spent much of the time from 40 onwards in Italy, Asia, Syria,

Armenia, and Media. Alexandria may have been his winter resort of choice, but the great lovers managed to survive long periods apart. If one cannot believe that the war arose from Cleopatra's witchcraft or Antony's lusts, it also stretches credibility that after nine years Octavian and his supporters suddenly noticed that Antony was having sexual relations with Cleopatra. Antony appears to have regarded his relationship with Cleopatra as compatible with his marriage to Octavia, and with good reason, since for nearly eight years there was no significant political problem.

Whereas for moderns there is uneasiness when the private becomes part of the political sphere, the absence of such a clear division in Roman thought allowed for a politicization of marital relationships. Sex is, of course, different from marriage. Marriage was seen as a public and thus political relationship, whereas sex was a private matter. Nevertheless, there appears to have been increasing hostility towards wives taking any role in politics during the first century A.D., possibly resulting from the experience of court politics under the first imperial dynasty of Rome, the Julio-Claudians (Tiberius, Caligula, Claudius, and Nero). This concern extended beyond the issue of marriage into sex. In the imperial period, it mattered with whom the emperor had sexual relations, whereas it seems unlikely that anyone (outside those intimately involved) cared very much about the sexual activities of Republican men.

On the verge of the Actian war, Antony says as much in a letter to Octavian when complaints about his relationship with Cleopatra surfaced.[3]

> What's happened with you? Because I enter the queen? She is my wife. Did I begin this now or nine years ago? Do you then enter only Drusilla? Good luck to you if as you read this letter you have not entered Tertulla or Terentilla or Rufilla or Salvia Titisenia, or all. What does it matter where and in whom you are pleasured?

Given the shortness of the extract from Antony's letter, we have to be careful in understanding the target: is it that Octavian was complaining about Antony's sexual activities, as Antony suggests, or was he, as our later sources suggest, complaining that Antony was "dominated" by Cleopatra, who was, ultimately, the pretext for the war of Actium? Antony's reaction was disingenuous. He argued that the politicization of sex was a novel attack, but it had always been part of Roman invective, though normally such invective focused on certain types of homosexual activity, sleeping with other men's wives, subservience of a man to his lover, or a man being distracted by his passions (especially if they were for women of lower status) from his duty as a Roman.

Moreover, Cleopatra was not just a convenient woman with whom Antony could sate his desires. She was, as he states in the first line of his reply, his wife as well as queen of Egypt, and together they established a household. There are complications here, though we should not be too proper about them. Rome was a monogamous society, but, like many slave societies, that monogamy did not require men to limit themselves to a single sexual partner. Furthermore, the Romans had no sense of sex as sin. For the Romans, sex was a normal part of life. What needed regulating was reproduction, and for legitimate reproduction a man was expected to have but one wife at a time.

A wife was a central figure in the household of her husband, and her status and connections contributed to his status and connections. In his relationship with Cleopatra, Antony showed the Roman world that he was the kind of man who could form a household with a queen. Wives were partners, perhaps unequal partners, in the households of great men, and husbands and wives could be expected to speak in support of their spouses.[4] There was no attempt to hide the influence of women during the late Republic, and the political marriages of the period, such as that between Octavia and Antony, recognized the political importance of the role of women within these male-dominated households.

It was politics, not romance, that drove these relationships; love was a separate and perhaps minor issue, and (perhaps consequently) there was a certain toleration for extramarital relationships, among the social and political elite at least. Romans were not blind to love (far from it), and the period of the Roman revolution saw the production of some of the most intimate love poetry ever written, but neither men nor women expected to find that romantic relationship in marriage.

The attempt to bind the triumvirs closer together by the marriage of Octavia and Antony obviously failed eventually, but the dissolution of the marriage followed from the failure of the political relationship between the two men rather than being its cause. Indeed, the long-lasting nature of the relationship between Octavia and Antony suggests that, novel as it may have seemed, Antony could build a regal household with Cleopatra and maintain a Roman household with Octavia.

Antony's listing of the various women with whom Octavian was supposed to have had sex picked not on low-status women (no one cared whether Octavian had extramarital relations with such women), but on the wives of Octavian's closest associates, suggesting that those households were corrupted by Octavian's sexual proclivities. Antony was drawing a contrast with his own sexual relationships—which he presented as legitimate and respectable, since they were maintained within a household—and the adulterous relations of Octavian.

Legally, a Roman could normally only form a legitimate marriage (and thus create a household) with another Roman. Yet, given that Antony had extensive legal powers and Cleopatra was a queen, they were unlikely to be inconvenienced by such legal niceties; the powers that had allowed the triumvirs to kill without recourse to due process were certainly sufficient to make the necessary legal arrangements for Antony's marriage to Cleopatra. Antony could thus claim that Cleopatra was his wife and that their children were legitimate. He could similarly represent the relationship between himself and Octavia as legal (if bigamous).

And yet the very power that enabled Antony to behave in this novel way also changed the political importance of his household. Household formation was a practical activity with practical consequences. Fulvia's political prominence in the early triumviral period may have been historically unusual, but that was a reflection of the extraordinary authority exercised by Antony. The household was politically important because it was perceived, probably rightly, that leading men took counsel of their wives, their wives supported and represented them, and much was decided within the household. This hardly mattered in a republican system, when all important decisions were taken by magistrates in consultation with their peers, but in the triumviral period, the households of Antony and Octavian took on an unprecedented political role.

The focus on the relationship with Cleopatra was, therefore, not a perverse entry of the personal, amatory, and private into the arena of the political, rational, and public. Antony's decision to form a household with Cleopatra was a political act, tying the futures of Antony and Cleopatra together. By association, both were, theoretically at least, strengthened and they were not afraid to publicize their close personal tie, even issuing coins in which Cleopatra, the famous beauty, looked very like Antony (see fig. 6 below). The relationship meant that Cleopatra had real power in the Roman world, through the household of Antony. It also meant that Antony's relationship was a matter of political concern. By contrast, and Antony was quite right in this, the adulteries of Octavian were not an issue, since it could not be pretended that his lovers had any significant influence over the triumvir. Romans could worry about the threat of becoming subservient to Cleopatra, because she was a woman of considerable power and influence. It also meant that to attack Cleopatra was to attack Antony.

We are not telling love stories, but Antony's angry, short, explicit sentences show that sex was part of this story, as was the glamour and exoticism of the Egyptian queen. In answer to Antony's question,

FIGURE 6

Coin of Antony and Cleopatra. The coin shows the pair as partners in power; notably, they are depicted as looking alike.

however much he disliked the way in which his sexual behavior was drawn into the debate and however unusual it was for the philandering of a Roman male to attract serious political attention, it did matter with whom Antony took his pleasures, and Antony almost certainly knew that it mattered.

THE DONATIONS OF ALEXANDRIA

In 34 B.C., Antony celebrated his victory over the Parthians with a procession in Alexandria. He had the former Armenian king led through the city in silver chains. Antony himself rode through Alexandria in a chariot, acknowledging the crowds as he went. The centerpiece of the event was a presentation of the captives and the booty to Cleopatra, who sat on a golden throne on a sliver dais amidst her people.[5] Antony then held a feast for his soldiers and for the Alexandrians, and afterwards he spoke to the crowd. Cleopatra was named Queen of Kings. Cleopatra's son by Julius Caesar, Caesarion, was named King of Kings. These Persian titles established their dominance, at least in titular terms, over the East. His own children by Cleopatra were given realms: Ptolemy was given Syria, Cleopatra Selene received Cyrenaica (the land west of Egypt), and Alexander was awarded Armenia and the lands to the east as far as India.[6]

The "Donations of Alexandria" did not correspond to a traditional Roman way of acting. Although the procession and the presentation of the captives in the center of the city could be seen as imitating the Roman triumph, its location in Alexandria and Cleopatra's role in the ceremonial were innovative. The event represented a new political reality and an acknowledgment that the politics of 34 were very different from those of an earlier age. Ceremonials are a means by which political power is represented to the people and are, therefore, ideological: they present a particular view of the world to their intended audience. Antony and Cleopatra could not have acted as if their position was analogous to that of earlier generations of pharaohs and generals. A household led by the Queen of Egypt and a triumvir was unprecedented, and obviously so to a Roman or an Egyptian audience. As a consequence, Antony and Cleopatra were forced to invent ceremonials, adapting the political symbolism available to them for the current situation. One of those adaptations was to present Cleopatra as Isis and Antony as Osiris or Dionysus.[7]

Such experimentation is not, however, without political risk. Symbols always present a view of reality and give people the opportunity to think about that reality. Innovating within a political culture becomes necessary when power operates in ways which cannot easily be accommodated within that culture. Ceremonials are opportunities for asserting a symbolic unity of the people, but also for people questioning that unity and wondering whether they agree with or belong to the version of their world that is being presented to them.

A victorious Roman general would normally impose a settlement on a defeated people which would be submitted to the senate for discussion. Not only was this procedure ignored in this case, but Antony's appointment of family members was, in Roman terms, a startling innovation (though those familiar with Greek regal practices would have understood immediately what was happening). Furthermore, the benefits of such actions are not clear, especially since there does not appear to have been any suggestion that Cleopatra or her children would exercise any administrative control. Cleopatra's role in the ceremony and in the politics of the event was overtly passive; it was Antony who spoke to the people and Antony who made the arrangements. The Donations represented Antony's power.

The Donations of Alexandria were a piece of political theater. They employed Roman imagery in the triumphal procession, but also incorporated traditions of Egyptian and Near Eastern kingship that had considerable cultural resonance within the region. Antony, like other conquerors of the East before him, most notably Alexander the Great, used traditional representations of kingship in the region for his own political purposes. The Donations addressed different audiences, but those audiences, disparate though their cultural backgrounds may have been, would have been sufficiently familiar with each other's traditions that they would understand the messages that were being communicated.

The Donations could be understood within a tradition of Eastern kingship and Roman victory celebrations, and after centuries of Roman engagement in the East both Romans and provincials were familiar with these representations.

Antony was not pharaoh and did not represent himself as such. He was not even a Ptolemaic king. Cleopatra did not attempt to formalize his place within the Egyptian dynasty, nor does he appear on temples in Egypt in association with Cleopatra; she tended to have herself depicted with her son Caesarion. Antony remained an outsider and a Roman. Nevertheless, his association with Cleopatra and with Egyptian and Near Eastern kingship was a representation of the permanence of his rule, and his elevation of Cleopatra and his children by Cleopatra acknowledged that permanence. The Donations laid claim to the hegemony of the household of Antony and Cleopatra over the East into future generations in a markedly dynastic and un-republican way. But if the arrangements of the East were not republican, neither could Antony's rule be understood as being that of a king; neither crown nor diadem was accepted, and no new title was given.[8]

Antony's actions in deploying an established language of power in a new way were not very different in type or form than those of Octavian in monumentalizing his victory over Pompeius in the Forum of Rome or in having coins minted which proclaimed him as *divi filius*, son of the deified Caesar. We cannot imagine a steadfastly republican Rome recoiling in horror from an association with Hellenistic kingship in the case of Antony but nodding happily at the association of Octavian with the gods in the golden statues adorning Rome. Both are instances of the development of innovative ways of representing power, and in the elevation of these individuals above the norms of senatorial and Roman tradition they reflected the new political circumstances of the late first century B.C. Nevertheless, the Donations of Alexandria provided a cultural representation of a crucial distinction between Octavian and Antony. Antony's ceremony revealed the personal and political reality of his union with Cleopatra and the centering of their power in Alexandria. Antony could maintain support within Rome and provide rewards for his supporters, but patrimonial networks are by their nature communicative. A network located in Alexandria (two or three months away from the center of business in Rome) and involving a queen whose connection to Italian political life was at best slight ran the risk of being less responsive and having less appeal than a network based in Italy. If the network did not work for its members, then people might shift their loyalties.

Antony was bound to Cleopatra, personally and politically. Cleopatra was mother to three of Antony's children. Even if he had not been carefully constructing a language of power which centered on his relationship to Cleopatra, he could not have thrown her aside, nor is there any evidence that he saw a need to give her up. The relationship brought glamour and wealth to his household and enhanced his status. Cleopatra was essential to his regime.

THE END OF THE TRIUMVIRATE

By 33 B.C., the relationship between Antony and Octavian was strained. The details are beyond us, but it is clear that their conflict did not emerge from a single critical issue. Antony demanded that troops be sent to him from Italy. Octavian asked for half the spoils from the Eastern campaigns and complained that he had not agreed to the arrangements enacted at the Donations of Alexandria. Antony questioned the removal of Lepidus and Octavian's acquisition of the provinces of Sextus Pompeius and Lepidus. Octavian claimed, implausibly, that he would have spared Sextus Pompeius, and accused Antony of his murder. He also complained about Cleopatra and Caesarion, suggesting that Antony had behaved dishonorably in his war in Armenia.[9] Much of this was old news.

The arguments appear to have been conducted largely in private or in the indiscreet gossip of the Roman aristocracy. Envoys were sent to and fro carrying irritating and irritable messages between the pair. One may imagine that the Roman political elite continually discussed the behavior of the two men. Still, they did not come to blows, nor did they have a legal or political issue that needed immediate resolution. Although the triumviral powers were due to expire at the end of 33, there appears to have been little suggestion that either man would relinquish his power or that Antony would return to Rome to resume a "normal" political career.

In 32, two associates of Antony, Gnaeus Domitius and Gaius Sosius became consuls. On January 1, in the traditional address of the new consul, Domitius took the opportunity to praise Antony and to criticize Octavian. Octavian was not in the senate to hear him. He did, however, reply soon. A session of the senate was called, and Octavian appeared surrounded by soldiers. The consuls listened to Octavian refute their allegations and the session ended.

Overnight, the consuls fled.[10] The formal ending of triumviral powers and Octavian's use of soldiers may have caused increased nervousness and fear of an escalation into violence. But even so, war was not inevitable. There was nothing approaching a casus belli.

Nevertheless, for some, it was time to choose. Some went from Rome to Antony; some came from Alexandria to Octavian. Those who arrived in Rome complained about Cleopatra, and the suggestion was made that Antony intended to give her Rome. Many probably hoped for a reconciliation and imagined that those who were loyal to both men might bind the disputants together once more. It was from the defectors that Octavian was made aware that Antony's will was lodged with the Vestal Virgins (temples were used for safekeeping of documents and money, as such property was under divine protection). Against all law, Octavian extracted the will from the vestals and read it to the senators. Key to Octavian's case was the discovery of a clause, which seems of no note in itself, stating that Antony wished to be buried in Alexandria alongside his queen. In response, the senators put on their military cloaks and voted war on Cleopatra.[11]

Octavian's charge was that Cleopatra was taking over the networks of power that governed the empire. The will provided some slight evidence in support of that accusation: Antony was turning from Rome to Cleopatra, and his tying of his household to Cleopatra could be represented as a usurpation of Roman authority in the East. With Cleopatra's usurpation, a geographical division was created between Rome and Alexandria, and Rome's position as the center and beneficiary of empire was threatened. If Cleopatra was to join with Antony in his power, then

Roman men would be subordinate to her, which might cause discomfort. Further, the Donations of Alexandria had made clear that Antony intended the relationship to Cleopatra to be long-lasting and dynastic: their children would succeed.

Octavian responded to the perceived threat posed by Cleopatra by organizing the cities and communities of Italy to take an oath to follow him in the coming war as their leader (*dux*). All Italy, he claimed, stood behind his campaign.[12] Octavian ascribed to Italy a political and cultural unity that positioned Italy as the center of a great empire. In the old Republic, it was Rome that mattered, and everything of importance occurred in the political world of that great city; in Octavian's new geography of power, it was Italy, including the towns and colonies in which the veterans had been settled and the communities who had made their peace, or were to make their peace, with the triumvir. The emphasis on Italy reflected a triumviral geography of power in which the patrimonial network of Octavian's influence spread beyond Rome itself. By emphasizing Italy, he was also standing in opposition to the exoticism of Egypt.

In reality, of course, the war was between Antony and Octavian, and Antony had considerable support within Italy. One presumes that many who favored Antony remained in Italy and that veterans of the various campaigns had fond memories of him, but political rhetoric and political reality are often different. Antony could not call upon his supporters in Rome and Italy, nor could his supporters offer Antony much practical help. Octavian was able to make his rhetoric real: the resources of Italy would be thrown against Antony and his Egyptian ally.

THE BATTLE OF ACTIUM

After the flight of the consuls and the initial diplomatic posturing, the military campaign began late in 32, but it was only in the spring of 31 that the two sides were ready for war. Octavian gathered his troops and organized his fleet at Brundisium in southern Italy. Antony sailed to Greece to secure the westernmost of his territories. He sent garrisons into the Peloponnese and located his fleet at Actium.

Actium lies on the southern side of the narrow inlet to the Ambracian Gulf which stretches inland more than 50 km (see Map 6). It is one of the few good harbors along the west coast of Greece, and although isolated by land, by sea it is within easy reach of Italy and the Peloponnese. Locating the fleet at Actium gave Antony considerable room to maneuver, allowing him to strike at Octavian's towns and troops in the Adriatic. Antony's strategy mirrored that adopted after the Perusine war, when he established a base in western Greece and used his naval superiority to launch an invasion at Brundisium. Yet, in 31, Antony did not enjoy naval superiority and Octavian was able to contend for control of the sea. Rather than being a stage for the launching of an invasion of Italy, Antony was to find himself imprisoned in the Ambracian Gulf.

Agrippa seized the initiative. He bypassed Actium and seized Methone, in the southwest Peloponnese. From there he was able to launch a series of raids into Antony's territory, harassing Antonian forces. Octavian crossed the Adriatic, probably landing somewhere in modern Albania, and prepared to strike at Antony's fleet at Actium.[13] As Antony dashed to Actium to join his troops and the bulk of his fleet, Octavian made his way south via the island of Paxos to establish a base on the northern side of the Gulf, a few kilometers to the north of Actium itself. Octavian tried to bring Antony's army to battle, either on land or on sea, but Antony had fortified both sides of the entrance to the Gulf, and Octavian could not storm the fortifications without considerable risk. Antony's forces were yet to be assembled and he refused to give battle, summoning troops, presumably by circuitous land routes, to his camp at Actium. Both sides awaited their opportunity and gathered their strength.[14]

Agrippa, however, was never one to sit still. He took the opportunity to raid the Peloponnese and establish a base at Leucas. This provided Octavian with control over the southern approaches to Actium. Antony was boxed in by sea, and Agrippa's naval control over the Gulf of Corinth meant that even circuitous land routes were endangered from raiding.[15] Having assembled his troops, Antony had to feed them, and if the sea lanes were closed, food needed to be hauled a very considerable distance.

This part of Greece can be fiercely hot in the summer. The atmosphere is humid. The low-lying land on which Antony was camped was probably

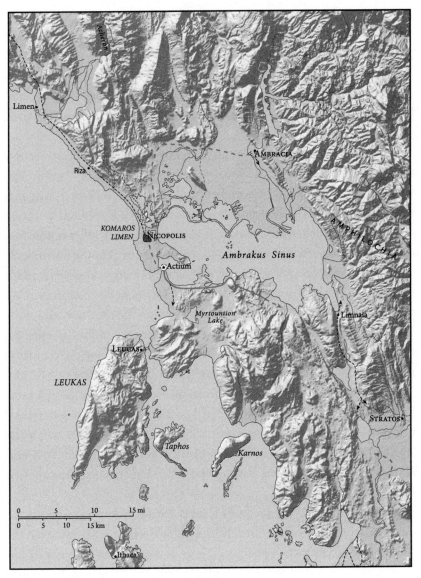

MAP 5
Actium and Environs

particularly unpleasant, whereas Octavian's troops to the north were camped on an elevated section of the plain and will have benefited from the sea breezes that blow down each afternoon. Much of the land south of the Gulf is marshy today, and in antiquity the area was malarial. The provision of clean water was also difficult, and draining the wastes from the camp in the relatively unmoving waters of the Gulf almost impossible. As the supply chain struggled, large numbers of increasingly hungry men remained stationary on the marshy plain. In the summer heat, short of food and fuel, living in insanitary conditions, the army began to suffer from disease. Antony could no longer wait. He was trapped and his army was dying.

Antony now offered battle on the northern shore. But waiting was now to Octavian's advantage. He must also have known that Antony was running out of time and needed to move his troops. Practically, that meant that either Antony would have to inflict a decisive land defeat on Octavian or his fleet would need to break out. The only other option was a complicated overland retreat which would require Antony burning his ships (his major military asset) and then withdrawing over difficult roads with a hungry and diseased army under harassment by land and sea. To fight on land, Antony needed to face Octavian on the northern side of the Gulf, on the flat land near modern Preveza. Hence, Antony marched his troops out and lined up before Octavian's fortifications. Skirmishes resulted, but Octavian was not prepared to commit to battle.

This must have been a tactical decision. Octavian and Agrippa must have weighed their options and decided on a sea battle. Octavian's refusal to fight gave notice that Antony would have to fight at sea. Octavian and Agrippa had enjoyed naval success against Sextus Pompeius, whereas Antony was untried at sea. It seems possible that they felt they enjoyed naval superiority.

Unable to draw Octavian into a land battle, Antony evacuated his outposts from the north of the Gulf. Antony's retreat acknowledged the superiority of Octavian's position. There is a story that the Antonians then held a council of war and, characteristically, Cleopatra, frightened by omens, is said to have had the decisive voice; she decided that they should extract what they could and flee.[16] The story is unlikely. There was nothing much for Antony and his council of advisors to discuss by that point. The fleet was their major military asset, and without naval support the army would be lost anyway.[17] If Antony could inflict a decisive naval defeat on Octavian and Agrippa, he would secure Greece and have a launch point for an invasion of Italy. He could reverse the situation and deprive Octavian of supplies. Even if he merely held off Octavian and extracted his fleet more or less intact from its current situation, Antony would be able to fight on. His fleet could contest the Adriatic, he could hope to extract his land forces, and he could summon reinforcements from across the East. Win or draw, Antony and Cleopatra would have more favorable circumstances in which to continue the war. As soon as Antony retreated his forces from the fortifications north of the Gulf, both sides began preparations for a potentially decisive naval engagement.

After several days waiting for the right wind and sea conditions, on September 2, 31, Antony and Cleopatra sailed out of the straits of Actium. Octavian and Agrippa were waiting for them. Antony's fleet assembled before the mouth of the Gulf and compacted their lines to prevent Octavian's ships slipping among them. A great wall of wood faced Octavian and his fleet. They waited. Neither side made a move. Octavian may have been expecting Antony to turn his ships to the south, exposing their flanks and forcing their formation to loosen as they made for the open sea. Antony made no such error. Octavian then extended his lines and sent out squadrons to outflank Antony's fleet. Threatened with encirclement, Antony took advantage of the maneuver and attacked.[18]

Antony's fleet was composed of larger, heavier ships. They had more missiles, and their greater height gave them an advantage at close quarters. Octavian's ships were smaller and lighter. They were more maneuverable, but were in danger of being overwhelmed if they could be caught. For an extended period, the battle was indecisive. Neither side could inflict great damage, but Antony's ships, slower as they were, could not escape.

Legend has it that as the battle was still in the balance, Cleopatra took fright and fled, and Antony followed her.[19] Legend sees the decisive moment as being a woman's weakness and Antony's failure being his trust in and love for Cleopatra. Legend is likely wrong. One favorable outcome of the battle for Antony and Cleopatra was to break out of the Gulf, to retreat and to fight another day. Tactically, Cleopatra and Antony had to force their passage from the Gulf and fight their way into open sea. The winds on that part of the coast build in the afternoon before falling in the evening. As the battle developed and morning turned to afternoon, Antony and Cleopatra must have watched for the wind, waiting for the opportunity to set sail and outrun Octavian's ships. But choosing the moment to hoist sail was difficult. Enough time had to be allowed so that the fleeing ships could escape Octavian's fleet.[20] The maneuver required the fleet to coordinate their dash. But the moment they would break off the battle and turn to the sea was a moment of danger. If the formation broke up or the ships turned to present their flanks to Octavian's prows, Octavian would have his chance, and if he could prevent the majority of the ships from leaving, he would have his victory. Perhaps the maneuver even required a rearguard of sufficient strength to hold off Octavian's fleet while the majority turned, raised sail, and fled.

When Cleopatra saw a chance, she went. Antony followed and made good his escape, but the majority of the fleet was unable to break away. Even though this is presented as the decisive moment in the war, the battle was not yet lost. Antony's fleet fought on. The very fact that they continued to fight suggests that Antony and Cleopatra's flight was not a surprise, nor the panic of a weak woman followed by the impulsive act of a man blinded by his passion. Even after the departure of Cleopatra, closely followed by Antony, the situation cannot have seemed hopeless. Still the Antonians looked for their opportunity to make for open sea.

The formation held together, and Octavian's fleet could not break them. Antony's reduced fleet held off Octavian, but as the day wore on, the chances of escape lessened. Sometime towards evening, the wind would drop, and the Antonians would be becalmed, and then their position would be lost. Octavian compressed the Antonian lines, making it yet more difficult for them to flee, and then he sent for fire from the camp.

Octavian ordered that blazing missiles be sent into the enemy fleet. He launched jars filled with charcoal and pitch. The oily tar was lit, and fires started on the wooden boats. The marines rushed to put the fires out, pouring first their drinking water and then sea water over the pitch. But perhaps Antony's soldiers were inexperienced in the dark arts of naval warfare, since they did not appear to know that pitch floats. Throwing water on the burning pitch spread the fire through the ship. They tried beating out the flames and even throwing the dead onto the fires. But it was of no use. The fires spread and soon were out of control. Octavian's fleet stood off and watched Antony's ships burn.[21] The battle was over.

Antony's army was already in retreat. Their position was hopeless. They could try the difficult road through the mountains and hence onwards to Macedonia, or they could march along the Corinthian Gulf, now controlled by Agrippa's fleet. Either way, the road ahead was long and hard. Even if they could hold off Octavian's troops, they needed to find food. This was an impossible march for a diseased army. The prospect of escape was negligible. Antony's legions surrendered.[22]

THE DEATH OF LOVE

Antony and Cleopatra may have paused briefly to see whether their army would escape, but once news of the surrender reached them, they sailed for Egypt. Octavian killed or spared the leading Romans he had captured among Antony's troops as he saw fit and sent at least some of his troops back to Italy, a sure sign of confidence. He built himself a great victory monument on the spot where he had pitched his tent. The monument was adorned with the prows taken from Antony's fleet and was dedicated to Apollo. A whole new city was to follow. Nicopolis, the City of Victory, stretched across the hillside overlooking the sea in which Octavian had secured his triumph. Games were instituted so that every five years the Roman world would come to celebrate Octavian's victory and remember the fate of Antony and Cleopatra. Octavian presented Actium as a historic moment that changed the Roman world.

The rest of the Roman world made up their minds. Theoretically, Antony had still had plentiful resources. Many of his legions had not been committed and remained in Syria and Africa; client kings owed him loyalty and could muster troops to defend his cause. Cleopatra had money and ships, though her fleet was inconveniently placed in the Red Sea. Yet, once the scale of the defeat of Actium became obvious, everyone could calculate that the war was effectively over. There was no honor in martyrdom, and no cause to die for. Antony had lost and Octavian would win. Antony's allies defected. The kings of the East sought to make peace. The Romans who commanded Antony's provinces sought reconciliation with Octavian. Only Egypt remained.

The strategic situation must have been obvious to Antony and Cleopatra. There was little they could do to match the power that Octavian now had at his disposal, and so they returned to Alexandria to await the arrival of their conqueror. There were diplomatic exchanges, but they were fruitless. Antony and Cleopatra had little to bargain with and Octavian had no reason to treat with them. The end was delayed by a mutiny among the discharged troops, as ever demanding reward, which forced Octavian to return to Brundisium, but it was only a stay of execution. It bought Antony and Cleopatra a winter and spring to prepare. They were set on resistance, gathering what forces they could, and they diverted themselves from the onrushing disaster by spending much of the winter in doing what they did best, holding extravagant dinners, conspicuously displaying and consuming their wealth. They formed a new dining club for themselves and their friends, the Partners in Death.[23] In 30, Octavian's forces closed in on Egypt.

Egypt was not an easy country to invade, being protected by its deserts, but Antony was faced with the task of defending the country from east and west (see Map 5). The army based in Cyrenaica, which had been under Antony's command, had defected. Antony had appointed Cornelius Gallus, an equestrian, perhaps in the hope that one of the lesser aristocracy might prove loyal. Instead, Gallus launched an invasion of Egypt. Antony had been expecting Octavian's forces to come through Pelusium, in the east, and was forced to march rapidly in the opposite direction. Gallus seized the border city of Paraetonium. Antony hoped that he could persuade the troops to return to his fold. He failed, and as he camped outside Paraetonium, he received news that Octavian had indeed invaded.[24]

Antony marched on Octavian. His cavalry caught Octavian's troops on the outskirts of Alexandria and drove them back. He followed up the victory with an infantry assault, but was unable to inflict serious damage. Nevertheless, he was elated, claiming that he could turn around even this dire situation. Yet, outnumbered and beleaguered from all sides, he cannot

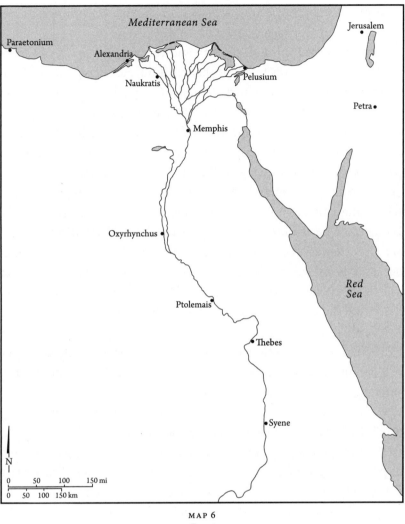

MAP 6
Egypt

realistically have expected anything but death. The next day Antony ordered the navy from Alexandria. As the fleet met Octavian's superior forces, they raised their oars and surrendered. On land, Antony led the infantry into battle. They were defeated and retreated back to the city.[25]

Cleopatra had seen the defection and the defeat and knew that the end was close. She had already transported at least some of her wealth to her mausoleum, which had been built so that once the gates were closed they could not be reopened. Now, she went to the mausoleum herself and closed the gates. The queen was ready to die.

The news spread through the city and reached Antony. It is easy to believe that Antony was told that she was dead. He fell on his sword. As he lay bleeding, there was further news. Cleopatra still lived. Antony demanded to be taken to his queen and he was carried through the streets of the city. When Antony reached the mausoleum, he was winched up to the windows and Cleopatra and her servants hauled him inside. Antony was reunited with Cleopatra and died in her arms.[26]

Cleopatra did not immediately follow him. Octavian's representatives entered the city, seemingly to negotiate, perhaps even to suggest that Cleopatra or her children might be spared (as, in fact, all were, other than Caesarion). Octavian's representatives were allowed into the mausoleum and they seized the queen, removing from her a dagger with which she tried to kill herself. They transported her from the mausoleum to the palace, and there she was placed under careful watch while they awaited Octavian.[27]

There is a certainly fictional tale of the meeting between Cleopatra and Octavian in which Cleopatra, the great seductress, tried out her charms on the young conqueror, who manfully resisted. He was no Caesar and certainly no Antony, but was of sterner, more Roman discipline. But there is little reason to believe that Cleopatra's intentions had changed.[28] She performed funerary rites for Antony and retired to the palace. There she prepared a great meal and dressed in her regal costume. She then sent a letter to Octavian. By the time Octavian received the letter, Cleopatra was dead. Octavian broke into the room to find Cleopatra's two maids arranging a diadem on the queen's head. The tableau was carefully constructed. The Romans were meant to find the queen in her majesty. Her maids were themselves dying, killed by whatever had poisoned their mistress.

The means of death are mysterious. There is some suggestion that there was a poisoned pin, but the legend places more emphasis on a snakebite, the snake or snakes smuggled in among figs or in a water jar. Isis was associated with snakes. It would have been a fitting way for the last pharaoh and the embodiment of Isis to pass to the land of the dead.[29]

Cleopatra was buried next to Antony, and thus Antony's desire to be lie in death alongside his queen was fulfilled.

EMPIRE AND RESISTANCE

The deaths of Antony and Cleopatra saw the birth of the myth and the start of monarchic imperialism. Actium was not, however, a moment that changed the world, and still less were the suicides decisive in the shaping of history. It seems unlikely that Rome would have developed in radically different ways had Antony emerged as victor at Actium. The dispute was over control of a network that had fragmented around two loci of power, that of Antony and Cleopatra in Alexandria and that of Octavian in Rome. It is improbable that a victory for Antony would have led to a lessening of the power of that network. Antony was, if anything, more realistic and more radical in his representation of the change from the republican to the imperial system, and more eager to experiment with different representations of that change. Alexandria might have come to play a more prominent role in the Roman imperial settlement, and the first dynasty of Rome would have been led by the children of Antony and Cleopatra, but Rome and Italy were still the geographical centers of power, and one presumes that Antony, whatever his love for his queen, would have spent many of his years in Rome.

The significance of the deaths of Antony and Cleopatra lies precisely in myth.[30] Antony and Cleopatra could be reimagined as opponents of empire, and that opposition was built into their lives and lifestyles. As they were painted as fools for love, orientalized, sexualized, feminized, and doomed, so those qualities came to be associated with an anti-imperial, anti-Roman stance. As the empire became more of a totalitarian state in which the emperor controlled all aspects of society and politics, so the values of Antony and Cleopatra could be made to represent an ideological opposition. No matter the reality, the legacy of Antony and Cleopatra was to make their opponents the enemies of love and to make lovers the enemies of empire.

13.

THE INVENTION OF AUGUSTUS

THE BATTLE HAD NOT ended the war between Antony and Octavian, but the latter stages were played out as a tragedy: everyone knew who was going to die, and it was just a matter of how it was going to happen. For Octavian, there was other business to settle. The war had divided Caesarian loyalties. There was the question of what was to be done with Antony's friends and Antony's troops. Moreover, Octavian had spent almost all his career in the West. His ventures to the East had been brief, and he was thus an almost unknown figure in the region.

Whereas much of the Roman West was divided into provinces which had Roman provincial governors, arrangements in the East were more complicated and varied. Many of the lands east of what is now Greece had only come late into the Roman imperial sphere. The Romans had, for a variety of reasons, been reluctant to make many of these newly conquered territories into provinces. Instead, and especially after Pompey's conquests in the 60s, the Romans delegated authority to a number of local kings. These kings were often dependent on Roman power. They were expected to contribute troops to Roman expeditions and to show their loyalties through financial donations, a procedure which enriched the Roman commanders if not always benefiting the treasury to the same extent.

One of the advantages of the system of dependent princelings for Roman aristocrats was that it enabled them to build personal relationships with the monarchs (very personal in the case of Cleopatra). Such relationships were prestigious; being seen in the company of kings displayed the importance of the individual. The relationship also tended to be lucrative, since the monarchs would be generous in ensuring that their "friends" would remember them and represent their interests. The disadvantage of the system came when Rome's political elite divided. At that point, the local kings were faced with difficult choices, balancing options which may have had implications obscure to them. Like everyone else caught up in civil war, however carefully the alternatives were weighed, the kings were faced with the possibility of being on the losing side. In the war between Antony and Octavian, the choice facing the kings was limited, since they were in Antony's sphere and had been reliant on him for a decade. There can have been no doubt that Antony would have removed any who were disloyal, and neutrality was hardly an option. Octavian, however, had little record of being understanding or magnanimous toward his former enemies. The kings will have feared for their kingdoms and their lives.

The political structure of the Roman East was made more complex by the presence of numerous Greek cities. Greek cities (*poleis*, singular *polis*) had a distinctive political structure: they were ruled by committees of magistrates, normally serving for limited periods; a council of (normally) landed aristocrats; and an assembly of citizens. They differed from Rome in having magistrates who were limited in the powers at their disposal and relying much more on the collective bodies of council and assembly. Most of these cities were constitutionally democracies, but controlled democracies, with the richer elements of society exercising a great deal of authority. These *poleis* normally ruled quite small territories, creating a patchwork system of political powers through much of the region. After the conquests of Alexander the Great, the *poleis* worked in conjunction within the various kingdoms of the region, creating networks of relations between the royal courts (which were the military powers of the region) and local communities.

Octavian presented the cities with a new problem. With previous Roman governors, there was always a sense that they were representatives of the greater power that was Rome, and cities responded to Roman domination in familiar ways, sending embassies, trying to win friends among the Roman elite, and granting honors to prominent individuals who might be persuaded to act on their behalf. Octavian's power, however, was personalized and did not obviously work through the institutions of Rome; seeking the support of senators seemed somewhat redundant if all the key decisions were going to be made by Octavian. It was also evident that Octavian, unlike the various governors, was not going to go away after a short tenure of office. The cities needed to develop a relationship with their new master.

The victor of Actium wasted no time. After his previous victories, he had been notably brutal, even by the blood-soaked standards of the time. We lack details of how he treated those aristocratic Romans who had fought alongside Antony; we are merely told that some he killed, some he fined, and some he spared. The stories of those who died are redolent of the cruelties of Octavian after the defeat of Cassius and Brutus and after Perusia. The cruelty is that of a tyrant—gratuitous, psychological, and fatal. It sent a message about the nature of Octavian, in case anyone had forgotten. At a later date, the Emperor Augustus, as he had by then become, was to represent the war of Actium as one of Italy against the East and himself as the conservative and conventional representative of traditions and order. At the time, however, there appears to have been little attempt at respectability or at disguise of his violent power.

Octavian now asserted himself in the East. The kings had to be put in their places. Many had received gifts, often extensions of territory, from Antony, who had made use of his alliances with the various kings to raise troops and resources for his various campaigns and rewarded the kings with gifts of territory. These gifts were now rescinded. Three kings were removed from office, and one was executed. One can only imagine that those retained were suitably grateful and eager to overlook any territorial adjustments in the perhaps unexpected circumstance of their continued power, especially as Octavian redistributed the realms of the supplanted to those who had shown him loyalty and friendship.

The most prominent of the kings of the East (other than Cleopatra) was Herod of Judaea. Herod had been raised up by Antony when the old regal dynasty had been removed by Antony's general Sosius because of their support for the Parthians. Herod was something of an outsider to the traditional power networks in Judaean society and appears to have been resented and to have faced much internal opposition. Confident in his alliance with Antony, he had taken opportunities to remove all his political and dynastic rivals, including recalcitrant high priests from the Temple. He had also opportunistically extended his kingdom, and in so doing had clashed with the Arab princedom ruled by Malchus. It was a local war with Malchus that had delayed Herod from joining Antony at Actium. When news of Octavian's victory reached Herod, he killed the current high priest of the Temple, sent his own family into relative safety in his desert fortress at Masada, and set off to visit Octavian.

Octavian received Herod on Rhodes. When Herod entered Octavian's presence, he refused to behave as a supplicant and beg for mercy. He did not put on clothes of mourning or abase himself, but entered proud and in his finery. He did, however, remove his diadem, the mark of his kingship. He then spoke. He was, he claimed, a great friend of Antony. He would have been at Actium with him, but had been delayed by the Arab war. Nevertheless, he had sent Antony food and money. Herod was loyal to his friend and loyal to his benefactors. He was, he asserted, a man the powerful could trust. If Octavian would take him into his friendship, Herod would be loyal to his new friend.[1]

Herod (if the account is to be believed) dealt in political realia. The political equation for Eastern kings had been simple. It was still simple. The calculation for Octavian was also simple. If he was briefed properly, he would have known that Herod had many enemies in Judaea and that he had survived by periodic purges of those enemies. If Octavian killed him, there was no obvious successor (Herod had ensured this) and there was certainly a chance that Judaea would descend into civil war. Octavian preserved Herod, and Herod was to repay him generously. When Octavian came to Judaea, he was lavished with gifts, and Herod took care to spread the liberality to soldiers and any others who might support his cause. Herod's gratitude was worth far more than his head on a pole.

Octavian spent much of the late summer and winter of 31–30 in Asia Minor and Greece. It would seem likely that he was both laying plans for the final stages of the war against Antony and building relations with the Greek cities, the elites of which were anxious to ingratiate themselves with the new Caesar. Octavian's primary need was money, and the Greek cities found themselves paying for their prior friendship with Antony as they had paid Antony to secure his friendship. Gradually, however, Octavian and the Greek communities developed new and innovative political relations. A new political culture, a specifically imperial way of doing political business, began to operate in the East.

IN THE CITY OF ALEXANDER

The first signs of this new political culture emerged in Egypt. The defeat of Antony and Cleopatra and the subsequent death of Cleopatra brought an end to the dynasty. Octavian was never likely to have restored the Ptolemaic dynasty by appointing one of Cleopatra's children to the throne. The war had been too brutal and the propaganda too ferocious to allow him that option. He would, thus, have to reduce Egypt to a province. Such a process was conventional; Octavian would need to appoint a governor and make provisional arrangements in Egypt itself. Those arrangements would then be ratified by the senate and possibly by a law in Rome. But there was an important preliminary question to be settled: the fate of Alexandria.

Roman armies had a tradition of exemplary destruction. After the great wars of the past, some of the finest cities of the Mediterranean had been razed to the ground. Carthage had been destroyed, reduced to emptiness for a century. Corinth, one of the oldest and grandest urban settlements, had been similarly treated. Athens itself had been brutally sacked by Sulla's troops, bringing widespread destruction to this most historic of cities and extracting as much of its wealth as could be looted. In the West, Spanish and Gallic cities had suffered similar fates, their destruction more casually recorded in the sources. Many must have feared that Alexandria would have joined that roll of horror.

Alexandria was one the great cities of antiquity, great in its history, its architecture, its size (perhaps more 300,000 people), and its culture. It was the second largest city of the Mediterranean (after Rome). Destroying the city would have sent a message to Octavian's enemies and indeed to all the powers of the East and West. Later, in his imperial conquests, Octavian employed exemplary brutality. The war of Actium and Alexandria had been fought against an enemy whom Octavian had denigrated ferociously. The literature that was to circulate around Actium deployed cosmic imagery to suggest that the war had been fought between different gods and moralities and that it was a war for Roman and Italian culture. Much was made of the "threat" of Cleopatra and Egypt. Wiping out the great city of the Ptolemies had a logic to it. But this was not the road Octavian took; he spared the city.

Octavian gave three reasons for not destroying Alexandria. The first was respect for the god of the city. Serapis was an unusual deity in that he had both Greek and Egyptian attributes and is sometimes suspected of being an invention of the Ptolemaic dynasty, an artificial god for an artificial city. But Greeks and Egyptians believed in their gods, and although they might discover elements of the divine world and elaborate on mythic elements in stories, they did not consciously invent their deities. Serapis was complicated. The god is most often represented as similar to Zeus, with whom he was sometimes associated, but also to Apis the bull-god, worshipped in the old Egyptian capital of Memphis; Amun (a ram god); and Osiris, husband of Isis. Through these associations, Serapis played a role in the ruler cult in which the pharaoh had certain divine characteristics. The association of Antony with Osiris in at least some of his Egyptian representations shows that Romans were able to work within this repertoire of symbolic associations and were open to the idea of associating a man and the divine. Where Antony led, Octavian could follow.

The twinned cults of Isis and Serapis had also spread beyond Egypt. They reached Rome in the early first century B.C., and one of the first acts of the triumvirs had been to build a new temple to Isis and Serapis in Rome. We will never understand the full significance of Serapis to contemporary Romans, and the cult was clearly a matter of some controversy. It may have been a cult with appeal to populist elements in Roman culture, a cult of the plebs, and this would explain why Antony and Octavian had looked to sponsor it. Octavian, who would be confident that all his words and deeds would be rapidly transmitted back to Rome, found an interest in honoring the god, and in so doing established an association between himself and a god who, somewhat unusually for ancient deities, had a pan-Mediterranean appeal.

A second reason for sparing the city was his devotion to Alexander. The young Octavian had already made use of Alexander imagery. The youthful conqueror of the East was something of an obsession for contemporary Romans. We have two versions of an Alexander story in biographies of Julius Caesar. In 67 or 66, Caesar was in Spain, and in one version he was reading the life of Alexander the Great and burst into tears because Alexander had achieved so much by the time he was Caesar's age and Caesar had achieved so little. In the other version, the same sentiments were expressed but the feelings were inspired by Caesar's falling into a fit of melancholy on encountering a statue of Alexander in the city of Gades (modern Cádiz).[2]

The story is almost certainly untrue, a literary premonition of greatness, but it shows that Alexander was the standard against which the ambitious measured their success. Similarly, on his return from his conquests, Pompey the Great (and it is no coincidence that he took the name Magnus, "great") allowed portraits of himself to be made in which his round, somewhat corpulent face was topped with a slight tuft that recalled Alexander's hairstyle. Before Actium, Octavian was already experimenting with an image that associated the youthful triumvir with both Apollo and Alexander. After Actium, Alexander became a more suitable model for the still-young Roman, a conqueror clearly blessed by the gods, a man to whom the East had fallen, a king of notably and capricious violence, and an individual who had traversed the thin line between the greatest of men and the divine.

In Alexander's city, Octavian commissioned statues of himself in the very image of the great king. One of these is the so-called Meroe head (see fig. 7), now in the British Museum. The head shows Octavian as Alexander. Most of Alexander's portraits show him with his neck uncomfortably twisted, probably symbolizing some far-off focus on the divine, and with a distinctive slight tuft Octavian's head is similarly angled, and his hair is depicted with the hint of a tuft. We may assume that it is this image, repeatedly replicated, with which Octavian introduced himself to his Egyptian subjects as the new Alexander.

FIGURE 7
The Meroe head: The head depicts the young Octavian
as the successor of Alexander the Great.

When he was in Alexandria, Octavian went to visit the Sema, the tomb of Alexander and, indeed, of the Ptolemaic dynasty. The body was brought forth. It was enclosed in a sarcophagus, but Octavian had the sarcophagus opened so he could gaze on Alexander's face. Octavian laid a golden crown on the corpse and scattered flowers on the tomb. But Alexander had been dead for nearly 300 years, and even with the best of embalming techniques, the body was fragile. The new Alexander broke a chunk off the old Alexander's nose. The Alexandrians, perhaps somewhat nervously given the damage to their most precious of kingly relics, asked Octavian whether he would like to see the bodies of the Ptolemaic dynasty. Octavian replied that he had wished to see a king, not corpses.[3] The line was so good that he repeated it when he was asked whether he wished to visit the Apis bull (Egyptians, uniquely for classical cultures, used animals to personify their gods); he replied that he normally worshipped gods, not cattle.

The third reason for sparing Alexandria was Octavian's friendship with Areios. Most Roman aristocrats of the period were fluent in Greek culture, and since the middle of the second century B.C., and perhaps even earlier, Greek philosophers especially had been welcomed to Rome and had helped create an aristocratic cultural milieu. Philosophers would find themselves invited to stay with the rich and powerful and to engage in learned discussions in the luxurious houses and villas that were springing up in Southern Italy. A pet philosopher was as much a mark of elite status as fine gardens, Greek (or Greek-style) statuary, and educated speech. It is thus no surprise to find an Alexandrian philosopher in Octavian's circle, and it does warn us off from thinking about culture and conflict in this period in nationalistic terms. Areios displayed Octavian's learning to the Alexandrians, showing that he valued the traditions of Greek education and culture. Octavian was no barbarian conqueror.

Octavian explained all this in a speech to the people of Alexandria; one presumes that they had been briefed beforehand. He spoke to them in Greek. The choice of language was significant: Roman conquerors (like those of other imperial nations) expected the conquered to learn their language and tended to address the defeated in Latin. Speaking in Greek and honoring one of their own, Octavian sent a clear message: he was someone the Greeks could deal with. He was in the familiar tradition of Alexander the Great.

Octavian slipped rapidly into the existing traditions of rulership in Egypt. He may have claimed not to worship cattle, but in the temple of Buchis in Upper Egypt he is depicted worshipping the bull-god Buchis. The depiction was part of a sequence of inscriptions showing rulers sacrificing to the god that stretched over a thousand years. Roman money was invested in temples and cult sites. Octavian was depicted on temples in traditional pharaonic form. A document from the small Egyptian city of Oxyrhynchus dated to the "first year of Caesar" (30 or 29 B.C. in our terms) contains an oath to serve in a temple from four temple lamplighters. They swore by Caesar, god and son of a god.[4] Octavian had been using the title "son of the deified" since the deification of Julius Caesar. On his coinage, he appeared as "Caesar, son of the deified" (*divi filius*).

The lamplighters of Oxyrhynchus clearly knew this and incorporated the title into their traditional oath, but they also incorporated Octavian into their traditional system of rulership in which he was a god in his own right.

Octavian celebrated his rapprochement with the people of Alexandria by investing in their city. The best evidence for this comes not from Alexandria but from Rome. In the middle of St Peter's Square in the Vatican stands an obelisk. Originally the obelisk came from the Egyptian city of Heliopolis (City of the Sun), where it had stood for centuries with many others as an act of dedication to the sun. The obelisk was then moved to Alexandria; it was removed from Alexandria and sent to Rome, probably by the emperor Caligula, and much later moved to the center of St Peter's Square. Detailed examination revealed various holes which had been used to pin bronze letters to the obelisk. The inscription would have read:

> By the order of the Imperator Caesar, son of the Deified, Gaius Cornelius, son of Gnaeus, Gallus, Praefectus Fabrum of Caesar, son of the Deified, made the Julian Forum.

Cornelius Gallus is a figure to whom we will return presently. He had led troops from the West into Egypt in 30 and rendered Octavian the service of distracting Antony from Octavian's own invasion.

The Julian Forum in Alexandria, the building of which probably dates to 30–29, was the centerpiece of a major civic remodeling in the city with which we can associate another landmark building of the period, the Caesareum. Originally, the temple was probably designed by Cleopatra to honor her lover and the father of one of her children, Julius Caesar. It was thus an Alexandrian equivalent to the temple of Divus Julius that Octavian was constructing in Rome. But the Caesareum was to become the temple of all Caesars, associating the deified Caesar with his successor.

Octavian was treading a path between divine and human, drawing on a number of traditions of ruler cult in the East—notably that of Egypt, but also the cultic associations of much of the Hellenized East—and on

Roman religious traditions that invoked Romulus and Aeneas, both founders of Rome and both gods in their own rights, and which had been revived in the deification of Julius Caesar. The lamplighters of Oxyrhynchus were not eccentric conservatives who failed to understand the new Roman regime and its different *mores*, but were in keeping with the mood of the times in swearing their oath by the new god Caesar.

In either late 30 or early 29, Octavian set out for Rome. Instead of sailing direct, he made steady progress around the Mediterranean and was met by embassies from various communities in Asia Minor. The people of Ephesus and Nicaea requested the right to dedicate temples to Roma (the personification of the city of Rome) and Julius Caesar. The people of Pergamum and Nicomedia requested permission to consecrate temples to Octavian himself (probably in association with Roma). The people of Pergamum also received permission to hold sacred games in honor of Octavian. Quasi-divine honors such as these had been granted before, notably to Hellenistic kings and to some Roman governors, but nothing quite so organized and thorough as what was now developing.[5]

For moderns raised within the great monotheistic traditions, worshipping a man seems perverse, a sign of the corruption of pagan traditions and religions. For the ancients, it made sense. There were traditions of men becoming gods, most notably Hercules. The gods were generally held to be among men regularly. Everyone had a spirit, which had something of the divine about it. In Egypt, the pharaoh had been a personification of a divine spirit, which was akin to being a god. Similar ideas had circulated in the Near East for centuries: kings had a special relationship with the divine, and that was why they were kings. Yet, and in spite of all these precursors to ruler cult, allowing oneself to be worshipped and taking the attributes of the divine was a radical step. In so doing, Octavian was announcing that he was different from all previous representatives of Roman power.

Rome had long had close relations with the communities of the East, who must have understood very well how Rome worked: Rome was not, after all, very different constitutionally from a Greek city-state. Rome was ruled by a council (the senate) of aristocrats of roughly equivalent status. Yet, in the invention of honors that followed the defeat of Antony, the cities were recognizing an indisputable political fact: Octavian was not like the other senators. Nor was he like the kings who had ruled the East in the centuries after Alexander. Octavian was special. He was a god. Although the various embassies were sent from the councils of the Eastern cities, and thus the impetus behind such honors would appear to have come from the cities themselves, it is difficult to believe that the different communities came up with similar ideas and acted in similar ways without some discreet prompting or encouragement from the regime.

With his power confirmed, the East fervent in its displays of loyalty, and loaded with the wealth of Egypt, Octavian crossed the Adriatic and returned to Italy. The senate had had nearly two years since Actium to prepare for the victor's return. They were ready to respond with appropriate rapture.

CELEBRATING VICTORY

The senators proved inventive in honoring Octavian. In the immediate aftermath of Actium and the capture of Alexandria, they competed to pass resolutions of honor and praise. He was voted a triumph for his defeat of Cleopatra. A victory arch was to be erected at Brundisium, from which he had set off on his war and to which he would return. The arch was to be decorated by trophies which displayed arms captured during the war. Another arch was to be built in the Forum at Rome. The temple of the Deified Julius (perhaps still under construction) was to be adorned with prows from the ships captured at Actium. A festival was to be held every five years in honor of Octavian. Details are lacking, but we would expect that it would include prayers and sacrifices, games (probably gladiatorial), and theatrical events, all of which thanked the gods. Octavian's birthday was to be a day of thanksgiving (more public sacrifices). The day when his victory was announced was also to be another day of thanks. For his return to the city, it was decreed that the Vestal Virgins, the senators, and all the people of Rome (including children) would go to meet him on the road. Senate and people were to be seen to be united in expressing their gratitude to Octavian.[6] The day of the fall of Alexandria was declared a lucky day, and the Alexandrians were ordered to restart the calendar from that day, as obvious a declaration of a new era as one could have.

There were some slight constitutional adjustments. Octavian was given some of the powers of the tribunes. The choice of tribunician powers was significant. The tribunes were the defenders of the rights and privileges of the Roman plebs. Octavian was to be their new representative. In the courts, he was to have the deciding vote. In religious ceremonies, priests were to add his names when asking for blessings on the senate and people of Rome; Octavian had become the third element of the state. The authorities decreed that at public and private dinners everyone was to pour a libation for Octavian. These were honors without precedent.

In the summer of 29, Octavian returned to Rome and there was yet another round of honors. Octavian's name was to be included in the public hymns alongside the gods. He was to be allowed to wear a crown such as was worn by those holding a triumph on all festival occasions. He was allowed to appoint priests to the sacred colleges even if there were no vacancies. The senate also closed the doors of the temple of Janus. This last ceremonial marked an end to war.[7] The city came to meet Octavian (though he had asked that the people be excused the duty). The consul sacrificed oxen in honor of his return, another unprecedented religious act. Octavian spoke to the people. Every adult man was given 400 sesterces as a gift, certainly more than enough to support a man for a year. He praised Agrippa, his admiral. He gave gifts to the troops. He also gave money to the children of Rome on behalf of his nephew Marcellus, aged 12 or 13 at the time. The association was the first hint that Octavian was envisaging a dynasty. Octavian refused the gold crowns that the peoples of Italy had collected for him, but even so, Rome was flooded with money. Not only were there the gifts offered by Octavian to the people, but the soldiers returning with him had the wealth of Egypt burning holes in their purses. Interest rates are said to have fallen from the normal 12 percent to 4 percent, and the price of goods rose.[8]

Octavian was granted the position of *princeps senatus*, first man of the senate, in 28, which meant that his opinion would be called for first in senatorial debates. The title *princeps*," meaning "first man," was an old one. The leading men of the senate were sometimes known as *principes*, the first men of the state. It was mainly an honorific title and carried with it no power. But later, certainly by the end of the reign of Augustus, the title came to have greater significance. Augustus's position was constructed around a range of powers and titles, but there was no one title that defined what he was. The word we use, "emperor," comes from the military acclamation of a successful general as *imperator*, which had a fairly narrow set of associations. *Princeps* emerged as an informal way of acknowledging his preeminence, and the term *principatus* ("principate") came to be used by Romans to describe both the period of leadership of an individual (what we would call a "reign") and the system of government established by the early emperors.[9]

And then Octavian held his triumphal celebrations. For three days, he and his troops marched through the city, offering sacrifices and displaying their loot. The first day was taken up by a triumph granted for campaigns in Dalmatia conducted in 35–34; Octavian had never had the leisure to hold his celebratory procession. The second day was devoted to Actium. It seems likely that posters depicting the victory were carried through the city. The third day was to celebrate the Egyptian victory. The centerpiece should have been Cleopatra in chains, but they had to make do with an effigy. Her twins by Antony, Alexander Helios and Cleopatra Selene, were marched through the city. Her son by Caesar, Caesarion, was, of course, dead. Traditionally, the captives would have been executed at the end of the procession, but Octavian showed clemency. The wealth of Egypt was carried in carts for the people to see. Then Octavian himself rode through the city, followed by his fellow consul and the senators.[10] It seems likely that technically Octavian celebrated two triumphs, the Dalmatian triumph and the Alexandrian triumph, and since celebrating victories in a civil war was in bad taste, the middle day was simply a procession. But very quickly, the technicality seems to have been forgotten.[11]Octavian was not finished. He dedicated a temple of Minerva. The senate house, which had probably been undergoing renovation for some time, was now opened and renamed the Curia Iulia after Julius Caesar, an irony which was surely not lost on contemporaries. The Curia was given an old wooden statue of Victory that had been taken from the city of Tarentum. The statue was adorned by spoils from Egypt. At each meeting of the senate, libations were poured to the goddess, and the senators would be reminded of Octavian's defeat of Antony. More of the wealth of Egypt ended up in the temple of the Deified Julius, located in the heart of the old Roman Forum, which was now completed and consecrated. Other items went to the oldest and most revered temple in Rome, that of Jupiter Capitolinus, and still more was sent to temples of Juno and Minerva.

Octavian also held victory games on a lavish scale. Wild and domestic animals were slaughtered in the arena, including a hippopotamus and a rhinoceros, neither of which had been seen in Rome before. Roman aristocrats took part in the races in the hippodrome. One senator fought as a gladiator. Octavian staged a battle between captured Suebians (Germans) and Dacians (from north of the Danube).[12] He even invented a new form of entertainment, the Lusus Troiae ("Trojan games"), at which aristocratic youths competed in equestrian events.

Nothing like this had ever been seen in Rome. The scale of the events, of the buildings, of the triumphs, of the games, of the gifts to the people, of the honors granted and received were unprecedented and marked out the return from the East as a major historical event.

The lavish games and the equally lavish honors sent messages to the politicians and people of Rome. After Actium and the deaths of Antony and Cleopatra, Octavian was without question the political master of Rome, but his next move was unpredictable, and there was every reason to be fearful. There was a possibility that Octavian would launch a fresh purge on his return, as others had done before him. The voting of lavish honors was not so much a mark of thanks to the victor as a sign of insecurity. The senators were desperate to assert their loyalty. But Octavian was also sending reassuring messages to the senators and to the people of Rome. Perhaps the most important symbolic act was to close the doors of the temple of Janus. Traditionally, the doors were opened when the Roman people went to war, and in fact the doors of the temple had only rarely been shut over the previous centuries. The closure symbolized a new era of peace. We cannot know whose decision it was to close the temple (or whether it was negotiated), but it suited both parties, expressing a fervent hope that the time of war was over and that there could be a resumption of normality.

Yet, if there was a reassurance in the end of war, the past was not truly forgotten. Octavian did not suddenly drop his violent radicalism. Notably, Octavian cemented his relationship with the plebs with his generous gifts, leaving them in no doubt that he was their protector and benefactor. Nor did he draw a veil over his victories and the violence that had divided Roman society, which might have provided the losers with a chance to mourn. Instead, Rome was to unite in the celebration of victory. The triumphs were one aspect, perhaps easily ignored by the disaffected, but the continuous replaying of the victories in the days of thanksgiving, the marking of the day in the calendar, and the monumentalizing of the victories in Rome meant that Actium and Alexandria could neither be forgotten nor ignored. The senators also required ordinary Romans to make offerings for Octavian at their private banquets. The rule may not have been enforceable, but one can only imagine what those mourning the dead of Actium thought of being required to make offerings on behalf of the man responsible for the deaths of their loved ones.

One of the oddities of Octavian's Rome was the presence of Cleopatra. While there was some attempt to obliterate the memory of Antony, Cleopatra remained within the monumental heart of the city. She was there in the Egyptian artefacts, in the buildings and in their ornamentation, in the prows of ships that lay before the temple of the Deified Julius. She was represented in the donations to the temples, which added further grandeur to some of the most significant sites of Roman religion. She was there in the public proclamations of the poets. Most notably, Octavian did not remove her from the temple of Venus. Caesar's temple of Venus Genetrix, Venus the Mother, retained its golden cult statue, and everyone knew that when they stared at the face of Venus, they were looking at Cleopatra. She was not to be forgotten. Octavian would not allow her to be forgotten, and because of her importance in the presentation of the regime, she became something of a wicked stepmother of empire, her career justifying the authoritarian regime that Octavian was to develop and the fiercely moralizing stance that the regime adopted in later years.

Yet, if Cleopatra's presence in Rome was striking, it was Octavian's personality that dominated the new city. Many of the honors granted to him were religious. His name was included in hymns. Offerings were made for him. On the Palatine hill, Octavian was building himself a new house. The house was integrally connected to a new temple of Apollo, Octavian's favored deity, to whom the victory at Actium was attributed. This temple was opened to great acclaim in 28.[13] The white marble columns of the hillside were a victory monument in themselves and provided a new home for the god. The temple of Vesta was also incorporated into the new complex. It took little imagination to think of the Palatine as housing three gods, Apollo, Vesta, and Octavian.

On the Campus Martius, Agrippa was constructing a magnificent new temple, the Pantheon. It was dedicated in 27, in Agrippa's third consulship. The original idea had been to have a statue of Octavian at the center of the temple. It would thus have been a temple to a living man, a clear sign that the Romans were expected to acknowledge their young master as a god. Already, there were some statues to Octavian around the city in gold and silver, metals normally reserved for statues of the gods. The statues had been dedicated by Octavian's friends and by the peoples of the empire.[14]

The Roman Republic was a republic of citizens. Its political culture emphasized equality. This equality was to modern eyes peculiarly hierarchic: the leading men of the state were "more equal" than others, and the population was grouped into various orders. But there was at least a myth of equality that was formally recognized. The senators also, for all their divisions and internal status competitions, were meant to operate as a collective, honoring each other and their individual achievements, advising, cooperating, and working together for the benefit of Rome. Of course, some people had become great, possibly even too great. But Octavian was different again. He was not like the others, not even like Marius, Sulla, Pompey, or Caesar. That further elevation left the Romans struggling for an appropriate political language, and it is perhaps unsurprising that they adopted the language of the divine and that Octavian chose to experiment with this imagery. Octavian assumed the role of a god among men. In the presence of a god, the basic premises of the Republic were redundant, since there was no one who could claim to be his equal or even aspire to equality.

Living with a god can be difficult, and being a god presents its own challenges, as the reign of the emperor Caligula was to prove two generations later. In 28–27, Octavian began to modify his position. The Pantheon became a temple to all the gods. The statue of Octavian was placed not in the center of the temple but in its entrance, and it was matched by a statue of the temple's builder, Agrippa. The gold and silver statues were melted down and turned into coin. The imagery of divinity, so prominent in the immediate aftermath of Actium and in Octavian's negotiations in the East, suddenly slipped into the background.

Octavian was reinventing himself, accepting some of the concerns of tradition, looking for partners in power (even if only Agrippa in the first instance), and paying lip service at least to the notions of equality. It is difficult to believe that Octavian changed tack voluntarily. In spite of his victories and his political dominance and the dead who littered his history and the monuments with which he displayed his power and reshaped the city, Octavian met resistance in Rome. Not everyone was as grateful to the new Caesar as the official proclamations would have us believe. Octavian also had to face the fundamental problem of how his career would develop and continue. The triumvirate had expired. Antony and Lepidus were dead. Rome could continue in its state of emergency and Octavian could rule with absolute power in the fiction that he was working to restore the Republic, but it would be a very obvious fiction. If he was to normalize politics in Rome and secure his own position, he needed to establish some sort of new order. The same conundrum that had arisen after earlier periods of civil disturbance arose in 28. Almost in default of other options, Octavian was being pressed toward a restoration. After all that had happened, the Republic was clearly dead, but resurrection still seemed a possibility.

THE REPUBLIC REVIVED

Even in 30, there were signs of opposition to Octavian in Rome. But whereas a few years earlier, one might have expected voices to be raised in the senate house or prominent politicians to have made absolutely clear their opposition to the regime by publicly and loudly removing themselves from the city, the opposition to Octavian was driven underground. While the public proclamations of the political class were of unfailing loyalty and friendship, no one was truly deceived. Of course, identifying the dissidents is difficult. If we imagine that some were brave enough to make explicit their views (though they are not recorded in the tradition), others carefully cloaked their politics, making use of opportunities to discomfort the regime where possible. We can only detect hints of the deals and disputes by which the new regime made its way and almost nothing of the anger that likely animated the political relationships of the new regime.

In 30 or thereabouts, Marcus Lepidus was disappeared. He was accused of conspiring with Junia, sister of Brutus, to assassinate Caesar on his return to Rome. The involvement of Junia connects the supposed plot to the republican assassins, suggesting a desire to rid Rome of a tyrant. Lepidus was the son of the triumvir, also Marcus Lepidus, who had been living in internal exile since Octavian extracted him from his legions in 36. Lepidus was Pontifex Maximus, effectively the highest priest of Rome, and seems to have been a focus for Octavian's contempt until his death, probably in 12 B.C.[15] The younger Lepidus was a significant political figure, probably offended by the way in which his father was being treated, and Junia, though a woman, had importance from her family name and her historical associations. Lepidus was killed, perhaps even without trial, detected in his conspiracy by Octavian's representative in Rome, Maecenas. The fate of Junia is not known.[16]

A second episode is more complex. In 30 or 29, the Roman general Marcus Licinius Crassus was campaigning in Macedonia. Crassus was the son of the prominent Roman politician of the same name who had been the ally of Pompey and Caesar. He was fighting a number of tribes—the Bastarnae, the Moesians, and the Getae. In the battle against the Bastarnae, Crassus found himself personally engaged, which was unusual from a Roman general, and he killed the opposing king, Deldo. This was an almost unheard-of achievement, and qualified Crassus for a special honor, the *spolia opima*. Octavian attempted to block the award.

Octavian used a technicality. Crassus had been appointed to his governorship by Octavian, and legally the power to govern the province had been delegated to him. Octavian alleged that only those who battled under their own authority were eligible for the *spolia opima*. This sent people scurrying to the history books and they found an exception. Back in the mists of Roman legend, the *spolia opima* had been awarded to a man called Cossus. All authorities claimed that Cossus was a tribune who would have been under the control of a senior magistrate. Octavian was overseeing the repair of the Temple of Jupiter Feretrius in Rome where the spoils had supposedly been dedicated, and the reconstruction turned up a linen cloth on which it was written that Cossus had dedicated the *spolia opima* while consul. Few would have believed the conveniently discovered document, certainly not the historian Livy, but no one could accuse Octavian of forgery.[17]

The anecdote shows us that Octavian was insecure. He was concerned that this scion of the Roman aristocracy would have an honor that he did not. Crassus was clearly neither an opponent nor a realistic rival. He had been entrusted with a major command and appointed personally by Octavian. Still, Octavian could tolerate no competition in his effort to monopolize honors.

In 28, Octavian embarked on a process of normalizing his own position. He took the consulship together with Agrippa. He had been consul throughout the years of emergency of 31, 30, and 29. For much of that period Octavian had been away from Rome, and the consul who had remained in Rome had had to do much of the work of the city by himself. After his return to the city, however, Octavian appears to have largely ignored his colleague in office. Each consul was attended by lictors, who carried the fasces (the rods and axe) which represented the consular imperative to discipline Roman citizens, but in his sequence of consulships since 31 Octavian had insisted that all the lictors accompany him. The measure accurately reflected the imbalance of power within the supposedly collegial magistracy, but it was also tokenistic: Octavian was displaying his monopoly of power. This now changed.

In 28, instead of having all the lictors wait upon him, the old custom was restored. Agrippa was Octavian's fellow consul both for this year and for 27, and from January of 28, half the lictors went to Agrippa. The restoration of the lictors was constitutionally and legally meaningless, but symbolic; it was a step toward more normal politics. Sometime in 28, Octavian declared an end to the emergency that had beset the Roman state for more than a decade.[18]

Technically, the emergency was associated with the triumviral period in which the three men had taken powers to reconstitute the Republic, but once the triumvirate had lapsed, the legal basis of the emergency was unclear, perhaps resting in Octavian's consular power, perhaps in the decrees of the senate against Antony. In fact, it seems unlikely that anyone really cared. But in 28, Octavian began the process of ending the emergency. Civic rights were restored. The restoration was celebrated on a golden coin (see fig. 8). The coin showed the consul with a box of scrolls at his feet, handing one of them out to a grateful citizen. On one side of the coin, the legend reads "Imperator Caesar, son of the Deified, in his sixth consulship." On the other side, the coin reads "He restores the laws and rights of the Roman people." There is no mention of Agrippa, either as consul or as an active partner in the political actions. Octavian was still not prepared to have anyone share his position at the forefront of Roman politics, even his most trusted associate. But the restoration of laws meant that there were to be no more extrajudicial killings. There were to be no more confiscations of property. The time of war was over. One must presume that the triumvirs' tasks were finally complete.

In his final testament to the Roman people, *Res Gestae Divi Augusti* (The Acts of the Deified Augustus), published in A.D. 14 as a funerary monument, the emperor was to conclude the account of his career by drawing attention to these events.

> In my sixth and seventh consulships, after I had extinguished civil wars, when by universal consent I had control over all things, I transferred the Republic from my control to the judgment of the senate and people of Rome.[19]

Octavian and Agrippa had first to ensure that the Republic was in a fit state to take over the running of "all things." They held a census in which

FIGURE 8

The Aureus of 28 B.C.: This gold coin was issued by Octavian to commemorate his restoration of the laws and rights of the Roman people.

the Roman people were counted (4,063,000 citizens).[20] There was a ceremonial purification of the Roman people. Octavian and Agrippa also revised the senatorial rolls.

There may have been more than a thousand senators in 28. Some of these men had found their way into the senate through traditional means, having served in the junior magistracies. But others had been directly appointed into the senate as political favors. Some may have secured places under Caesar, others under the triumvirs. Octavian let it be known that he was examining the qualifications of those sitting in the senate and sought voluntary retirements. Some, for whatever reason, obliged. Octavian and Agrippa then asked senators to vouch for each other's worth, in the hope that some would find themselves embarrassed and withdraw. Finally, the two of them directly supervised the rolls and removed those whom they felt were not to standard.

The procedures were designed so as not to seem partisan, but they were controversial. Those removed were offended. Octavian supposedly put on a breastplate when presiding over the senate and had ten friends act as bodyguards. Many of those removed had owed their status to services provided to Octavian or to Caesar, and their rejection at this point was a betrayal.[21] But Octavian and Agrippa felt it was important that the senate should recover some of its former prestige, and they were prepared to risk unpopularity and sacrifice some of their supporters in the process.

In January of 27, Octavian came to the senate. He laid down his consulship and took the traditional oath that he had behaved justly and abided by the laws. He had previously avoided taking the oath, since the laws had not applied to him. Then, before the newly restored senators, he took up his seventh consulship. Agrippa was his colleague, taking his third consulship.

On January 13, he spoke to the senators. This was a key moment. If the surviving accounts are to be believed, it marked the next and final stage of the normalization of Roman politics. Octavian laid down his control over the provinces of the empire. The senate and people were now to decide on the provincial governors. Through these acts, Octavian relinquished control of the vast armies at his disposal and the wealth of the empire. The senators reacted by granting him new honors. An oak wreath was to be displayed on his new house, a distinction given to those who saved the lives of citizens. The doors of his house had laurel trees planted alongside them; laurel was the symbol of Apollo, but also of victory. A golden shield was displayed in the senate house to proclaim the four cardinal virtues of Octavian: *virtus* (virtue/manliness/courage), *clementia* (mercy), *iustitia* (justice), and *pietas* (dutifulness).[22]

Octavian had almost certainly prepared the ground for this announcement. He and Agrippa had been working toward this day for at least a year. But it was not exactly a fix. Not everything was decided on that day, and three days later, the senate convened again. At this debate, the settlement was detailed. Octavian was given control over most of Spain, Gaul, Germany, Syria, Cyprus, Egypt, Phoenice (modern Lebanon and coastal Syria), and Cilicia (in eastern Turkey). With some significant exceptions, these were the major military provinces of the empire. The exceptions were Macedonia, Dalmatia, and Africa (modern Tunisia). The senators responded to this settlement with yet another honor. They gave Octavian a new name. On January 16, the boy who had been born Octavius and had reached maturity as Caesar became Augustus.[23]

The events of 28–27, culminating in the January settlement , were a refiguring of Octavian's power. The extraordinary powers of the triumviral period were laid aside, the senate was reformed, and the laws were given force once more. This was institutionally a thorough restoration of republican governance. Octavian recognized and restored the sovereignty of the senate and people. The senate responded with lavish honors. Still, the events remain paradoxical. There was never any intention that the newly named Augustus would step aside and retire from the political fray. He remained the dominant figure in Roman politics. He had a huge provincial command. He continued as consul, and was to hold the consulship every year until laying down the office in June of 23 B.C.

In retrospect and from antiquity onwards, many, including the historian Cassius Dio, have seen the January debates of 27 as marking the birth of empire.[24] Yet Dio also saw the paradox of dating the formation of the monarchy to the moment of celebration of the restoration of the Republic. The reality was more complex and messy, as politics so often is. The restoration of the Republic, meaning the traditional style and mechanisms of Roman government, was real enough, but it took a decade or more for the Roman political class to work out how to operate in the paradoxical situation of the restored Republic with a single dominant figure. In January of 27, the Romans invented Augustus. Over the next years, they had to understand the implications of what they had achieved.

14.

THE AUGUSTAN REPUBLIC

A S THE SENATORS MADE their way home after the historic events of January 16, 27 B.C., they might have been forgiven for wondering what, in the end, they had achieved. The events of the previous three days had a marked a restoration of the traditions of Roman politics and thus of the Republic, and yet Augustus remained an anomaly, no more compatible with the conservative traditions of Roman political culture than his adoptive father had been.

At one level, the solution looked like a repetition of history. The crises of the last century of the Republic had shaken Rome, but after each crisis the Roman political system had restored itself in a recognizably similar form. The key elements of Roman political culture were the sovereignty of the people and the dominance of the aristocracy. The Roman revolution had challenged that hierarchy. The soldiers had overthrown the Republic and terrorized the aristocracy. Many of those aristocrats had been killed; others had been deprived of their property. The triumviral period had seen an enormous redistribution of wealth within Roman Italy as well as very large-scale movements of population as colonies of veterans were sent out. By 30, Octavian had stood at the heart of a political network which controlled vast resources. He was undisputed master of the Mediterranean world.

Augustus may have been the dominant figure, but there were practical questions as to how Rome could be governed. He continued to rely on the landed aristocracy to officer his army, to act as priests, to serve in the courts on juries, to administer the city, and to act as junior magistrates.

The concentration of power in his hands was such that it was possible that he could have swept away the accumulated traditions of five centuries of republican governance and started again with a blank page, but Augustus was a traditional Roman, brought up in a conservative, hierarchic culture. Rome was not just a city, but it was also that conservative culture and tradition. To sweep away the senate and its traditions would have entailed the end of the order with which Rome was inextricably associated and would be the equivalent to establishing Rome afresh, as a new city, free of the old traditions and also its glorious past. A new Rome was not unthinkable, but it was perhaps that prospect that led to some turning against Antony. In the first century B.C., with Rome as the political, cultural, religious, and economic center of a great empire, shifting to a new city would be a radical act, imaginable, but very unlikely.

However, the Roman political imaginary was not completely conservative. If the history of Rome itself did not provide her leaders with the ideas they required, they could always look to the Greek world and its varied histories of city-states, confederations, and kingdoms. The Romans had experienced, if only remotely, foreign traditions of government that they could potentially adapt and reinvent for their own purposes. To a great extent, that is what we start to see with the Augustan experimentation with divine imagery. The experiment drew on traditions of divine monarchy from Egypt, Persia, and the Hellenistic kingdoms, but it was unlike all of those traditions: it was new, distinct, and Roman, and was to develop a peculiar ideology and infrastructure all of its own. Roman monarchy was more absolute and violent, and less bound by rules of decorum. It was also in many respects antitraditional. In 27, in the center of Rome, surrounded by the monuments of the city, the built environment of tradition, before the ranks of the senators in their brilliant white togas, fringed with those purple bands, before the gods and their ancient temples, could Augustus have dared envisage a whole new way of being Roman?

There is precious little evidence that Augustus was an innovative thinker, an ideological mastermind moving his political pieces across the board. Ancient historians like to imagine him plotting and planning his new state, perhaps even sitting with his closest advisors, Agrippa and

Maecenas, and engaging in abstract discussion as to how to run Rome. Yet, like most other revolutionaries, he was bound by the past and tried to find solutions to contemporary difficulties from that past. Like most other politicians, he muddled through, seeking particular solutions for particular issues. Like most peoples, the Romans needed to be secure in their political life and to be reassured in the times of uncertainty. Revolutions were difficult, since the world was turned upside down and the traditions on which people relied to navigate their way through social and political life came into question. People had an urge for certainty, but certainty could only come from having a social and political order they understood, and that meant an order familiar from history. Augustus promised the Roman people peace. That meant not just an end to civil wars (symbolized by the closing of the doors of the temple of Janus and the various triumphal celebrations), but an end to social disorder.

But the contradictions in the political situation in 28–27 were obvious. The problems that Augustus faced were new and systemic. They could not be ignored, nor could they be wished away. As a result, the modes of politics that emerged in answer to those problems were themselves revolutionary. The Roman revolution was nothing if not pragmatic. The revolution stemmed not from a grand utopian vision but from the power relations at the heart of Roman society. The breaking of senatorial power by the military made possible the rule of the triumvirs. The political leadership was faced with a set of particular and intensely practical problems as to how to meet the demands of their supporters and maintain their own power. Those practical problems drove their experimentations with non-Roman ways of representing their power and of governance; the differences between how Antony and Octavian worked their political relationships were far less striking than their similarities.

Nevertheless, Octavian was gradually drawn back into a more conservative mode; restoration became the central element of the new regime's program, whether restoration of temples, political institutions, or morals. Augustus associated himself with a conservative political culture. Almost ever since the Augustan age, conservative thinkers have been tempted to take the Augustan program at face value, to read into the new name a new start, and to disassociate the conservative Augustan regime from the violence of Octavian's rule. In the light of the moral conservatism, it is easy to ignore the paradox at the heart of the state. Augustus may have said traditional words and enacted traditional rules, but his very presence at the center of politics and his power to act and speak in such a way were against all tradition. Modern historians can seemingly forget the man and his history, the political context that underlay his power, and focus on his later actions. It is difficult to believe that contemporary Romans could have suffered such amnesia.

The republican restoration of 28–27 was the first stage of this new conservative policy. For Octavian to revive the old political culture, he had to restore the majesty of the senate. For the system to work, the senate needed to support and advise the consuls and to give moral weight to their actions. That could only happen if the senate had authority itself. But giving the senators authority and restoring their power inevitably threw the position of Augustus into question. Although the restoration of the senators' power was necessary for the Augustan regime, the greatest obstacle to the restoration of senatorial power was Augustan power.

The most profound challenge to the regime lay in this paradox. Augustus needed to resolve his own position. His dominance had no parallel within the traditions of Roman political history, and he had no intention of following Sulla who, after his conservative reform of the state, had stepped down from office. In January of 28, Octavian's rule was based in the unclear but absolute authority of the emergency. In reality, it stemmed from military power and popular support. The emergency gave him legal powers which were above the traditions of the law, even though that legal power was exercised through the institution of the consulship. With the declaration of the end of the emergency, those powers became anomalous. In the circumstances of victory, unusual powers are unjustifiable, a paradox that has beset many dictatorial and authoritarian regimes. In the transformation to Augustus, those legal powers were laid aside. In practical terms, however, Augustan power depended not on law but on money and the potential for violence. The constitutional adjustments had little effect on the realities of power.

Law had been a traditional means of providing a regime with legitimacy. Since the regime could not rely upon law to justify and explain Augustan power, legitimacy was claimed by reference to Augustus's specific personal qualities. It was these personal qualities which elevated Augustus above the norms of senatorial equality. It is in this light that we must understand the symbols of honor given to Augustus: the marks of distinction for his house, his association with the gods, and the shield in the senate house which celebrated his particular virtues. Augustus himself noted the change when he claimed that after 27 he held power in the same manner as other magistracies and his powers did not exceed those of his several colleagues in those magistracies, but that he had *auctoritas* ("authority").[1] *Auctoritas* was a political quality, but also a personal virtue. Augustan justification of his rule moved from a political-legal-violent representation of power to become a moral claim, residing in the personal authority of the man.

Augustan rule was institutionalized in the holding of successive consulships. There had been repeated consulships before, notably those of Marius in the late second century, but those were always held in a situation of emergency. The exceptional qualities of Marius and the needs of the Roman state justified the innovation. The threat to Rome was somewhat less obvious in 27, and hence the justification for Augustus's repeated consulships was not clear. The post-emergency excuse for Augustan hegemony could only be his exceptional moral and leadership qualities, but the very essence of the senatorial system was the sharing of magistracies and the equality of the senators (within their own hierarchy). Augustus remained an uncomfortable and anomalous presence.

Yet, the personalization of politics had other implications. If Augustus had a personal moral authority, that authority needed to be displayed through his moral discipline and his leadership. Augustus continued to stress those moral-political qualities throughout his reign, primarily through excellence in the military arena, but he also extended his leadership into all spheres of Roman life, including religious life and the family. The new order of Augustan Rome required discipline and needed to excise those elements of disorder that had brought chaos over the previous century. Only thorough social reform would return peace to the people of Rome.

But there would be a price for such peace, and it was a price the Augustan regime was reluctant to divulge to its critics. The new disciplines of the Augustan regime worked against traditional freedoms. It was and is an uncomfortable political reality that a certain amount of disorder is integral to the working of a (pseudo-) democratic system. The playing out of politics in the Republican period was disorderly; elections were hard-fought; elite competition could be vicious and personal. To take disorder out of the system was to remove an essential element of traditional politics. Peace and order could be secured. The price, though, was the end of freedom and the dominance of Augustus.

A MILITARY REGIME?

If traditional Roman political history had tended to emphasize the play of relations within the aristocracy, other forces retained a key presence in Roman political life. The senators conducted these negotiations surrounded by the new monuments of victory and continuously aware (as if they could ever forget) of the fate that had befallen Octavian's enemies. But more telling was that Augustus retained control over the army.

Augustus was given control of a range of provinces, in the majority of which there were significant military forces. The justification for retaining what was a very large army was the necessity of fighting in these various provinces, and Augustus had the prestige and military experience to lead these wars. Of course, he could not be in all these provinces at once, and he ruled many through legates, hand-picked loyalists to whom he could entrust these key forces. Nevertheless, Augustus and Agrippa and later the key male figures in the Augustan family spent much of their time with the Roman legions in the provinces, and Augustus maintained power over this key constituency.

The demands on the soldiers were great. The 28 legions, 140,000 Roman males, were required to serve away from Italy not just for a few years but for the full term that could be required of them, 16 years. Their reward was regular pay and irregular bonuses, though these last were to be systematized later in the reign. With a census population of just over 4,000,000, somewhere around 11 percent of Roman manpower was serving in the legions at any one time. It was these men who were the most direct beneficiaries of Augustan rule, and if we add to those 140,000 the veterans discharged from the army and given generous settlements in the aftermath of the various civil wars, we have a military constituency both numerous and powerful.

The legions were not the only troops at Augustus's disposal. His first act after the settlement of 27 was to institute a guard paid twice as much as the ordinary legionaries and based in Italy. The praetorian guard had existed long before. Republican generals had a personal guard to protect them. Julius Caesar had made extensive use of a large personal guard. It seems likely that the Augustan praetorians numbered about 5,000 men. It was thus a significant military force. Although the number of troops actually stationed in Rome was quite small, since Augustus dispersed them into various camps in Italian cities, it was not normal for a consul to have any soldiers to call upon. The troops were thus a visible reminder of the origins of Augustan power and of the continued importance of the military within Roman politics.[2]

The events of January 27 marked the resumption of the normal processes of Roman politics, but the politics that resumed could not be normal. The mechanisms of Rome's politics and much of its culture remained republican, dominated by tradition and the values of the aristocracy. Power, though, remained firmly in the hands of Augustus. Nevertheless, this paradox at the heart of the regime provided a space for political debate. The regime's political methodology required adherence to the old rules and playing the old game, so that Augustus would be seen not to be a tyrant. But the old rules made obvious the friction between the idea of a restored Republic and a Republic dominated by Augustus. If the senators walking away from the senate house in January 27 were uncertain as to what had been achieved and about the nature of the new political order, it was this very uncertainty that made politics possible.

THE POLITICS OF THE RESTORED REPUBLIC

Late in 27 B.C., Augustus left Rome to embark on the task of administering his provinces. He journeyed first to Gaul with the intention of launching an invasion of Britain.[3] But the plans for the invasion were, for some reason, put on hold. Instead, Augustus conducted a census in Gaul. At the end of the year, Augustus left Gaul and went to Spain, where he remained until 24, leading a campaign in the Pyrenees. In spite of being consul throughout the period, he never found it necessary to visit Italy.[4] Once the war was over, he discharged at least some of the troops and established a colony in Spain.

While Augustus was away, his business in Italy appears to have been largely conducted by Agrippa. Agrippa was engaged in building on the Campus Martius in Rome. His major construction was the Saepta Julia. This building was where the Roman electoral assembly would meet to vote on laws and to elect the junior magistracies. Instead of naming the Saepta after himself, he chose to name it after Augustus. In the same period, he built a bathhouse (one of the most expensive public buildings in the Roman city) and something called the Basilica of Neptune, in which the iconography celebrated Augustan naval victories. Agrippa also presided at the marriage of Augustus's daughter Julia to Marcellus, Augustus's nephew, and after a fire in Agrippa's house, he moved into Augustus's Palatine residence. Agrippa was not only acting as Augustus's deputy, but he was being marked out as a man who shared his authority. His removal to Augustus's house, which, of course, had been distinguished by many honors by the senate in 27, made that house look even more like a royal palace.[5]

But matters were not all straightforward for Augustus and his associates; probably in 25, politics claimed the life of Cornelius Gallus, former prefect of Egypt. Octavian had left him as governor of the province when he had set off for Rome in late 30. This may have been a practical decision, but it would also have been controversial. Gallus, who incidentally was a notable and influential poet, was not a senator but an equestrian. A province of the size and importance of Egypt would normally have been placed under the control of a senator.

Gallus had a busy time as prefect of the new province. He was in charge of establishing Roman government and put down a major revolt. By April 15, 29, Gallus was erecting victory inscriptions in which he claimed to have subdued the revolt in a fifteen-day campaign, capturing five cities and then leading his armies beyond the borders of Egypt into Ethiopia and establishing Roman hegemony in the region.[6] Gallus returned home after what would appear to have been a successful governorship, but he had enemies waiting for him.

A certain Valerius Largus levelled charges against Gallus. Those charges are obscure. He is said to have erected statues and inscriptions to himself through Egypt, which is certainly possible, but excessive self-promotion was hardly a crime in Roman law. The first round of the dispute was enough for Augustus to break his friendship with Gallus. At this point, matters became yet more serious for Gallus, and he was indicted, though the charge is not clear. Somewhat improbably, Gallus is said to have been plotting revolution. Gallus was convicted, exiled, and deprived of his property, which was voted to Augustus. Gallus committed suicide. Augustus is reported to have wept on hearing the news of Gallus's suicide, a somewhat surprising outbreak of emotion for a man who had killed so many so easily throughout his career.

Valerius Largus did not enjoy his success. He was approached by a man carrying a writing tablet and accompanied by a crowd of associates. The man asked Largus whether he knew him. Largus affirmed that he did not. The man called the crowd to witness the declaration. In a similar manner, Proculeius, a senior member of the Augustan inner circle, took to clamping his hand over his own mouth whenever he encountered Largus, showing that it was unsafe to speak in Largus's presence.[7]

The death of Gallus offers us a window into the continuing uncertainties and latent violence of the early Augustan period. Gallus, in himself, cannot have been a threat to the regime. He was a relatively lowly figure within the political hierarchy. Perhaps we might imagine that he had spoken out of turn and said things that should not be said, and that these inappropriate remarks were reported by Largus. Gallus was a trusted member of the Augustan circle; only a man in whom Augustus had complete faith would have been given the governorship of Egypt. But, as so many were to find over the coming decades, the imperial age required new disciplines. Whatever Gallus said or did, it was such that Augustus felt that he had to reprimand his friend. But then the senators moved in. Gallus was not one of them, and even if the condemnation of Gallus was dressed up as a show of loyalty to Augustus, the complicated politics were such that those hostile to Augustus were probably gleeful at the opportunity to remove an arrogant beneficiary of the new regime.

Imperial politics changed the dynamics of friendship, and as friendship was central to the political culture of Rome, the fall of Gallus pointed to a wider shift. The Roman elite valued their ability to speak openly and honestly, but the Gallus episode suggested that the age of free speech was over. Faced with whatever accusations were levelled at Gallus, the Augustan senators decided, as their colleagues under later emperors were to do, that they had no choice but to condemn and thereby show their own loyalty. To be seen to be on Gallus's side would mark them out as enemies of the regime. With Augustus away from Rome and unable to intervene, the fall of Gallus had its own ghastly and inevitable dynamic. Although perhaps no one quite realized it at the time, the moment Augustus signaled his disapproval of Gallus, the man was dead.

In early 24, Augustus returned from Spain, having been away for the best part of three years. The senators responded to news of his return in what was becoming a traditional manner, voting him new and yet more extensive honors, both religious and political. An altar was built to Augustan Peace to celebrate both his victories and his return. He was also raised above the compulsion of the laws, a significant privilege not for any extra power it provided but because it further emphasized his special status. As if to further to mark the increasingly regal nature of Rome, honors were granted to Tiberius, the son of Livia Drusilla (Augustus's wife), and Marcellus, son of Octavia (Augustus's sister). Tiberius was allowed to embark on official offices five years below the normal minimum age and was immediately elected to the senate. Marcellus, who had recently married Julia, Augustus's only child, was appointed straight into the senate among the second rank of Roman magistrates (as a praetor), and he was to be allowed to stand for the consulship a decade ahead of time.[8] In the paradoxical world of the

Augustan Republic, traditional republican magistracies were preserved and were a central element in the presentation of the regime, yet these magistracies were granted by the senate to members of Augustus's family and for no reason other than to honor the proto-monarch.

The paradoxical nature of Augustan power created tensions. Nobody, least of all the senators, could have been unaware that the elevation of family members and the concentration of power in the hands of a single man were eroding the restorationist claims of the regime. The conservative political culture of Rome was being undermined to the extent that it was becoming increasingly difficult to ignore the monarchic and tyrannical nature of Augustan power. The paradox that must have been evident to all in January 27, when the Augustan Republic was invented, had been less obvious when Augustus himself was away, but with Augustus in Rome, there could be no pretense that this was the Republic as normal. Over the following two years, those latent tensions were to emerge as a major political crisis.

THE CRISIS OF THE AUGUSTAN REPUBLIC

In January 23, Augustus, still only 39 years old, became consul for the eleventh time. He had now held the magistracy for an unprecedented nine successive years. At some point early in the year, Rome was afflicted by one of the periodic epidemics that ravaged the city's population. Such diseases are no respecters of status, and Augustus fell ill. The fever did not respond to treatment, and Augustus weakened. It seemed that he would die. He summoned those closest to him and the officials of the state. He entrusted the various official account books to his fellow consul. These included details of military dispositions and the financial accounts; it is notable that the other consul did not have access to this information beforehand. He gave his signet ring to Agrippa. He thus clearly marked the return of civil powers to the appropriate and empowered magistrate, and showed that Agrippa was to be his personal and political heir.[9]

As the end came closer, his doctor, Antonius Musa, became desperate. He prepared a cold bath and plunged the dying Augustus into it.

Remarkably, the rapid cooling of the body worked, and the fever was broken.

Augustus's illness focused attention on what would happen after he was gone. There were murmurings in the senate. It was suggested that Augustus had left an heir to the throne, bequeathing the state to a successor. Of course, in law and in practical terms, one could not bequeath a republic; an empowered magistrate would have to be replaced by another magistrate after passing through a due constitutional process. Augustus could name a personal heir, as he had been named as Caesar's heir, but the political implications of such a naming were unclear and informal (though they would undoubtedly have been significant). The appointment of a successor would demonstrate that Rome was a monarchy.

Augustus was forced to act. He came to the senate house bearing his will and offered to read it out. No one would let him. Not only would any person who demanded that the will be read be demonstrating their lack of trust in the most powerful and influential man in the state, but the very fact that he had made the offer meant that whatever was in the will would not be damaging. Also, a will was a private document and meant to be private until it was read after the death of the testator. The Romans used their wills to reward their friends and attest to their loyalty. The will was a testament to one's social relations and thus a document of great significance to Romans. Senators were unwilling to be seen to be forcing Augustus to reveal the contents of this intensely personal document.

There were two possible "heirs" to the imperial position, young Marcellus and Agrippa, Augustus's partner in power. The model of later imperial succession would suggest that Marcellus should succeed even though he had held no office and had no political or military experience, being the closest male family member and married to Augustus's daughter. But Augustus was never a sentimentalist, and even in A.D. 14 he seems to have planned his succession so that the most powerful and experienced member of his family would succeed, a man who had the personal authority and the political weight to manage the first transition of imperial power. In the political context of 23, Augustus's only practical political heir was Agrippa (see fig. 9).

Agrippa was a general, a man of vast military experience. He had been engaged in extensive building activities within the city of Rome, and one would assume that he had a high reputation among the lower classes of the city. He had been acting as an informal deputy while Augustus had been in Spain. Although his family background was not particularly elevated, Agrippa would have had far more chance of securing the loyalty of the various armies than the aristocratic but inexperienced Marcellus, and it was to Agrippa that the signet ring was passed.

The significance of such an act is not clear to us today and may not have been clear to the political commentators of 23, but it opened up the possibilities for political speculation. Something was meant by it. It did signify a passing of an extralegal authority to Agrippa. It would seem to mean that even if Augustus had died, Rome would not be rid of Caesarian supervision, since Agrippa would have a claim on Augustus's political position. Yet, if the Augustan regime was exceptional in the history of

FIGURE 9

Marcus Vipsanius Agrippa: Agrippa was Augustus's leading general
and after 23 B.C. his likely successor and acknowledged partner in power.

the Republic, the emergence of a successor would make it seem less like an exception and more like a repeatable institutional innovation. As the political temperature rose in Rome, Agrippa set sail for the East to take up duties supervising Augustan provinces. Once more, he was acting as deputy, but his extraction from Rome, like Augustus's long sojourn in Gaul and Spain, removed him from any personal attacks, and his absence rendered him less oppressive to the republican-minded senators.[10]

Augustus was under pressure. In July 23, he left Rome for an ancient sacred site in the suburbs of the city to celebrate a festival, the feriae Latinae. At the festival, on July 1, he laid down his consulship and appointed Lucius Sestius in his place. Sestius had been a supporter of Brutus and still publicly honored the tyrannicides. The appointment of such a man was hardly by chance. Augustus was proclaiming that the Republic was indeed restored and that this was normal government.

However, it was not quite business as usual. Augustus took yet another power, that of the tribunes (*tribunicia potestas*). He did not hold the office, but he exercised its powers and responsibilities. Augustus marked his political territory. He would remain the defender of the people, and thus, constitutionally and legally, he would limit the authority of the consuls. In some ways, this returned the regime to the dynamics of the triumviral period, when the triumvirs claimed that they intervened in order to protect the rights of the people against the power exercised by a senatorial minority. The senators may have maneuvered Augustus into laying down his consulship, but he was not going to step aside.

As this political drama played out, Augustus was hit by a human trag-edy. Marcellus died. He, too, had developed a fever and Musa had dumped him in cold baths, but to no avail. Even if Agrippa would have succeeded to Augustus's political position had Augustus died earlier in the year, Marcellus was still intended as the eventual successor. His death robbed Augustus of any close male relatives. Marcellus was cremated, and his ashes were interred in the Mausoleum of Augustus on the Campus Martius on the banks of the Tiber. The Mausoleum was to become a family tomb, a fitting monument to Rome's first monarchic family in five centuries (see fig. 10). The new theatre that was being built at the foot of the Capitoline Hill, a structure hugely impressive even today after centuries of reuse, was named the theatre of Marcellus (see fig. 11).

Four or five years later, Virgil published the *Aeneid*, his great mythical epic of the foundation of Rome. In one of the prophecy scenes of the poem, Virgil takes his hero, Aeneas, to the underworld, and offers him a parade of the heroes who will transform the community Aeneas is about to found from an obscure settlement of refugees into a world empire.[11] But the prophecy ends not with glorious Augustan imperial victories, as one might expect and as do other prophetic episodes, but with the appearance of the ghost of the young Marcellus and a narrative of his funeral on the Campus Martius. Marcellus was to have been the greatest of Romans, but even the gods were jealous and took Marcellus from the Roman people. Those who die young, leaving hopes unfulfilled, are often the focus of posthumous adulation, the "what-might-have-beens" of history who would have solved all our problems if only they had lived. But this is a very royal fantasy, especially since—unlike, for instance, John F. Kennedy—Marcellus had not achieved anything at the time of his death.

FIGURE 10

The Mausoleum of Augustus on the Campus Martius. The Mausoleum became the tomb of the imperial family. Marcellus's ashes were interred here in a grand ceremony in 23 B.C.

FIGURE 11

Theatre of Marcellus: Augustus ordered that this new theatre, under construction in 23 B.C., be named in honor of his late nephew.

Even as the regime monumentalized the family in ever more impressive ways, building itself into the urban fabric of Rome, Augustus's hold on power was starting to look tenuous. The death of Marcellus shook the regime. If Virgil captures anything of the popular emotion on the occasion of Marcellus's funeral, the ceremony offered a demonstration of the incipient monarchism in Rome and suggests that many, especially among the plebs, were behaving as if there were a monarchy. Flattering though such an outbreak of public emotion may have been, it was also dangerous. The senators who watched the funeral and observed the public emotions would have been aware that Marcellus had been only a boy; the regime that had been sold to them as the Republic restored had something uncomfortably close to a royal family. The display of public grief and mourning for one so young and politically inexperienced attested to a public willingness to accept that monarchy. The twin dynamics of the Augustan Republic, at once monarchic and republican, were exposed.

Augustus's resignation of the consulship may be seen as a response to a growing political crisis. Sending Agrippa away from Rome to the East removed him from an immediate political confrontation with the senators and provided Agrippa with a clear role in the imperial state, but if an imperial heir was an anomaly in a restored Republic, so was Augustus himself. His presence in Rome was unnecessary if the Republic had been restored, especially now that he was no longer consul. Augustus himself was seeming evidence of the monarchic nature of the government. His duties lay in the provinces, where he still had gubernatorial authority, rather than in Rome, where he had laid down his day-to-day responsibilities. If the senators could now send him away from the city, they would be able to resume control properly and without imperial interference for the first time since Caesar's crossing of the Rubicon in 49.

To add to this confused political mix, Augustus was now faced with a momentous political trial. The trial concerned Marcus Primus, former governor of Macedonia, where he had probably succeeded Crassus. The province was far from peaceful, and Primus had campaigned against the Odrysians, a local tribe. The campaign was successful, but Primus was campaigning beyond the borders of his province and was, strictly speaking, breaking the law. On his return to Rome, probably in 23, he was put on trial. Primus was close to the Augustan court. His province was an important one and had a significant military establishment. It is difficult to believe that Augustus would have allowed a potential dissident to take the position. Furthermore, his defense was taken up by Lucius Murena, a man very close to Augustus. Primus's defense, though, was potentially embarrassing. He claimed that he ventured out of his province because he had been ordered to do so in a message from either Marcellus (who could be presumed to have spoken for Augustus) or Augustus himself.

But neither Augustus nor Marcellus had any such authority. Marcellus was, in Roman terms, a boy without any official role. He had no power to transmit instructions to a senior Roman magistrate. In fact, even Augustus had no such power. Marcellus's involvement would be primary evidence of what Augustus had just so publicly denied, that he was building an extralegal dynasty in Rome. If Augustus had sent the message, then the situation was better, since Augustus was consul, but still his actions were monarchic, since they ignored traditional prerogatives of the senate over military policy.

This was a political trial, brought about by enemies of Primus who wished to destroy his career. If the jurors voted to acquit, they would be saying that it was likely that Augustus and Marcellus were acting as royals. If they voted to condemn, they would be ending the career of a man close to the Augustan circle. Much to everyone's surprise, Augustus appeared in court. The presiding judge called on him to give evidence. Augustus denied that any such message had been sent. Murena was furious and demanded to know who had summoned Augustus to court and on what basis he was acting as a witness. Augustus told him, "the Republic." He was acting in defense of the state. In fact, however, he was acting to deny politically uncomfortable truths. He could not be seen to be ignoring senatorial prerogatives, and still less to have delegated authority to Marcellus. The jurors voted. Some voted to acquit, but the majority could not bring themselves to tell Augustus that they thought he was a liar. Primus was ruined.[12] Augustus had sacrificed the political career of a man who was, as far as we can tell, a friend and certainly closely connected with the imperial inner circle.

Soon after, probably in 22, there was a conspiracy to assassinate Augustus. We can never know the truth of such plots. The two main alleged conspirators were Fannius Caepio and the aforementioned Lucius Murena. Before they could be apprehended, both men fled the city. They were tried in absentia, the case against them being presented by Tiberius, son of Livia (Augustus's wife).[13] It was his first major public duty. Even in these circumstances, Tiberius could not secure a unanimous conviction, leading Augustus to pass legislation stating that the jurors' individual verdicts would henceforth be published. The new law massively increased the likelihood that he would secure convictions in a political trial. Caepio was seized in flight, brought back to the city, and killed. His father responded by freeing the slaves who had attempted to defend his son in his attempted escape. Another slave, who had deserted Caepio, was led through the forum with a notice round his neck and then crucified. Caepio's father was making a public display of faith in his son and thus of opposition to Augustus. The implicit accusation was that Augustus had murdered Caepio.

It is less clear how Murena met his death. Murena was very well connected; his family sat close to the center of the imperial court. One brother, Proculeius, was the man who had actually captured Cleopatra and a friend of Cornelius Gallus. Murena's sister was Terentia, who was the wife of Maecenas, one of Augustus's closest associates. Terentia was widely believed to be Augustus's lover. It seems very likely that another brother was supposed to be consul in 23, but died on the verge of taking office.[14] One of these brothers had taken command in the Alps a few years before.

The disposal of Primus and Murena (and perhaps Gallus) showed that Augustus would abandon friends to serve his political ends. Those who had been around Augustus for a long time would hardly have been surprised by such ruthlessness, but Roman politics still adhered to the notion that a network of friendships and favors bound the political order together. The fall of Murena especially was shocking and caused divisions in the Augustan inner circle. Maecenas had told Terentia that her brother was under investigation, and Terentia told her brother, who then ran.[15]

Maecenas and Terentia may have been showing familial affection, but in a world in which family and politics were so tightly entwined, such actions could be read as a betrayal.

Those who had acted as jurors in the two key political trials had been at best unconvinced by Augustus. The regime had shown its teeth, but in so doing, it exposed the falsities of the republican restoration. There were obvious signs of dissidence and opposition from the senatorial aristocracy. The project of an Augustan Republic on which Rome had embarked from 28 seemed ruined.

Augustus still had options. He had soldiers and money. But to use the army would be to bring civil war back to Rome. It would also mark Augustus as a tyrant. The pragmatics of power (money, troops) worked in Augustus's favor, and in any calculation of political resources, the senators would have recognized Augustan preeminence, but throughout the late Republic they had shown themselves to be remarkably unmoved by such calculations. The senators relied on their authority and traditions, their right to rule, and a perception that ultimately there was still no alternative to senatorial dominance. For Rome to be Rome, Augustus needed to reach an accommodation with the senators. This was a game of political brinkmanship in which the threat of political assassination or a resumption of large-scale civil violence lurked in the shadows. Nevertheless, in 22, as Augustus prepared to head off to his provinces, the senators could be excused for thinking that events were moving in their direction and that Augustan power was crumbling.

Three years later, Augustus returned with his positioned immensely strengthened. If the Republican senators thought they were winning, they were about to be taught another lesson in the harsh realities of political conflict.

15.

ANARCHY AND POWER

ELECTIONS FOR THE CONSULSHIP were normally held in the middle of the preceding year. Augustus, having just resigned the consulship of 23 B.C., had not stood for the consulship of 22. Responsibility for the governance of the city passed to other men. Augustus had not, however, followed Agrippa to his provinces, though plans may have been afoot. For the first January since 32, when the consuls led the senate in the customary oaths and sacrifices for the new year of 22, they were not led by Caesar.

The year did not open well. The winter storms were severe and the Tiber flooded. Rome was affected by thunderstorms, and some prominent statues were struck by lightning. The floods brought disease in their wake, and the supplies of food to the city dried up. There was hunger in the city.

The plebs responded by rioting. They stormed into the Forum and shut the senators into the senate house. They threatened to burn the building down unless the senators offered the dictatorship to Augustus. The lictors who accompanied the consuls and carried the fasces were extracted from the senate house and marched off to find Augustus. The consuls were thus deprived forcibly of their symbols of office. When they reached Augustus, the plebs demanded that he act as dictator and take over the grain supply. He demurred, dramatically tearing his clothing and baring his breast, suggesting that he would be killed if he accepted the dictatorship. In the end, however, he did take on the management of the grain supply. He was, after all, the protector of the plebs and their refuge in times of trouble. Five days later, the granaries were full.[1]

Augustus had been careful to maintain a close relationship with the plebs of Rome. Throughout his career, he had sought to appear as the defender of plebeian interests, associating himself with the powers and responsibilities of the tribunes, the representatives and protectors of the people. As early as 36, he had assumed some of the symbols associated with the tribunes. In 23, his stepping down from the consulship was balanced by his taking of tribunician powers—a political act by which Augustus had asserted that even if he was no longer leader of the senate, he would continue to be the protector of the people.

Augustus also spent money. He had paid out 300 sesterces from the will of Julius Caesar to more than 250,000 recipients. Similar numbers received 400 sesterces in 28 as the victory bonus from Actium and Alexandria. In 24, on his return from Spain, he paid another 400 sesterces. Four hundred sesterces was probably enough to support perhaps two people in Rome for a year at a very basic level. In 23, Augustus provided twelve grain rations for the Roman population, again for 250,000 or more men.[2]

The total amount paid out by Augustus to Rome's population alone was enormous. The three cash payments amounted to 75,000,000 sesterces, 100,000,000 sesterces, and 100,000,000 sesterces. We have to add to this total the 40,000,000 sesterces worth of grain bought in 23.[3] In a six-year period after Actium, Augustus had invested more than 240,000,000 sesterces in the direct support of 250,000 plebs, so that each registered male would have benefited by 960 sesterces. If we guess that the basic subsistence costs for a Roman were in the region of 200–300 sesterces per year, the Augustan contribution to the family budgets of the poor was considerable.

But this was not the end of the money Augustus pumped into the Roman economy. The building projects undertaken by Augustus and Agrippa were extensive. Many of the free inhabitants of Rome were in search of work, and in an age before mechanization, porterage and the building trade were major employers.[4] In normal periods, perhaps as much as 10–18 percent of the male urban population would be working in construction.[5] The first decades of the imperial period were far from normal, with Agrippa and Augustus transforming the monumental face of Rome. The money provided through wages was not, of course, charitable, but it must have been obvious to those on the various sites, cutting and transporting the stone, moving the wood and brick, building the walls, decorating and finishing the buildings, providing the statues for the temples, working the metal fittings, and providing or repairing the building equipment, that the vast construction industry was heavily dependent on Augustan expenditure. And this is before we start counting the shopkeepers and food sellers who were secondary beneficiaries from Augustan investments. If Augustus were to disappear, the work on which all they survived would also disappear.

Although much of the new architecture consisted of ornamental or prestige buildings, such as theatres, arches, monuments, temples, and the Augustan palace itself, some was utilitarian. Agrippa focused on aqueducts, repairing and improving the Aqua Marcia and building the Aqua Julia, the Aqua Virgo, and the Aqua Alsietina. In so doing, he improved the availability of water, perhaps by more than 50 percent.[6] Water was a key resource and fresh, clean water a major benefit to the urban population, rich or poor. The city of Rome had grown rapidly over the preceding century and far outstripped its infrastructure. The limited supplies of water to the Republican city must have forced people to use insanitary water, limit their water usage, and devote considerable time and energy to securing and transporting any water they needed. The aqueducts were major pieces of engineering that cut across the Italian countryside, bridging inconvenient valleys. If anyone ever doubted the commitment of Agrippa to the people of Rome, they only had to use the new water. The aqueducts were political statements. No one else could invest in such magnificent ways in the support of the plebs of the city.

Elite historians are used to deprecating the imperial policy of "bread and circuses." It is seen as buying popularity (and thus a form of corruption) or distracting the population from the realities of the political situation. But in a society as unequal as that of Rome, where many of the people were very poor, starvation was a real threat. Agrippa and Augustus demonstrated that they would use state resources to protect the plebs and improve their lives. Between 28 and 23, they invested heavily and spectacularly in the plebs and on a level with which individual senators or even the senate as a collective body could not compete.

Ultimately, the politics of the belly is quite straightforward: the poorer the population, the more dependent it will be on the provision of basic necessities, and those who provide the people with money, food, and water will win support. The best hope for the poor is that the political class will feel that they depend on them in some way and thus seek to secure their favor through social provision. Augustus's spectacular investment in the welfare of the plebs of Rome recognized and acknowledged the entitlement of Roman citizens to these benefits of imperial wealth, but it would be naive to imagine that the investment was politically neutral or driven by a disinterested theory of citizenship and communitarianism; Agrippa and Augustus were contracting for the support of the plebs. It would be similarly naive to believe that they did so without calculating that the plebs might play a crucial role in the politics of the city in some future conflict with the senators, even if the grounds of that conflict could not be envisioned at the time; the wise politician stores favors.

The use of the financial resources at their disposal to build support among the plebs effectively brought the plebs within the patrimonial network established by Augustus. As the soldiers had been bought, so the plebs were secured. The contrast between Augustan investment in the plebs and the senators' traditional and marked disdain for the plebs lay in large part in the senators' view that their status depended primarily on their fellow aristocrats rather than the poor. Augustus and Agrippa, by contrast, knew that the senators were unreliable allies. In 22–19, Augustus was to reap the rewards of his investment in the plebs.

In 24, Augustus provided for the people of Rome. This was an unusual gratuity in its magnificence and scale, but was seemingly primarily political in motivation. In 23, Augustus provided extra grain for the people of Rome. This act of generosity was not related to a political event, and it seems likely that Augustus was responding to problems in the harvest in Italy in the previous year. A harvest failure would have led to an increase in the grain prices on the markets of Rome and potentially caused hunger in the city, from which political unrest would inevitably follow. We have no information that would allow us to guess at the harvest of 23. In 22, probably early in the year, there was flooding in the Tiber valley. Very heavy rains might have washed out the early grain harvest. We likely have two poor harvests in three years, and possibly three.

Roman agriculture was quite sophisticated. Roman farmers grew a variety of crops. They guarded against risks when they could. They invested in technologies when they would help. They had food processing facilities that allowed grapes to be turned into wine and olives into oil such as enabled the preservation and transportation of foodstuffs. But like all agricultural regimes, and Mediterranean regimes in particular, Roman farming was vulnerable to fluctuations in rainfall and temperature. Crops could fail if there was too little water or too much. There were poor harvests perhaps once every four years, and years of near complete crop failure perhaps once a decade. Repeated crop failures do not allow the farmers the time and resources to recover and restock, especially if the harvest failure is so severe that people move off the land temporarily in search of food and work.[7] In such a crisis, the most obvious destination for the hungry was Rome.

The population of Rome had been able to use its political power to extract a secure supply of food from the Roman political elite: it was for that reason that a grain dole was established in the late Republic and continued to function through the Roman imperial period. Nevertheless, that dole was not enough to feed the whole population of the city, being distributed to probably 200,000 men. Many would not have been able to find their way onto the registers, nor would the dole have been enough to feed their families. Such people depended on the market.

Imagine that a small farmer in a normal year sold 50 percent of his crop and ate the other 50 percent. If a yield was down by 50 percent, he would still eat the same amount but would have nothing to market. If the farmer normally marketed 70 percent of the crop and ate 30 percent, a 50 percent crop reduction would leave him eating 60 percent of his crop and marketing the remaining 40 percent, but the marketed goods would amount to only 20 percent of the normal crop. Those in the city would see a shortage of food in the market without there having been a catastrophic crop failure. Large farmers would be in a similar situation, having to hold back a much higher proportion of their crop to feed their workers than in a good year.

Both small and large farmers would compensate for the smaller volumes for sale by raising prices, and those prices would be met because of the shortages in the market, but under such conditions the market could fail completely. The farmer (or more likely the grain merchant) has to decide when to bring his grain to market and at what price to sell it. Even without a more than rudimentary understanding of the laws of supply and demand, he might decide to dramatically raise the normal price. Two things would then result, neither of which are good. The grain might remain unsold because the buyers refused to buy it or could not afford it, or the grain would be sold at the inflated price, further encouraging hoarding and price inflation. One could have a situation in which there was grain in the granaries and even in the market (at a price), but people were going hungry.

Augustan intervention in 23 recognized that the Roman population were entitled to food and that the Augustan Republic would provide for its people. He bought the grain and then distributed it. The farmers got their money and the people their food. But in 22, Augustus was no longer in charge. The consuls did not intervene. They may not have had the money to hand. They may not have seen the need. They may not have been willing. The senators were, after all, major landowners, and had not much history of empathy with the plight of the poor. They were likely to be on the side of those who had grain to sell. The people could also make that calculation, and in classical food riots the target was always the rich landowners, who were suspected of holding onto grain in order to make a profit from the misfortunes of others.

The consuls had no military forces at their disposal and no police. We need not imagine tens of thousands of angry, hungry, pro-Augustan plebs appearing suddenly in the Forum; a few thousand would have been ample to trap the senators and intimidate them into submission. The only person who might have been able to easily combat such a crowd and protect the senators was Augustus, who had his personal guard, but he was seemingly reluctant to send his praetorians to the Forum to protect the senators and discipline a crowd which was about to identify Augustus as their savior.

Locked into the senate house, the consuls gave up their lictors, the symbols of their *imperium*. The crowd led the lictors to Augustus (who must have been in the city) and offered him the dictatorship. Of course, the crowd was not formally constituted and was not a legal body, but the fundamental principle of republican government was the sovereignty of the people, and this was a clear expression of popular will. Politically, Augustus could have taken the dictatorship, and the finer points of the legal position would have been resolved; the trapped senators could have been rapidly persuaded to ratify an Augustan dictatorship. But Augustus refused the dictatorship in dramatic style, baring his breast.

This was a world without microphones and without mass media; communicating with large and angry crowds required the dramatic gesture, a kind of political mime. The meaning of this gesture was clear: appointment to the dictatorship would mean his death. We could read the gesture as a commitment to constitutionalism, suggesting that he would rather die than accept such an office, and such a gesture would fit with the fond image that many have had of Augustus as a constitutional reformer trying to balance his power with that of the traditions of Rome. Augustus later hinted that his refusal was an exercise of self-deprecating modesty in keeping with the moral traditions of Rome.[8]

Yet, such views are fantastic. Augustus was likely making a different political point, alluding to the fate of the last dictator, of Caesar, at the hands of the senators.[9] He was suggesting that he was on the side of the plebs and their protector against the senators who threatened them all, and it was as the protector of the plebs that he now intervened again in the governance of Rome by taking on the grain supply. Augustan modesty was the modesty of the great; the man could refuse office because real political power lay elsewhere. But it was also calculated: to have taken the dictatorship would have confirmed the critiques of his enemies and have returned to the situation at the end of the triumviral period. The Augustan Republic would have failed, and there would, potentially, have been unpleasant consequences.

Augustus solved the problem of the grain supply. To do so, he invented the new office of curator of the grain supply. His intervention was such a success that within five days supplies were back to normal. The speed of the restoration should give pause for thought. If we imagine that

Augustus got down to work straightaway and wrote to the provinces to secure grain (notably Africa, Sicily, Sardinia), then the letters would hardly have arrived within five days. Ships would have to be found for the emergency supplies of grain. The grain would have to be loaded, sailed across the Mediterranean, unloaded at Puteoli or Ostia, and then carted or put on barges to the city. That process would take many weeks. How then was Augustus able to alleviate the shortage in five days?

There are various possibilities. The first is a conspiracy theory. Since Augustus had charge of the key grain-producing province of Sicily, he already had significant grain at his disposal. Aware of the growing crisis and guessing at the complete inability of the senators to resolve the problem, he might have been holding back grain from the market. A second possibility is that Augustus was able to get grain flowing to the market by influencing those who held grain in Italy. Augustus was never a man it was safe to refuse. A further possibility is that once Augustus had control over the grain supply, those with grain would have made the perfectly sensible calculation that he would either requisition their stocks or find other stocks with which to flood the market. The price would fall once those new stocks arrived. The moment had come to sell.

By whatever means Augustus used, the crisis was resolved. It was resolved so quickly that the plebs would likely have been confirmed in their suspicion that the senators were either incompetent or wicked, artificially boosting the price for their own benefit. In early 22, we see a polarization of Roman politics, with Augustus confirming his place as the defender of the rights and interest of the people against the senators.

THE POLITICS OF ABSENCE: THE AUGUSTAN REPUBLIC WITHOUT AUGUSTUS

Augustus left Rome for Sicily towards the middle of the year, but his removal from the political scene did not bring peace to the city. Rome was in turmoil after the violence of the food riots and the conspiracy of

Caepio and Murena.[10] The next major political flashpoint was the consular elections, probably delayed until late in the year—certainly they did not take place while Augustus was still in the city.

The elections were violent, which was not unusual in Rome. Yet, the violence of 22 seems not to have been between the supporters of the candidates, but violence offered by the supporters of Augustus, who was not a candidate in the elections. Elections were held via a popular assembly and would be conducted by arranging the crowd into groups (centuries) who then voted in order by passing across "bridges." Such assemblies were potentially difficult to control, and although the presiding magistrate would do his best to maintain order, he was always in danger of being shouted down. The crowd managed to prevent the proper running of the assembly and either voted for Augustus or refused to elect more than one consul, holding the other position open for Augustus.[11]

A presiding magistrate would be brave indeed to refuse the manifest will of the people and reject the election of Augustus, since he could assume that either the crowd or Augustus himself would react badly to such a show of independence. It is likely that an embassy was sent to Augustus on Sicily to ask him once again to act as dictator and to offer him the open consulship. Augustus refused. Yet, the people had demonstrated their dislike of the settlement of 23: they wanted Augustus to remain at the heart of Roman politics, and were prepared to force the senators to accept Augustan dominance.

For the senators, the events of 22 had been dire. They had been forced to acquiesce in an Augustan display of power and their own obvious impotence in the face of the crowd. The next year, 21, was little better. The new consul, Marcus Lollius, entered office alone. His first task was to hold elections for a colleague. These elections were also violently disputed. Augustus was summoned back from Sicily to restore order. He refused and instead summoned the candidates to him. They were told to stay away from Rome during the vote, and eventually (after further violence) one of them was chosen. The business of Rome was the responsibility of the magistrates of the city, notably the consul, but Lollius had been unable to control events, and Augustus's summoning the candidates to Sicily was an act of political authority that clearly signaled both the inferiority of the candidates and Augustan supervision of the state.

Augustus's reluctance to return to Rome may have had little to do with the politics of the city. Returning in 21, he would have been in a stronger position than in 23, able to dictate terms to the senators once more, but the political problems that he had faced from 24 to 22 would have remained, and the paradox of the Augustan Republic would be no more comfortable. But Augustus had bolder plans. Agrippa had been sent to the East in 23 because of troubles with the Parthians. The Parthians were unfinished business for the Romans and were an opportunity for Augustus to secure a spectacular military success. Agrippa was summoned back, and Augustus embarked for Greece.

Agrippa's return to Rome in 21 brought him back to the city for the first time since his rapid departure in 23. Later, historians speculated that his retreat had something to do with hostility towards Marcellus and rivalry for the imperial succession, but the accounts of Augustus's illness point the other way, to Agrippa being the likely successor to the political leadership of the Augustan group; anyhow, Marcellus had died soon afterwards. Agrippa's absence was probably partially strategic, to remove him from the vision of the more republican senators, but also practical, since from Lesbos Agrippa was able to manage more effectively those eastern provinces that were under imperial control and make preparations for Augustus's grand expedition to the East. On his return to Rome, Augustus and Agrippa took the next logical step in confirming Agrippa's status as the chosen successor of Augustus. Agrippa married Julia, Augustus's daughter and the widow of Marcellus. Agrippa was thus brought into the center of the dynasty as he was at the center of the political circle. The marriage confirmed the arrangements of 23.

In spite of Agrippa's return, the populace continued to be restive. There was rioting in 21 over the election of a temporary magistrate to look after the city during a festival, but even after the festival the people were not quelled.[12] The elections of 21 for the consulship of 20 may well have been affected, and again they produced just one consul. In 20, Gaius Sentius Saturninus was elected and Augustus was offered the other position. Saturninus assumed the consulship alone in 19. Agrippa had probably left Rome in 21. He went first to Gaul and then to Spain, where the victories of Augustus in the mid-twenties B.C. were proving less conclusive than had been thought.[13]

The violence continued at Rome. A bodyguard was appointed for Saturninus, and an embassy was sent to Augustus. Augustus took the unusual and unprecedented step of appointing one of the envoys as consul, though on what authority and according to what procedure is unclear. Once more the plebs demonstrated to the senators that Augustan power was necessary for the state to function, and once more Augustus exercised power to bring order to the city of Rome.[14] The legal basis of Augustan hegemony mattered little; what mattered is that he was needed and that he had sufficient authority that his decisions were upheld.

From 22 to 20, the plebs took to the political stage as a violent, disruptive, and pro-Augustan force capable of imposing their will on the senators. It seems possible that Augustan influence lay behind this political emergence. Somehow the plebs acted to prevent a second consul being elected. One suspects that some form of political organization must have lain behind these actions.

In his absence, Augustus's power was growing. The senators' difficulties in dealing with the plebs and repeated demonstrations in Augustus' favor were lessons in the realities of power. Augustus could threaten his senatorial opponents with the crowd more effectively than with the latent threat offered by the soldiers, posted on the frontiers out of sight, but surely not out of the minds of the senators. If the streets of Rome were threatened by anarchy, it was Augustan power that preserved order. In an obvious breach of established customs and procedures, Augustus was able to summon consular candidates, issue instructions to those candidates, and, in extremis, appoint consuls. The basic processes of the Republic depended on and were subverted by Augustus. The Augustan Republic could not manage in the absence of Augustus.

In 19, the senators were to face yet another and perhaps even more serious challenge to their authority. But by that time, Augustus was on his way home, basking in the glory of his "victories" in the East.

THE "CONSPIRACY" OF EGNATIUS RUFUS

Little is known about the background of Egnatius Rufus. He emerged on the political scene in 21 B.C. when he was elected as aedile. Aediles had responsibility for maintaining the streets of Rome and for putting on games. In both roles, there were opportunities to win popular favor. As aedile, Rufus established fire brigades in order to protect the city; such a seemingly straightforward act launched him onto a path of political radicalism that eventually led to his death.

Fires were a considerable danger to the city of Rome. With limited supplies of water and no water under pressure, putting out even small fires could be difficult. In the condensed streets of Rome, where the multistory apartment blocks might be separated by only the narrowest of alleys (70 centimeters was the minimum width for an alley), fire could easily jump from building to building. There were, of course, neither fire regulations nor easy emergency access from the upper stories of buildings. Stopping a major fire required making firebreaks by pulling down buildings, and even so, there was every chance that a fire would burn across the rubble. There were also no organized fire brigades. If a fire broke out, one was reliant on one's neighbors organizing themselves, finding buckets, locating the nearest water supplies, and bringing the axes and tools needed to save the day. If it was anything more than a minor incident, the chances were slim of getting enough water to the fire quickly enough to prevent a major conflagration.

Rufus's fire brigades were an extension of his duty as aedile to protect the fabric of the city of Rome. He organized his own slaves into brigades, which, to be effective, he must have then distributed through the city. They also must have been numerous. He also recruited others into the brigades and paid wages.[15] The brigades were effectively an organized crowd which Rufus could then deploy in political meetings. Furthermore, the brigades won Rufus popular support, and the people rallied behind him.

Any politician who sought the support of the plebs or who tried to organize non-elite groups of the population was viewed with suspicion by the political elite as a rabble-rouser. But, bolstered by his success, Rufus ran for the next office in the career structure, the post of praetor. Successive magistracies were technically illegal (though the law had not stopped Augustus). The law was ignored in the face of the declared will of the people, and popular sovereignty remained a principal doctrine of Roman political life. Laying down his aedileship, Rufus supposedly issued a statement that he had handed over the city to his successor intact. The political elite, who had collective responsibility for the city, took offence.[16]

During the next year, 19, Rufus announced his attention to run for the consulship. The elections were presided over by Sentius Saturninus, who was acting as sole consul at the time (probably before Augustus's appointee to the post, Lucretius Vespillo, had managed to return to take up his appointment). Saturninus, who either earlier or at this point was voted a bodyguard, made clear that he would refuse the candidature of Rufus. Technically, the presiding magistrate at an election had to accept a candidature for the individual to be allowed to stand. Saturninus was within his rights, but such a refusal went against the will of the plebs. His actions were a reassertion of the powers of the consul in the face of popular discontent. Rufus was not his only target, however. He also banned some individuals for running for the praetorship, and it is difficult not to imagine that these vetoed candidates were related somehow to Rufus. There can be no doubt that these decisions resulted in violence on the streets of Rome. One of our sources, Velleius Paterculus, even compares the actions of Saturninus to those of ancient heroes of Rome in defense of the Republic, but we do not know precisely what happened.[17]

The next event in the story is mysterious and suspicious. Rufus was discovered in a conspiracy to assassinate Augustus. As a result, Rufus and his unnamed and unnumbered supporters were killed. We can hardly ever know whether ancient conspiracies were real or excuses to remove political opposition. In this case, one assumes that the "conspiracy," to have any credence, must have planned to remove Augustus after his return to Rome on October 12, 19. Rufus's enemy, Sentius Saturninus, was already dead by the time Augustus returned to Italy. Saturninus's disappearance from the political scene is not necessarily suspicious, and it is possible that he died from natural causes, but Velleius's comparison of Saturninus to the ancient heroes of Rome would be hyperbolic unless something very dramatic had happened. No source makes explicit mention of the murder of a consul (and it would surely have been a major event), and Rufus was accused of conspiring against Augustus, not murder. Saturninus's death was at the very least convenient for Rufus.

It was also, coincidentally, good news for Augustus, since it removed a man who had shown himself both able and independent. Saturninus had demonstrated that he was capable of leading his fellow senators; his death allowed Augustus to replace this independent, confident, and powerful figure and insert his own man into the consulship for what was to be an important few months at the end of 19. His replacement was Marcus Vinicius, a prominent Augustan general who had won a major victory in Germany.[18] Vinicius was a man without elevated ancestry, from a new family on the Roman political scene.[19] In later life, Vinicius and Augustus played dice together, and Vinicius's son and grandson were to have brilliant careers.[20] Vinicius was clearly a loyalist and very close to Augustus.

One has to wonder what Rufus would have to gain from the murder of Augustus; he could not hope to challenge Augustan control of the military, and even if he rivaled Augustan popularity with the plebs, the senators would not be likely to acquiesce in his dominance. There is no such doubt as to Augustus's motives for removing Rufus. Rufus challenged his monopolistic support among the plebs, and Augustus would tolerate no rivals. Further, killing Rufus sent a message to the senate and people of Rome. To the people, Augustus was asserting his power and showing them that he would tolerate no indiscipline. The plebs needed the Augustan network, and they owed Augustus loyalty; that loyalty could not be offered to others. Even if there was a mutual dependency between the regime and the plebs, the hierarchical organization of their political network required the lesser men in the network to follow the lead of Augustus and Agrippa.

To the senators, Augustus was sending a more complicated message. In the first instance, whether or not there was a conspiracy, the killing was an assertion of Augustan power. He could remove a prominent and popular politician should he so wish. But he was also identifying with the senatorial cause in removing a man who had threatened the senators and the consul over the previous years. The intervention of Augustus restored political order and demonstrated that the senators could rely upon him, or more sinisterly, that that the senators needed him for their protection. After their political disputes in the early 20s in which the senators seem to have struggled against Augustan dominance, and the violent years after 23 when the senators found themselves unable to control their own members or the streets of Rome, Augustus offered the senators respect, order, and security. One expects that the senators made clear their gratitude. But Augustus's protection came at a price.

The removal of Rufus opened the way for a new political settlement. Augustus was returning from the East with a major diplomatic success, and the senators were not slow to demonstrate their support and loyalty with another round of honors. But whereas in 24 Augustus could be seen as being in himself the greatest threat to senatorial government, in 19 not only might the senators have been looking nervously at the plebeians, but Augustus himself could pose as the guarantor of order.

The Augustan Republic remained paradoxical, since Augustus himself could not be reconciled with the traditions of republican government, but the paradox was not just an unfortunate hangover from the triumviral period. The experience of 23–19 showed that the Augustan Republic was necessary. It was Augustus who held back the revolutionary energies of the Roman plebs and who kept the armies in check in the provinces. It was Augustus who maintained the hierarchies of Roman society. Only in a limited sense was the old Republic to be preserved. It was obvious that Rome could not be a republic with Augustus: Augustan power was monarchic. On the other hand, without Augustus the social hierarchies that were embedded in the old Republic could not survive. The Augustan paradox had been played out for the conservatives of Rome, and the choices of the traditionalists now seemed bleak.

VICTORY IN THE EAST

In 23 B.C., Augustus had received an embassy from Phraates of Parthia and had also heard his rival for the throne, Tiridates, who came in person. Both were brought before the senate to plead their disputes.

Tiridates was clearly hoping for Roman intervention against Phraates. Phraates was, of course, equally anxious to avoid a Roman invasion. It was after these embassies that Agrippa was sent to the East to prepare the ground for a major expedition.[21]

Augustus delayed his own departure to the East, but probably set out by the second half of 21. He spent some time in Sparta before heading to Athens. In Athens, he fell out with the locals. The statue of Athena spat blood at him, or so it was said, and he left early to winter in Samos, which was anyhow convenient for the continuation of his journey to Syria.[22]

Phraates now knew that Augustus and his armies were coming. Much of the detail of Parthian political history has not been recorded, but we may assume that the quarrel with Tiridates was not settled and that at least some of the Parthian aristocracy, seeing the way in which events were likely to develop, would have sided with Tiridates. Phraates was thus in a weak political position. To keep his throne, he made peace. The standards captured by the Parthians in 53 were returned. The Romans captured in that war were sent home, though some had probably settled happily in Parthia after all the time that had passed. The Romans intervened in Armenia (a disputed territory between Rome and Parthia) to impose their candidate for the throne, and Tiberius was sent with an army to enforce Rome's wishes. Augustus then engaged in a grand settlement of the East, establishing kings in some of the smaller states of the region.

The Eastern expedition was both a nonevent and a great victory for Augustus. Phraates had retained his throne, but had been forced to make diplomatic concessions; most importantly, Roman hegemony had been acknowledged. Augustus could and did make the case that the conflicts on the frontier which had been ongoing for three decades were resolved with the establishing of lasting Roman hegemony in the region, something Crassus and Antony had singularly failed to achieve. Although there had been no battles and no war, and thus the Parthian events did not fulfil the traditional Roman criteria for a triumph, the very fact that Phraates had been forced to symbolic concessions without war was impressive. The Romans saw the Parthians as the heirs of the Persians and thus the successors to one of the great empires of antiquity, an empire that had threatened Greece in the fifth century. Persia's defeat by the Greek city-states and the humiliation of the Persians more than a century later by Alexander were key moments in classical history. Augustus had now secured Rome's hegemony over that empire (or so he claimed), and this was in itself a major step in Rome's ultimate goal of world conquest. All this had been achieved by the mere threat of force and within a few months of his arriving in Syria.

Augustus was to make much of his victory. He had been victorious in Gaul and Spain, in the far west of the world, and now his authority was acknowledged through the far east. The standards were brought to Rome to be set up in a temple of Mars Ultor (Mars the Avenger) in the grand new Forum that was being constructed in the centre of the city, though they may have been temporarily located on the Capitol, in another temple of Mars, while the larger temple was being built.[23] Further honors were granted to Augustus. His birthday became a festival day, with sacrifices and games. The day on which he returned to Rome, October 12, was marked in the calendar as Augustalia, another day of sacrifices. An altar to Fortuna Redux (Fortune Returned) was established at the gate by which Augustus entered the city.[24] Augustus rode into the city on horseback, in a parade which was not a triumph in the traditional Roman sense, but was meant to look like one. The Roman political elite slipped easily into what was becoming a customary pattern of honoring the returning conqueror. The people and senators engaged in the choreographed acclaiming of Augustus.

Augustus returned in 19 in a strong position. The senators had been battered by political events, by the repeated violent political interventions of the plebs, which had demonstrated beyond doubt that the people did not trust the senators and preferred Augustan rule. The senators had seen elections spiral out of control and had relied on Augustan authority to provide them with their consuls. Augustus, meanwhile, had been successfully engaged in the making of cities and of kings and in the extension of Roman power to the furthest reaches of the known world. The anarchic period beginning in 23 had demonstrated senatorial impotence and Augustan power. Augustus was returning to provide what the senators themselves could not: security and order. But what came with that order was an acceptance of the new disciplines of the imperial system. The stage was set for the grand political bargain by which the Roman elite exchanged liberty for security. In so doing, they accepted Augustan imperial monarchy.

16.

THE AUGUSTAN ORDER

B Y 19 B.C., THE senators knew what was expected when Augustus returned from his conquests. There had been honors voted after Actium and on his return to Rome following the death of Cleopatra. The senators had voted yet more honors when Augustus came back victorious from Spain in 24. So in 19, the senators racked their collective imagination and voted temples, sacrifices, and religious honors. All were to be seen as united in their happiness at the return of "Fortune," which came with Augustus's arrival in Italy. If many were secretly delighted by his leaving in 22, they were publicly ecstatic at his return.

The day after Augustus returned to Rome, the senate voted honors to Tiberius and Drusus, the sons of Livia, Augustus's wife (see fig. 12). Tiberius was born on November 16, 42, into the distinguished family of the Claudii. In 39, his mother, Livia, had divorced her husband at the request of Octavian, who simultaneously divorced his wife Scribonia (on the very day on which she gave birth to Julia, Augustus's only child). Livia then married the young triumvir. She was pregnant at the time with Drusus, who was born in early 38. Tiberius began his official career by prosecuting Caepio in 22 for conspiracy against Augustus and was then in command of the army in the East that intervened in Armenia.[1] In late 19, although a man of some military experience, he was still very much starting out on his career. He was, however, raised to praetorian status (treated as if he had performed a praetorship). Drusus was permitted to stand for office five years ahead of the normal time.[2] These were dynastic moves, like the elevation of Marcellus in 24. Tiberius and

Drusus were being identified as key to the future of the regime, and their elevation was central to Augustus's reassertion of his presence in Roman politics in October 19.

The third figure in the dynastic arrangements was, of course, Agrippa. Agrippa was married to Julia, and their first son, Gaius, was born in 20. He was to be followed by Julia in 19, Lucius in 17, Agrippina in 14, and Agrippa in 12. Even before Augustus returned to Rome, Agrippa had left for Gaul. He fought a small war there before heading to Spain to fight against a supposedly defeated tribe, the Cantabri. It was not an easy war, and Agrippa had to deal with ill-disciplined troops. Nevertheless, he brought the war to an end and was voted a triumph, an honor he refused. Although others had been allowed triumphs under the Augustan Republic, the list of nonimperial holders of triumphs comes to an abrupt end in 19 B.C.[3] Agrippa's refusal of the honor indicated correct behavior towards Augustus for future generals. From now on, the emperor was to have a monopoly on military glory, and the title with which successful

FIGURE 12
Livia, wife of Augustus and mother to Tiberius and Drusus.

generals were acclaimed, *imperator*, gradually came to be associated with the monarch.

This moderate refusal of honors was not, however, Agrippa taking a step back into the political shadows. He was not modest and he had no intention of retiring. His place in the family was made yet more secure by the marriage of his daughter (by a previous marriage), Vipsania, to Tiberius. In 18, the tribunician power that Augustus had taken in 23 ran out. This power, exceptional in almost every way, carried the patina of a republican magistracy in being voted and time-limited, though it had not been collegial. This anomaly was corrected in 18, when Agrippa and Augustus took the office jointly. Agrippa's elevation established him as a partner in the Augustan regime and at the center of a dynasty which would survive Augustus's death. While there had been doubt as to what would have happened if Augustus had succumbed to his illness in 23, the arrangements of 19 made clear that the Augustan household would continue to dominate Roman political life with Agrippa at the helm, aided by Tiberius and Drusus.

A further aspect of the arrangements of 19 was a clarification of the relationship between Augustus and the consuls. In the turbulent years from 22 onwards, Augustus had frequently acted as if he held consular power. In 19, he formally took consular powers. In practical terms, it seems to have meant very little.[4]

The reforms of 19 and 18 marked a shift in Roman politics. There was not, as constitutional historians have imagined, a third grand settlement, revising the earlier settlements of 27 and 23, in part because there was a lack of obvious negotiation and of obvious parties with whom Augustus could negotiate. The consuls were Augustus's men. They were responsible for easing through the changes in his position which took place, remarkably quickly, in late 19. By the time Agrippa was awarded the tribunician power in 18, Augustus had laid out his dynastic plans for a new political order.

By 18, Augustus was dominant in all areas of conventional political life. Moreover, the Augustan regime was determinedly and openly dynastic. If the elevation of Marcellus had proved something of an embarrassment, there seem to have no similar reservations as the young

Tiberius and the even younger Drusus were marked out for high office. All this, of course, was conducted under the benign influence of Agrippa, whose sons were the direct male descendants of Augustus. If there were rumors of competition between Marcellus and Agrippa, there is no such gossip surrounding Tiberius and Drusus; they were junior figures in an imperial house dominated by Augustus and Agrippa. The political future of Rome was taking shape within the Augustan palace, and the Augustan family was planning for generations to come.

BUYING ROME

Augustan power depended, as it had always done, on the regime's control of key political constituencies. That control was intimately related to Augustan exploitation of the empire and its resources; imperial money was the key to the regime's stability. The patrimonial network established in the wake of the wars of 44–43 monopolized power and resources. By 19 B.C., a whole generation of Romans had grown up dependent on that network. The historian Tacitus, reflecting from a century later on the Augustan regime, describes the process:

> When he had enticed the army with gifts, the plebs with grain, and the rest with the sweetness of leisure, little by little, he pushed on to take to himself the functions of the senate, the magistrates, and the law, without opposition, since the most fierce had fallen in war or through proscription, the other nobles, somewhat more eager for servitude, were elevated by wealth and honors and having benefited from the new regime preferred safety and the present to the old and dangerous. The provinces nodded at this new state of affairs, having feared the power of senate and people on account of the contestation of the powerful and the greed of the magistrates, by which legal remedies were rendered useless, overthrown by violence, favors and, most of all, money. . . .[5]

One of the most direct ways in which the rewards of empire were distributed to the people was through colonization.[6] Colonial settlements had come to be associated with the discharge of soldiers from the legions during the last decades of the Republic, and Augustus also settled veterans in colonies at the end of campaigns.[7] But other Augustan colonies had no obvious military origins.[8] Augustan colonization was on a very large scale. We do not have complete lists of colonies, and those outside Italy can only be identified occasionally, but it is likely that there were more than 60 Augustan colonial settlements, which would have involved somewhere between 300,000 and 600,000 male settlers, though not all of these would have been citizens.

Even after the civil wars, looking after the soldiers was a political and financial priority. Augustus claimed to have spent 860,000,000 sesterces on finding land for veterans. The difficulties of organizing settlements encouraged a shift away from discharge bonuses being paid in land to cash prizes. Some veterans may have preferred cash, since it allowed them to return to Italy and their families with the resources to resettle rather than leaving them in the provinces. From 7 B.C. onwards, Augustus put an additional 400,000,000 sesterces into funding cash benefits to veterans.[9] In total, Augustus discharged more than 300,000 veterans with cash or land benefits. But this was not the end of his generosity. In his *Res Gestae*, Augustus tells us that in 29 he gave each of his colonists 1,000 sesterces in celebration of his victory of Actium, and it is likely that he repeated his financial generosity during the various tours of Italy that he undertook irregularly during his reign.[10]

Augustus also had to meet the running costs for the legions. Augustus had 28 legions for most of the period from 30 B.C. to A.D. 14, amounting to about 140,000 men, probably just over 10 percent of the total adult manpower of Rome in any one period. That percentage increased toward the end of the reign, when troops were raised for the Pannonian revolt and the German wars, perhaps to as much as 14 percent of total Roman manpower.[11] Terms of service were made more regular, with a norm of 16 years of service, later increased to 20.[12] Eventually, Augustus established a new military treasury to fund pay and rewards to the soldiers and primed it with his own money. The treasury was funded by a 5 percent tax on inheritances, which proved unpopular—rich Romans saw no reason why their wealth should be taxed for the benefit of the soldiers.[13]

Augustus also continued to support the plebs. After 23, there were further donations in 11 B.C. (400 sesterces per man) and in 5 B.C. and 2 B.C. (240 sesterces per man).[14] On his death, a further 40,000,000 sesterces was to be distributed to the Roman people (presumably the plebs of Rome), perhaps 160 sesterces each. Cumulatively, the total provision was more than 500,000,000 sesterces, a sum that must have awed the senators, especially as it was in addition to the monies spent on the grain dole, the aqueducts, and the shows.

If buying the support of the soldiers (and their families) and the plebs was relatively straightforward, the position of the elites of Rome was more complex and conflicted. The senators regarded themselves as the natural and traditional rulers of Rome. That position had been usurped by Augustus. But this was an era of personal politics: what mattered was the status of individuals and the ability of those individuals to acquire positions consonant with their familial prestige.

Such individualism opened the elite to Augustan manipulation; Augustus needed to make individuals feel recognized and honored. By allowing the aristocrats to share in the benefits of imperial power securely and to enjoy their wealth without threat of revolution, he associated their status with his success and thereby implicated them in the regime. If the honors could be provided, then Augustus just needed to do the little things. He needed to remember names. He had to send presents on birthdays. He had to honor family events. He had to participate in debates as if he were talking with equals, not subordinates. He had to work on the personal relationships which eventually sustained the political relationships that maintained the regime.

Augustus controlled public appointments, and that effectively made him a gatekeeper on the path to political success. He had the ability to raise up an individual, smoothing his path to high office, or to hinder the careers of those he disliked. There was probably little need to use that power aggressively or negatively to weed out those who might be ill disposed toward the regime, and in the later years of the Augustan reign many consulships were held by members of old and distinguished families. But the very fact that these men were allowed to rise and enjoy success was evidence that the Augustan Republic could function and that a senator of distinguished lineage could have a successful career under Augustan tutelage.[15]

Augustan support implicated the well-connected with the network, making opposition seem self-destructive. As a result, Augustan policy toward the senators adopted, consciously or unconsciously, their preexisting hierarchy. There was no need to pack the senate with supporters, since eventually the senate would be composed of men who owed their positions to Augustus and whose ambitions depended on imperial support.

It was when Augustus questioned the individual status of senators, such as in his revisions of the senatorial rolls, that he ran into significant difficulties.[16] Augustus had reformed the senate in 28 as part of his restoration of the Republic. He returned to the issue of senatorial membership in 18. This time he devised an elaborate system. Thirty men were selected by Augustus. They each selected five men, and then a lottery was used to reduce that 150 to 30. Those 30 became the first tranche of senators, and the Augustan 30 were returned to the pool. The senatorial 30 then selected another 150 and a lottery was used for a second group of 30, who were then to select another 150 until the number of senators reached 300. Any who are inclined to think of Augustus as a great statesman should reflect on this system. The results were chaotic and corrupt. Deserving and senior figures were passed over by forgetfulness or the lottery. One senior senator found that he had been removed from the roll while his son was on the list. He tore his clothes to show the wounds he had suffered while serving Rome (a display of the nude, scarred body, which had some precedent in Republican Rome). Another son begged to be allowed to step down for a father who had been passed over. Despairing of the process, Augustus took the lists in and made his own selection (and further deselections).[17]

Augustus returned to the problem five years later with another brilliant idea. This time he established a new census level qualification for senators. If there had been a requirement during the Republic, it was probably set at 100,000 sesterces. Augustus raised the level to 1,000,000 sesterces. Immediately, there were problems. Augustus must have seen the census level as a benchmark of financial and social respectability and expected that some families would not make the grade.[18] But he appears not to have predicted which families would have difficulties. Families with distinguished lineages found themselves embarrassed, and Augustus felt himself obliged to donate money to these poorer but respectable senators. One guesses that the processes of giving and receiving were far from socially comfortable.[19]

The logic behind these reforms was not to remove those who were opposed to the Augustan regime but to find ways of increasing the prestige of the senate. Although individual senators might have been offended by their omission from the various lists (either accidentally or by design), as a group the senators' status was made more select. The political stresses resulted not from the honoring of the collective of the senate but from the dishonoring of individual senators. The personal nature of political ambition, which worked so well for the regime elsewhere, in this instance worked against Augustan reforms.

If the political functions of the senate were reduced by Augustan hegemony, Augustus enhanced its administrative roles. He established offices with particular responsibilities normally fulfilled by small boards of officials: public buildings, roads, aqueducts, the banks and channel of the Tiber (which was notoriously prone to flooding in the winter rains), and the grain supply all came under the care of special senatorial magistrates. The senatorial career was now made more complex, and senators began to represent themselves in new ways. Augustan senators laid claim to status through their holding of offices (rather than from political and military achievements or family background), but their need for offices implicated the aristocrats in the Augustan system, making them dependent on that system for their status.[20] Subtly, the nature of the Roman elite was being shifted.

Soldiers, plebs, and senators were slowly implicated in the system, becoming dependent on its money or being won over by its honors. The reality of Augustan dominance was that the network provided for everyone. As Tacitus puts it, all constituencies were reconciled, all opposition was seduced. Imperial power bought out the vestiges of the Republic. There was no pragmatic alternative to imperial power. It was this dominance that allowed Augustus to launch a cultural revolution to match the political revolution which had secured for the regime the resources of empire.

THE CULTURAL REVOLUTION

Revolutions are peculiar. Modern revolutionaries want to change the world. They do that by seizing political power, overthrowing the previous regime, and typically purging any vestiges of the old political order. But what can be done once power is seized? One can change politics, cutting off a king's head for instance, but to generate real change, one has to revolutionize society, to sweep away the old attitudes and ways that supported the king and his court. Cultural revolution is much more difficult than political revolution, and it is in cultural revolution that so many regimes have foundered and ended up wading through vast seas of troubles and blood.

Unlike modern revolutions, the Augustan revolution did not have an ideological scheme lying behind it. Its leaders were not, as far as we know, motivated primarily by an ideological commitment to change the world. Yet, that is not to say that they viewed their society as perfect, or nearly so. The century of civil wars that culminated in the victory of Augustus was demonstration enough of fundamental problems in the Roman political system. The Roman understanding of those problems was sociological, though not in the same way in which we think about society. The problems were attributed to what we might best regard as "moral decline."

For Romans, morals were essentially public virtues and customs. A moral decline was a degeneration in the ways in which people conducted themselves socially and politically. The scope of morality covered relations to the gods, to the family, and to the state; morals were political. The cause of the decline of political culture was related to the transformation of Roman society through the acquisition of the benefits of empire. Wealth generated luxury. A desire for wealth animated political decision-making. In their desire for wealth, Romans ceased to be good citizens and became competitive individualists, and this transformation affected all levels of society.

In its essentials, this understanding of Rome's moral degeneracy is a fiction, even a myth. It projected a golden age into the past, but although the Romans may have felt that they could locate that golden age in the third century B.C. or earlier, no period of Roman history, as far as we can see, could make the claim to have been the golden age of Rome. The historian is often engaged in a losing battle in the face of the seductive power of myths; truth is often less persuasive than a simple and well-constructed story that everyone can believe. For if the troubles of Rome in the first century were not the result of a simple and shared moral weakness, they might be more difficult to understand, more intractable, and more complicated. Simple stories are reassuring, and this story had many attractions for elite Roman moralists, because it also offered a simple solution to those political problems: a return to the morals of the past.

Roman political thinkers had difficulty imagining what a new world might look like, but they had less trouble reinventing the old world. Augustan attempts at restoration of a version of the old moral order had begun in 28–27. Reforms of the senatorial rolls, the holding of the census and associated ceremonials, and most spectacularly the program of restoration of temples conducted in 28 attest a willingness to bring back an old-fashioned social and religious order. But if these were largely institutional reforms, the extraordinary ambition of the Augustan program is hinted in the rather unusual context of a love poem.

Propertius, whose elegant love poetry enlivens our understanding of the culture of the early Augustan period, wrote a poem reflecting on the joy of his girlfriend, Cynthia, when a "law" was withdrawn. The two lovers had wept at the prospect of legislation that would somehow separate them. But, Propertius concludes triumphantly, "Caesar is great in war, but conquered nations are worth nothing in love."[21] We cannot reconstruct what a law that would separate a man and his lover might look like. One would presume that it placed a requirement on Roman men and women to marry and that this requirement was supported by penalties sufficiently severe that even the most confirmed avoider of marriage would be obliged to abide by the law. The proposed law may also have made adultery a criminal offence. Propertius imagines his marriage procession making its mournful way along the street outside the house of Cynthia and weeping at his lost life of love. There appears to have been no possibility that Propertius and Cynthia could marry: marriage was antithetical to the life of a lover.

Propertius draws a clear ideological division in the poem. The law was about the military, designed to force Romans to produce legitimate children to serve in Rome's legions: Propertius asserted "None from my blood will be a soldier." Propertius claims that love is beyond the power of Caesar. Caesar can have his armies, but he cannot control love. The realm of love is, in Propertius's poetry, a realm of relative freedom from Augustan control.

It seems that Propertius was not a lone eccentric voice. The law failed in the assemblies, and we may presume that other lovers spent the night after the law's withdrawal celebrating as only lovers can. Propertius's poem was published in the mid-20s B.C., and the failed legislation must date to early in that decade. But if Propertius celebrated the lovers' triumph over Caesar, Caesar himself was not one to give up. After 19, newly powerful, he returned to his program of moral reform and proved to Propertius and Rome's other lovers that in love too Caesar was powerful.

The program of legislation was extensive. Initial legislation passed in 18 was sometimes modified later or extended. Furthermore, the imperial regime took this moral conservatism to its heart, pushing forward the imperial family as a model of good morals, encouraging the representation of traditional values in Roman art, and sponsoring behaviors that fitted the moral message; he appears to have claimed that the women of his family made his clothes (weaving being a traditional activity for the Roman matron), though tradition does not record what the imperial princesses thought of such enforced labors.[22] Legislation was passed which regulated or tried to influence the freeing of slaves; conspicuous luxury; the types of clothing to be worn; the marital choices of senators, their children, and their grandchildren; to whom property might be bequeathed; sexual behaviors; and treason.

The regulation of sexual activity was based on a morality very different from that of modern traditions. Marriage was for the production of children and the continuing of a family line; love had nothing to do with it. Roman men and women were encouraged to be married. Augustus passed a law in 18 by which a woman was required to remarry within six months after divorce. After the death of her husband, she was given a year's grace. Later, in A.D. 9, the law was amended to provide a period of grace of 18 months after divorce and two years after being widowed. The penalties related, it seems, to rights to receive inheritances and to make bequests.[23] Men were also to be punished for being unmarried, and rights to inheritance were similarly limited. A property tax was introduced, especially on the property of the unmarried wealthy. It looks also as if the unmarried were banned from the theatre.[24]

Both men and women were to be rewarded for having children. Women who had three children (and freedwomen who had four children) were made legally independent; women could not normally conduct legal business without a male representative. Men running for political office who had children were allowed to advance more quickly through the senatorial career. But the privileges were not limited to the political elite. When Augustus toured the various regions of Italy, probably visiting colonies and other communities and cementing his political relationship with their peoples, he gave 1,000 sesterces to the fathers for each child. Given that the annual salary of a soldier was 900 sesterces, this was a substantial amount of money, and assuming that there might be as many as 1,000,000 citizen children in Italy at any one time, it would also be a significant expenditure, though it is unlikely that these payments were systematic.[25]

The legislation was deeply controversial. There were demonstrations against it which were sufficiently vigorous that Augustus was forced to reform the laws, perhaps even in two different amendments.[26] At one demonstration in the theatre, late in Augustus's reign, he bounced the children of Germanicus and Agrippina on his knee to show the benefits of fatherhood (and great-grandfatherhood in this case).[27] In A.D. 9, there were further demonstrations in the theatre, and Augustus subsequently assembled the Roman equestrians in the Forum and harangued them on the subject.[28] Augustus also read to the senate in 18 B.C. the speech of Quintus Caecilius Metellus Macedonicus "On Growing the Population," first delivered in 131 B.C.[29] We have only a few words of it preserved, but that is enough to establish its tone:

> If we were able to do without a wife, citizens of Rome, we would all avoid
> that nuisance; but since nature has so arranged it that it is not possible to
> live comfortably with nor to live in any way without, we must make
> arrangements for our preservation over the duration rather than for our
> short-term pleasures.[30]

The point of reading the speech was to associate his attempted reforms with the old traditions of Roman morality, and even if Metellus had not succeeded in reforming Roman marital practices, the speech served Augustus's purposes in making his intervention conservative and familiar rather than innovative and invasive. Augustus could respond to his critics that his attempt to regulate the private lives of the citizens had parallels in Roman tradition, and the version that Dio gives of Augustus's speech to the childless in A.D. 9, though we cannot know whether it is accurate, replayed the themes of Metellus's speech in accusing the childless of endangering the very future of Rome and in putting pleasure ahead of the duty of procreation.[31]

Another law was passed making adultery a criminal offence. Adultery was defined as a married woman having sexual relations with a man who was not her husband, and both parties were judged to be guilty. A man could legally have sexual relations with a woman who was not his wife, provided that she was not married to someone else. Prostitutes were an exception to the law, and either by this law or by another law had to register. The issue related to the behavior of the young especially, but also to the production of legitimate children.[32] Adultery was punishable by loss of property and exile. Augustus laid a duty on a husband to prosecute a wife suspected of being guilty of adultery, and if he failed to do so after 60 days from the discovery of the alleged act, others were allowed to take up the case. If a woman was found guilty, her husband was obliged to divorce her or risk prosecution himself.[33]

These laws suggest moral panic. Although moralists throughout history have declaimed against the times and claimed that their era is more corrupt than any other, the evidence for such claims is normally flimsy. In Rome, for instance, there does not appear to have been a register kept of adulterous relationships which would be susceptible to statistical analysis. However, there was clearly a focus on the politics of the bedroom in the late Republican and early imperial periods that it is difficult to parallel from other Classical periods (or from many later times). The issue was not necessarily behavior, for who can estimate for any historical period the prevalence of illicit sexual acts, but that people worried about adultery.

The poetry of the time maintained a fascination with the politics of love and with the idea that love was not limited by the bonds of marriage or to the marital relationship. The poets drew a contrast between traditional *mores* and the life of love. The admittedly anecdotal accounts of the lives of the great men of the period, Julius Caesar, Mark Antony, and Augustus himself, emphasize the freedom with which they pursued their sexual desires in relations which were frequently adulterous in the Roman as well as the modern sense.[34] There were suggestions that Augustus had a taste for virginal girls and that very young women were procured for his pleasures.[35] There were also lascivious stories of a long-lasting affair with Terentia, wife of Maecenas. In the furor that followed the passing of the adultery laws, it was even claimed that in 16 B.C. Augustus was eager to leave Rome in order to take up duties in Gaul so as to continue his relationship with Terentia away from prying eyes.[36] If Augustus had carried on a semipublic relationship with his friend's wife over a 15-year period, after the passage of a law on adultery that relationship suddenly became criminal. It takes little imagination to think that once the formerly private lives of prominent men and women were subject to official sanction, Augustus's own bedroom arrangements would themselves attract hostile commentary.

Whatever their personal behavior, few politicians, ancient or modern, will stand up for the rights of adulterers. But the implications of the issue in Rome went far beyond the bedroom. Augustus was asserting a vision of Roman society and using the law to enforce that vision. It was the duty of Roman men and women to procreate. They were to make children for the Roman state: boys to fight, girls to be mothers of the next generation of soldiers. Romans worried about their population and its decline; they worried that there would not be a new generation of soldiers to maintain the empire. The personal lives of Romans were to be bent to that imperial goal. Discipline was to be enforced.

The regulation of Romans' marital lives was an extension of state power into the households of citizens. The unpopularity of the laws was due in large part to their practical effects on the ways in which Romans organized their lives. There are numerous personal reasons for individuals not to embrace the married state, of course. But Romans also operated a partible inheritance system, meaning that each legitimate child would expect an equal share of the family estate. The implications of such a system are that preservation of status over the generations was relatively easy if a family had only two children, but became progressively more difficult the more children the family had. Furthermore, because marriage was status-led and status ultimately followed wealth, an only child had a good chance of marrying a child of a family superior to that of her parents. The system would tend to mean that some smaller families would rise socially and economically while other larger families would fall.

One way of managing this social and economic elevator was to plan marriage. Augustan legislation, though, insisted on marriage. If any man delayed marriage in order to accumulate sufficient property to make a good match or to limit the chances of having a big family, or perhaps even to make allowances for an overly fertile sibling, he would fall foul of the Augustan legislation and not be able to inherit. If they could not inherit, the chances of the sons of a large family accumulating wealth in order to make a suitable match were limited. Some or even many Roman men made efforts to evade the law, contracting very long engagements or becoming engaged to girls not old enough to marry, and Augustus later closed loopholes in the legislation. Some may even have practiced family limitation strategies within marriage, such as abortion or infanticide, sexual restraint or nonreproductive sex, though we know almost nothing about how married couples behaved in the Roman bedroom.

One guesses that opposition to the Augustan laws was animated at least as much by the principles involved as by practical considerations.

Some might have taken the view of Metellus and regarded wives as an unfortunate inconvenience that would force uncomfortable adjustments to their style of life; Roman women expected to play a part in a household, and some at least may have taken a dim view of any concubines kept by their husbands. Other men perhaps lived a life of the demimonde, as reflected in the love poetry of the age, and marriage may have been incompatible with such a life. For others, the assertion of state power would have been intolerable. Roman myth-history may have glorified the subsuming of the individual to the interests of the state and patriotic, dutiful self-sacrifice, yet to demand that people procreate for the good of Rome was a startling invasion of individual liberty. Furthermore, the boys to be born were to fight in Augustus's armies and in Augustus's wars in the service of the Augustan state. The demands of the imperial regime were to put men and women in bed together, and this may not have been the most powerful of aphrodisiacs. As Propertius asserted, there would be no soldiers from his blood, no children to support the Augustan imperial vision. Others probably felt the same.

The laws opened a window into the bedrooms of the Romans that rendered men and women vulnerable to malicious prosecution. If in previous generations someone might gossip that the wife of his enemy slept around, under Augustus one might take her to court. Friendships between men and women risked being misinterpreted and the two being ruined. We may also wonder at the standards of proof required in court. There would be no photographers hanging around outside seedy hotels to provide the required evidence. Courts did not normally concern themselves with deciding issues "beyond reasonable doubt." Malicious gossip could be enough. Situations which were once resolved within the confines of households now had the potential to lead to disgrace, exile, and financial ruin. As the historian Tacitus was later to note:

> The crowd became more dangerous, since every household risked its overthrow by the arts of the informers.[37]

What began as laws enforcing a supposedly age-old discipline and a morality with which few right-thinking men could disagree became chains tightening the hold of the imperial power on the Roman people.[38]

THE GOLDEN AGE

On May 23, 17 B.C., the senate met under the chairmanship of the consul Gaius Silanus to discuss aspects of the Secular Games that were to be held under the authority of Caesar Augustus and Marcus Agrippa. The Games were to mark the end of a *saeculum* (an age) and consequently the beginning of a new age, one which after the *saeculum* of war and civil strife that had just passed would be an age of hope and peace, a time that the regime advertised as a new golden age.

The Secular Games were an old tradition which, like many others, had fallen into abeyance in the late Republic. The exact rules that governed the games were a matter of some dispute. The previous Secular Games had been held in 146 and the Games before that in 249. The Secular Games may have been an innovation of 249, a moment at which the Roman state thought itself in danger from Carthaginians. There may have been a feeling that Rome had lost the favor of the gods and dramatic action was needed to restore their blessings. Oracular books were consulted, and the gods of the underworld and the ancestors were identified as those offended. Consequently, the rituals of 249 were funereal, seeking to honor all those who had departed from the previous generation and centered on the gods of the underworld. The oracle which instructed the Romans to conduct these rituals specified a gap of 105 or 110 years between Secular Games. This was so that everyone who had seen the games would be dead by the time the next ones were held. The games were to mark a whole generation of the Roman people passing away. This relatively small and gloomy event was to be transformed by Augustus and Agrippa.[39]

The decree of the senate issued on May 23 was an effort to maximize the crowd for what was intended as a grand public ceremonial. The senators permitted those who were unmarried and any who were subject to penalty under the law on marriage between the orders to attend the Games. It was desired that as many people as possible would be present, since no one alive would ever see such games again. They also gave instructions that the event be recorded on an inscription, and a fragmentary version of that inscription has come down to us.[40]

Our account begins on May 31 with a nighttime sacrifice of nine sheep and nine goats to the Fates and a public prayer declaimed by the presiding priest, Augustus. Augustus asked that the empire and majesty of the people of Rome be increased; that the people of Rome and its legions have safety and victory; and that benefits accrue to the College of Fifteen (who were the presiding priests over this event), to the citizens, to Augustus himself, and to his household and family. There was then a performance of some kind and a sacred banquet for 110 selected wives of Roman citizens.

The following day, Augustus and Agrippa sacrificed bulls to Jupiter. Theatrical performances followed, and then the College of Fifteen delivered a proclamation reducing the period of mourning which citizen women were expected to maintain after their husbands' deaths. When night fell, Augustus conducted another sacrifice, this time of cakes, to Ilithyia, the goddess of childbirth. On June 2, Augustus and Agrippa sacrificed cows to Juno and a prayer was offered on behalf of the women of Rome, a prayer almost identical to that offered by Augustus the previous day. The nighttime sacrifice was of a pregnant sow to Magna Mater (the Great Mother). All these events took place, as was traditional for the Secular Games, on an area on the banks of the Tiber.

The next day, June 3, the focus shifted to the Palatine Hill, where Augustus had his residence, and sacrifices of cakes were offered to Apollo and Diana. A hymn, composed for the occasion by the poet Horace, was sung by a choir of 54 boys and girls. The party then adjourned to the Capitol, where the hymn was sung once more. There followed more theatrical performances and then chariot racing. At the end of these festivities, the College of Fifteen announced seven days of theatrical events, in Greek and in Latin. On June 12, there was a show involving the hunting of wild beasts in an arena and chariot racing. After all this, one presumes, life returned to normal.

Augustus and Agrippa transformed the secular games into a major festival. The meaning of the event was also changed. No longer was it so much about assuaging the dead, but about the future of the Roman state. Prayers were offered for the increase of empire, for the legions, and for the people of Rome. Prayers were also offered for Augustus, his household, and his family, a clear indication that the dynasty had become an arm of the state (and we may note that there is no obvious reference to the senate or the magistrates). Instead of gods of death, we see sacrifices to a goddess of childbirth. There is an emphasis on women and fertility and the matrons who will give birth to and provide moral guidance to the future generation of Romans. Children figure in the singing of Horace's hymn. On June 3, the location and nature of the religious activities changed completely. The focus shifted to the temple of Apollo on the Palatine, a temple built by Augustus, associated with his victory at Actium, and architecturally tied to his own house. Furthermore, the central role of the College of Fifteen appears to have been an innovation, developed primarily to allow the two leading figures of that College, Augustus and Agrippa, to dominate proceedings. This was, without doubt, their show.

The hymn that the choir of children sang (twice), known as the Carmen Saeculare, has come down to us. Horace was a leading poet of the age, famous for his lyrical odes and satires. He was close to the Augustan circle, principally, it seems, through Maecenas. The Carmen opens with an address not to the gods of the Underworld but to Apollo and Diana. The themes are obviously Augustan: the gods are asked to care for mothers, to make strong the youth, and to give force to the laws on parenthood and marriage. The Fates and Magna Mater are requested to bring fertility to the fields. Then, attention shifts to Rome's foundation, not so much to the story of Romulus and Remus but to the tale of Aeneas's flight from Troy and his settling in Italy. The poet asks that Augustus may conquer, before, in quieter tones, the poem looks forward generally to new eras of Roman peace and prosperity.

The Secular Games were a performance of the regime's ideology. They linked key ideas: military success, peace, prosperity of the land, childbirth, divine blessings, and the disciplining of the Roman people through legislation. At the heart of the Games was a particular vision of Roman history, one which departed from the traditional story. The Games were intended to mark the passing of a whole population of Roman citizens. Onto this unusual idea was mapped the Greek conception of ages. In Greek mythology, there was the concept of a Golden Age, a type of primeval paradise in which men did not have to labor, the world was at peace, and all had what they needed. This primitive communist Arcadia went into decline and was followed by ages which were progressively worse, degenerating to the Iron Age, a time of violence and warfare.

The idea was a commonplace of Latin poetry by the late Republic, being used famously by Catullus, perhaps the leading poet of the late Republic, and Virgil, who was to write the great Augustan epic, the *Aeneid*.[41] The Catullan use was firmly in the context of the representation of a mythic world from which his contemporary world was in decline, and the Virgilian poem envisaged an unlikely reversal of history brought about by a messianic figure.

The decline narrative was fundamentally pessimistic, with each age being worse than what had preceded it, and the question that beset the Romans was to what new lows they would fall. The Secular Games marked a radical departure, since what was to follow the age that was drawn to a close by the Games was not an age yet worse, but a renewed Golden Age. The positive imagery of childbirth, peace, youth, and fertility (human and agricultural) recalled the age of leisure in the mythic accounts. Augustus and Agrippa were claiming to start history again, announcing their own Year Zero.

The allusions to Aeneas in the Carmen Saeculare point to an Augustan emphasis on this particular foundation myth. The story was widely used in Augustan art, appearing in the grand Forum of Augustus in the center of Rome and in the smaller but exquisite Ara Pacis (Altar of Peace) that was to be built later in the decade on the Campus Martius. Among the friezes of the Altar is a depiction of Italia (or Peace herself) surrounded by images of fertility that reference the renewed vitality of the Augustan peace (see fig. 13).

Aeneas was important for the regime in large part because the Julian family claimed descent from his son, Iulus, and in 19, the Aenean legend

FIGURE 13

The Italia Relief from the Ara Pacis: The relief depicts a goddess, probably Italia, who is surrounded by symbols of fertility. The relief symbolizes the prosperity that has returned to Italy with the Augustan Peace.

had received a full epic retelling from Virgil. Virgil's *Aeneid* is one of the masterpieces of Latin literature and is probably the most influential of all Latin poems. At the heart of the poem are the character of Aeneas and his troubles and travails as he journeys from Troy to Italy and then fights in Italy to establish his people in Latium. The *Aeneid* echoes the Homeric epics, and there are close parallels with the *Iliad* and *Odyssey*. Virgil's epic is evidently not meant to be read as true but to function as a kind of myth-history of the foundation of Rome, a metaphoric rethinking of Roman history. Aeneas is not just a founder of the new community in Italy, but also a personification, perhaps a representation of the Roman character. His literary creation provokes musings on Roman masculinity, the relationship between individual and politics, and the nature of fate. As Aeneas travels in search of his new land, he must give up his old land, his wife, and then his lover. He loses his father and sees his friends killed. He must fight for a city the very foundation of which lies many generations in the future. He is shown often as a flawed hero, whose behavior raises questions as to how a Roman should act. He is almost always described as *pius*, "dutiful." Dutiful Aeneas with his devotion to the gods, to the state that will come into being, to his people and his fate recalls his descendant and successor Augustus. The story of a city and people remade after a catastrophic war had obvious resonances. The analogies are never straightforward, but are always present.

Augustus offered Rome a new beginning. But there was no attempt to hide the nature of the new state that Augustus was proposing. The invented traditions of the Secular Games were monarchic and authoritarian. The events may have been presented to their Roman audience as if they were somehow part of the archaic fabric of religious traditions in Rome, but this was a new Rome dominated by Augustus and Agrippa in which the imperial family was a central element.

Augustus claimed that he was returning Rome to an old-fashioned ideal. In his *Res Gestae*, he paradoxically wrote,

> By passing new laws, I recalled the decayed practices of our ancestors now fallen from use and myself established practices worthy of imitation by our descendants in many areas.[42]

Innovation and conservatism make uneasy bedfellows in the Augustan reforms. Even in 131, Metellus had contented himself with making striking and encouraging speeches. The conservatives of old had set themselves against the morality of their own ages, presenting themselves as eccentrics. Roman reality was, as far back as we can see (and the Romans may have been fully aware of this), different, more complicated, and far from morally uniform. The difference with Augustus was that he had the power to make this eccentric vision of the past a promise for the future. He tried to use state power to reshape Roman society and its mores.

The new society on display in Augustan literature and ceremonial needed to educate its people into its values. The people were meant to watch the games and understand the *Aeneid* and be educated in their dutifulness to the gods and Augustus. They were meant to devote themselves to service of the Augustan state. The men were to fight and to marry, the women to bear children for the Augustan legions. All were to have before their eyes the promise of a new Augustan future, a new age of prosperity and imperial peace, a new age of imperial gold in service to the imperial destiny of global empire. This was and is a totalitarian vision, and a vision shared by many dictators and megalomaniacs over the ages.

Perhaps twenty years later, the poet Ovid was to complain that girls no longer valued his poems:

> They praise poems, but they seek great gifts.
> Provided he is rich, a barbarian pleases.
> Truly, now are the Golden Ages: with gold
> comes many offices, with gold love is won.[43]

Augustus and Agrippa, like so many politicians, were selling a myth. Not everyone bought it. The truth was that Rome, like most complex societies, worked on power and money, and Ovid mocks the pretence that it could be otherwise. He adopts a nostalgic fondness for the older life before the decline in morality, recalling an age when a poet could seduce a girl with a fine turn of phrase. Now, in the new Augustan age, gold rather than verse is the way to a girl's bed. Whatever the politicians might promise about the virtuous life and the girls might say about the lovely poetry with all its fine sentiments, ultimately it was only gold that mattered. Rome was not to be converted to ancient morality by the sentimentality and conservatism of the political class. It was too complicated and diverse a place for that. Ovid's vision of an age of gold was one in which everyone had their price—politicians, soldiers, plebs, and girls. It was a different and more realistic vision than that propagated by the regime.

17.

THE IMPERIAL MONARCHY

B Y 18 B.C., IT was clear that the Augustan regime was a family affair, and the senior male family members came to be seen more and more as partners in the enterprise. If republicans nursed the fantasy that Augustus was just a blip in a history of the Republic that went back to 509, the powerful court that gradually emerged around the emperor was an uncomfortable dose of realism. The concentration of authority in the hands of those closest to Augustus and the familial nature of that court pointed to a future of monarchic government. Those around Augustus were unlikely easily to give up power; those outside the Augustan circle were equally unlikely to amass the resources, political, financial, and military, that would enable them to challenge the Augustans.

The Augustan regime had advertised itself as an imperial regime, bringing order to Rome and the disciplines required to fulfil Rome's imperial mission. In 30, Octavian had control over all the armies of the empire. As part of the settlement of 28–27 by which Octavian and Agrippa regularized their position within the state, that command was temporarily given up. But regularizing political authority did not mean laying down authority, and in 27 Augustus received the grant of authority over a huge proportion of the empire, involving two of the three provinces that made up modern Spain, four Gallic provinces, Syria, Phoenicia, Cilicia (in Eastern Asia Minor), Cyprus, and Egypt. There was a significant Roman military presence in the senatorial provinces of Africa, Dalmatia, and Macedonia, but the rest of the senatorial provinces —one Spanish province, Numidia, Crete, Cyrenaica (Libya), Asia, Bithynia, and Pontus (three of the four provinces of Asia Minor), Greece, and Sardinia—were all without large military garrisons.[1] There were to be revisions of the settlement later, with Augustus giving up control of Cyprus and the most southerly and peaceful province of Gaul (Gallia Narbonensis) but taking power in Dalmatia, which was at the center of a major expansion of Roman power to the line of the Danube.

It is likely that members of the Roman elite queried the need for a single dominant military leader. The question need not often have been explicit, but was clearly implicit in the political interactions of the period. Under the guidance of the senators, Rome had grown from a small city state to the mistress of a huge empire. If Rome had achieved so much under the Republic, there must at least have been a suspicion that monarchy would undermine Rome's imperial drive.

Augustan answer to such critics was the promise of world conquest, and it was a promise on which Augustus at least claimed to have delivered. The *Res Gestae Divi Augusti* (Achievements of the Deified Augustus), Augustus's final, self-justificatory account of his life, included a preface which made clear the military nature of the regime:

> Below is a copy of the Achievements of the Deified Augustus by which he subjected the lands of the world to the people of Rome.[2]

Augustan militarism and imperial expansionism were at the ideological center of the imperial regime as the resources of empire were the regime's financial foundation.

Augustus and Agrippa had been heavily involved in military matters from the first years of the Augustan Republic. In 27, Augustus left Rome for Gaul with the intention of invading Britain. He was, however, distracted by events in Spain. In 26, the Romans were fighting major wars in the Alpine region (under the command of Terentius Varro); in Spain against two tribes, the Astures and Cantabri (under Augustus); in Germany (under Marcus Vinicius); in Arabia Felix (under Aelius Gallus), probably in 26; and probably also in Dalmatia-Pannonia (under Marcus Primus). Although the Romans declared victories in these wars, many of the conflicts continued until 22–21 and, in some cases, for longer.[3]

At home, the Roman audience was repeatedly reminded of the various military successes. The repeated declarations of victory and success in campaigns may have alleviated the doubts of the skeptical, but the Augustan generals were doing no more than Republican generals had done: reporting their victories and expecting to be rewarded with celebrations and honors, no matter if the defeated peoples were not completely pacified. Glory followed victory, and military success justified political authority. The regime emphasized Rome's historical mission of imperial conquest. Virgil was to put into the mouth of Jupiter the prophecy that to the Romans was promised "empire without limits" in space or time.[4] Augustus's reassertion of his political authority in 19 was underpinned by the unprecedented military successes of the previous years.

But it was not just the grand public monuments and the epic poetry of the period that advertised Augustan militarism. Late in the reign, an exquisite intaglio was produced, known as the *gemma augustea* (see fig. 14), which was showed the triumphant and divine Augustus reclining in the midst of gods and welcoming a returning, victorious generous, while, on the lower scene, the human cost of Rome's imperialism was displayed: soldiers manhandle women (with clear allusions to rape), captives are prepared for slavery or execution, and barbarian tears are shed. The Romans glorified their wars, but they did not romanticize them.

In 16, in the aftermath of the rush of legislation and the Secular Games, Agrippa and Augustus resumed the program of imperial expansion. They concentrated their efforts on the West and the Danubian region. Tiberius and his brother Drusus were sent to gain military experience and win glory in the Alpine region, fighting through a politically disparate region controlled by numerous small tribes that the Romans named Rhaetia (mostly modern Austria). The Alpine tribes supposedly brought troubles upon themselves through acts of banditry, raiding, and the killing of male Romans they captured, including any of the unborn whom they mystically divined to be males. Drusus and Tiberius not only conquered the tribal lands but engaged in a systematic degradation of local political and social structures. They deported and enslaved large numbers of male inhabitants, reducing the population of significant stretches of territory.[5] The war continued into 14 and beyond, though

FIGURE 14

The *gemma augustea*: The intaglio shows a returning general being welcomed by a divine Augustus.

little is known of later campaigns, and in 6 B.C., Augustus built a victory monument at La Turbie in the Maritime Alps, to the east of modern Nice. It was an unusual design, a tower 35 meters high. The associated inscription listed 45 conquered tribes.[6]

Expansion into Germany also began in earnest after 17 and was led by Augustus himself until 13.[7] The war was sparked by yet more barbarian atrocities, or accusations of atrocities: an alliance of three German tribes arrested the Romans in their territory, crucified them, and then launched raids into Gaul.[8] When Augustus left, Drusus, who had presumably moved on from the Alpine war, took his place.[9] In 12, Drusus struck out across the Rhine. It is difficult to trace the route of his invasion, as we know very little about the place names of Germany in this period (see Map 7). But Drusus reached the North Sea, probably marching through modern Holland, establishing fortresses in a line roughly south of Bremen, perhaps 300 km from the Roman bases along the Rhine.[10]

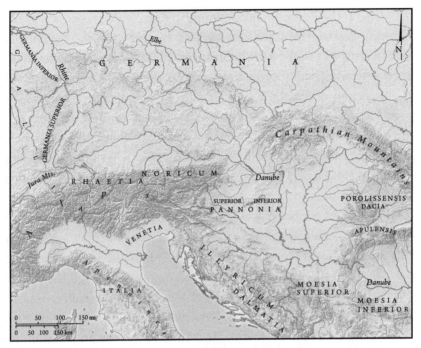

MAP 7

The Roman North

In 17, tribes from the Upper Danubian region struck south toward the Mediterranean. Further east, separate invasions of Macedonia sought to push the Romans back. The Roman client king in Thrace also suffered a tribal incursion. It is not obvious what caused this widespread movement or whether there was coordination between the various groups. The Danube was a major conduit of trade, and the peoples of the Upper and Lower Danube had reasons to maintain diplomatic contacts. The challenge posed by Rome was unprecedented. The Romans had been exerting pressure and expanding across the whole region for more than a decade, and the accumulated experience of resisting and being defeated by Roman legions may have encouraged a more coordinated approach, but the Romans were not easily stopped. They drove north to the line of the Danube and declared their control over the whole Balkan and Macedonian region.[11] The establishing of military bases and a provincial system did not, however, bring peace.[12] Roman victories were fragile.

By late 14, the Romans once again proclaimed victory, but late in the following year Agrippa was appointed to command in the region. His appointment was supposedly because the Pannonians were planning to revolt once more, but it presumably reflects the generally unsettled and rebellious state of Pannonia, which made further intervention necessary, from a Roman viewpoint at least. Agrippa wasted no time and attacked during the winter. The Romans had the advantage of professional troops, permanent camps, and well-organized logistics. Agrippa's campaign consolidated Roman power south of the Danube. His work done, Agrippa made his way back to Rome.

Agrippa never reached the imperial city. He died in Campania in 12 B.C.[13] Agrippa had been at Augustus's side since 44. He had either led or been next to Augustus in the wars against Lucius Antonius, Sextus Pompeius, and Antony. As consul, he had supported Augustus through the crucial years of 28 and 27, which gave shape to the Augustan Republic. He had fought in Gaul and Spain and prepared the ground for Augustus's campaigns against the Parthians. He had deputized for Augustus in the mid-20s, when Augustus himself had been in Spain, and subsequently in the difficult years after 23. Agrippa had taken charge of many of the largest and most prestigious building projects in Rome. After the death of Marcellus, Agrippa had been brought into the heart of the dynasty, marrying Julia (Augustus's daughter) and providing Augustus with grandchildren. He had been at Augustus's side when they celebrated the new Golden Age and had been granted the powers of the tribune in 18, a grant which was renewed in 13. In 13 or earlier, he was also granted powers in the provinces which equaled those of Augustus. Formally, Agrippa had the same powers as Augustus and was at the time of his death his partner in power.

Augustus travelled to Campania to be with his friend. He led the funeral cortege to the center of Rome, where the body was laid out in the Forum. Augustus himself pronounced the funeral oration, a fragment of which was discovered on an Egyptian papyrus in the university library in Cologne in 1970. The document is in Greek but is a close translation of the Latin original, and it seems likely that the speech was officially distributed to the provinces.[14] The fragment we have emphasizes the constitutional powers that Agrippa was granted: no one was his superior in power, not even Augustus. Even as the language used was rooted in the constitutionalism of Augustan politics, the predominance of the Augustan regime was advertised. Agrippa was then placed on his pyre and the ashes were committed to the Mausoleum of Augustus on the Campus Martius in Rome.

When Agrippa's will was read, it was announced that he had given estates to Augustus (not just those in Italy, but estates that he had somehow accumulated in the provinces). The people received gardens and a bathhouse, together with the funds necessary for them to be enjoyed without charge. A sum of 400 sesterces was distributed on Agrippa's instructions to each member of the plebs. There were funeral games which, according to the Roman custom, featured gladiatorial combats, and these were repeated in 7 B.C.[15] The public grief, the rituals and the ceremonials were a display not only of the importance of Agrippa, but also of the success of the regime in monopolizing power; few men had had careers of such prominence as Agrippa, with the magisterial posts, the armies led, the buildings constructed, but it was a new type of career, an imperial career in which he was always second to Augustus.

Augustus had lost his leading general and his political partner in power. But whereas two decades earlier this would have been a disaster for the regime, by 12, Tiberius (see fig. 15) and Drusus were in a position to take on the role of Augustus's old friend. With almost unseemly haste, Tiberius was divorced from Vipsania (Agrippa's daughter) and married to Julia (Agrippa's widow and Augustus's daughter). The marriage marked Tiberius as the leading figure in the imperial family after Augustus himself, and the program of imperial expansion continued without pause.[16]

In Germany, Marcus Lollius was drawn into battle and lost a legion.[17] Drusus, however, continued the campaign into 10, and for at least part of the year Augustus and Tiberius joined him in Gaul.[18] Drusus was consul in 9. He probably entered his consulship in Rome and left early in the year for Germany for the new campaigning season. He fought his way yet further east, crossing the Weser, probably on the line of the forts established in the preceding season, and reaching the Elbe, 100 km further east. He was the first Roman general to get so far into Germany (see Map 7). Legend has it that on crossing the river Drusus met an extremely tall woman who

FIGURE 15
Tiberius. After the death of Agrippa, Tiberius took up his role as the second man in the state and the
husband to Augustus's daughter, Julia.

predicted his death and ordered him to return home. He erected trophies
to celebrate his victory and obeyed the divine messenger, but on the way, as
she had promised, he grew sick. Tiberius rushed to his brother's side, probably from his own campaigns in Pannonia, and found him still alive, but
by the time the party had reached the Rhine, Drusus was dead.[19]

The Germans may have felt that after the death of Drusus, the Romans
would hold off, concentrating their major commanders elsewhere. But
Tiberius was transferred from the Danubian campaigns, and Augustus
himself returned to Gaul to supervise. With Augustus in Gaul and
Tiberius crossing the Rhine in force, there could be little doubt that the
Romans intended to prosecute the war vigorously. The Germans sued for
peace. But Augustus and Tiberius chose to treat them as a single people
and demanded that all the tribes agree to the settlement. When unanim-
ity could not be reached (and one wonders by what procedures the various tribes could have reached a common position), they arrested the

German ambassadors and imprisoned them. German resistance crumbled.[20] Tiberius was, however, still in the field in the following year, though he had returned to Rome during the winter to enter into the consulship.[21]

If the peoples of the Danubian region believed that Agrippa's death would lead to a reprieve, they were to be proved wrong. The Pannonians did indeed revolt, but Tiberius, who had been persuaded into Agrippa's widow's bed, also slipped, perhaps rather more comfortably, into Agrippa's military role and undertook campaigns in Pannonia. The Pannonians were again defeated, and Tiberius embarked on a program of deportation and enslavement, very much as Drusus and he had done in Rhaetia a few years earlier.[22] However, even this did not bring an end to the wars, and in 11, Tiberius marched south into Dalmatia to defeat another revolt and returned to Pannonia for yet another campaign.[23] Although Tiberius went to Gaul in 10, an incursion across the Danube by the Dacians, a tribe who were to cause the Romans considerable problems for the next 120 years, sparked further trouble in Pannonia. Tiberius returned to reassert Roman authority. His campaigns continued into 9, whereupon the Romans once more declared victory and peace.[24]

The death of Drusus was a considerable blow to the dynasty. His death was marked by an outpouring of public grief. Honors were granted to his mother, Livia, as a consolation.[25] For the second time in five years, Rome's people mourned. They mourned not for the loss of a statesman, as they had with Agrippa, but for a prince, showing their loyalty to and a personalized relationship with the imperial family. The funeral was another display of unity, community solidarity, and imperial political hegemony.

The deaths of Agrippa and Drusus made the dynasty less secure. The safety of the regime depended on there being a potential successor at the side of Augustus, a man of sufficient experience and political weight that he could negotiate the transition from the Augustan regime to whatever might follow. More prosaically, the potential benefits of conspiracy suddenly increased. Whereas before 9, the success of a conspiracy would depend on removing from power or killing Augustus, Agrippa, Tiberius, and Drusus, after 9, the potential targets had been halved. There was, however, another generation of potential imperial leaders emerging.

Gaius Caesar, son of Agrippa and Julia, was born in 20 B.C. His brother, Lucius, was three years younger, born in 17. These boys were rapidly brought to the fore. Both Gaius and Lucius were adopted by their grand-father in 17. Although this shows an expectation that they would be Augustus's heirs, they were too young to be considered as his immediate political successors; Rome expected its emperors to be leaders of men, and it was not until centuries later that the concept of a boy-emperor became acceptable. Germanicus, the oldest son of Antonia and Drusus, was born on May 24, 15. It would be also many years before he could take his father's place at the side of an emperor. Lucius, Gaius, Germanicus, and Tiberius's own son, Drusus (born on October 7, 13), were the next in line to become Rome's leaders, but they needed time to assume their designated roles. In the meantime, Augustus was reliant on Tiberius.

THE MALCONTENTS

After 19 B.C., opposition was also pushed into the margins. We are told, enigmatically, that Augustus often wore a breastplate when he entered the senate because he feared assassination and that around 18 "many" were accused of conspiracy against Augustus and Agrippa (both then and later) and some were executed.[26] Augustus was on campaign for much of the period from 16 to 8, but once more he faced trouble. There were conspiracies, though we have no names and no details and thus no evidence by which to assess the seriousness of the threats posed. But the conspiracies were sufficient to persuade Augustus to change the law, tightening the chains that bound the Roman political class. Romans customarily tortured slaves in order to extract evidence of criminal wrongdoing; a slave's evidence, it seems, could only be relied upon if extracted under such circumstances. But it was illegal to use evidence obtained from slaves under torture to implicate their masters. The law gave masters security in what was said and done within their own house-holds. Under the Empire, however, when all interests were subordinated to the state, this legal protection was evaded. Augustus ordered slaves of a suspected conspirator to be transferred to the state so that they could be tortured and their evidence used: at one stroke, the potential conspirator's household became a potential source of informants.[27]

The problem with such conspiracies is obvious. There is a fine line between dangerous talk and conspiracy. For emperors, there was a judgment to be made as to when expressed discontent became sedition. Suppressing a conspiracy came at a political cost: opposition was made public; the facade of unity and happy consensus was shattered; isolated but disgruntled individuals would see that they were not alone. Others might be inspired to follow where previous attempts had failed. Violently removing political enemies left a legacy of trouble for emperors. It was an act of tyranny which ironically provided evidence in support of those disposed to conspire to remove the tyrant.

The only conspiracy about which we have much detail comes from much later, from about A.D. 4, when there is a report of a major conspiracy centering on Gnaeus Cornelius. We know about the conspiracy precisely because Augustus broke from his usual policy. He did not kill Cornelius and his supporters. This was no outbreak of compassion from a leader suddenly concerned by the ghosts of the many who had fallen in the Augustan quest to obtain and maintain power, but was an attempt to break the cycle of violence. We have an entirely fictional dialogue between Augustus and Livia, preserved in different versions in the writings of the first-century political philosopher Seneca and in the third-century historian Cassius Dio. As a result of Livia's advice, Augustus supposedly called together the conspirators, warned them, and sent them on their way.[28] Cornelius was even consul the following year, A.D. 5. Whatever we make of the truthfulness of the ancient accounts, the episode suggests that the regime was trapped in a vicious cycle of violence and opposition from which there was no obvious escape.

The laws regulating family formation and sexual behavior were to remain a point of contention, leading to a major demonstration in A.D. 9 by the equestrians. Augustus addressed the crowd, praising those who had fathered children and offering them further distinctions or honors and, probably, cash. The childless had a contrasting treatment, being accused of acting as libertines, putting their own pleasures before the interests of Rome, comparing them to murderers for not fathering the next generation, and temple robbers for not producing children who would take up the duties of honoring the gods.[29] Nevertheless, the consuls of the year passed a law, the Lex Papia Poppaea, modifying the provisions of earlier legislation and moving towards a regime of reward rather than punishment; as it happens, neither of the consuls was married.

We can see opposition in the literary sphere. Ovid, the last of the renowned Augustan poets, ended his days in exile. He was exiled by decree on two charges; one related to a poem, the other to an unspecified "error." Ovid tells us all this in a long poem that begs for mercy and recounts his faults, the second poem in a collection called the *Tristia*, "Sad Ones."[30] In this poem, Ovid teases his readers. He will not speak of the error because it would open up old wounds. But through that very act of not speaking, his audience, some of whom would presumably have known the error, would be forced to recall and evaluate it, while others, like us, are left to speculate and invent an error sufficient to have caused a well-known poet to be threatened with death and then exiled.

The poem is, however, known: the *Ars Amatoria*, Ovid's guide to love. In this poem, Ovid takes on the persona of the "teacher of love," directing his lessons to both men and women who wish to find lovers. Ovid is not running a marriage bureau. Marriage was a family matter in which wealth, social status, prospects, and the general utility of the alliance were central to the decision to marry. Ovid is interested in finding partners for sexual intrigues. He warns the readers off adulterous relationships, since these are illegal ("We sing of safe sex; there will be no crime in my verse"),[31] but the warning is formulaic and everything in the text points to the potentially adulterous nature of the liaison ("All women are liable to be caught").[32] The man must get into the house of the girl, and for that he needs to befriend the husband; the girl needs to find a way of distracting the attention of a potentially jealous spouse.[33] The *Ars Amatoria* is an adulterer's handbook in an age when adultery was a criminal offence.

But in *Tristia* 2, even as Ovid's abjection moves from an admission of his wrongdoing to a plea for clemency and a prayer for the imperial house, the poet seems to lose track and patience and inserts an angrier tone. He quotes the *Ars Amatoria* and notes that he warned his readers off respectable married women (conveniently forgetting the supposed vulnerability of all women to his techniques). He asks Augustus whether he has even read the poem. He recites instances of sex and violence from the mythic history of Rome, of which there is an abundance. He recounts all the places where boy might meet girl in Rome—the theater, the circus, the lavish porticos with which Augustus and Agrippa had adorned the city, the temples of Jupiter and Juno and Mars and Isis—and points out that all these buildings remain open. The whole of the city becomes a possible scenography of dissidence. Sex was written into the fabric of Roman culture, and Ovid set about uncovering the city of sex. He remembers the mythic stories of divine lust and rape. He produces a long list of respected poets who wrote tales of love and adultery. Tellingly, he wonders why Augustus should bother about light verse and an insignificant poet when he had Pannonians and Thracians and Parthians to conquer. With all that to occupy him, he worries about love poetry?

Ovid's apology slips into accusation. He punctures the ideology; he shows the tyrannous nature of Augustan power. He portrays it as arbitrary and cruel, like the arbitrary acts of the gods. He shows a Rome that is decadent, but one which has always been decadent. Augustan Rome is a city in which even a minor figure like Ovid could become an enemy of the state for the crime of unauthorized love. When Ovid looks at Augustus, his political power, his wealth, his armies, he sees someone so far beyond the norms of political life that he seems a god among men; Ovid's poetry of sex was throwing twigs at a political colossus. But the colossus responded by exiling the poet.

The relationship of power to ideology is intimate. Power seeks to legitimate itself through ideology. To question a regime's ideology brings into doubt the social benefits that the regime offers. Opposition invites exclusion. In totalitarian regimes, many may adhere to the grand ideas of the regime, but others who regard the official ideology as nonsense will find contingent advantage in going along with the regime. The Augustan regime implicated its people in its political structures, involved them in its imperial mission, and invited the people to celebrate its successes and mourn its losses, both in war and in the domestic sphere of the imperial family. Individuals were encouraged to acquiescence by the benefits they received from the regime. A republican-minded senator, finding himself and his family enriched, finding peace and security comforting, being rewarded with positions of authority in the provinces and magistracies at home, perhaps being treated with honor by the emperor himself, might find reasons not to express his distaste for the regime. Open opposition could bring no benefit. As a result, opposition was forced down two separate paths: it could be radicalized into political conspiracy or reduced to irony. In either case, official toleration was limited. We may pretend to wonder with Ovid why a leader so respected and so honored and with universal support would concern himself with a naughty poet of sex. But all Romans knew the answer: the regime allowed no opposition.

CRISIS AT COURT: THE FALL OF TIBERIUS

In spite of the rumbling opposition, no doubt irritating in its own way, and the loss of Agrippa and Drusus, the regime still had control of the mechanisms of power. In 8 B.C., Augustus renewed the constitutional arrangements of 18 by accepting the power of the tribune for a further ten-year period. Tiberius was consul for a second time in 7, and Augustus celebrated with a gift of money to the soldiers and the veterans in the colonies, renewing his links with the military. Tiberius was granted a triumph, allowing him to parade through the streets of Rome as Augustus's partner in power, a great Roman military leader, and the presumed successor of the emperor.[34] But Augustus himself was to be yet further honored. His birthday was now to be marked by annual games held in the Circus Maximus. The Roman month of Sextilis was renamed August, following on from the commemoration of Julius Caesar through the naming of July. These were spectacular honors, more suited to gods than to men.

As the new consuls of 6 B.C. took their official oaths, Tiberius was granted tribunician power. He was now in the same position that Agrippa had enjoyed, junior partner in Augustus's regime. Tiberius was preparing to leave Rome for Armenia, where the king had died and the region was unsettled. Armenia had been the scene of Tiberius's first military adventure, and there was an imperial logic to launching a grand campaign in the East as a means of further elevating his political status and demonstrating once more that the demands of the empire required the imperial family.

But Tiberius never got to Armenia. Something happened. Behind the closed doors of the imperial court, there must have been an argument, and Tiberius lost it. Rather than wait on events, live to fight another day, and employ his undoubted political resources, Tiberius begged to be allowed to retire. The dispute went public, though publicity was probably inevitable in the tight-knit world of Roman politics. Livia intervened on behalf of her son, perhaps trying to broker an agreement with Augustus, who openly complained at his desertion and refused Tiberius permission to retire. Tiberius starved himself for four days before Augustus relented.

Tiberius left Rome for Rhodes. He had been to Rhodes on one of his earlier trips to the East and enjoyed himself. He found himself a small house, without all the usual paraphernalia of the villa of a great Roman, and took to wandering into the town and chatting with the townsfolk. He had, it seems, retired.[35]

Tiberius's withdrawal must have been a great political shock. It was almost without precedent in Roman political life: only the very old or the politically isolated withdrew from politics, and Tiberius was neither. For a Roman man of his status, involvement in political life was not a career choice—it was part of his identity. Withdrawal from that life was a rejection of the fundamental social values of Rome and its hierarchy. It could be read or justified as a reaction to a state so corrupt that there was no place there for the good man. Later, there was speculation that he was tired of his wife, Julia, appalled by her infidelities. Yet, in 6 B.C., Julia sat at the heart of the imperial family. If the relationship between Tiberius and Julia was the subject of speculation or gossip, it would hardly seem enough in itself to drive Tiberius from Rome.

It cannot be a coincidence that 6 saw the emergence of Gaius (see fig. 16) and Lucius (see fig. 17) on to the public stage. Gaius, aged 14, was appointed to a priesthood, a major honor for a Roman senator. And then, in the elections for the consulship of 5 (which would have been held in the summer of 6), the people elected Gaius consul. We cannot know whether the election of Gaius predated Tiberius's retreat or was a response to it. Whatever the case, his popularity likely contributed to Tiberius's disaffection.

The election of one so young was, of course, unprecedented. He was even younger than Octavian had been when he took up his adoptive father's legacy and launched himself on Roman political life. Augustus responded in republican fashion by rejecting the election, reprimanding the people for their show of support for the young man.[36] Augustus pointed out to the people that he himself was still alive, and there was no need to throw such responsibilities on someone so young. At some point, he publicly reprimanded both Gaius and Lucius for their lifestyles, which seemingly fell short of the expectations of Roman discipline. But if these events caused Augustus embarrassment, they also signaled the mood of the plebs and the direction of Roman politics; it mattered little to the crowd that Gaius was so young. The outward republicanism of the constitutional arrangements had no obvious influence on the voters' behavior. What mattered was that he was the grandson of Augustus. The election was a manifestation of a royalist ideology.

FIGURE 16
Gaius Caesar, son of Julia and Agrippa and grandson of Augustus.

For Tiberius, the evidence of the popularity of Gaius was bad news. In traditional terms, there could be no contest between the two. Tiberius was a two-time consul, a general of many years' experience, and a man who had been at the heart of the Augustan circle for his whole adult life. Gaius was a boy. Nevertheless, the expectations of the people were obvious. Augustus may have restrained the crowd's enthusiasm, perhaps as much for the benefit of the watching senators as anything else, but the election made clear that the question was not whether Gaius would emerge as Augustus's successor, along with his brother Lucius, but when.

Once Gaius and Lucius assumed the imperial position, then the role of Tiberius would be that of loyal supporter and advisor, an Agrippa to their joint Augustus. It was obvious that the senior man might find this role difficult and that being asked to take second place in the Augustan regime to boys so young could be understood as an offence against Tiberius's *dignitas*. Even if Tiberius had left Rome before the electoral demonstration in favor of his wife's eldest son, as an experienced

FIGURE 17
Lucius Caesar, son of Julia and Agrippa and grandson of Augustus.

315

politician he would have understood the way the politics were shaping and known that this dispute had only one outcome. As the boys grew older, Tiberius would find his position progressively weakened and would watch as his wife's children supplanted him.

The problem that beset the imperial family in 6 was both personal and ideological. Rome had not had a monarchy for five centuries. Romans were, of course, very familiar with how kingship worked, observing the long traditions of monarchy in the Greek world, but the Augustan Republic was not a straightforwardly regal system. Augustus had given his power the veneer of a magistracy, and the imperial position, even after Augustus, retained republican characteristics, being ratified by law. In an Augustan Republic, it might be expected that imperial power should pass to the senior man in the state, and Tiberius was clearly that man. But Tiberius was now challenged by a boy whose only claim to power was his grandfather. We have, thus, two contrasting systems of legitimation in play.

Although many senators might have sympathized with Tiberius, what they saw was the same structural problem that had condemned the senators themselves to secondary status. A republic judges great men on their achievements (at least in theory), whereas in a monarchy (again in theory) greatness depends on birth. Tiberius's prospects were best served by the Augustan Republic behaving like a republic and treating him as the senior man, but the electorate had behaved as if they were living in a monarchy and had shown their preference for authority passing down the family line. Although neither the monarchists nor the republicans were clearly in the right, given the paradoxical nature of the Augustan Republic, the flouting of Tiberius's expectations had a certain justice to it. Tiberian preeminence did not stem from his innate brilliance, which had been identified from an early age by his stepfather, but arose from the monarchic features of the regime. The logic of the political culture that had raised him up was about to consign him to secondary status. Whatever the justice of his position, by late 6, Tiberius was gone.

Augustus was now 57, not old as such but of an age when he was no longer expected to be long in the front line of Roman political life. But he was not about to follow his son-in-law into retirement. He himself took the consulship for 5 to reassert his authority and his leadership of Rome. He used his position to advance Gaius and Lucius. Gaius was introduced to the senate. The young man was to gain the experience he so patently lacked by watching from the side of his grandfather. The following year Lucius was awarded the same privilege of early entry into the senate. Gaius was also elected as consul, but for five years in the future, when he would be twenty. Lucius was given the same advanced notice of his consulship. Although allowing an early candidature had become a normal means of advancing a member of the imperial family, the actual election of Gaius was an innovation, and one that reflected the unstable political situation following the retirement of Tiberius. It had become necessary to fix the future. Augustus was asserting that it would be a future under the authority of the Julian dynasty. The early election nailed the boys into a future leadership role in Roman politics and provided the electorate with a further opportunity to display their support for the regime and for the boy, just in case it crossed anyone's mind to challenge the dominion of the Augustan family.

Over the next years, Augustus made ample use of ritual, ceremonial and spectacular, to assert the hegemony of his dynasty over all aspects of Roman political life. In one instance, also in 5 B.C. (or just possibly 4), the equestrians gathered in some type of informal assembly and in a supposedly spontaneous demonstration of support acclaimed Gaius, and perhaps at the same time Lucius, as *principes iuventutis*, the first among the young, a title that paralleled Augustus's own assumption of the title *princeps senatus* (first man of the senate) in 28.[37]

Augustus also sought to secure the support of the plebs. After more than a decade in which he had found little need to spend money on the plebs, he had distributed the bequest of Agrippa in 13, and then 400 sesterces each to at least 250,000 plebs in 12 to celebrate his election as Pontifex Maximus, following the death of the long-disgraced Lepidus. In 5 B.C., a new disbursement celebrated the emergence of his grandsons onto the political scene. The population of the city, 320,000 recipients, were awarded 240 sesterces each.[38] Still, the position of the regime was fragile. Gaius and Lucius needed to grow up; Augustus had to live a little longer until they were of age. Both were teenagers and without political experience or political weight. One suspects that if Augustus had died before 2 B.C., Tiberius would have rapidly returned to Rome to assume the imperial position. The boys were still not viable successors to the imperial position. Such uncertainties are reflected in the treatment of Tiberius. A path was left open for his return in spite of the public nature of the breach within the imperial family. The tribunician power that Tiberius had been granted just before his departure was not withdrawn and Julia was not divorced from her estranged husband, so formally at least he remained at the center of the imperial household. Nothing was done to formalize Tiberius's retirement into an exile, even as Julia's sons rose in political status.

But Augustus did not die. In 2, he was once more consul. It was his thirteenth consulship. Augustus also gave out another gift, also of 240 sesterces, but this time to only the 200,000 men in receipt of the grain dole. He staged a spectacular celebration to mark the long-delayed opening of the Forum of Augustus and the Temple of Mars Ultor (Mars the Avenger) at its heart. The Temple of Mars Ultor (see fig. 18) was a dynastic monument. It had been vowed 40 years earlier as a reward to Mars for the vengeance exacted on the assassins of Caesar. The Forum celebrated the martial achievements of the conquering heroes of times past who had guided Rome on its journey from village to imperial power.[39] The Forum was a representation of the Augustan vision of Roman history, martial and imperial and a representation of family history, with Mars and Augustus at its heart.

Augustus staged a magnificent program of events. There were chariot races. The aristocratic youth of the city performed the "Trojan games," supervised by their future leaders, Gaius and Lucius, as well as their younger brother, Agrippa Postumus. Two hundred and sixty lions were killed in the arena. Elsewhere, there were gladiatorial bouts. There was a dramatic reenactment of a naval battle between Persians and Athenians, probably the battle of Salamis, which the "Athenians" won for a second time. Finally, a circus was flooded and a hunt staged in which 36 crocodiles were killed.[40]

The extravagance of the games reflected the wealth and power of the empire. There were, of course, the human lives to be thrown away in the spectacular combats. Bringing such volumes of water to the city to stage a mock naval battle was in itself a spectacular engineering triumph. But we should also consider the animals. The lions were presumably brought from Africa. They needed to be trapped, secured, transported to the sea, and then shipped, all without the aid of a tranquillizer dart. The crocodiles must have been captured on the Nile and then transported to Italy. These exotic creatures were symbolic of the power of an empire that could govern such distant lands and bring such creatures to be viewed by the Roman crowd: the world was plundered for entertainment. The crocodiles also represented Egypt, and in their hunting the Roman audience were provided with a narrative of Augustan power which ran from the conquest of Egypt to the dynastic triumph of the Augustan family. The audience was invited to join together in a communal celebration of empire, conquest, Rome, and the Augustan family.

The people responded according to the script. As Augustus remembers it:

> The senate, the equestrian order, and the whole people called me *pater patriae* (father of the nation) and this was inscribed on the entrance to my house, on the senate house, and in the Forum of Augustus beneath the four-horsed chariot voted to me by the senate.[41]

FIGURE 18

The Temple of Mars Ultor is the centerpiece of the Forum of Augustus built in the heart of Rome. It was vowed to Mars by Octavian in return for his support against the assassins of Caesar and became a monument to Augustan imperialism.

Other accounts suggest that it was the plebs who came up with the idea: they sent a deputation to Augustus while he was staying outside the city at Antium and offered him the title of *pater patriae*. Augustus refused, but when he was next in the theater, the offer was repeated by a crowd wearing laurel wreaths. Next, Valerius Messala spoke in the senate and offered Augustus the title once more. This time, a tearful Augustus accepted the honor.[42]

The Forum of Augustus was given a place in Roman ceremonial life. When cohorts of boys became eligible for military service, they were to assemble in the Forum, presumably to be impressed by the military heritage of Rome and to be encouraged to offer themselves up to the legions.[43] Governors and legionary commanders were supposed to start their journeys to the provinces from the Forum. The senate was instructed to hold debates on the granting of triumphs in the Forum, and those awarded triumphs were supposed to dedicate their triumphal crowns to Mars in this temple.[44] The standards returned by the Parthians in 20 were dedicated to Mars and relocated to the temple. The Forum functioned as the ceremonial heart of the military empire.

The events of 2 B.C. portrayed Rome at peace with itself, happily under the authority of the father of the nation, controlling and expending the resources of empire. There was a renewed confidence to the regime. Gaius was to be sent to the Danube to gain experience with the legions. Lucius would undoubtedly follow when the time was right. The boys were old enough to embark on public life. The succession was secure and the family once more settled. Moreover, Augustus was not yet dead. With every year, his sons grew more plausible as leaders and the regime's future more clear. The storm, it seemed, had been weathered, and the regime had survived its dynastic crisis. Tiberius's path back to power was slowly being closed off, and the Roman people, those of a monarchic disposition at least, could begin to imagine a smooth transition of power from the aged Augustus to his glamorous grandchildren.

Then, events turned.

18.

DEATH OF AN EMPEROR

A T SOME TIME DURING 2 B.C., a praetor was dispatched to the senate to read a letter from Augustus. Few could have expected its contents. Augustus told the senators that he had banished his only daughter, Julia. She was sent from Rome to the small island of Pandateria, a prison island in the Tyrrhenian Sea. The charges were outrageous: Julia held wild parties; she and her companions caroused in the Forum, and even on the speaker's platform itself; she committed adultery. But this was no ordinary adultery. Julia was supposedly wildly promiscuous. She had aristocratic tastes. Her lovers included Iullus Antonius, the son of Mark Antony; Sempronius Gracchus, from the family of the brothers Gracchi who had been at the center of so much turbulence in the last decades of the second century; Quintus Crispinus, a noted moralist; Appius Claudius, from perhaps the most noble house in Rome; a Scipio; and others, both senatorial and equestrian, whom the tradition does not name.[1] Iullus Antonius was executed; conspiracy was added to his sexual crimes. The others were exiled, as was laid down by law as the punishment for adultery. After her exile, Julia was denied all luxuries and deprived of almost all male company. Augustus received a report on the appearance of any man who was to be sent to her or who was to be posted to her guard. The implication is that her desire was such that even on her island prison, she would seduce her captors and engage in debauches.[2] Augustus sent her a deed of divorce on behalf of Tiberius.

This mix of sex and politics is the very stuff of an imperial court. But the ancient commentators concentrate on the sex, in spite of the very obvious truth that within a monarchy sex and politics are inextricably intertwined. Julia had been given to her various husbands for straight-forwardly political reasons. Born in 39, on the very day on which Octavian had divorced her mother, she had been at the heart of the Augustan regime all her life. It seems unlikely that she was politically naive. She cannot have believed that her sexual behavior was a private matter. Similarly, any men associated with her would have been aware of the consequences of any illicit sexual relationship with the daughter of Augustus, a woman who was, after all, married.

The accusation of sexual promiscuity was an easy charge to lay against prominent women. It was fundamentally misogynistic, making the assumption or the charge that any woman who might wish to pursue a political agenda and develop a circle of male friends, for whatever reason, would employ her sexual wiles to entrap unfortunate and defenseless men. Accusations of sexual misdemeanors were easily made, but not easily disproved.

Roman women of this period were not restricted to the home. They had friends. They went to parties. They had social relationships. A prominent woman would be expected to manage unofficial political business. Julia probably maintained a separate house from those of her husband and father, possibly on a lavish scale. Her friends will have been drawn from the highest echelons of Roman society. These will have been men and women of status and independence. Julia was powerful in part because of those friends, but also because of her access to Augustus and the other great men of the imperial family. She was also mother to the boys who were expected to inherit the empire. It was quite obvious that Julia was a power broker in Roman politics. Aspiring politicians would assume she could influence their prospects. It is not difficult to believe that she acquired a glamorous, powerful circle who expected to share in her political good fortune when her father eventually passed on. It was this circle that was crushed in 2.

The fall of Julia had no obvious cause. We may be confident that many people dismissed the stories of gross immorality that circulated. A freed-woman of Julia's, Phoebe, hanged herself when Julia's disgrace became known, which was taken as evidence of the immorality that had infected her household; Scribonia, Julia's mother, in a gesture that was both political and personal, accompanied her daughter into exile, as if to deny the stories that were being peddled. Others had to decide what to believe. Five years later, the people demonstrated in Julia's favor, demanding that she be recalled; she was not disgraced in the popular view. Augustus refused.[3]

There was a schism at the heart of the imperial family between Tiberius and Julia and her sons. The politics of that schism were brutal. Even 14 years later, on his accession, Tiberius dealt bloodily with the unfinished business of Julia and her circle. But although it is easy to see how Tiberius and Julia might end up at daggers drawn and tempting to see Tiberius's hand behind the fall of Julia, in 2 Tiberius was himself in disgrace on Rhodes, his influence weakening by the month, and, one presumes, his ability to compete politically with Julia's circle reduced. Tiberius's time seemed to have passed, and he was not the immediate beneficiary of Julia's fall. He remained on Rhodes, and there was no dramatic return for the cuckolded spouse. If Tiberius's supporters had engineered her disgrace, it is not obvious that Tiberius won anything from it.

The dispute is most likely to have originated in the relationship between Julia and her father. Julia was gathering supporters among the aristocracy, the kind of men whose loyalty would be essential should her father, now over 60 and old in Roman terms, die suddenly. Such an operation required tact. Julia's planning for the political situation after the death of her father may have seemed to anticipate the event, and one can see that, at a human level, such activities might have been irritating for the aging emperor. At a political level, Julia's powerful political group could easily be seen as eager for a post-Augustan future. Still, this hardly seems enough for what happened next. Augustus's actions betray a vitriol that suggests that whatever Julia had done, he saw it as a betrayal.

Allegations of sexual misconduct were the easiest way to ruin a royal princess, but if the fall of Julia was a political dispute that went wrong and was purely a result of political intrigues in the court, one would have to wonder why the charges of sexual misconduct were brought. The charges would seem to heighten the political damage, increasing the levels of political embarrassment. Was it better for Julia, the mother of the presumed successors to Augustus, to be seen as a sexually promiscuous adulteress than as a political opponent to her own father? If the charges were just the means by which Julia's enemies struck at her, once has to wonder why Augustus did not see through the stratagem. The complaints of her father also appear to have a consistency to them. The information is anecdotal and thus cannot entirely be trusted, but Augustus behaved as if he was convinced the issue was one of sex rather than politics. Whatever Julia and her friends did or did not do, it seems unavoidable that we conclude that the sex scandal was not an excuse—it was the heart of the matter.

The charges of immoral sexual conduct carried an ideological weight. The Augustan regime had sponsored an association between morality and the political community. Perhaps from 28, when the first reforms of the Republic were attempted, but certainly from 18, the Augustan regime had associated itself with moral reforms. A restoration of moral values was seen as the way to civic peace and imperial success. Augustus justified his own position and legitimized his regime through those reforms (conducted while Augustus was censor or acting as "overseer of laws and customs").[4] The Augustan monarchy had set itself in a conservative mode, and there is little doubt that Augustus had encountered severe opposition as a result.

It is not difficult to imagine that Julia and her circle were more relaxed about moral issues than Augustus. The politics of monarchy allowed for displays of status, extravagance, and luxury that would separate the lives of the royals from those of the ordinary people whom they ruled.[5] The path that Antony and Cleopatra had taken to assert their monarchic claims was still one that was open to the protean Roman imperial monarchy. In the rather stern moral environment of the later Augustan period, Julia and her supporters could hope to capitalize on the evident discontent with the regime's moralizing and offer an alternative view of Roman monarchy. In such circumstances, a more luxurious lifestyle was a political statement, and a contentious one. A relaxed attitude to sexual morality could also be seen as a political choice, aligning Julia more closely with the behavioral politics of Propertius and Ovid than with the traditions of the old Republic.

Many matters were involved in the exile of Julia, and to reduce her fall to a single point of contention is to mislead. Augustus and Julia were father and daughter. Their relationship was inevitably both public and private. The world of court politics was undoubtedly labyrinthine in its complexity. The argument was about the future of the monarchy and moral behavior and the nature of Roman political culture. By exiling Julia, Augustus reasserted the vision of Rome and its monarchy that he had been propagating for nearly 30 years. In the evidently vicious internal politics of the Augustan court, Julia's exile was an extreme way of attempting to close down the argument. It was also an assertion of power: Augustus showed that however glittering and well-connected the circle that surrounded Julia, he would determine the future course of Roman monarchy and therefore of Rome itself.

Given what was at stake, Augustus did not win the argument simply by exiling Julia. The later popular demonstrations in favor of Julia can be linked to the demonstrations against the marriage legislation as a rejection of central elements of Augustan ideology.

Julia's disgrace had no obvious dynastic implications. The fundamental choice was between a future in which Gaius and Lucius were to succeed their grandfather and one in which Tiberius was to become emperor, but the sudden fall of Julia did not hinder the rise of her sons. Both Gaius and Lucius were advanced further up the political ladder. Lucius Caesar, the younger brother, was sent to Gaul to meet provincial notables and become familiar with one of the key provinces of the Empire. Gaius was sent to the Danube, but then he moved to the East. Armenia had been unsettled since 6 B.C., when Tiberius had been designated to intervene. An alliance had formed between the Parthians and the Armenians that threatened Roman hegemony, though Augustus had not felt the need to dispatch an army until Gaius was ready to assume his imperial role. Gaius was meant to intimidate the Parthians and the Armenians. In a replication of events of 20, the Parthians were faced with a bellicose prince intent on winning glory, and they made the same decision as they had 20 years earlier—they made peace. The Armenians, however, decided on war.[6]

The Parthians were not the only ones intimidated by Gaius's presence in the East. Tiberius may have been behaving as if he was committed to the quiet life, but few will have believed his protestations of fatigue. He had not completely given up on the political game, nor had Rome entirely forgotten about him. Governors found it politic to visit Rhodes on the way east and pay their respects to the former heir-designate. But as the boys matured, the fortunes of Tiberius fell. The citizens of Nemausus (Nîmes) in Gaul decided to overthrow their statues of Tiberius. Normally, this would have been a treasonous act, but it seems likely that Lucius was at least sympathetic to their actions and could protect those who were engaged in this political vandalism.[7] From Gaul, Lucius could not touch Tiberius; Gaius, on the other hand, had wide authority in the East, though one cannot imagine that he could have moved against Tiberius without the approval of Augustus.

There were rumors that Tiberius was plotting, perhaps even corrupting centurions to take action against Gaius. If Gaius "detected" Tiberius in a plot against his own life, he could have been forgiven for striking him down without reference to his grandfather. Tiberius left Rhodes and sailed to meet the young Caesar. The older man was forced to beg for forgiveness, a humiliation which marked a shift in the political balance of power.[8] A story circulated that when Gaius was holding a dinner party, someone stood up and volunteered to sail to Rhodes and bring back the head of "the Exile." The East was becoming dangerous for Tiberius, and he petitioned to be allowed to return. Augustus let him come back to Rome, probably in A.D. 2, on condition that he remain out of politics.

But in A.D. 2, Lucius fell ill. The illness was short, and he died in Marseilles on August 20. He was only 19.[9] The convenience of the death led to rumors that Tiberius was behind it. Worse was to come. Gaius was campaigning in Armenia. The commander of an enemy garrison lured him to a conference and then attacked him. Gaius was wounded. The Romans pressed the siege and continued the war, defeating the Armenians. Gaius was acclaimed "*imperator*" by the troops, the standard acclamation for a victorious general. But Gaius was ailing.[10] He wrote to Augustus asking to be allowed to retire. Augustus acquiesced reluctantly, but demanded that Gaius return to Rome. On April 23, A.D. 4, Gaius died.

THE RETURN OF THE EXILE

Augustus now had few choices. Tiberius and the youngest son of Agrippa and Julia, Agrippa Postumus, were adopted by Augustus. Tiberius was obliged to adopt Germanicus, his nephew, who was married to Agrippina, the daughter of Julia and Agrippa. The family reorganization established three potential heirs to the imperial regime, but only Tiberius had experience and authority, and Augustus now treated him as his partner in power. Tiberius was immediately sent off to Germany to reassert the regime's military nature. He remained, however, at the heart of Roman politics; the Parthian ambassadors, who arrived in Rome to repair their king's relationship with Augustus, were received by Augustus and the senate, but then told that they must see Tiberius as well.[11]

Germany was the main theatre for Roman expansionism, and Tiberius pushed the Roman frontier further to the east. But in A.D. 6, the Danubian provinces exploded in revolt. The German wars required a continual supply of manpower, and Tiberius turned to Dalmatia for reinforcements. Having raised units to meet the levy, the Dalmatians now had an army (if one technically under Roman authority), and a leader emerged, a man named Bato. He urged the newly raised troops to turn against their masters, and some initial success encouraged the Breucians, a Pannonian tribe led by another Bato, to join the revolt. The Moesian governor, Severus, marched against them, but his "victory" left the Pannonians in the field and Severus himself in retreat. The Dalmatian Bato marched south; he too was supposedly defeated by the Romans, but the Roman forces retreated from the province.

The empire needed Tiberius, and he marched south to protect Italy. The war intensified. A Roman colony was destroyed, and the Romans estimated that 800,000 rebels were under arms.[12] Germanicus was drafted into service and given an army recruited by an emergency levy not just on the free population but also on the slaves and freed.[13] Notably,

Agrippa Postumus, who had reached an age suited for military service, was not called upon.[14] Tiberius now had ten legions (50,000 men), 70 regular cohorts (35,000 men), 14 cavalry units (7,000 men), 10,000 veterans drawn back into the army by the emergency, and levies from the Thracian king, which together amounted to more than 102,000 men. The total normal establishment for the empire was probably about 250,000 men.

The war made obvious Augustus's dependence on Tiberius, and, however this was managed, Tiberius used his power to resolve the vestiges of dynastic opposition to his rule. With Julia in exile and Gaius and Lucius dead, Agrippa Postumus was the most obvious potential challenge to Tiberius. Even though Agrippa had been adopted by Tiberius, he was in a vulnerable position, and his enemies moved against him. He was exiled from Rome.[15] The charges laid against him related to his morals, with a suggestion that his behavior was inappropriate, that he was fierce (a quality that had a hint of madness) and crude.[16] It takes only a little speculation to imagine that Agrippa was raging against being passed over. Agrippa's sister, Julia, was also removed. She was accused of adultery, but her husband, Lucius Aemilius Paulus, one of the most prominent aristocrats of Rome, was convicted of conspiracy.[17] Augustus also razed Julia's palatial house.[18] She was pregnant when she was exiled. Augustus ordered the baby, his great-grandchild, to be killed. Julia herself lived on until 29, dying an exile.[19]

By late 8, the war in Pannonia had progressed sufficiently that Tiberius was able to return to Rome as a conquering hero. Augustus, now in his 70s and increasingly frail, left the imperial palace and came to the suburbs to meet him. Everyone must have realized that the old emperor was escorting the future emperor into the city.[20] Germanicus continued to campaign in Dalmatia into the following year. Tiberius joined him in the summer, and eventually they brought an end to the war.[21] Germanicus returned to Rome to report the victory to the Roman people, and the senators responded with the normal feast of honors. Augustus and Tiberius were granted a triumphal procession through the streets of Rome, though they probably declined to hold the procession.[22] Triumphal arches were voted, but if these were the major honors, the lesser but perhaps more significant grants were to Germanicus. He was a young man, 24, but was given the rank of praetor, the second most senior magistracy, and the right of giving his opinion first after the former consuls. Such honors followed the patterns of rapid career advancement that been set with Marcellus, Tiberius, Drusus, Gaius, and Lucius.[23]

With the emergence of Germanicus, the future of the family seemed once more assured. Augustus was now too old to lead the troops himself, but Tiberius at 51 was in the prime of his political and military career. He had the support of his nephew Germanicus, and Tiberius's own son, Drusus, would soon be of an age to take on military responsibilities. The future must have seemed bright and securely imperial, even if, five days after the celebratory announcement in Rome of victory in Pannonia, there was news of a catastrophe in Germany.

THE GERMAN REVOLT

In Germany, the previous years of campaigning had pushed the frontier from the Rhine to the Elbe, bringing a vast swath of what is now western Germany within the Empire. Perhaps for the first time in a decade, the Romans did not campaign in A.D. 9, concentrating on the establishing of political and institutional structures. The new governor, Varus, an experienced general close to the Augustan inner circle, decided that the time had come to regularize the administration of Germany and levy taxes.[24] To make his administration work, Varus summoned the leading men of Germany to advise him. This was perhaps the first time so many of Germany's leaders had ever been gathered together, and they had an excellent opportunity to conspire.

The revolt was led by Arminius, a man who was very close to Varus. The plan was careful and coordinated. An uprising in a remote part of Germany was reported, and Varus gathered troops and allies to resolve what seemed like a small local difficulty. On the march, his German friends started to disappear; they made excuses and set off home. Simultaneously, small, more remote Roman outposts were attacked and the troops massacred. By the time Varus realized that he was facing a major revolt, he was deep in suddenly hostile territory. He stopped the advance, loaded up his army, and began to fight his way back to the Rhine. The soldiers packed up their slaves, women, and possessions and began a slow, heavily encumbered march through the German forests.

The Germans knew which way the Romans would be going; they chopped trees and laid them across the road. The Roman line was long, and the Germans struck at any perceived weak points. The Romans could form up for battle, but then they could not progress.[25] As more and more of the troops were wounded, the march became yet slower. Even Varus himself was injured. In desperation, the Romans fortified a camp, burning the wagons they could no longer defend. Unencumbered by their baggage, they were in a better position to fight their way back home, but after four days they were still trapped in the German forests.

Varus gathered his senior officers to take counsel. As their men guarded the camp, news came from the general's conference. Having considered the options available to them, Varus and his officers had committed suicide. Resistance ended. Some tried to flee, but the Germans cut them down, leaving their bodies to rot on the forest paths. Others were captured, tortured, or sacrificed.[26] Three legions, their support troops, their slaves and their womenfolk, and all the camp followers were lost. Perhaps somewhere between 20,000 and 30,000 were killed. All Germany east of the Rhine was gone.[27]

The news was received with shock in Rome. Augustus put on mourning and is said to have banged his head against a doorframe crying out "Quinctilius Varus, return the legions!"[28] Tiberius was immediately dispatched to the Rhine.[29] Meanwhile, Augustus embarked on a program of conscription. But there was a reluctance to serve, possibly for a good part of a man's lifetime, and be engaged in the long and hard wars that had been taking place in Germany. Some avoided the draft, and Augustus reacted by depriving them of their citizenship and their property. Veterans were encouraged back into the army and freedmen conscripted. These hastily raised cohorts were sent to Gaul to shore up the defenses on the Rhine.[30] In 11, Tiberius and Germanicus went on the offensive once more; the Romans knew no other way of fighting.[31]

The Arminius revolt was the last great war of the Augustan period, and it stretched Roman military resources to the limit. The Pannonian revolt had been suppressed and all the territory lost had been regained, but the war in Germany was a major defeat. The losses of men were heavy, and after the strains placed on Rome by the Pannonian revolt, they were not easily made up. Conscription into the cohorts sent to the Rhine was deeply unpopular, and Rome was never to recoup the lost lands.

Although the revolts damaged the imperial family's record of military success (even if the tradition quite effectively lays most of the blame on the incompetence of Varus), in the longer term, politically, the wars were not a disaster for the regime. They demonstrated to the Roman people the necessity of military discipline. They provided Tiberius with the opportunity to reassert his military credentials. They allowed Germanicus to take command for the first time and associated the young man with military successes. Indeed, Germanicus and Tiberius could pose as the saviors of Italy in their suppression of the Pannonian revolt and as the restorers of Rome's military reputation in their campaigns after 11. In 14, the regime could point to Germany and Pannonia as justification for imperial continuity and to Tiberius as the leader Rome needed to ensure imperial security.

THE DEATH OF AUGUSTUS

In A.D. 13, Augustus announced that he would no longer attend public banquets. He asked the senators not to visit him at home to pay their respects, or at least not to visit so often.[32] The following year, he left Rome to accompany Tiberius on the first stage of his journey for yet another campaign in the north. Augustus fell ill and went to his villa in Campania to recuperate. He rallied, and Tiberius continued on his journey. Augustus crossed to Neapolis (Naples) to watch the games. But he had not fully recovered. Ill once more, he travelled to his ancestral villa at Nola, and Tiberius was summoned.

Augustus knew that he was dying. He called for those close to him to witness his parting. In Greek verse, he asked that they applaud the life of a man who had played his role so well, and sent them away. Livia remained at his bedside. On August 19, A.D. 14, Augustus, first emperor of Rome, passed away peacefully. He had lived 75 years, 10 months, and 26 days. Thirteen days after his death was the 44th anniversary of Actium.[33]

Tiberius might not have reached Nola to attend the deathbed, but by the time Livia and he broke the news to the waiting empire, they were in complete control. Tiberius assumed command of the praetorian guards and prepared to journey to Rome. Even before the funeral, he had received oaths of loyalty from the consuls, the prefect of the Praetorian Guard, and the prefect of the grain supply. Perhaps there were also oaths taken at popular gatherings and by the soldiers stationed in Rome. Tiberius had written to the legions and the governors in the provinces. He was everywhere accompanied by soldiers.[34] The political reality was clear: Tiberius had succeeded Augustus, as had long been predicted.

There was no republican restoration and no thought of such a restoration. There was no viable resistance in Rome to the Tiberian accession. The only possible threats to Tiberius came from inside his own family, and these were rapidly disposed of. Agrippa Postumus, Julia's surviving son, was killed, the first victim of the new regime.[35] Tiberius also sent troops to kill Sempronius Gracchus, one of the alleged lovers of Julia. He was an enemy for whom even 14 years of exile was insufficient punishment.[36] Julia killed herself. There were mutinies in the Danubian legions and in Germany, and it looked briefly as if Germanicus might make an attempt on the throne, but the young man was loyal to the imperial family.[37] In any case, the soldiers might have marched to secure the throne for a different emperor, Germanicus, from whom they might have been able to demand rewards and better terms and conditions, but they were certainly not going to march for a return to the Republic. Whatever the private discussions and evaluations of the career of Augustus, the senators and equestrians, plebs and soldiers united in their grief at their collective loss, and the new emperor smoothly supervised the transition of Augustus from first man of Rome to Divus Augustus, the second god of the new dynasty.

This peaceful accession was one of the great successes of the Augustan regime. With the benefit of hindsight, Tiberian rule seems to have been the obvious outcome of the Augustan period. After all, we know that Augustus was the first Roman emperor in a sequence of emperors that was to last until at least A.D. 475, and much longer in the East. We know that adopting Tiberius (who was from the family of the Claudii) into the Julian family led to the formation of what we know as the Julio-Claudian dynasty, a dynasty that was to bring us characters such as Gaius Caligula, Claudius, and Nero. But this could scarcely have been predicted in 28 B.C., when Octavian and Agrippa started on their formation of the Augustan Republic.

If the Augustan Republic was always a paradox, it was a useful paradox and one which the regime maintained. Even when Tiberius was returned to the forefront of Roman politics with the death of Gaius Caesar, he and Augustus were careful to advertise the republican vestiges of their regime. Tiberius succeeded because he was Augustus's adopted son, because he was the sole surviving son of Livia, and because he was the leading man of the Augustan family. But he was also the leading general of his generation, who had led Rome's armies in Armenia, Rhaetia, on the Danube, and in Germany. He had defeated the Pannonians and restored the vestiges of Roman pride on the German frontier. In the militarized political culture of Rome, he was by far the most honored and successful general.

Tiberius was also the most experienced politician. He had been consul in 13 and 7 B.C. He had held tribunician power alongside Augustus both before and after his "retirement." By the time of Augustus's death, a decade had passed since Tiberius was dramatically restored to the heart of the imperial family and Roman politics. Tiberius could claim with considerable confidence that he was the leading man of the state, the only man with the experience and authority necessary to succeed Augustus.

Nevertheless, even if Tiberius sought legitimacy for his accession from his career and this appealed to more conservative and republican representations of imperial power, the reality of the political situation was straightforwardly monarchic. The later years of the Augustan period had shown that the Roman people were ready to acquiesce in monarchy. More and more extravagant honors had been voted to

Augustus so that any suggestion of republican equality between emperor and senators would seem risible. The rapid elevation of Gaius and Lucius, boys whose only claim on power was lineage, was a clear sign of the emergence of monarchy in Rome. Julia and her children lived as princesses and princes, with lifestyles of luxury that perhaps had more in common with the court of Cleopatra than with the households of the stern Roman moralists of old. It was only their misfortune that kept Gaius and Lucius from attaining the throne instead of the vastly more experienced Tiberius.

In A.D. 14, Tiberius, probably with the agreement of Augustus, chose to play on the republican elements of the Augustan system, perhaps to differentiate his claims from those of other members of his family, perhaps to assert once more the perceived necessity of a strong leader in Rome to combat the military dangers lurking in the further reaches of the empire. As a consequence, Tiberius remained trapped in the paradox of republican monarchy and spent much of the early years of his reign seemingly deferring to the senators, much to their bemusement and frustration. The senators could also see the reality of imperial power: Tiberius controlled the army and the empire. He controlled wealth almost beyond the imagining of his fellow senators, as well as the key military and political positions. All eyes looked to Tiberius, for no one could afford to offend him. Whatever he might say to the senators and however he might defer to their collective wisdom, there was only one man who counted, one man who ruled.

Tiberius's position was anomalous in the long history of Rome. By all accounts, he was a conservative man, steeped in the moral and intellectual traditions of the past, but when he finally succeeded Augustus, politics had been transformed and the world around him was imperial. The Republic was but a memory—a powerful memory, which captured the imaginations of many of his contemporaries and perhaps even caused some among the senators to drift into nostalgic reveries for that age of freedom and glory, but if after A.D. 14 there was any serious political movement in favor of a real republican restoration, we cannot see it in our histories.[38] There had been a revolution and there was no going back.

ROME'S REVOLUTION

In the 57 years between the murder of Caesar and the death of Augustus, almost five centuries of republicanism had been swept aside. In itself, that justifies the use of the term "revolution." Part of the difficulty of understanding Rome's revolution is that we tend to think of politics in terms of institutions. It is a habit we have picked up from the Greeks. We understand revolutions as moments when the institutional frameworks of government are transformed. Kings are decapitated, or their soldiers and representatives sent back across the ocean. Democracies emerge (sometimes). But the Roman revolution was not an institutional revolution. The senators continued to meet. The magistrates continued to serve in much the same numbers and with much the same powers. The Roman electorate continued to assemble. From an institutional perspective, one might look at Rome in A.D. 14 and wonder quite what had changed over the preceding five decades.

And yet, there was a revolution. When Brutus and Cassius raised their daggers over the bloody corpse of Caesar, they confidently expected the restoration of an old order of senatorial rule. Over the next years, the soldiers asserted themselves in Roman political life. The aristocracy of Rome was traumatized by triumviral violence. The old political order was bloodily deposed. Its restoration after 28 B.C. was partial and conditional. The senators had lost control over the armies, over the wealth of empire, and over the plebs of Rome. Progressively, Augustan monopolization of the realia of power (money and violence) allowed the emperor to control the senators themselves, deciding who would rise and who would fall.

The senators survived because they were able to make themselves part of the new regime. There was no grand plan, no blueprint for the emergence of a new order. The imperial regime worked with its own logic: the extraordinary concentration of power in the hands of Augustus and his associates simply overwhelmed any institutional or individual resistance. Individuals were forced to cooperate with and acquiesce in the regime's power, since there was no viable alternative. From 43 B.C., the regime had established a patrimonial network that came to dominate all aspects of political life. It was this network, not exactly an institution, not exactly an insurgent group, but a significant political force nonetheless, that drove Rome's revolution.

The Augustan regime presented a dazzling face to posterity. After decades of violence, the regime celebrated order and peace. It sponsored art and architecture that glorified the city and the imperial family. There is every reason to believe that Augustus enjoyed genuine popular support; the plebs and the soldiers had few reasons to mourn the Republic's passing. But that peace and order came at a cost. The imperial system secured the acquiescence of its people through violence and corruption. In the face of Augustan power, the rights and privileges of free citizens, perhaps abused under the Republic, became an irrelevance under the empire. The imperial regime controlled such resources that its power became almost absolute, and after Augustus and, indeed Tiberius, gave birth to tyrants whose excesses were limited only by their imaginations. Augustan Rome was a totalitarian state that sought to control the lives of its citizens, rendering them subservient to an imperial and military ideal. The new Golden Age of Augustan Rome was intended as an age of iron discipline in which the bedrooms of the citizens were turned over to the furtherance of empire. Opposition was marginalized, forced into shadowy conspiracies or literary subversions. If the political order was shaped so as to support the military endeavors in the provinces, the soldiers remained a mainstay of Augustan power. We might like to imagine that the soldiers were a distant political reality, an uncomfortable truth which the authorities did their best to dismiss to the margins of civilian political life. As we have seen, however, Augustus and his household were generals as much as politicians, and it was with the army that they won the authority and prestige and wealth that allowed them to govern Rome. In the grand political bargain that the Augustan regime forced upon the Roman people, it was not just peace that was offered but military success and imperial glory. The price of that promise was paid by the peoples of Spain, Rhaetia, Germany, Dalmatia, Pannonia, Thrace, Armenia, and Africa.

In any evaluation of the Augustan achievement, we need to count the corpses: the dead of the civil wars, of the proscriptions, of the various conspiracies against the regime, but also of the wars of expansion that consumed so many lives, Roman and non-Roman. Historians and politicians have too often allowed themselves to be awed by Rome's empire, and by the Augustan age in particular. Before we praise the Caesars and their civilization, we should consider what was taken from the Roman people in exchange for those imperial benefits. We should remember that dissident voices, such as those of the Christians, were often silenced. We might think of the numerous aristocratic victims of the emperors who found themselves on the losing side in the vicious politics of the imperial court. We should reflect on the vast and increasing inequalities of imperial society which divided aristocrat from slave, rich from poor. In sum, we should consider the value of the liberty lost in exchange for the supposed peace of an imperial age.

TIMELINE

DATES	EVENT
B.C.	
133	Tribunate of Tiberius Gracchus.
124	First tribunate of Gaius Gracchus.
123	Second tribunate of Gaius Gracchus.
112–106	War with Jugurtha.
107	First consulship of Gaius Marius.
106	Birth of Cicero.
105	Roman defeat at Arausio.
104	Second consulship of Gaius Marius.
103	Third consulship of Gaius Marius.
102	Fourth consulship of Gaius Marius.
	Defeat of the German tribes at Aix-en-Provence.
101	Fifth consulship of Gaius Marius.
	Defeat of German tribes at Vercellae.
100	Sixth consulship of Gaius Marius.
	Birth of Julius Caesar.
	Repression of the tribune Saturninus.
90–89	Social War.
88	Consulship of Cornelius Sulla.
	Sulla's march on Rome.
87	Marius's march on Rome.
86	Seventh consulship of Gaius Marius.
	Death of Marius.

84	Sulla's return to Italy. Outbreak of civil war.
82	Battle of the Colline Gate. Defeat of Marian forces in Italy.
80	Sulla steps down from office.
78	"Revolt" of Marcus Lepidus.
	Pompey sent to Spain to fight Sertorius.
73–71	Revolt of Spartacus.
70	Consulship of Pompey and Crassus.
67	Pirate war fought by Pompey.
66–62	Pompey in the East.
63	Consulship of Cicero.
	Conspiracy of Catilina.
	Birth of Gaius Octavius (later to become Augustus) (September 23).
60	Consulship of Julius Caesar. Formation of the alliance between Pompey, Crassus, and Caesar.
59–49	Caesar in Gaul.
58–57	Exile of Cicero.
53	Violence between Clodius and Milo.
	Death of Crassus at the battle of Carrhae.
52	Death of Clodius.
	Burning of the senate house.
	Sole consulship of Pompey.
49	Caesar crosses the Rubicon, sparking a resumption of civil war.
48	Caesar defeats Pompey at the battle of Pharsalus.
	Caesar appointed dictator.
	Death of Pompey.
47	Caesar in Egypt. Liaison with Cleopatra VII.
46	Victory at Utica in North Africa.
45	Caesar defeats Pompey's sons at Munda in Spain.
	Caesar returns to Italy.
44	Caesar assassinated (March 15).
	Consulship of Mark Antony.
	Caesar's adoption of Gaius Octavius, who is afterwards known as Caesar Octavian.

Decimus Brutus in Cisalpine Gaul (from April).
Brutus and Cassius leave Italy for the East.
Cicero begins his sequence of speeches against Antony
(from September).
Antony secures an army from Macedonia (by October).
Octavian begins to gather troops (October).
Antony marches against Decimus Brutus and the civil war
begins.

43   Consulships of Hirtius and Pansa.
The senate declares war on Antony.
First battle of Mutina (April 14).
Second battle of Mutina (April 21). Death of Hirtius.
Death of Pansa (April 23).
Antony and Ventidius join forces at Vada (May 5).
Lepidus's legions defect to Antony (late May).
Embassy to the senate from Octavian's legions
(July–August).
Octavian's march on Rome.
First consulship of Octavian.
Death of Decimus Brutus.
Conference between Antony, Octavian, and Lepidus at Bononia.
Launching of the proscriptions.
Passing of the Lex Titia, brings the triumvirate into being
(November 27).
Death of Cicero (December 7).

42   First battle of Philippi. Death of Cassius (October 3).
Second battle of Philippi (October 23).
Death of Brutus (October 24).
Birth of Tiberius (November 16).

41   Consulship of Lucius Antonius.
Antony meets Cleopatra at Tarsus.
Colonization program in Italy begins.
Perusine war.

40   Peace of Brundisium. Antony marries Octavia.

39   Ventidius defeats Labienus and the Parthians.

Herod made king in Judaea.

Birth of Julia (October 30).

Marriage of Octavian and Livia.

38   War between Octavian and Sextus Pompeius.

Birth of Drusus.

37   Antony campaigns against the Parthians and their allies.

36   Octavian and Lepidus invade Sicily (July).

Battle of Naulochus (September 3).

Lepidus deposed.

Octavian's army mutinies.

35   Death of Sextus Pompeius.

Antony campaigns in Armenia.

Octavian campaigns in Dalmatia.

34   Donations of Alexandria.

33   Second consulship of Octavian.

32   Consulships of Gnaeus Domitius and Gaius Sosius. The consuls flee to Antony.

War between Antony and Octavian.

31   Third consulship of Octavian.

Battle of Actium (September 2).

30   Fourth consulship of Octavian.

Octavian invades Egypt.

Death of Antony (August 1).

Death of Cleopatra (August 12).

Conspiracy of Marcus Lepidus.

29   Fifth consulship of Octavian.

Octavian returns to Rome (summer).

28   Octavian consul (sixth time) with Agrippa (second consulship).

Octavian celebrates three triumphs (August 13–15).

Octavian and Agrippa begin the process of regularizing the political order.

Laws and rights of the Roman people restored.

27   Octavian consul (seventh time) with Agrippa (third time).

Octavian lays down control over the provinces
(January 13).
Octavian given the name Augustus (January 16).
Augustus leaves Rome for Gaul.

26   Eighth consulship of Augustus.
Augustus in Gaul and later in Spain.
Roman campaigns in the Alpine region begin.

25   Ninth consulship of Augustus.
Augustus campaigning in Spain.
Death of Cornelius Gallus.

24   Tenth consulship of Augustus.
Augustus returns to Rome.

23   Eleventh consulship of Augustus.
Illness of Augustus.
Agrippa sent to the East.
Death of Marcellus.
Trial of Primus.
Augustus lays down the consulship (July 1).
Augustus awarded tribunician power.

22   Conspiracy of Caepio and Murena.
Augustus offered the dictatorship after a riot.
Augustus in Sicily where he is once more offered the
dictatorship.

21   Augustus appoints a consul.
Agrippa returns to Rome. Augustus heads East.
Agrippa marries Julia.

20   Augustus makes peace with the Parthians. Return of the
standards.
Birth of Gaius.

19   Consulship of Saturninus.
"Conspiracy" of Egnatius Rufus.
Augustus returns to Rome (October 12).
Birth of Julia the Younger.
Agrippa campaigns in Spain.

18   Agrippa awarded tribunician power.

	Augustus and Agrippa launch a program of social reforms.
17	Birth of Lucius.
	Secular Games.
	War in Pannonia begins.
16	Augustus campaigning in Gaul and Germany.
	Tiberius and Drusus campaigning in Rhaetia (until 14).
15	Birth of Germanicus, son of Drusus.
14	Birth of Agrippina.
	Agrippa campaigns in Pannonia.
13	First consulship of Tiberius.
	Drusus takes over the war in Germany.
	Death of Agrippa.
	Birth of Drusus, son of Tiberius.
12	Birth of Agrippa Postumus.
	Julia marries Tiberius.
11	Tiberius campaigns in Pannonia and Dalmatia.
10	Drusus joined by Tiberius and Augustus in Germany.
9	Drusus consul.
	Death of Drusus.
7	Second consulship of Tiberius.
6	Tiberius granted tribunician power.
	Tiberius retires to Rhodes.
	Gaius "elected" consul.
5	Twelfth consulship of Augustus.
	Gaius and Lucius declared *principes iuventutis* (first among the young).
2	Thirteenth consulship of Augustus.
	Games held for the opening of the Forum of Augustus.
	Augustus acclaimed *pater patriae* (father of the nation).
	Fall of Julia.
	Gaius sent to the Danubian provinces.
	Lucius in Gaul.

A.D.

1	Gaius consul and sent to the East.
2	Tiberius allowed back to Rome.
	Death of Lucius (August 20).
3	Demonstrations in Rome for the recall of Julia.
4	Conspiracy of Gnaeus Cornelius.
	Death of Gaius (April 23).
	Tiberius recalled to office.
	Tiberius adopts Germanicus.
	Tiberius campaigns in Germany.
6	Pannonian revolt.
8	Tiberius returns to Rome after asserting control in Pannonia and Dalmatia.
	Exile of Julia the Younger.
9	Demonstrations in Rome against marriage legislation.
	Germanicus announces the final victory in Pannonia.
	Revolt in Germany and the defeat of Varus. Germanicus and Tiberius sent to the German frontier.
	Exile of Agrippa Postumus.
11	Germanicus and Tiberius go on the offensive in Germany.
12	Consulship of Germanicus.
14	Death of Augustus (August 19).

CAST OF CHARACTERS

T HIS LIST ENCOMPASSES ONLY significant individuals mentioned in the book. It is organized in alphabetical order by the name by which the individual is most often known. Thus, the Emperor Tiberius Claudius is under Tiberius, though his family name is Claudius.

Marcus Vipsanius **Agrippa**: Close friend and supporter of Augustus who came to be his chosen successor and deputy.

Agrippa Postumus: Grandson of Augustus, son of Agrippa and Julia.

Agrippina: Granddaughter of Augustus, daughter of Agrippa and Julia. Wife to Germanicus.

Lucius Domitius **Ahenobarbus**: An admiral who fought alongside Sextus Pompeius and later defected to Antony.

Alexander Helios: Son of Cleopatra and Antony.

Lucius **Antonius**: Brother of Mark Antony who fought the Perusine war against Octavian.

Mark **Antony**: Triumvir.

Bato: Dalmatian military leader who led the revolt against Rome.

Bato: Pannonian tribal leader who led the revolt against Rome.

Junius **Brutus**: Leading assassin of Caesar.

Fannius **Caepio**: Conspirator of 22 B.C.

Caesarion: Son of Cleopatra and Julius Caesar.

Quintus **Calenus**: Supporter and representative of Antony.

Decimus **Carfulenus**: Leading officer in Octavian's armies.

Gaius **Cassius**: Leading assassin of Caesar.

L. Sergius **Catilina**: Conspirator of 63 B.C. who was suppressed by Cicero.

Cato (the younger): Leading senator and moralist who fought on the Pompeian side during the civil war and committed suicide after his defeat by Caesar at the battle of Utica.

Quintus **Catulus**: Consul of 78 B.C. and a leading figure of the post-Sullan era.

M. Tullius **Cicero**: Leading politician and orator who led the senators in the period after the death of Julius Caesar.

Lucius **Cinna**: Consular ally of Marius in the war against Sulla.

Cleopatra VII: Queen of Egypt, lover of Julius Caesar and wife of Mark Antony.

Cleopatra Selene: Daughter of Cleopatra and Antony.

Clodia: daughter of Clodius and Fulvia, who was briefly married to Octavian.

Publius **Clodius**: Popular leader who clashed with Cicero and Milo and was murdered in 52 B.C.

Cornelia: Daughter of Cinna, first wife of Caesar.

Gnaeus **Cornelius**: Relative of Pompey, involved in a conspiracy ca. A.D. 4.

Cornificius: Octavian's general during the Sicilian war.

Licinius **Crassus**: Leading politician who fought Spartacus and was later allied with Caesar and Pompey. Killed at the battle of Carrhae in 53 B.C.

Licinius **Crassus**: Prominent general who campaigned successfully in Macedonia.

Decimus Brutus: Assassin of Caesar who was later besieged in Mutina and leader of the Republican armies against Antony.

Publius Cornelius **Dolabella**: Consul of 44 B.C. and ally of Mark Antony.

Drusus: Son of Livia and brother of Tiberius.

Egnatius Rufus: Popular politician and supposed conspirator against Augustus.

Fulvia: Wife to Clodius and later to Mark Antony.

Gabinius: Republican governor in Syria who intervened in Egyptian dynastic disputes.

Gaius Caesar: Grandson of Augustus (later adopted by him), son of Agrippa and Julia.

Cornelius **Gallus**: First prefect of Egypt and noted poet who fell out with Augustus early in the 20s B.C. and subsequently killed himself.

Germanicus: Eldest son of Drusus, married to Agrippina, adopted by Tiberius; fought in Pannonia and Germany.

Gaius Sempronius **Gracchus**: Brother of Tiberius Gracchus and reforming tribune of 123 and 122 B.C.

Tiberius Sempronius **Gracchus**: Reformer and tribune murdered in 133 B.C.

Sempronius **Gracchus**: Supposed lover of the elder Julia and enemy of Tiberius.

Herod: King in Judaea, appointed by Antony and retained by Octavian.

Aulus **Hirtius**: Consul of 43 B.C. and commander at the battle of Mutina.

Julia (1): Wife of Marius, aunt of Julius Caesar.

Julia (2): Daughter of Augustus.

Julia (3): Daughter of Julia and Agrippa, granddaughter of Augustus.

C. **Julius** Caesar: Victor in the civil wars against Pompey; dictator. Assassinated in Rome in March 44 B.C.

Junia: Sister of Brutus who was involved in a conspiracy, ca. 30 B.C.

Quintus **Labienus**: General of Julius Caesar who defected to the Pompeians and then joined with Brutus and Cassius, before leading troops against Antony with the support of the Parthians.

Marcus Aemilius **Lepidus** (1): Consul of 78 who led a revolt against the Sullans and was suppressed by Pompey.

Marcus Aemilius **Lepidus** (2): Triumvir.

Marcus Aemilius **Lepidus**: (3): Son of the triumvir, disappeared in 30 B.C.

Livia Drusilla: Wife of Augustus, mother of Tiberius and Drusus.

Livius Drusus: Tribune of 122 B.C. who was in competition with Gaius Gracchus.

Lucius Caesar: Grandson of Augustus (later adopted by him), son of Agrippa and Julia.

Maecenas: Political advisor to Octavian and member of the Augustan inner circle.

Claudius **Marcellus**: Son of Octavia and thus nephew of Augustus who married Julia (Augustus's daughter) and hence achieved political prominence before his premature death in 23 B.C.

Gaius **Marius**: Leading general of the late second century B.C. who fought a civil war against Cornelius Sulla.

Menodoros: Admiral who defected from Sextus Pompeius to Octavian.

T. Annius **Milo**: Politician who challenged and eventually killed Clodius.

Monaeses: Parthian noble who defected to Antony.

Lucius Terentius Varro **Murena**: Supposed conspirator of 22 B.C. and intimate of the Augustan inner circle.

Antonius **Musa**: Doctor to Augustus.

Octavia: Sister to Augustus, married to Antony, mother of Marcellus.

Marcus **Octavius**: Tribune who threatened to veto Tiberius Gracchus's land law and was consequently deposed from office.

Lucius **Opimius**: Consul of 122 B.C. who led the senators against Gaius Gracchus.

Ovid: Poet of the later Augustan era, notable for his love poetry; exiled late in the reign of Augustus.

Pacorus: Parthian prince who led armies against Antony.

Vibius **Pansa**: Consul of 43 B.C. and commander of Republican forces at the battle of Mutina.

Quintus **Pedius**: Friend and relative of Octavian, elected as consul in late 43 B.C.

Phraates: Parthian king.

Munatius **Plancus**: Caesarian general who supported the republican cause until Octavian's march on Rome.

Gnaeus Pompeius Magnus (**Pompey** the Great): Leading general of the late Republic. Defeated by Caesar in the civil wars.

Sextus **Pompeius**: Son of Pompey the Great who held Sicily against Octavian and the triumvirs.

Asinius **Pollio**: General and friend of Antony.

Marcus **Primus**: General, victorious in Thrace, but then prosecuted in Rome, sparking the conspiracy of Caepio and Murena.

Gaius **Proculeius**: Friend of Octavian who accompanied him to Alexandria and was then a prominent figure in the early imperial decades. Brother of Terentia (wife of Maecenas) and Lucius Terentius Varro Murena.

Propertius: Poet; author of four books of elegies, many of which concerned love.

Sallust: Latin historian of the late Republic.

Salvidienus Rufus: Triumviral general executed after the Perusine war.

Saturninus: Tribune of 100 B.C. who was suppressed by Marius.

Gaius Sentius **Saturninus**: Consul of 19 B.C. who clashed with Egnatius Rufus.

Scipio Nasica: Senator and Pontifex Maximus who led the opposition to Tiberius Gracchus.

Scribonia: Wife of Octavian, mother of Julia.

Sertorius: Marian general who led a revolt in Spain during the 70s B.C.

Spartacus: Thracian gladiator who led a slave revolt.

Cornelius **Sulla** Felix: General and dictator who staged a coup in 88 B.C. and thereby launched a series of civil wars from which he emerged victorious.

Publius **Sulpicius** Rufus: Tribune of the plebs who clashed with Sulla and thereby brought about Sulla's first march on Rome.

Terentia: Wife of Maecenas, lover of Augustus.

Tiberius: Second emperor of Rome, son of Livia.

Tiridates: Claimant of the Parthian throne.

Valerius Largus: Informer of the early Augustan period.

Quinctilius **Varus**: Governor of Germany who suffered a disastrous revolt and defeat.

Publius **Ventidius**: Friend of Antony who raised legions on his behalf in 43 B.C. and subsequently supported his campaigns in the East.

Marcus **Vinicius**: Consul of 19 B.C., close friend of Augustus and leading general.

Vipsania: Daughter of Agrippa, married to Tiberius.

Virgil: Poet of the Augustan age; author of *Georgics, Eclogues,* and the *Aeneid.*

NOTES

CHAPTER 1

1. See the discussion in Aloys Winterling, *Politics and Society in Imperial Rome* (Malden, MA: Blackwell, 2009).

2. In the nineteenth century, it was a norm of writing about the late Republic to postulate a significant ideological division at the heart of Roman politics, a division between *populares* and *optimates* that paralleled contemporary class divisions. Cicero in his speech in favor of Sestius (*Pro Sestio*) appears to postulate a fundamental division of political style between politicians who are *populares* and politicians who are *optimates*. The terms have a complex set of meanings and associations but are perhaps best understood as equivalent to "democratic" and "aristocratic." But although democratic and aristocratic values might on occasion be opposed, sovereignty in Rome depended ultimately on the citizenry, so that all politicians were in the last analysis democratic (*popularis*), whereas the social hierarchies of Rome were such that political leaders were by definition aristocratic (*optimas*). Consequently, these labels were for stances or styles which sat within the conventional frameworks of republican political culture; the *populares* were not "a voice from outside." See also Margaret A. Robb, *Beyond Populares and Optimates: Political Language in the Late Republic* (Stuttgart: Franz Steiner Verlag, 2010). My suggestion here is not that *optimates* and *populares* should be resurrected as distinct political groups (as they were thought of in the nineteenth century), but that there was likely to be a significant number of Roman citizens who were excluded from or not committed to the dominant political culture and were thus outside its remit.

3. Revolutions often deploy a language of power drawn from the past. Indian rebellions looked back to religious traditions and pre-British systems of rule to give their politics a focus. See Dipesh Chakrabarty, *Provincializing Europe: Postcolonial Thought and Historical Difference* (Princeton, NJ: Princeton University Press, 2008), and Ranajit Guha, "The Prose of Counter-Insurgency," in *Selected Subaltern Studies*, 45–84, edited by Ranajit Guha and Gayatri Spivak (New York: Oxford University Press, 1988).

4. Leading historians have worried about this absence of discussion of issues and, indeed, of ideological debate. Peter A. Brunt, *The Fall of the Roman Republic and Related Essays* (Oxford: Oxford University Press, 1988), 273–275, observed that "[t]here was no doctrine or programme to give the peasantry a sense of solidarity, and the leaders sought not . . . to secure clearly conceived social changes," while Erich Gruen, *The Last Generation of the Roman Republic* (Berkeley: University of California Press, 1974), argued that it was events rather than social issues or ideologies that brought about the end of the Republic. See also Josiah Osgood, *Caesar's*

Legacy: Civil War and the Emergence of the Roman Empire (Cambridge, UK: Cambridge University Press, 2006).

5. See Livy's "Preface" to his histories and Sallust, *Bellum Jugurthinum.*

6. Peter A. Brunt, "The Lex Valeria Cornelia," *Journal of Roman Studies* 51 (1961): 71–85. Peter A Brunt, "'Augustus' e la 'Republica'," in *La Rivoluzione romana: Inchiesta tra gli antichisti*, 236–244 (Naples: Jovene, 1982), simply denies any real change, arguing that Augustan domination was fundamentally republican. See also Brunt, *The Fall of the Roman Republic*, 9. The great book of the twentieth century on the transition from republic to empire is Ronald Syme's *The Roman Revolution* (Oxford: Oxford University Press, 1939), and Syme wrote (p. 7) that "In all ages, whatever the form and name of government, be it monarchy, republic, or democracy, an oligarchy lurks behind the façade; and Roman history, Republican or Imperial, is the history of the governing class."

7. See, for example, Karl Galinsky, *Augustan Culture: An Interpretive Introduction* (Princeton: Princeton University, Press, 1996), 8, and Thomas Rice Holmes, *The Architect of the Roman Empire* (Oxford: The Clarendon Press, 1928).

8. In addition to the works cited above, see Pierre Renucci, *Auguste le révolutionnaire* (Paris: Boutique de l'histoire, 2003), Klaus Bringmann, *A History of the Roman Republic* (Cambridge, UK, and Malden, MA: Polity Press, 2007), and Francisco Pina Polo, *La crisis de la República (133—44 a.C.)* (Madrid: Editorial Síntesis, 2004) for eulogistic accounts of Augustus.

9. Galinsky, *Augustan Culture*, entitles his first chapter "The Augustan Evolution." See also Thomas Habinek and Alessandro Schiesaro, "Introduction," in *The Roman Cultural Revolution*, xv–xxi, edited by Thomas Habinek and Alessandro Schiesaro (Cambridge, UK: Cambridge University Press, 1997), p. xvi, and Andrew Wallace-Hadrill, "*Mutatio morum*: The Idea of a Cultural Revolution," in *The Roman Cultural Revolution*, 3–22, edited by Thomas Habinek and Alessandro Schiesaro (Cambridge, UK: Cambridge University Press, 1997), and Andrew Wallace-Hadrill, *Rome's Cultural Revolution* (Cambridge, UK: Cambridge University Press, 2008).

10. For analyses of the theory of revolution in relation to Rome's equivalent, see the collection of essays *La Rivoluzione romana: Inchiesta tra gli antichisti* (Naples: Jovene, 1982).

11. It used to be believed that Roman republican politics was governed by aristocratic networks which controlled defined numbers of clients who could be relied upon to vote as instructed by their aristocratic leaders (an aristocratic politics of faction). The model falls on the notable lack of evidence for the operation of such factions. See Karl-Joachim Hölkeskamp, *Reconstructing the Roman Republic: An Ancient Political Culture and Modern Research* (Princeton, NJ, and Oxford: Princeton University Press, 2010). What I am proposing is very different, partly because I see large networks as vast, distinctly imperial redistributive systems from which members of all social classes drew benefits.

12. Daniele Manacorda, "Le anfore di Pompeo Magno," in *Studi di archeologia in memoria di Liliana Mercando*, 137–143, edited by Marina Sapelli Ragni (Turin: Soprintendenza per i beni archeologici del Piemonte e del Museo antichità egizie, 2005). Michael H. Crawford, "States Waiting in the Wings: Population Distribution and the End of the Roman Republic," in *People, Land and Politics: Demographic Development and the Transformation of Italy 300 BC–AD 14*, pp. 631–643, edited by Luuk de Ligt and Simon Northwood (Leiden and Boston: Brill: 2008), argues that the dynasts of the late Republic developed quasi-state institutions with productive capacities.

13. Tacitus, *Annales*, 1.2–3.

14. We may draw comparisons with the "patrimonial networks" that have been identified as distributing power and resources in contemporary African states. See, for comparison, Patrick Chabal and Jean-Pascal Daloz, eds., *Africa Works: Disorder as a Political Instrument* (Bloomington: Indiana University Press, 1999), and Patrick Chabal and Nuno Vidal, *Angola: The Weight of*

History (London: Hurst, 2007). Once the triumviral network had taken over the Roman state, there was no need to abolish Rome's traditional institutions.

15. Lucan, *Pharsalia* 1.72–80.

CHAPTER 2

1. Appian, *Civil Wars*, 2.111

2. Cicero, *Pro Milone*.

3. Suetonius, *Divus Julius*, 30. The opinion is taken from a quotation from Caesar himself.

4. For the repeated emphasis on *dignitas* see, Caesar, *Bellum Civile*, 1.7–9.

5. Suetonius, *Divus Julius*, 32; Plutarch, *Life of Julius Caesar*, 32 has the phrase, but without the supernatural influence.

6. Suetonius, *Augustus*, 79.

7. Suetonius, *Divus Julius* 78.

8. Suetonius, *Divus Julius*, 80.

9. Livy, 1.56–60.

10. Appian, *Civil Wars*, 2.115.

11. Suetonius, *Divus Julius*, 81.

CHAPTER 3

1. Romans took the names of their fathers so the son of a Julius Caesar would also be called Julius Caesar and a daughter would be called Julia. Although brothers might be differentiated by taking different first names (Sextus, Gaius, Marcus), sisters would often carry the same names.

2. Plutarch, *Life of Tiberius Gracchus*, 5–7.

3. See Plutarch, *Life of Gaius Gracchus*, 2 and 5, for evidence of the poverty of soldiers. For the poverty of the peasantry, we rely heavily on the archaeological material. See Dominic W. Rathbone, "Poor Peasants and Silent Sherds," in *People, Land and Politics: Demographic Development and the Transformation of Italy 300 BC–AD 14*, 305–332, edited by Luuk de Ligt and Simon Northwood (Leiden and Boston: Brill, 2008); William V. Harris, "Poverty and Destitution in the Roman Empire," in *Rome's Imperial Economy: Twelve Essays*, 27–54, by William V. Harris (Oxford: Oxford University Press, 2011).

4. For Scipio Aemilianus, see Alan E. Astin, *Scipio Aemilianus* (Oxford: Oxford University Press, 1967). Scipio Aemilianus was by birth one of the Aemelii, a family associated with the conquest of Greece. By adoption, he was one of the Scipios.

5. Land was the most valuable resource, and Romans were traditionally cautious about the accumulation of land in the hands of individuals. Pliny, *Natural History*, 18.7 suggests that in the earliest period two *iugera* (about 0.5 hectares) was the norm for the amount of property that an individual could own, an amount that also appears in Varro, *Res Rusticae*, 1.10 and Livy, 6.36 and 8.21. See also Emilio Gabba and Marinella Pasquinucci, *Strutture agrarie e allevamento transumante nell' Italia romana (III–I secolo a. C.)* (Pisa: Giardini, 1979), 55–63. Two *iugera* was an amount considerably below that necessary to support a family.

6. See also Dionysius of Halicarnassus, *Roman Antiquities*, 4.13.

7. See Saskia T. Roselaar, *Public Land in the Roman Republic: A Social and Economic History of Ager Publicus in Italy, 396–89 BC* (Oxford: Oxford University Press, 2010). One of the earliest distributions was of the territory of Veii in Tuscany in 393 B.C.; see Livy, 5.30.

8. For colonial distributions of land, see Gianfranco Tibiletti, "Richerche di storia agraria romana," *Athenaeum* 28 (1950): 183–266, John K. Evans, *"Plebs Rustica*: The Peasantry of Classical Italy," *American Journal of Ancient History* 5 (1980): 19–47, 134–173; and Edward Togo Salmon,

Roman Colonization under the Republic (London and Southampton: Thames and Hudson, 1969), 95–109.

9. See Fiona C. Tweedie, "The Case of the Missing Veterans: Roman Colonisation and Veteran Settlement in the Second Century B.C." *Historia* 60 (2011): 458–473.

10. The motives of Tiberius Gracchus are endlessly debated. Plutarch, *Life of Tiberius Gracchus*, 8–9, makes reference to a pamphlet published by Gaius Gracchus which claimed that his brother had been motivated by the seeming depopulation of Tuscany and the farming of the land by barbarian slaves. Plutarch also quotes a speech of Tiberius in which he notes the poverty of the soldiers. Both motives are mutually compatible.

11. Appian, *Civil Wars*, 1.7.

12. Appian, *Civil Wars*, 1.8, claims that Tiberius Gracchus limited the amount of public land that could be held by individual Romans to 500 *iugera* per person, with an allowance of 250 *iugera* for each son. The implication is that the powerful in Rome had built up considerable estates of public land. Appian, *Civil Wars*, 1.7, says that such land had been treated as if it were private.

13. Plutarch, *Life of Tiberius Gracchus*, 10–12; Appian, *Civil Wars*, 1.12–13.

14. Plutarch, *Life of Tiberius Gracchus*, 18–20; Appian, *Civil Wars*, 1.16–17.

15. Plutarch, *Life of Tiberius Gracchus*, 19.

16. Appian, *Civil Wars*, 1.21, 1.23; Plutarch, *Life of Gaius Gracchus*, 5–7.

17. Grain was provided at the fixed price of six and a third asses (a low denomination copper coin) per *modius*. That amount was probably a traditional price. See Livy, *Periochae*, 60; Cicero, *Pro Sestio*, 55, though Livy, 30.26 has a grain distribution from the late third century at 4 asses per *modius*. See Fik Meijer, "Cicero and the Costs of the Republican Grain Laws," in *De Agricultura: In Memoriam Pieter Willem De Neeve*, 153–163, edited by Helena Sancisi-Weerdenburg (Amsterdam: J. C. Gieben, 1993). The figure appears to have been within the normal range for Greek prices of this period. See Kenneth W. Harl, *Coinage in the Roman Economy, 300 B.C.– A.D. 700* (Baltimore: John Hopkins University Press, 1996), 455, n. 10. The measure was not to provide cheap grain and thus subsidize the poor, but to protect the poor from rapid changes in food prices and speculation on the price of food by ensuring that food was available at a reasonable price.

18. Peter Garnsey, *Famine and Food Supply in the Graeco-Roman World: Responses to Crisis* (Cambridge, UK: Cambridge University Press, 1988).

19. Plutarch, *Life of Gaius Gracchus*, 7. The guaranteed supply of grain increased the food security of the urban population, and the program of public works pumped money into the economic system. Taken together, these policies were very similar to those adopted by modern states in order to alleviate poverty; see Jean Drèze, "Famine Prevention in India," in *The Political Economy of Hunger* II, 13–122, edited by Jean Drèze and Amartya Sen (Oxford: Oxford University Press, 1990).

20. Plutarch, *Life of Gaius Gracchus*, 9; Velleius Paterculus, 1.15; Salmon, *Roman Colonization*, 118–120. A colony was also founded at Fabrateria, south of Rome, on land seized after a supposed revolt in 124 B.C.

21. Appian, *Civil Wars*, 1.24.

22. Plutarch, *Life of Gaius Gracchus*, 9.

23. Appian, *Civil Wars*, 1.24; Plutarch, *Life of Gaius Gracchus*, 11.

24. Appian, *Civil Wars*, 1.25.

25. Plutarch, *Life of Gaius Gracchus*, 13.

26. Plutarch, *Life of Gaius Gracchus*, 16–17; Appian, *Civil Wars*, 1.26.

27. Sallust, *Bellum Jugurthinum*, 5.

28. Sallust, *Bellum Jugurthinum*, 3.

29. Sallust, *Bellum Jugurthinum*, 26.

30. Plutarch, *Life of Gaius Marius*, 3.

31. Plutarch, *Life of Gaius Marius*, 4.

32. Plutarch, *Life of Gaius Marius*, 5.

33. Plutarch, *Life of Gaius Marius*, 7. Marius seems also to have drawn support from the Roman trading community in Utica. Utica was a major African port and must have contained a sizeable Roman community, who were probably supportive of those traders killed earlier in the war by Jugurtha. See Sallust, *Bellum Jugurthinum*, 63.

34. Livy, *Periochae*, 67.

35. Livy, *Periochae*, 67.

36. For the census levels, see Dominic W. Rathbone, "The Census Qualifications of the *assidui* and the *prima classis,*" in *De Agricultura*, 121–152, edited by Sancisi-Weerdenburg. See also Arthur Keaveney, *The Army in the Roman Revolution* (Abingdon: Taylor and Francis, 2007).

37. Plutarch, *Life of Gaius Marius*, 34–35; *Life of Sulla*, 7–9; Appian, *Civil Wars*, 1.55–56.

38. Appian, *Civil Wars*, 1.57.

39. Appian, *Civil Wars*, 1.58–60.

40. Plutarch, *Life of Gaius Marius*, 38–39.

41. Appian, *Civil Wars*, 1.62–64.

42. Appian, *Civil Wars*, 1. 64–70; Plutarch, *Life of Gaius Marius*, 41–42.

43. Appian, *Civil Wars*, 1.71.

44. Appian, *Civil Wars*, 1.71–74; Plutarch, *Life of Gaius Marius*, 43–44.

45. Appian, *Civil Wars*, 1.79–80.

46. Appian, *Civil Wars*, 1.84–85.

47. Appian, *Civil Wars*, 1.84–85.

48. Appian, *Civil Wars*, 1.87–91.

49. Appian, *Civil Wars*, 1.92–94.

50. Some of the reported casualty figures may be pure guesses, but we have no preserved figures for several of the battles and sieges, and most of the figures we have represent only the losses of the Marians.

CHAPTER 4

1. There has been ferocious argument over the nature of Roman politics since Fergus Millar suggested in a series of articles that both the constitutional form and the practice of politics in Rome were democratic. See especially Fergus Millar, "The Political Character of the Classical Roman Republic," *Journal of Roman Studies* 74 (1984): 1–19; "Politics, Persuasion and the People before the Social War (150–90 B.C.)," *Journal of Roman Studies* 76 (1986): 1–11; and "Political Power in Mid-Republican Rome: Curia or Comitium?" *Journal of Roman Studies* 79 (1989): 138–150. The reaction has overturned much of Millar's case. See, for example, Henrik Mouritsen, *Plebs and Politics in the Late Roman Republic* (Cambridge, UK: Cambridge University Press, 2001), and Karl-Joachim Hölkeskamp, *Reconstructing the Roman Republic: An Ancient Political Culture and Modern Research* (Princeton, NJ and Oxford: Princeton University Press, 2010).

2. See, for instance, Christopher S. MacKay, *The Breakdown of the Roman Republic: From Oligarchy to Empire* (Cambridge, UK: Cambridge University Press, 2009), 8; Laurence Keppie, "The Changing Face of the Roman Legions (49 BC–AD 69)," *Papers of the British School at Rome* 65 (1997): 89–102; and Arnold Toynbee, *Hannibal's Legacy: The Hannibalic War's Effects on Roman Life* (Oxford: Oxford University Press, 1965). See also Peter A. Brunt, *The Fall of the Roman Republic and Related Essays* (Oxford: Oxford University Press, 1988), for a systematic debunking of earlier theories.

3. Given the absence of other social structures through which power could be diffused, Roman networks were probably more important than their modern counterparts. For states operating through networks, see Patrick Chabal and Jean-Pascal Daloz, eds., *Africa Works: Disorder as a Political Instrument* (Oxford and Bloomington: Indiana University Press, 1999), and Patrick Chabal and Nuno Vidal, *Angola: The Weight of History* (London: Hurst, 2007). For modern networks in contemporary Africa, see Salwa Ismail, *Political Life in Cairo's New Quarters: Encountering the Everyday State* (Minneapolis and London: University of Minnesota Press, 2006.

4. For rankings and social locations, see Francis X. Ryan, *Rank and Participation in the Republican Senate* (Stuttgart: Steiner, 1998), 52–71.

5. One might imagine that lower down the social hierarchy the networks provided self-help groups that operated more intensely within particular socioeconomic categories than across them.

6. Plutarch, *Life of Julius Caesar*, 1.

7. Suetonius, *Divus Julius*, 1.

8. Plutarch, *Life of Julius Caesar*, 5. Women who had reached a certain age and status were sometimes given funeral orations.

9. Plutarch, *Life of Julius Caesar*, 6.

10. Appian, *Civil Wars*, 1.105–106.

11. Sallust, *Histories*, 1.77; Appian, *Civil Wars*, 1.108–115.

12. Pompey's career had been unusual in that he had not held any of the lower magistracies, and thus his candidature was probably illegal. It is a measure of the practicality with which the Roman elite approached the constitution that they chose to ignore the law in this clearly exceptional instance.

13. Plutarch, *Life of Julius Caesar*, 1–2.

14. For ancient piracy, see Philip De Souza, *Piracy in the Graeco-Roman World* (Cambridge, UK: Cambridge University Press, 1999).

15. Much of our knowledge of these events comes from Cicero's speech in favor of the law, *De Imperio Cn. Pompei*.

16. Sallust, *Bellum Catilinae* 31; Cicero, *In Catilinam* 1.

17. Cicero, *In Catilinam* 3.

18. Cicero, *In Catilinam* 4.

19. This debate forms the central element in Sallust's account, the *Bellum Catilinae*.

20. See Cicero's speeches *De Imperio Cn. Pompei* and *De Lege Agraria*.

21. Cicero, *Pro Archia*.

22. Cicero, *De Consulatu suo*.

23. On Clodius, see W. Jeffrey Tatum, *The Patrician Tribune: Publius Clodius Pulcher* (Chapel Hill: University of North Carolina Press, 1999).

24. Suetonius, *Caesar*, 9–10. Plutarch, *Life of Caesar*, 9. Plutarch, *Life of Cicero*, 28–29.

25. Cicero, *De domo suo*. Cicero also engaged in a memorable and vicious character assassination of Clodius's sister, *Pro Caelio*.

26. As detailed in Cicero, *De domo suo*.

27. Cicero, *Pro Milone*

28. See, for example, James A. Froude, *Caesar: A Sketch* (London: Harper and Brothers, 1890).

29. Georg W. F. Hegel, *The Philosophy of History* (New York: Cosimo, 2007 [German ed., 1899]), 19–20.

30. See the comments by Christian Meier, *Caesar* (New York: HarperCollins, 1995), 18–20.

31. See the commentary on Caesar's ambition by Montaigne, *Essays* II 36 in Michael Andrew Screech, ed. and trans., *Michel de Montaigne: The Complete Essays* (London: Penguin Books, 1987), 855.

32. Suetonius, *Caesar*, 40–44. See also Martin Jehne, *Der Staat des Dictators Caesar* (Cologne: Böhlau, 1987).

33. Caesar, *Bellum Civile*, 1.7–9; Meier, *Caesar*, 18–20.

34. Caesar, *De Bello Gallico*, 1.1, commenced his description of his conquest of Gaul with one of the most famous sentences in Latin: *Gallia est omnis divisa in partes tres* (Gaul is divided into three parts), which is clear, authoritative, but also reflective of a hazy Roman understanding of the geography of Gaul.

CHAPTER 5

1. Appian, *Civil Wars*, 3.7; 25.

2. Cicero, *Ad Atticum*, 15.4

3. *Philippic* 1.11.

4. Born Gaius Octavius, on adoption he became Gaius Julius, son of Gaius, Caesar Octavianus. Moderns tend to pick up the last element so as to differentiate him from his uncle in their narratives.

5. Appian, *Civil Wars*, 3. 9–39.

6. Cicero, *Ad Atticum* 15.12.

7. Appian, *Civil Wars*, 3.43.

8. Appian, *Civil Wars*, 3.43–44.

9. Appian, *Civil Wars*, 3.29–39.

10. In addition to *Philippics* 4 and 5, our two main narrative sources are Cassius Dio, 46. 1–28, and Appian, *Civil Wars*, 3. 50–60.

11. Cicero, *Philippic* 4.15.

12. Cicero, *Philippic* 5.22; 34.

13. There was no fixed number of senators, but Caesar had rewarded his supporters with seats in the senate. By 30 B.C., possibly after another round of irregular conscription to the senate, there may have been as many as 900 senators, though the numbers preserved in our sources are vague.

14. Cicero, *Philippic* 2, 30–62, and especially 61, where Antony is described as being "in sinum quidem et in complexum tuae mimulae". The "complexum" is an explicit sexual reference, though it is quite difficult to render into English, "lap" being rather tame.

15. Our two main narrative sources have slightly different versions of what resulted. In general, Appian's account is to be preferred; it is more detailed and more internally consistent, and appears to pay more attention to the chronology of the unfolding events.

16. Appian, *Civil Wars*, 3. 61. In *Philippic* 6, delivered to the people summarizing the debate in the senate, Cicero claims that the ultimatum was, indeed, equivalent to a declaration of war.

17. Appian, *Civil Wars*, 3. 63. Compare with Dio, 46. 30, in which Antony asked for the appointment of the assassins, Junius Brutus and Cassius Longinus, as consuls (surely an ironic request) and rewards for his own troops comparable to those offered to Octavian's men. Both Appian's and Dio's accounts are somewhat confused.

18. Dio 46. 36. Antony's spies could pretend to the townsfolk that they were soldiers and to the soldiers that they were townsfolk, but once these groups were divided, the spies became obvious.

19. Appian, *Civil Wars*, 3. 63.

20. Cicero, *Philippic* 5.38.

21. Appian, *Civil Wars*, 3. 65; Dio 46. 36.

22. Dio 46. 31.

23. Nevertheless, the senate did not limit their demands to their own, and the workmen of the city were conscripted to provide arms and equipment for the new levies of troops.

24. Dio 46. 32.
25. Appian, *Civil Wars*, 3. 68.
26. Appian, *Civil Wars*, 3. 68–71 for a narrative account of the battle.
27. Cicero, *Ad Familiares*, 10.30.

CHAPTER 6

1. Cicero, *Ad Familiares*, 11.13.
2. Appian, *Civil Wars*, 3.73.
3. Cicero, *Ad Familiares*, 11.13; 11.10.
4. Cicero, *Ad Familiares*, 11.13.
5. Cicero, *Ad M. Brutum* 1. 3.
6. Appian, *Civil Wars*, 3.74.
7. Dio 46.39.
8. Cicero, *Ad M. Brutum* 1. 4 (April 27).
9. Appian, *Civil Wars*, 3.73–76; Cf. Dio 46.40.
10. The timeline here is difficult. Rome is 440 km from Mutina. If we assume that it took five days for messages to move between Mutina and Rome, then even if the senate were certain that Pansa would take no further part in the war, and indeed that his wounds were likely to be fatal, it is unlikely that any instructions could have reached Decimus Brutus and Octavian before April 26. If such decisions could only be made after the death of Hirtius, then instructions from the senate could only have been received in Mutina by April 30. It thus seems possible that the decision to transfer Pansa's legions was made locally.
11. Cicero, *Ad Familiares*, 11.13b.
12. Cicero, *Ad Familiares*, 11.10.
13. Cicero, *Ad Familiares*, 10.30.
14. Cicero, *Ad Familiaries*, 11.9.
15. Cicero, *Ad Familiares*, 11.10.
16. Cicero, *Ad M. Brutum*, 1. 10, would appear to have blamed Decimus Brutus for bungling the aftermath of the battles of Mutina.
17. Cicero, *Ad Familiares*, 11.13.
18. Cicero, *Ad Familiares*, 11.10.
19. Appian, *Civil Wars*, 3.81; Cicero, *Ad Familiares*, 10.24.
20. Cicero, *Ad Familiares*, 10.11.
21. Cicero, *Ad Familiares*, 11.13.
22. Cicero, *Ad Familiares*, 10.21.
23. Cicero, *Ad Familiares*, 10.34.
24. Cicero, *Ad Familiares*, 10.17.
25. Cicero, *Ad Familiares*, 11.12.
26. Cicero, *Ad Familiares*, 10.34.
27. Cicero, *Ad Familiares*, 10.34a.
28. Cicero, *Ad Familiares*, 10.34a.
29. Cicero, *Ad Familiares*, 10.35.
30. The alert reader will note that Plancus claimed to have put down a mutiny of a Tenth legion in his army in *Ad Familiares*, 10.11. Although legions should have been numbered according to a strict sequence, it is possible that there were two Tenth legions, though two Tenth legions fanatically loyal to Antony strains credibility. The most economical explanation would be an error somewhere in the historical account.

31. Appian, *Civil Wars*, 3.84.
32. Cicero, *Ad Familiares*, 12.8.
33. Appian, *Civil Wars*, 3.85.
34. Cicero, *Ad Familiares*, 10.32.
35. Cicero, *Ad Familiares*, 11.13a.
36. Cicero, *Ad Familiares*, 10.24.
37. Cicero, *Ad Familiares*, 11.10; Appian, *Civil Wars*, 3.80.
38. Cicero, *Ad Familiares*, 11.20.
39. Cicero, *Ad Familiares*, 11.21.
40. Appian, *Civil Wars*, 3.88. Cassius Dio, 46.39–43, as is characteristic, conflates various events and suggests that Octavian, sometime before the May 29 compact between Lepidus and Antony, had made peace with Antony. But no hint of such a reconciliation had reached Cicero by the end of July, which is very unlikely. Further, on that understanding it becomes very difficult to explain Octavian's inactivity over the late spring and early summer: what was he waiting for?
41. Appian, *Civil Wars*, 3.86. Appian has two embassies, the first of which is about money and the second of which is about Octavian's political position, but Dio only has one.
42. The account here combines Appian, *Civil Wars*, 3.88, and Dio, 46.43. Although there are differences between the two accounts, it seems clear that they describing the same incident, and in broadly similar ways.
43. Appian, *Civil Wars*, 3.92.

CHAPTER 7

1. For modern evaluations of Sextus Pompeius, see Anton Powell and Kathryn Welch, eds., *Sextus Pompeius* (London: Duckworth, 2002), and Kathryn Welch, *Magnus Pius: Sextus Pompeius and the Transformation of the Roman Republic; Roman Culture in an Age of Civil War* (Swansea: Classical Press of Wales, 2012).
2. Appian, *Civil Wars*, 3.94.
3. Appian, *Civil Wars*, 3.9–20; 32–39.
4. Velleius Paterculus, 2.69.5: "Then by the Pedian law, which the consul Pedius (Caesar's colleague) carried, those who had killed the elder Caesar were forbidden fire and water." The forbidding of fire and water was an archaism which meant literally that none within Roman territory were allowed to offer the named individuals fire or water. Such a decree meant exile from Italy.
5. Appian, *Civil Wars*, 3.95; 4.27; Dio 46.49.5.
6. Appian, *Civil Wars*, 3.96. Dio 46.50–55 seems hopelessly confused about the chronology of these events.
7. Appian, *Civil Wars*, 3. 97–98; Dio 46.52–53.
8. Appian, *Civil Wars*, 3.95–96; Dio 46.47–48.
9. Appian, *Civil Wars*, 4.2; Dio 46.54–55.
10. Appian, *Civil Wars*, 4.3; Dio 46.55–56.
11. Appian, *Civil Wars*, 4.6.
12. Appian, *Civil Wars*, 4.7.
13. Most of our understanding of Roman law comes from much later compilations that preserved fragments of earlier laws, and since the Lex Titia did not form part of the repertoire of late antique law, the various codes do not preserve its terms.
14. Sulla's title appears on a fragmentary inscription *CIL* VI 40951 = VI 31609 as [L. Cornelius L. f. Sulla] Felix d[ict r(ei publicae) co[nstituendae]. In spite of the fact that everything in the

square brackets is scholarly assumption, the restoration is reasonable. The possibility of a longer title comes from Appian, *Civil Wars*, 1.98, but is scarcely persuasive.

15. Carsten H. Lange, *Res Publica Constituta: Actium, Apollo and the Accomplishment of the Triumviral Assignment* (Leiden and Boston: Brill, 2009), 23, suggests that the Lex Titia will have been explicit as to the purpose of the triumvirate: to punish Caesar's assassins, to end the civil war, and to restore government. If so, only the last of these made it into the title of their office.

16. See, for example, the decree reported in Joyce Reynolds, *Aphrodisias and Rome* (London: Society for the Promotion of Roman Studies, 1982), no. 8.

17. Appian, *Civil Wars*, 4.8–10.

18. *Res Gestae*, 1–2.

19. See Peter Garnsey, "The Lex Iulia and Appeal under the Empire," *Journal of Roman Studies* 56 (1966): 167–189.

CHAPTER 8

1. Appian, *Civil Wars*, 4.8–11. There is some doubt as to the veracity of the decree, but even if Appian (who wrote in Greek and notes, unusually, that he had translated the text from a Latin original) had been fooled by his Latin source's invention, it provides a plausible insight into triumviral thinking.

2. Dio 47.3. Livy, *Periochae* 120, has only the 130. It is possible that he knew only the first list.

3. Appian, *Civil Wars*, 4.17. In addition to the citations below, see Valerius Maximus, *Memorable Deeds and Sayings*, notably 5.7.3; 6.7.5–7; 7.3.8.

4. The obvious distance between the rhetorical assurances of the triumviral decree and the events that followed might be one reason to regard the decree as an invention. But we have enough experience of horrors perpetrated on the people by politicians acting in the name of the people to recognize a political trope that resonates through the ages.

5. Appian, *Civil Wars*, 4.12.

6. Appian, *Civil Wars*, 4.17. A tribune was sacrosanct, and so his killing was a religious and political crime.

7. These stories are also in Valerius Maximus, *Memorable Deeds and Sayings*, 9.11.6–8.

8. Appian, *Civil Wars*, 4.12–30.

9. Appian, *Civil Wars*, 4.36–45.

10. *ILS* 8393. See also Valerius Maximus, *Memorable Deeds and Sayings*, 6.7.2. See now Josiah Osgood, *Turia: A Roman Woman's Civil War* (Oxford and New York: Oxford University Press, 2014).

11. Appian, *Civil Wars*, 4.19; Dio 47.11; Livy, Fr. 60; Plutarch, *Life of Cicero* 48; Valerius Maximus, *Memorable Deeds and Sayings*, 5.3.4.

12. Dio 47.13.

13. Appian, *Civil Wars*, 4. 5. One might suggest that his 300 is made up of the listed 280 and 17 marked down for early assassination.

14. The number of important senators may have been as few as a hundred. Absolute numbers given for the senate are 300 (for times past), 600 (for the Augustan senate), and "more than a thousand" (for the senate in the early Augustan period).

15. Suetonius, *Augustus* 27.2.

16. Dio 47.14.

17. Appian, *Civil Wars*, 4.31.

18. We do not need to resort to the moral explanations offered by Appian. Appian is committed to seeing the events of this period as being the work of a very small group which caused general revulsion.

19. Livy, *Periochae*, 89.
20. See Israel Shatzman, *Senatorial Wealth and Roman Politics* (Brussels: Latomus, 1975).
21. Appian, *Civil Wars*, 4.32–34. Dio 47.14 has a more complex tax regime, but one which can be made compatible with that of Appian.
22. Dio 47.16. Additionally, the triumvirs requisitioned slaves for the navy (Dio 47.17).
23. For recruitment and manpower, see Peter A. Brunt, *Italian Manpower 225 B.C.–A.D. 14* (Oxford: Oxford University Press, 1971) and Elio Lo Cascio, "Recruitment and the Size of the Roman Population from the Third to the First Century B.C.E.," in *Debating Roman Demography*, 111–137, edited by Walter Scheidel (Leiden and Boston: Brill, 2001).
24. For offers of money to the troops, see Appian, *Civil Wars*, 3.43–44; 3.48; 3.90. Appian, *Civil Wars*, 4.3 also tells us that the troops were promised lands in settlements that were to be established in 18 Italian towns. It is unclear whether this was part of the 20,000 sesterces that had been offered.
25. Appian, *Civil Wars*, 4.3. The calculation for 43 legions of 4,500 men gives us 193,500 soldiers, which at 20,000 sesterces each makes 3,870,000,000 sesterces.
26. See Luciano Canfora, "Proscrizioni e dissento sociale nella repubblica Romana," *Klio* 62 (1980): 425–437.
27. See the data collected in Shatzman, *Senatorial Wealth and Roman Politics*.
28. Based on an assumption of about 4,000,000 free citizens as reflected in the census figure for 28 B.C., which would be made up of 1,000,000 free adult males and 3,000,000 women and children.
29. Appian, *Civil Wars*, 4.16. Dio 47.7–8 rather unconvincingly attempts to excuse Octavian from the worst of the excesses.

CHAPTER 9
1. Appian, *Civil Wars*, 4.53–56; 4.83–86.
2. Appian, *Civil Wars*, 4.82.
3. Appian, *Civil Wars*, 4.106.
4. Appian, *Civil Wars*, 4.107–108.
5. Appian, *Civil Wars*, 4.111–113.
6. It seems probable that Appian or his sources were attempting to deflect the blame for what happened next from Brutus. There is some suggestion of history repeating itself, as Pompey's troops at Pharsalus had rushed into battle against the wishes of their general.
7. Appian, *Civil Wars*, 4.128–130.
8. Appian, *Civil Wars*, 4.131.
9. Appian, *Civil Wars*, 4.138.

CHAPTER 10
1. Plutarch, *Life of Antony*, 26–27 (trans. Robin Waterfield).
2. Cicero, *De Lege Agraria*, 2.27.
3. Appian, *Civil Wars*, 4.3, lists only Capua, Rhegium, Venusia, Beneventum, Nuceria, Ariminum, and Vibo. In addition to the stray references from Appian and some indications in other sources, we have a list from a collection of treatises on land surveying known as the *Corpus Agrimensorum*, one book of which is the *Liber Coloniarum*, which would appear to be a later revision of an Augustan list of colonies. See also Pliny, *Natural History*, 3.46–63.
4. Appian, *Civil Wars*, 5.12.
5. Dio 48.4 recounts that on January 1, 41, on the very day that he became consul, Lucius Antonius held a triumphal procession in Rome. This double achievement had few precedents, and

Antonius appears to have cited the general Marius. Dio is derisive, given the comparative scale of Marius's and Lucius Antonius's achievements.

6. Appian, *Civil Wars*, 5.19.

7. Dio 48.5.3.

8. Dio 48.5. Romans had three main elements to their names: the praenomen (Lucius), the gentilicium or clan name (Antonius), and the cognomen or associated name. Cognomens could be awarded to or even chosen by individuals. *Pietas* carries meanings of duty to family, loyalty to the state and others, trustworthiness, and reverence for the gods. For Lucius's republicanism, see Appian, *Civil Wars*, 5.19, 5.39 and 5.43.

9. Dio 48.10–13. The account of events in Dio is no less confused, seemingly reliant on a pro-Octavian source.

10. Appian, *Civil Wars*, 5.19.

11. Appian, *Civil Wars*, 5.19.

12. Appian, *Civil Wars*, 5.14.

13. Appian, *Civil Wars*, 5.22.

14. Appian, *Civil Wars*, 5.14.

15. Appian, *Civil Wars*, 5.20.

16. Appian, *Civil Wars*, 5.39.

17. Appian, *Civil Wars*, 5.43–44; 45. Appian tells us that he was translating Latin *hypomnemata*. This word was used of official documents which summarized the acts of magistrates. It is possible that Appian accurately records Lucius's own political justification.

18. Appian, *Civil Wars*, 5.15–16.

19. Appian, *Civil Wars*, 5.18.

20. Dio 48.8–9; Dio claims that such violence was replicated throughout Italy.

21. Appian, *Civil Wars*, 5.18.

22. Suetonius, *Augustus*, 1.

23. Suetonius, *Augustus*, 13.

24. The title of imperator was awarded by acclamation from the troops to a successful general and was later confirmed (or not) by the senate.

25. Dio, 48.13.

26. Appian, *Civil Wars*, 5.34.

27. Appian, *Civil Wars*, 5.35.

28. Appian, *Civil Wars*, 5.36–37.

29. Appian, *Civil Wars*, 5.46–47.

30. Appian, *Civil Wars*, 5.48–49.

31. Dio 48.14.4. Human sacrifice was rare in Rome, and the number 300 has the feel of an estimate. Nevertheless, all accounts agree that Octavian took revenge.

32. Suetonius, *Augustus*, 15.

33. Appian, *Civil Wars*, 5.52.

34. Dio 48.16.2.

35. Appian, *Civil Wars*, 5.52.

36. Appian, *Civil Wars*, 5.56–57.

37. Appian, *Civil Wars*, 5.59–63.

38. Dio 48.28–30; Appian, *Civil Wars*, 5.65.

39. Virgil, *Eclogue*, 1.70–73.

40. Virgil, *Eclogue*, 1. 6; 18.

41. Propertius, 1.1.1–6.

42. Propertius, 1.21–22.

CHAPTER 10

1. Appian, *Civil Wars*, 5.71–75.
2. Appian, *Civil Wars*, 5.78–92; Dio 48.46–47.
3. Appian, *Civil Wars*, 5.96–100; Dio 49.1.
4. Appian, *Civil Wars*, 5.98–110; Dio 49.3–5.
5. Appian, *Civil Wars*, 5.111–112.
6. Appian, *Civil Wars*, 5.113–114; Dio 49.6–7.
7. For Roman warships, see Michael Pitassi, *Roman Warships* (Woodbridge: Boydell and Brewer, 2011).
8. Appian, *Civil Wars*, 5.117–121; Dio 49.9–10.
9. Appian, *Civil Wars*, 5.133–144; Dio 49.11; 49.18.
10. Appian, *Civil Wars*, 5.123–126; Dio 49.12.
11. Appian, *Civil Wars*, 5.128; Dio 49.13–14.
12. The privileges foreshadow a constitutional innovation of the developed Principate when Augustus took the power of a tribune without actually holding the office.
13. Dio 49. 14–15.
14. Dio 49.18.6–7.
15. Dio 48.24.
16. Dio 48.25–26.
17. Dio 48.39–40.
18. Dio 48.40.
19. Dio 48.41.
20. Dio 39.22.
21. Dio 49.19–21.
22. Dio 49.23.
23. Dio 49.27–30.
24. Dio 49.33.
25. Dio 49.39–40.
26. Dio 49.34.
27. Dio 49.35.
28. Dio 49.37.
29. Dio 49.38.

CHAPTER 12

1. See Sally-Ann Ashton, *Cleopatra and Egypt* (Malden, MA: Blackwell, 2008), xi, who acknowledges the failure of her attempt to find the "real" Cleopatra. The impossibility and futility of stripping away the myth does not stop the many valiant attempts; see recently Michel Chauveau, *Cleopatra: Beyond the Myth* (Ithaca, NY and London: Cornell University Press, 2002); Joann Fletcher, *Cleopatra the Great: The Woman Behind the Legend* (London: HarperCollins, 2009); and Stacy Schiff, *Cleopatra: A Life* (New York: Little, Brown, 2010), who writes "to restore Cleopatra is as much to salvage the few facts as to peel away the encrusted myth and the hoary propaganda" (p. 7). Somewhat more realistic in aim is Stanley M. Burstein, *The Reign of Cleopatra* (Westport, CT: Greenwood, 2004). For Augustan uses of the myth, see Robert A. Gurval, *Actium and Augustus: The Politics and Emotions of Civil War* (Ann Arbor: University of Michigan Press, 1995). Diana E. E. Kleiner, *Cleopatra and Rome* (Cambridge, MA: Belknap Press of Harvard University Press, 2005), sees Cleopatra as a "superstar" of the Roman world, whose life was mythic even as she lived it. For images of

Cleopatra, see Peter Higgs and Susan Walker, *Cleopatra of Egypt: From History to Myth* (London: British Museum, 2001).

2. Dio 49.34.1.

3. Suetonius, *Divus Augustus* 69, quoting a letter of Antony.

4. See the discussion in Riet van Bremen, *The Limits of Participation: Women and Civic Life in the Greek East in the Hellenistic and Roman Periods* (Amsterdam: Gieben, 1996), of households as avenues through which women and men participated in public life.

5. Dio 49.40.

6. Dio 49.41; Plutarch, *Life of Antony*, 54.

7. Plutarch, *Life of Antony*, 24 and 54, for Cleopatra as Isis.

8. See Rolf Strootman, "Queen of Kings: Cleopatra VII and the Donations of Alexandria," in *Kingdoms and Principalities in the Near East*, 139–157, edited by Ted Kaizer and Maria Facella (Stuttgart: Steiner, 2010), for a similarly sympathetic reading of the Donations.

9. Dio 50.1.

10. Dio 50.2.

11. Dio 50.4.

12. *Res Gestae*, 25.

13. Dio 50.11.

14. Dio 50.12–13.

15. Dio 50.13.

16. Dio 50.15.

17. John C. Carter, *The Battle of Actium: The Rise and Triumph of Augustus Caesar* (London: Hamish Hamilton, 1970), 213–214, comes to the same conclusions.

18. Dio 50.31.

19. Plutarch, *Life of Antony* 66; Dio 50.31–33.

20. For the probable role of the winds in the battle, see Carter, *The Battle of Actium*, 217–223.

21. Dio 50.34.

22. Dio 51.1.

23. Plutarch, *Life of Antony*, 71.

24. Dio 51.9.

25. Dio 51.10; Plutarch, *Life of Antony*, 76.

26. Dio 51.10; Plutarch, *Life of Antony*, 76–77.

27. Dio 51.11; Plutarch, *Life of Antony*, 78–79.

28. Dio 51.12.

29. Dio 51.14; Plutarch, *Life of Antony*, 86.

30. For the myth, see Lucy Hughes-Hallett, *Cleopatra: Queen, Lover, Legend* (London: Bloomsbury, 1990).

CHAPTER 13

1. Josephus, *Antiquities*, 15.6. Josephus's account is detailed, but we must suspect some invention.

2. Suetonius, *Caesar*, 7; Plutarch, *Life of Caesar*, 11.

3. Dio 51.16; Suetonius, *Augustus*, 18.

4. *P. Oxy.* 1453.

5. Dio 51.20–21.

6. Dio 51.19. The way Dio expresses the honors suggests that he is quoting from an official decree.

7. Dio 51.20.

8. Dio 51.21.

9. Dio 55.9. *Res Gestae*, 14; *Res Gestae*, 7. See, for example, *Res Gestae*, 13 for Augustus's use of *princeps*.

10. Dio 51.21.

11. The Fasti Triumphales Barberini, a listing of triumphs held in antiquity, has entries for August 13 and August 15, 29, for triumphs over Dalmatia and Egypt, but makes no mention of the Actian "triumph."

12. Dio 51.22.

13. Dio 53.1; Propertius, 2.31.

14. Dio 53.22; 53.27.

15. *Res Gestae*, 10; Dio 54.27; cf. 54.15.

16. Velleius Paterculus, 2.88.

17. Livy, 4.20; Dio 51.23–37.

18. Dio 53.2.

19. *Res Gestae*, 34.

20. It seems very likely that Octavian and Agrippa changed the way in which the census worked. Previously, the census had counted only men. Although there is considerable scholarly disagreement, the balance of the argument would seem to point to the census being extended to count women and probably children.

21. Dio 52.42; Suetonius, *Augustus*, 35.

22. Dio 53.2–11; *Res Gestae*, 34; Ovid, *Fasti*, 1.589–90; *Fasti Praenestini* (January 13).

23. *Augustus* would appear to mean "revered," but it also has connotations of increase, suggesting that Augustus would increase the Roman state.

24. Dio 53.17.

CHAPTER 14

1. *Res Gestae*, 34.

2. Dio 53.11.

3. Dio 53.22.

4. Dio 53.28; *Res Gestae*, 12.

5. Dio 53.23; 27.

6. Friedhelm Hoffmann, Martina Minas-Nerpel, and Stefan Pfeiffer (ed.), *Die dreisprachige Stele des C. Cornelius Gallus: Übersetzung und Kommentar* (Berlin and New York: Walter de Gruyter, 2009).

7. Suetonius, *Augustus*, 66.2; Dio 53.23–24.

8. *Res Gestae*, 12; Dio 53. 28.

9. Dio 53.21.

10. Dio 53.22.

11. *Aeneid* 6. 752–885.

12. Dio 54.3. Velleius Paterculus, 2.91.

13. Suetonius, *Tiberius*, 8.

14. The story of the brother is complicated. There are various inscribed consular lists which do not mention Varro; one of the lists, the Fasti Capitolini, lists a Varro Murena as consul for January 23, but something (lost in a gap in the inscription) happened to him.

15. Suetonius, *Augustus*, 66.3.

CHAPTER 15

1. Dio 54.1; *Res Gestae*, 5; Suetonius, *Augustus*, 52.

2. The rations were such as to feed an adult man, and we can estimate the value of the twelve rations at about 80 sesterces.

3. *Res Gestae*, 15.

4. Although slave gangs were likely contracted in for some building projects, slaves were relatively expensive assets, and free labor was better placed for irregular and seasonal work.

5. Janet DeLaine, "Bricks and Mortar: Exploring the Economics of Building Techniques at Rome and Ostia", in *Economies beyond Agriculture in the Classical World*, 271–296, edited by David J. Mattingly and John Salmon (London: Routledge, 2000). See also Janet DeLaine, *The Baths of Caracalla: A Study in the Design, Construction, and Economics of Large-Scale Building Projects in Imperial Rome* (Portsmouth, RI: Journal of Roman Archaeology, 1997): 201.

6. Romilda Catalano, *Acqua e acquedotti romani: Fontis Augustei aquaeductus* (Naples: Arte Tipografica, 2003), 60.

7. See Peter Garnsey, *Famine and Food Supply in the Greco-Roman World: Responses to Crisis* (Cambridge, UK: Cambridge University Press, 1988), and Tom W. Gallant, *Risk and Survival in Ancient Greece: Reconstructing the Rural Domestic Economy* (Oxford and Stanford: Stanford University Press, 1991).

8. *Res Gestae*, 5.

9. This is how Dio 54.1 interprets the events, though he is puzzled by this piece of political theatre since he is of the view that Augustus was an absolute monarch from as early as 31.

10. For the chronology of events, we rely heavily on the narrative in Cassius Dio, but for some reason he is not certain about dates from 22 to 19. The chronology has to be pieced together.

11. Dio 54.6.

12. Dio 54.6.

13. Dio 54.11.

14. Dio 54.10.

15. Dio 53.24.

16. Dio 53.24.

17. Velleius Paterculus, 2.91–92.

18. *Res Gestae* 12 has the leading men of Rome and the consul Lucretius going to Campania to meet Augustus on his return. In *Res Gestae* 11 there is reference to sacrifices held on October 12 in the consulship of Vinicius and Lucretius. In *Res Gestae* 6, Augustus says that he received the duty of Curator Morum (Manager of Morals) in the consulship of Vinicius and Lucretius. It looks as if Saturninus was no longer consul when Augustus reached Italy and that Vinicius was consul by October 12 or very soon thereafter.

19. Dio 53.26.

20. Suetonius, *Augustus*, 72.

21. Dio 53.33.

22. Dio 54.7; Plutarch, *Moralia* 207 F (Sayings of the Romans).

23. Dio 54.8; *Res Gestae*, 29.

24. *Res Gestae*, 11.

CHAPTER 16

1. Suetonius, *Tiberius*, 8–9.

2. Dio 54.10.

3. The nonimperial trimphators were Calvisius Sabinus, C. Carrinas, and L. Autronius Paetus, all in 28; Licinius Crassus in 27; Sextus Appuleius in 26; Sempronius Atratinus in 21; and Cornelius Balbus in 19.

4. Augustus does not even mention the honor in the *Res Gestae*.

5. Tacitus, *Annales* 1.2–4 (excerpts).

6. *Res Gestae*, 28.

7. Dio 53.25–26.

8. See Nicola K. Mackie, "Augustan Colonies in Mauretania," *Historia: Zeitschrift für alte Geschichte* 32 (1983): 332–358, who suggests that these colonies were to accommodate veterans from the Spanish wars; Barbara Levick, *Roman Colonies in Southern Asia Minor* (Oxford: Oxford University Press, 1967); Dio 54.7; 54.23; Andrew Burnett, Michel Amandry, and Pere Pau Ripollès, *Roman Provincial Coinage*, Vol.1, *From the Death of Caesar to the Death of Vitellius (44 B.C.–A.D. 69)* (London: British Museum Press, 1992), 1650; Harikleia Papageorgiadou-Bani, *The Numismatic Iconography of the Roman Colonies in Greece: Local Spirit and the Expression of Imperial Policy* (Athens: Research Centre for Greek and Roman Antiquity, 2004); Suetonius, *Augustus*, 25.

9. *Res Gestae*, 16.

10. *Res Gestae*, 15.

11. Velleius Paterculus, 2.113. These figures are calculated on a total adult male population of 1,300,000. There is considerable debate about the total Roman population, and the figures here are based on a "low count" for the Italian population. A high count would effectively triple the number of men available (and also the total population for Roman Italy). Academic historians are roughly equally divided between high and low counters. My opting for a low count is based on estimating the servile population for Italy, which I think must have been considerably more than 20 percent of the total population of the peninsula, based on comparison with figures from Roman Egypt. If this is the case, a high count would suggest about 13,000,000–14,000,000 free citizens in Italy (excluding Sicily) in 28 B.C. with about 3,000,000 slaves, to make a total population of about 17,000,000, rising to above 20,000,000 by the end of the Augustan period. These are figures not matched until the mid-nineteenth century and are, I think, too high for Augustan Italy.

12. Dio 54.25.

13. Dio 55.25; 28.

14. *Res Gestae*, 15.

15. Peter A. Brunt, "The Lex Valeria Cornelia," *Journal of Roman Studies* 51 (1961): 71–83.

16. Suetonius, *Augustus*, 53–57.

17. Dio 54.14.

18. Dio 54.26.

19. Dio 55.13.

20. This can be seen in the developing fashion for senators to list their offices in inscriptions; see *Inscriptiones Latinae Selectae*, 914; 928; 932.

21. Propertius, 2.7.1–8.

22. Suetonius, *Augustus*, 73.

23. Ulpian, *Rules*, 13–14.

24. Gaius, *Institutes*, 2.111; *Gnomon of the Idios Logos*, 24–32; FIRA I 40.

25. Suetonius, *Augustus*, 46.

26. Dio 56.1–10. Dio gives the account under A.D. 9, when there was a major reform, but he may be combining two reforms of the legislation in his account.

27. Suetonius, *Augustus*, 34.

28. Dio 56.1–10.

29. Livy, *Periochae*, 129; Suetonius, *Augustus*, 89.

30. Aulus Gellius, *Attic Nights*, 1.6.1.

31. Dio 56.2–9.

32. Dio 54.16–17.

33. The terms of the law are scattered around a number of sources and not easily reconstructed. See Michael H. Crawford, *Roman Statutes*, II (London: Institute of Classical Studies, 1996): 781–786, n. 60.

34. Suetonius, *Augustus*, 69. Typically, Suetonius sees Augustan adultery as driven not by lust but by policy. He slept with the wives of the great men of Rome so as to understand better what their husbands were thinking and saying. It is an excuse I recommend to politicians everywhere.

35. Suetonius, *Augustus*, 71. The difference between Roman and contemporary morality is illustrated by the fact that Suetonius places as much emphasis on Augustus's fondness for dice as his habit of deflowering virgins.

36. Dio 54.19.

37. Tacitus, *Annales*, 3.25.

38. Tacitus, *Annales*, 3.28.

39. Zosimus, 2.6. The text is clearly of an Augustan version of the oracle.

40. *Corpus Inscriptionum Latinarum*, 6.32323.

41. Catullus, 64; Virgil, Eclogue 4.

42. *Res Gestae*, 8.

43. Ovid, *Ars Amatoria*, 2.275–279.

CHAPTER 17

1. Dio 53.12.

2. *Res Gestae*, Preface.

3. Dio 53.22–26; 53.29; 54.3–5; 54.11; 54.29; Strabo, 16.4; *Res Gestae*, 26.

4. Virgil, *Aeneid*, 1.261–296.

5. Dio 54.22; 54.24.

6. AE (1973) 323.

7. Dio 54.19.

8. Dio 54.21.

9. Dio 54.25.

10. Dio 54.33.

11. Dio 54.20.

12. Dio 54.24.

13. Dio 54.28. Dio suggests that Agrippa was on his way home, but coming via Campania seems a somewhat roundabout route.

14. For the text, see Michael Haslam, "Augustus' Funeral Oration for Agrippa," *Classical Journal* 75 (1980): 193–199.

15. Dio 54.29; 55.8.

16. Dio 54.31.

17. Velleius Paterculus, 2.97.

18. Dio 54.36.

19. Dio 55.1–2.

20. Dio 55.6.

21. Dio 55.8.

22. Dio 54.31.

23. Dio 54.33.

24. Dio 54.34; 55.2; Velleius Paterculus, 2.98 notes a war in Thrace which seems to have lasted three years.

25. Dio 55.2; 55.5.

26. Dio 54.12; 54.15. Suetonius, *Augustus*, 19, provides names of conspirators ranging from major political figures, such as Lepidus and Caepio and Murena, to a Lucius Audasius, a supposed forger; an Asinius Epicadus, who was of Illyrian origin; a slave called Telephus, who thought he was about to become emperor himself; and an unnamed servant of an unnamed soldier, who just appeared in Augustus's bedroom carrying a large knife. The list is hardly impressive.

27. Dio 55.5.

28. Dio 55.14–22. Seneca, *De Clementia*, 1.9.

29. Dio 56.1–10. The speeches are reported extensively in Dio and attested in Suetonius, *Augustus*, 34. Augustus clearly also associated his reforms with that of age-old morality (see Suetonius, *Augustus*, 89, and p. 000. See also Dio 54.19 for earlier discontent.

30. Ovid, *Tristia*, 2.

31. Ovid, *Ars Amatoria*, 1.32–34.

32. Ovid, *Ars Amatoria*, 1.269–270.

33. Ovid, *Ars Amatoria*, 1.579–580.

34. Dio 55.6; *Res Gestae* 16. Dio dates the gift to the soldiers to 8 B.C., while in the *Res Gestae* the gift to the veterans is 7 B.C.

35. Suetonius, *Tiberius*, 10–11; Dio 55.9.

36. Dio 55.9.

37. *Res Gestae*, 14; Dio 55.9.

38. Dio 55.10; *Res Gestae*, 15.

39. See Joseph Geiger, *The First Hall of Fame: A Study of the Statues in the Forum Augustum* (Boston: Brill, 2008), Paul Zanker, *Forum Romanum: Die Neugestaltung durch Augustus* (Tübingen: Wasmuth, 1972), and Paul Zanker, *The Power of Images in the Age of Augustus* (Ann Arbor: University of Michigan Press, 1990), 194–195. For the Forum and literature, see Torrey James Luce, "Livy, Augustus and the Forum Augustum," in *Between Republic and Empire, Interpretations of Augustus and his Principate*, 123–138, edited by Kurt Raaflaub and Mark Toher (Berkeley: University of California Press, 1990).

40. Dio 55.11.

41. *Res Gestae*, 35

42. Suetonius, *Augustus*, 58.

43. It is not obvious how such a procedure would have been achieved. Greek cities had gymnasia which educated boys (known as ephebes), and the various age cohorts would leave the gymnasia at a ceremonial event. Roman education did not work in this way, having no centralized system. It seems likely, however, that Augustus was thinking of Greek customs.

44. Dio 55.10.

CHAPTER 18

1. Velleius Paterculus, 2.100; Dio 55.10.

2. Suetonius, *Augustus*, 65.

3. Dio 55.13.

4. *Res Gestae*, 6.

5. See the discussion of Catharine Edwards, *The Politics of Immorality in Ancient Rome* (Cambridge, UK: Cambridge University Press, 1993).

6. Dio 55.10A.

7. Suetonius, *Tiberius*, 13.

8. Dio 55.10A; Suetonius, *Tiberius*, 12.

9. See *Fasti Antiates*.

10. Dio 55.10A.

11. Suetonius, *Tiberius*, 15–16.

12. Dio 55.29–30; Velleius Paterculus, 2.110.

13. Dio 55.31.

14. Dio 55.22.

15. Dio 55.32

16. Tacitus, *Annales*, 1.3; Dio 55.32; Suetonius, *Augustus*, 64–65.

17. Suetonius, *Augustus*, 19. One of Julia's supposed lovers was Decimus Junius Silanus. He was exiled but was allowed to return to Rome under Tiberius on condition that he maintain a low profile: see Tacitus, *Annales*, 3.24.

18. Suetonius, *Augustus*, 72, records the destruction of the house as a way of discussing the simplicity of Augustus's own residences.

19. Tacitus, *Annales*, 4.71.

20. Dio 55.33–34; 56.1.

21. Dio 56.16.

22. *Res Gestae*, 4.

23. Dio 56.17.

24. Dio 56.18; Velleius Paterculus, 2.117–118.

25. Dio 56.19.

26. Tacitus, *Annales*, 1.60–62.

27. Velleius Paterculus, 2.117.

28. Suetonius, *Augustus*, 23.

29. Velleius Paterculus, 2.121.

30. Dio 56.23.

31. Dio 56.25.

32. Dio 56.27.

33. Suetonius, *Augustus*, 100; Dio 56.29–30; Tacitus, *Annales* 1.5; Velleius Paterculus, 2.123.

34. Tacitus, *Annales*, 1.7.

35. Tacitus, *Annales*, 1.6.

36. Tacitus, *Annales*, 1.53.

37. Tacitus, *Annales*, 1.16–54.

38. After the murder of Gaius Caligula, there was a brief moment when the senators appear to have considered a republican restoration, but as they could not control the army, the idea was quickly dismissed.

BIBLIOGRAPHY

Alston, Richard. "History and Memory in the Construction of Identity in Imperial Rome," in *Role Models: Identity and Assimilation in the Roman World*, 147–160, edited by Sinclair Bell and Inge L. Hansen. Ann Arbor: Michigan University Press, 2008.

Arendt, Hannah. *The Origins of Totalitarianism*. New York: Harcourt, Brace and Company, 1966.

Ashton, Sally-Ann. *Cleopatra and Egypt*. Malden, MA: Blackwell, 2008.

Astin, Alan E. *Scipio Aemilianus*. Oxford: Oxford University Press, 1967.

Beloch, Julius. *Die Bevölkerung der griechisch-römischen Welt*. Leipzig: Dunker and Humblot, 1886.

Bradford, John S. P. *Ancient Landscapes: Studies in Field Archaeology*. London: Bell, 1957.

Bringmann, Klaus. *A History of the Roman Republic*. Cambridge, MA: Polity Press, 2007.

Broughton, Thomas R. S. *The Magistrates of the Roman Republic*. Atlanta: American Philological Association, 1986.

Brunt, Peter A. "'Augustus' e la 'Republica'," in *La Rivoluzione romana: Inchiesta tra gli antichisti*, 236–244. Naples: Jovene, 1982.

Brunt, Peter A. *The Fall of the Roman Republic and Related Essays*. Oxford: Oxford University Press, 1988.

Brunt, Peter A. "The Lex Valeria Cornelia," *Journal of Roman Studies* 51 (1961): 71–85.

Brunt, Peter A. *Italian Manpower 225 B.C.–A.D.14*. Oxford: Oxford University Press, 1971.

Burgers, Gert-Jan. "L'archaeologia e l'Italia meridionale post-Annabilica: Una prospettiva regionale e diacronica," in *Modilità insediative e strutture agrarie nell' Italia Meridionale in età romana*, 249–266, edited by Elio Lo Cascio and Alfredina S. Marino. Bari: Edipuglia, 2001.

Burnett, Andrew, Michel Amandry, and Pere Pau Ripollès, *Roman Provincial Coinage*. Vol.1, *From the Death of Caesar to the Death of Vitellius (44 B.C.–A.D. 69)*. London: British Museum Press.

Burstein, Stanley M. *The Reign of Cleopatra*. Westport, CT: Greenwood, 2004.

Canfora, Luciano. "Proscrizioni e dissento sociale nella repubblica Romana," *Klio* 62 (1980): 425–437.

Carandini, Andrea, and Franco Cambi, eds. *Paesaggi d' Etruria: Valle dell' Albegna, Valle d'Oro, Valle del Chiarone, Valle del Tafone*. Rome: Edizioni di storia e letteratura, 2002.

Carter, John C. *The Battle of Actium: The Rise and Triumph of Augustus Caesar*. London: Hamish Hamilton, 1970.

Catalano, Romilda. *Acqua e acquedotti romani: Fontis Augustei aquaeductus*. Naples: Arte Tipografica, 2003.

Chabal, Patrick, and Jean-Pascal Daloz, eds. *Africa Works: Disorder as a Political Instrument.* Indianapolis: Indiana University Press, 1999.

Chabal, Patrick, and Nuno Vidal. *Angola: The Weight of History.* London: Hurst and Co., 2007.

Chakrabarty, Dipesh. *Provincializing Europe: Postcolonial Thought and Historical Difference.* Princeton, NJ: Princeton University Press, 2008.

Chauveau, Michel. *Cleopatra: Beyond the Myth.* Ithaca, NY: Cornell University Press, 2002.

Crawford, Michael H. *Roman Statutes, II.* London: Institute of Classical Studies, 1996.

Crawford, Michael H. "States Waiting in the Wings: Population Distribution and the End of the Roman Republic," in *People, Land and Politics: Demographic Development and the Transformation of Italy 300 B.C.–A.D. 14*, 631–643, edited by Luuk de Ligt and Simon Northwood. Leiden and Boston: Brill, 2008.

DeLaine, Janet. *The Baths of Caracalla: A Study in the Design, Construction, and Economics of Large-Scale Building Projects in Imperial Rome.* Portsmouth, RI: Journal of Roman Archaeology, 1997.

DeLaine, Janet. "Bricks and Mortar: Exploring the Economics of Building Techniques at Rome and Ostia," in *Economies beyond Agriculture in the Classical World*, 271–296, edited by David J. Mattingly and John Salmon. London: Routledge, 2000.

De Souza, Philip. *Piracy in the Graeco-Roman World.* Cambridge, UK: Cambridge University Press, 1999.

Drèze, Jean. "Famine Prevention in India," in *The Political Economy of Hunger II*, 13–122, edited by Jean Drèze and Amartya Sen. Oxford: Oxford University Press, 1990.

Eck, Werner. "Senatorial Self-Representation: Developments in the Augustan Period," in *Caesar Augustus: Seven Aspects*, 129–167, edited by Fergus Millar and Erich Segal. Oxford: Oxford University Press, 1984.

Edwards, Catharine. *The Politics of Immorality in Ancient Rome.* Cambridge, UK: Cambridge University Press, 1993.

Evans, John K. "Plebs Rustica: The Peasantry of Classical Italy," *American Journal of Ancient History* 5 (1980): 19–47; 134–173.

Fantham, Elaine. "Caesar against Liberty? An Introduction," *Papers of the Langford Latin Seminar* 11 (2003): 35–67.

Fletcher, Joann. *Cleopatra the Great: The Woman Behind the Legend.* London: HarperCollins, 2009.

Frank, Tenney. "Roman Census Statistics from 225 to 28 B.C.," *Classical Philology* 19 (1924): 329–341.

Froude, James A. *Caesar: A Sketch.* London: Harper and Brothers, 1890.

Gabba, Emilio, and Marinella Pasquinucci. *Strutture agrarie e allevamento transumante nell Italia romana (III—I secolo a.C).* Pisa: Giardini,1979.

Galinsky, Karl. *Augustan Culture: An Interpretive Introduction.* Princeton, NJ: Princeton University Press, 1996.

Galinsky, Karl, ed. *The Cambridge Companion to the Age of Augustus.* Cambridge, UK: Cambridge University Press, 2005.

Gallant, Tom W. *Risk and Survival in Ancient Greece: Reconstructing the Rural Domestic Economy.* Stanford, CA: Stanford University Press, 1991.

Garnsey, Peter. *Famine and Food Supply in the Greco-Roman World: Responses to Crisis.* Cambridge, UK: Cambridge University Press, 1988.

Garnsey, Peter. "The Lex Iulia and Appeal under the Empire," *Journal of Roman Studies* 56 (1966): 167–189.

Bibliography

Geiger, Joseph. *The First Hall of Fame: A Study of the Statues in the Forum Augustum*. Boston: Brill, 2008.

Gruen, Erich. *The Last Generation of the Roman Republic*. Berkeley: University of California Press, 1974.

Guha, Ranajit. "The Prose of Counter-Insurgency," in *Selected Subaltern Studies*, 45–84, edited by Ranajit Guha and Gayatri Spivak. New York: Oxford University Press, 1988.

Gurval, Robert A. *Actium and Augustus: The Politics and Emotions of Civil War*. Ann Arbor: University of Michigan Press, 1995.

Habinek, Thomas, and Alessandro Schiesaro. "Introduction," in *The Roman Cultural Revolution*, xv–xxi, edited by Thomas Habinek and Alessandro Schiesaro. Cambridge, UK: Cambridge University Press, 1997.

Harl, Kenneth W. *Coinage in the Roman Economy, 300 B.C.–A.D. 700*. Baltimore: John Hopkins University Press, 1996.

Harris, William V. "Poverty and Destitution in the Roman Empire," in *Rome's Imperial Economy: Twelve Essays*, 27–54, by William V. Harris. Oxford: Oxford University Press, 2011.

Harrison, Ian. "Catiline, Clodius, and Popular Politics at Rome during the 60s and 50s BCE," *Bulletin of the Institute of Classical Studies 51* (2008): 95–118.

Haslam, Michael. "Augustus' Funeral Oration for Agrippa," *Classical Journal 75* (1980): 193–199.

Hegel, Georg W. F. *The Philosophy of History*. New York: Cosimo, 2007.

Higgs, Peter, and Susan Walker. *Cleopatra of Egypt: From History to Myth*. London: British Museum, 2001.

Hölkeskamp, Karl-Joachim, ed, *Eine politische Kultur (in) der Krise?: Die "letzte Generation" der römischen Republik*. Munich: R. Oldenbourg, 2009.

Hölkeskamp, Karl-Joachim. *Reconstructing the Roman Republic: An Ancient Political Culture and Modern Research*. Princeton, NJ: Princeton University Press, 2010.

Hölkeskamp, Karl-Joachim. *Senatus populusque romanus: Die politische Kultur der Republik; Dimensionen und Deutungen*. Wiesbaden. Franz Steiner, 2004.

Holmes, Thomas Rice. *The Architect of the Roman Empire*. Oxford: The Clarendon Press, 1928.

Heuss, Alfred. "Rivoluzione: Relatività del concetto," in *La rivoluzione romana: Inchiesta tra gli antichisti*, 1–17. Naples: Jovene, 1982.

Hughes-Hallett, Lucy. *Cleopatra: Queen, Lover, Legend*. London: Bloomsbury, 1990.

Ismail, Salwa. *Political Life in Cairo's New Quarters: Encountering the Everyday State*. Minneapolis: University of Minnesota Press, 2006.

Jehne, Martin. *Der Staat des Dictators Caesar*. Cologne: Böhlau, 1987.

Jones, G. D. Barri. "Capena and the Ager Capenas: Part II," *Papers of the British School at Rome 31* (1963): 100–158.

Kaag, Mayke. "Ways Forward in Livelihood Research," in *Globalization and Development: Themes and Concepts in Current Research*, 49–74, edited by Don Kalb, Wil G. Pansters, and Hans Siebers. Dordrecht and Boston: Kluwer Academic Publishers, 2004.

Kalb, Don. "Time and Contention in the Great Globalization Debate," in *Globalization and Development: Themes and Concepts in Current Research*, 9–47, edited by Don Kalb, Wil G. Pansters, and Hans Siebers. Dordrecht and Boston: Kluwer Academic Publishers, 2004.

Keaveney, Arthur. *The Army in the Roman Revolution*. Abingdon, UK: Taylor and Francis, 2007.

Keppie, Laurence. "The Changing Face of the Roman Legions (49 B.C.–A.D. 69)," *Papers of the British School at Rome 65* (1997): 89–102.

Keppie, Laurence. *Colonisation and Veteran Settlement in Italy: 47–14 B.C.* London: British School at Rome, 1983.

Bibliography

Kleiner, Diana E. E. *Cleopatra and Rome*. Cambridge, MA: Belknap Press of Harvard University Press, 2005.

Lange, Carsten H. *Res Publica Constituta: Actium, Apollo and Accomplishment of the Triumviral Assignment*. Leiden and Boston: Brill, 2009.

La rivoluzione romana: Inchiesta tra gli antichisti. Naples: Jovene, 1982.

Levick, Barbara. *Roman Colonies in Southern Asia Minor*. Oxford: Oxford University Press, 1967.

Lo Cascio, Elio. "The Size of the Roman Population: Beloch and the Meaning of the Augustan Census Figures," *Journal of Roman Studies 84* (1994): 23–40.

Lo Cascio. Elio. "Recruitment and the Size of the Roman Population from the Third to the First Century BCE," in *Debating Roman Demography*, 111–137, edited by Walter Scheidel. Leiden and Boston: Brill, 2001.

Lo Cascio, Elio. "The Augustan Census Figures and the Population of Italy," *Athenaeum 93* (2005): 441–495.

Luce, Torrey James. "Livy, Augustus and the Forum Augustum," in *Between Republic and Empire: Interpretations of Augustus and His Principate*, 123–138, edited by Kurt Raaflaub and Mark Toher. Berkeley: University of California Press, 1990.

MacKay, Christopher S. *The Breakdown of the Roman Republic: From Oligarchy to Empire*. Cambridge, UK: Cambridge University Press, 2009.

Mackie, Nicola K. "Augustan Colonies in Mauretania," *Historia: Zeitschrift für Alte Geschichte 32* (1983): 332–358.

Manacorda, Daniele. "Le anfore di Pompeo Magno," in *Studi di archeologia in memoria di Liliana Mercando*, 137–143, edited by Marina Sapelli Ragni. Torino: Soprintendenza per i beni archeologici del Piemonte e del Museo antichità egizie, 2005.

Meijer, Fik. "Cicero and the Costs of the Republican Grain Laws," in *De Agricultura: In Memoriam Pieter Willem de Neeve*, 153–163, edited by Helena Sancisi-Weerdenburg. Amsterdam: J.C. Gieben, 1993.

Meier, Christian. *Caesar*. New York: HarperCollins, 1995.

Millar, Fergus. "The Political Character of the Classical Roman Republic," *Journal of Roman Studies 74* (1984): 1–19.

Millar, Fergus. "Politics, Persuasion and the People before the Social War (150–90 B.C.)," *Journal of Roman Studies 76* (1986): 1–11.

Millar, Fergus. "Political Power in Mid-Republican Rome: Curia or Comitium?" *Journal of Roman Studies 79* (1989): 138–150.

Morley, Neville. "The Transformation of Italy, 225–28 B.C.," *Journal of Roman Studies 91* (2001): 50–62.

Mouritsen, Henrik. "The Album of Canusium and the Town Councils of Roman Italy," *Chiron 28* (1998): 229–254.

Mouritsen, Henrik. *Plebs and Politics in the Late Roman Republic*. Cambridge, UK: Cambridge University Press, 2001.

Nicolet, Claude. *The World of the Citizen in Republican Rome*. Berkeley and Los Angeles: University of California Press, 1980.

Osgood, Josiah. *Caesar's Legacy: Civil War and the Emergence of the Roman Empire*. Cambridge, UK: Cambridge University Press, 2006.

Osgood, Josiah. *Turia: A Roman Woman's Civil War*. Oxford: Oxford University Press, 2014.

Papageorgiadou-Bani, Harikleia. *The Numismatic Iconography of the Roman Colonies in Greece: Local Spirit and the Expression of Imperial Policy*. Athens: Research Centre for Greek and Roman Antiquity, 2004.

Pina Polo, Francisco. *La crisis de la República (133–44 aC)*. Madrid: Editorial Síntesis, 2004.

Pitassi, Michael. *Roman Warships*. Woodbridge, UK: Boydell and Brewer, 2011.

Plutarch. *Roman Lives: A Selection of Eight Roman Lives*. Translated by Robin Waterfield. Oxford: Oxford University Press, 1999.

Powell, Anton, and Kathryn Welch (eds). *Sextus Pompeius*. London: Duckworth, 2002.

Raaflaub, Kurt A. "Caesar the Liberator? Factional Politics, the Civil War and Ideology," *Papers of the Langford Latin Seminar 11* (2003): 33–67.

Raskolnikoff, Mouza. "La 'rivoluzione romana' e gli storici sovietici," in *La rivoluzione romana: Inchiesta tra gli antichisti*, 51–65. Naples: Jovene, 1982.

Rathbone, Dominic W. "The Census Qualifications of the *assidui* and the *prima classis*," in *De Agricultura: In Memoriam Pieter Willem De Neeve*, 121–152, edited by Helena Sancisi-Weerdenburg. Amsterdam, J. C. Gieben: 1993.

Rathbone, Dominic W. "Poor Peasants and Silent Sherds," in *People, Land and Politics: Demographic Development and the Transformation of Italy 300 BC–AD 14*, 305–332, edited by Luuk de Ligt and Simon Northwood. Leiden and Boston: Brill, 2008.

Renucci, Pierre. *Auguste le révolutionnaire*. Paris: Boutique de l'histoire, 2003.

Reynolds, Joyce. *Aphrodisias and Rome*. London: Society for the Promotion of Roman Studies, 1982.

Robb, Margaret A. *Beyond Populares and Optimates: Political Language in the Late Republic*. Stuttgart: Franz Steiner Verlag, 2010.

Roselaar, Saskia T. *Public Land in the Roman Republic: A Social and Economic History of Ager Publicus in Italy, 396—89 BC*. Oxford: Oxford University Press, 2010.

Ryan, Frances X. *Rank and Participation in the Republican Senate*. Stuttgart: Franz Steiner Verlag, 1998.

Salmon, Edward Togo. *Roman Colonization under the Republic*. London and Southampton: Thames and Hudson, 1969.

Sen, Amartya. "Food, Economics, and Entitlement," in *The Political Economy of Hunger I*, 34–52, edited by Jean Drèze and Amartya Sen. Oxford: Oxford University Press, 1990.

Sen, Amartya. "Population and Reasoned Agency: Food, Fertility and Economic Development," in *Population, Economic Development, and the Environment*, 51–78, edited by K. L. Kiessling and H. Landberg. Oxford: Oxford University Press, 1994.

Sen, Amartya. *Poverty and Famines: An Essay in Entitlement and Deprivation*. Oxford: Clarendon, 1981.

Shatzman, Israel. *Senatorial Wealth and Roman Politics*. Brussels: Latomus, 1975.

Scheidel, Walter. "Human Mobility in Roman Italy, I: The Free Population," *Journal of Roman Studies 94* (2004): 1–26.

Scheidel, Walter. "The Slave Population of Roman Italy: Speculation and Constraints," *Topoi 9* (1999): 129–144.

Scheidel, Walter. "Progress and Problems in Roman Demography," in *Debating Roman Demography*, edited by Walter Scheidel, 1–81. Leiden and Boston: Brill, 2001.

Schiff, Stacy. *Cleopatra: A Life*. New York: Little, Brown, 2010.

Screech, Michael Andrew, ed. and trans., *Michel de Montaigne: The Complete Essays*. London: Penguin Books, 1987.

Storey, Glenn R. "The Meaning of *insula* in Roman Residential Terminology," *Memoirs of the American Academy in Rome 49* (2004): 47–84.

Strootman, Rolf. "Queen of Kings: Cleopatra VII and the Donations of Alexandria," in *Kingdoms and Principalities in the Near East*, 139–157, edited by Ted Kaizer and Maria Facella. Stuttgart: Steiner, 2010.

Syme, Ronald. *The Roman Revolution*. Oxford: Clarendon, 1939.

Syme, Ronald. *The Augustan Aristocracy*. Oxford: Clarendon, 1986.

Tatum, W. Jeffrey. *The Patrician Tribune: Publius Clodius Pulcher*. Chapel Hill: University of North Carolina Press, 1999.

Tibiletti, Gianfranco. "Richerche di storia agraria romana." *Athenaeum 28* (1950): 183–266.

Toynbee, Arnold. *Hannibal's Legacy: The Hannibalic War's Effects on Roman Life*. Oxford: Oxford University Press, 1965.

Tweedie, Fiona C. "The Case of the Missing Veterans: Roman Colonisation and Veteran Settlement in the Second Century B.C.," *Historia 60* (2011): 458–473.

van Bremen, Riet. *The Limits of Participation: Women and Civic Life in the Greek East in the Hellenistic and Roman Periods*. Amsterdam: Gieben, 1996.

Vanderbroeck, Paul J. J. *Popular Leadership and Collective Behaviour in the Late Roman Republic (ca. 80–50 B.C.)*. Amsterdam: Gieben, 1987.

Wallace-Hadrill, Andrew. "*Mutatio morum:* The idea of a cultural revolution," in *The Roman Cultural Revolution*, 3–22, edited by Thomas Habinek and Alessandro Schiesaro. Cambridge, UK: Cambridge University Press, 1997.

Wallace-Hadrill, Andrew. *Rome's Cultural Revolution*. Cambridge, UK: Cambridge University Press, 2008.

Welch, Kathryn. *Magnus Pius: Sextus Pompeius and the Transformation of the Roman Republic; Roman Culture in an Age of Civil War*. Swansea, UK: Classical Press of Wales, 2012.

Winterling, Aloys. *Politics and Society in Imperial Rome*. Malden, MA: John Wiley & Sons, 2009.

Wyke, Maria. *The Roman Mistress: Ancient and Modern Representations*. New York: Oxford University Press, 2002.

Zanker, Paul. *Forum Romanum: Die Neugestaltung durch Augustus*. Tübingen: Wasmuth, 1972.

Zanker, Paul. *The Power of Images in the Age of Augustus*. Ann Arbor: University of Michigan Press, 1990.

INDEX